THE
ENVIRONMENTAL
& SUSTAINABILITY
HANDBOOK

2013 Edition

The Green Guide for
Householders and
Businesses of all sizes

GREENER *TIMES*
>PUBLISHING

GREENER TIMES >PUBLISHING

The Environmental & Sustainability Handbook 2013 Edition

This is a:
GREENER TIMES GUIDE &
THE GREEN PAGES UK ™
RESOURCE DIRECTORY
Text, illustrations and design
copyright © 2013

ISBN 978-0-9575284-0-6

A CIP record for this book is available
from the British Library upon request

PUBLISHER
This edition published in
Great Britain by:
Greener Times Publishing Ltd
1D Kinnoull House
Friarton Road
Perth, PH2 8DF

GUIDE PRODUCTION
Editor - Designer:
Stephen Lings
Assistant Designer:
Craig Bruce

MANAGEMENT
Managing Director:
Gary W. Braybrooke
Technical Director:
Kenneth Campbell
Operations Director:
Dave Hunt
Editorial - Art Director:
Stephen Lings
Green Pages UK Compilation:
Big Green Book UK Team

PRINT PRODUCTION
Printed and bound in Britain by:
Stephens & George Print Group

DISTRIBUTION & SALES
Big Green Book UK Ltd
*A Not-For-Profit: Small Business
Environmental Network*
www.biggreenbook.com

preface

By Rt Hon Owen Paterson MP

Improving our environment for future generations is one of the great challenges we face as a society. The environment is about so much more than the just the flora and fauna of this land. It is about the communities we live in. Our communities sustain us and provide us with jobs, homes, schools, goods, services, families and friends. Communities can only be maintained if we work together in a sustainable manner.

We should strive for a healthy economy and a healthy environment, something many of the businesses in the Big Green Book will help us achieve. I believe that a healthy environment is essential to our future prosperity. We need to avoid growth that erodes our natural assets and encourage growth which conserve or enhances our natural environment, thereby ensuring that our ability to grow in the future is not undermined.

This handbook has a key role to play in this process. It showcases the very real opportunities a sustainable economy provides us with, consumer and business alike. It also enables homeowners and businesses to manage their own impact on their environment. Above all, it confirms the fantastic potential technology provides us with to live more sustainably without a major impact on our existing lifestyle.

This directory provides us with a framework to grow our economy while improving the environment. A framework which I hope you will take advantage of and that will place our communities on a firm footing for the future. Imaginative thinking, combined with British entrepreneurism, will see our environment, wildlife and economy thrive.

Rt Hon Owen Paterson MP
Member of Parliament for North Shropshire
Secretary of State for the Environment,
Food and Rural Affairs

contents

Part 1. Environmental Sustainability at WORK:

Green Pages UK: Your Regional Directories of Product and Service Providers.

The resource directory is designed to provide you with an easy-to-use guide to key small business providers.

contents

Part 2. Environmental Sustainability at HOME:

TOOLKIT HOME

Green Pages UK: Your Regional Directories of Product and Service Providers.

The resource directory is designed to provide you with an easy-to-use guide to key small business providers

Acknowledgements and Dedication

Another green book, and more people to thank for their tireless help with facts, suggestions, photocopied articles, checking and proofreading.

At Greener Times Publishing it would have been almost impossible to complete this project without the help and support of the Big Green Book Team's assistance and scrutiny of particular sections and the making of many useful suggestions for this new edition.

Many thanks are also due to our families who didn't complain when dinners were late and have endured hours of 'did you know this' conversations while this book was being written.

We would also like to dedicate this book to the Ecopreneurs of the future, and all the wonderful Ecopreneurs who never cease to inspire us, because being green is never black and white.

foreword

Small and Medium sized Enterprises (SMEs) are vital to the British economy: there are 4.5 million SMEs (source: BIS industry analysis 2011) making up 99% of the total number of businesses in the UK. They employ around 59.1% of the workforce and contribute nearly 50% of the country's Gross Domestic Productivity (GDP)

For these SMEs, Environmental Sustainability is an opportunity to become more competitive. This can be done by developing new and successful products based on social and environmental innovation; attracting or securing clients and investors with environmental and sustainability requirements; anticipating future regulations, and enhancing their overall management – human resources, quality, and environment.

The time for debating on the relevance of environmental sustainability is over. Now is the time for implementation. The people living on this planet need resources to meet their present needs without compromising the ability of future generations to meet theirs. This is the meaning of sustainable development. Environmental sustainability is the means to achieve sound and profitable sustainable development.

While there is an acceptance that environmental and sustainable business practices are the way forward, businesses need assistance to make this journey. There are many tools and initiatives available, but it is not easy for SMEs or homeowners with limited resources to decide which are relevant or the right ones to help them make greener choices. We hope that this handbook will enable you to take those first steps and chart your journey.

SMEs have specific advantages to implement environmental and sustainable development thanks to their size, flexibility and openness to innovation and change. They have shorter hierarchies that allow management to be receptive to employees; and also strong connections with their local environment and stakeholders. Approximately 94% of the Big Green Book: Small Business Environmental Network members are SMEs and entrepreneurs. Thanks to past and current Big Green Book's environmental and sustainability activities, several of these businesses have already engaged in, or strengthened, their 'Green Business' programmes. Big Green Book wants to further support these 'Green' engagements and is therefore pleased to launch this handbook in conjunction with Greener Times Publishing.

We invite anybody, and especially our SME and entrepreneur members, to use it. We also invite our larger members to help disseminate it to their business partners.

We would also encourage companies and individuals using this handbook to be active and give us feedback on what successes you may or may-not have achieved in becoming more sustainable. These will be a valuable addition to future editions of this handbook and contribute to the further development of good environmental and sustainability practices. Send your stories to: goinggreen@biggreenbook.com.

We wish you a fruitful reading. Thank you!

The Big Green Book: Small Business Environmental Network.
Business Engagement and Development Team

intro

A message from the author

As businesses large and small are realising that there is significant opportunity in the new green economy, too many are struggling to understand what they need to do to save money on energy costs, capitalise on incentives, prepare for new regulations and reduce their climatic impact. This book provides an introduction to the broad concept of Environmental Sustainability which under-pins this emerging low-carbon green economy.

Since the Brundtland report (*Our Common Future 1987*) up to the recent Rio Summit of 2012; The concept of Environmental Sustainability, which lies at the heart of moving towards a low-carbon green economic future, has largely remained an elusive conceptual framework. With many differing views and ideas of environmental sustainability around, it remains a fluid concept resulting in various definitions which have emerged over the past twenty five years; for some it has been at the starting point of going green and for others an end goal.

Where environmental sustainability starts and what its goals should be, and how these are to be achieved, is still very open to interpretation. What isn't in any doubt is that achieving a low-carbon green economy requires environmental sustainability to be at the core of creating significant advancements and opportunities in technology, processes and know-how.

Whether it is rising global temperatures or rising energy and fuel costs that motivate our actions, the need to make changes in our business decisions and our economy is increasingly urgent. With the UK an energy intensive economy, contributing one of the highest levels of greenhouse emissions per capita in the world, 'business as usual' can no longer be 'business as usual'. The future holds both risks and opportunities. Businesses should begin considering how rising fuel and energy costs, changing weather patterns, future regulatory requirements and consumer buying patterns might impact their present and future value. Business opportunities will grow for those providing goods or services that enable energy efficiency, provide renewable energy, mitigate climatic impact or help others adapt to a changing world.

The low-carbon green economy already exists with new markets emerging fast. Players include businesses of all sizes, government contractors, energy providers, venture capitalists, public sector entities, shareholders, green product manufacturers, developers of new low carbon solutions and green consumers.

UK businesses that are early adopters, and proactive about implementing environmental sustainability into their everyday business practices, stand to enjoy substantial competitive advantages in the future.

Businesses can take action now by:

• Anticipating rising fuel and energy prices by implementing a comprehensive programme to reduce energy and fuel use

• Identifying sources of local supply and manufacture to help take steps in reducing their supply chains carbon footprint and help support local sustainability

intro

• Engaging with government programmes designed to assist businesses with implementing environmental management policies

• Responding to both local and global environmental and sustainability requirements which will either affect them, their customers or suppliers

• Proactively addressing consumer and investor interest in transparency and environmentally sustainable products or services

Businesses that take action now stand a greater chance of being competitive than those who wait, because being on the front foot in an evolving environment has always made business sense.

I hope you find the handbook a useful introduction to what an emerging low-carbon green economy means for business and a starting point from which you can begin to make changes. Together, we can make a difference!

Welcome to a UK full of green opportunities and green businesses to help you live, work and build a greener environment.

" The Green Economy is a UK success story which shows that, quietly and without fanfare, the green business sector has become an economic force to be reckoned with!"

Stephen Lings

Author and Environmental Business Campaigner

Environmental Sustainability Equals Profitability

By taking steps towards greening your business, you can help yourself access a slice of the green economy.

Currently valued at £122 billion in the UK, this consists of between 5-10% per cent of GDP and £3.2 trillion worldwide.

This handbook offers practical advice, showing you how to grow your business by taking action to improve your green credentials.

By making your business more environmentally sustainable, green growth can lead directly to business growth.

" Over a third of the UK's economic growth in 2012 - 2013 is likely to have come from green business"
CBI. 2012

welcome

How to use this guide?

This Environmental and Sustainability Handbook is aimed at inspiring Small and Medium sized Enterprises (SMEs) and Homeowners; inviting them to engage in the environmental and sustainability journey, and providing them with the practical guidance to do so. In this handbook, some topics will be relevant to your activity, some others less so.

As Environmental Sustainability should be implemented progressively with a continuous improvement approach, you may feel it is too early to implement some steps. You can leave them aside and come back to them later, when your company or lifestyle is ready to advance more along the green footpath.

In this way we are encouraging a flexible use of this handbook – without overlooking any significant issue.

Greener Times Publishing in conjunction with the Big Green Book: Small Business Environmental Network; would like to congratulate you on picking up this handbook.

The fact that you are considering moving your business past environmental compliance and into a more environmentally sustainable business model says much about your core values and forward thinking.

We hope this handbook will help guide you to greening your small business for growth in the emerging greener economy.

This handbook has been developed to provide both a toolkit to assist Small-to-Medium sized Enterprises (SMEs) in taking their first steps towards achieving more sustainable outcomes in their organisations and also an easy-to-use UK resource directory of key product and service providers.

Notice

This Handbook is intended as an introductory and reference guide only; to basic environmental and sustainability principles, practices and actions for the workplace and home environment. It is not to be taken as a definitive textbook on business, lifestyle or guidance on Environmental or Sustainability implementation or understanding.

The information is designed to help any individual or business make simple informed decisions they can employ to help manage their costs and environmental impact. It is not intended as a substitute for any professional advice or services that may be required to conduct more detailed works of consideration [e.g. to implement or enact a firmer environmental policy, or to work towards an accredited Environmental Management Scheme (EMS), or to meet minimum legal environmental standards].

Contacts, Internet addresses and telephone numbers given in this handbook were accurate at the time of print. These as well as schemes, policies and regulations mentioned in this handbook are subject to change or may subsequently have been superseded. Therefore ensure that you always check that any information is still relevant or current before making any decisions that may affect your business, home or wellbeing – always seek professional support and advice.

intro

introduction & overview

Over the last ten years, with the steady increase in regulation, environmental sustainability has become part of a new economic model for businesses to remain robust.

For business success today means not just a healthy bottom line, but a healthy **triple bottom line** that takes financial, social, and environmental performance into consideration: the essence of sustainability. Many businesses also believe that they have a responsibility to help their community and make a positive contribution to the world.

The issues and opportunities motivating these organisations can also drive your business success. Consider consumer demand; consumers are increasingly concerned about environmental issues, and the marketplace for sustainable products and practices continues to grow. As consumers learn more about environmental and health threats from hazardous chemicals and climate change, they seek companies that address their concerns.

An increasing segment of UK consumers are highly motivated, well-informed, and concerned about environmental and health issues. Environmentally aware businesses that have reduced their **environmental footprint** are better positioned to meet this growing market demand.

The New Green Consumer

The Benefits of Greening Your Business

Environmentally-sustainable business practices can yield enormous rewards, both for the environment and the business.

Being green can:

Save money from reduced waste and increased efficiency.

Bring peace of mind from reduced concerns about health and safety liability.

Improve public relations.

Improve employee pride and morale.

Attract green consumers.

Attract motivated employees.

Differentiate your business from competitors.

Provide flexibility in uncertain times.

Minimise risk, financial and otherwise, from the impacts of climate change.

Demonstrate leadership and commitment.

73%

of consumers consider it important that companies have good environmental records

Think   Act   Save

Greening your business can be a way to conserve both the environment and your financial resources.

Environmental realities are also driving corporate sustainability efforts. There is little doubt that environmental issues, particularly climate change, are going to alter the regulatory and market landscape in the near future. Environmentally efficient companies will be better able to navigate these regulatory changes and be better positioned to weather negative events like energy price spikes.

Consumers are shying away from more toxic products, concerned by media reports of dangers such as chemical compounds leaching from plastic containers. Companies that have reduced their use of toxic chemicals will enjoy better public relations and be more likely to thrive over time as such issues continue to drive media reports and public concerns. These companies can also reduce their potential regulatory costs and liabilities, as laws that focus on hazardous material, do not apply to non-hazardous substitutes.

Climate change and toxic chemicals are just two concerns that will affect businesses in the near future. Other issues, such as unpredictable energy costs, drought and depleting natural resources, may also significantly impact business success. However, these challenges offer small business leaders a historic opportunity to make a difference and turn a profit.

What Makes a Company Sustainable?

The characteristics of a greener, more sustainable business include:

- Incorporating "green thinking" into the company culture.
- Eliminating inefficiencies.
- Minimising its impact on the environment.
- Streamlining its processes.
- Thinking long-term.
- Evolving and adapts to new information in a changing world.
- Seeking continual improvement.

Green Premium

Greening has become mainstream. Historical barriers to becoming more sustainable, such as higher costs and low consumer demand have largely been removed or significantly diminished. Today, for example, the UK government offers incentives for **renewable energy** and **hybrid vehicles**; organic product sales continue to grow by about 20% annually; and green product sales are expected to double over the next two years.

Small business owners who have been implementing sustainable strategies for decades are seeing these changes first-hand. The sustained success of these green small businesses and many others like them is evidence that greening can and does 'bring in the money'.

Guide Overview

The Environmental and Sustainability Handbook provides small business owners and managers with practical advice and tools to implement sustainable and environmentally-preferable business practices that go beyond compliance. The handbook offers a framework to strategically green your business and presents realistic opportunities to improve environmental performance.

To get your business on track to sustainability, The Environmental and Sustainability Handbook will help you:
- Understand the impact your business has on the environment.
- Develop and implement a strategy to minimise this impact.
- Explore opportunities to become more sustainable.
- Share your sustainability efforts with your customers.
- Continually strive for improvement.

Section 2 presents a five step greening strategy. Optional charts can help tailor your approach to fit your business.

Section 3 discusses opportunities for improving your environmental performance by area of environmental impact and offers guidance on communicating your greening efforts to the public.

Definitions of terms you may be unfamiliar with are in **Appendix A.**

Appendix B provides actionable samples to help you get started.

The journey to sustainability is unique for every business, and it's important to remember that lessons can be learned from those who have already forged a greener profitable path.

Remember: that any contacts for products or services to help you green your business are listed in the **Resource Directory- Part 3** of your handbook located towards the back of the book.

Steps to Environmental Sustainability

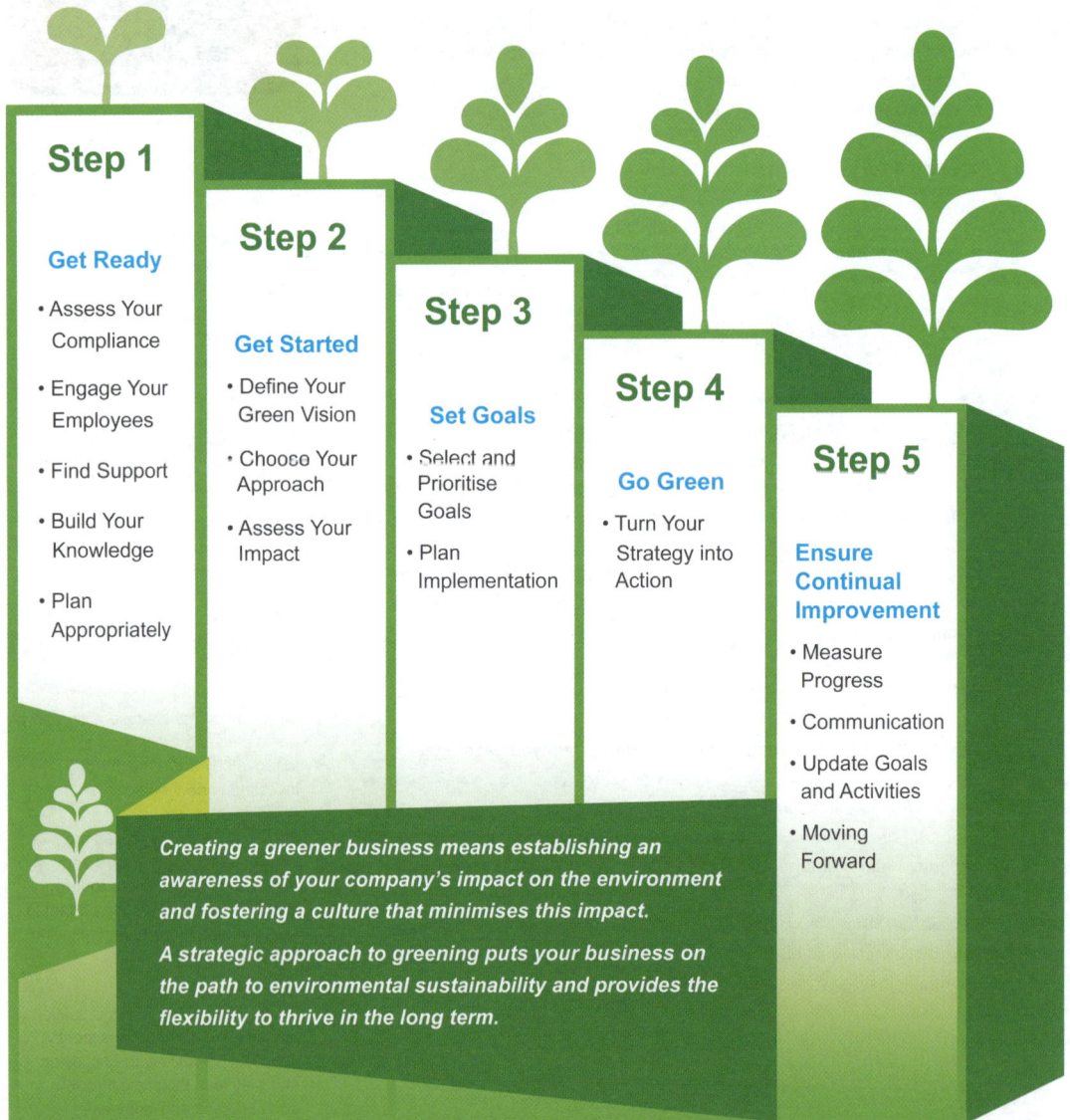

Step 1

Get Ready

- Assess Your Compliance
- Engage Your Employees
- Find Support
- Build Your Knowledge
- Plan Appropriately

Step 2

Get Started

- Define Your Green Vision
- Choose Your Approach
- Assess Your Impact

Step 3

Set Goals

- Select and Prioritise Goals
- Plan Implementation

Step 4

Go Green

- Turn Your Strategy into Action

Step 5

Ensure Continual Improvement

- Measure Progress
- Communication
- Update Goals and Activities
- Moving Forward

Creating a greener business means establishing an awareness of your company's impact on the environment and fostering a culture that minimises this impact.

A strategic approach to greening puts your business on the path to environmental sustainability and provides the flexibility to thrive in the long term.

steps
to environmental sustainability

This section presents a five-step strategy to help you create a more environmentally-responsible company and lay the foundation for a sustainable future.

After completing the five step strategy to environmental sustainability, how can you be sure you've achieved success and have started to become a more greener business?

You can when:

- *"Green thinking" is part of your company culture.*
- *Minimisation of environmental impact is just the way business is done.*
- *Working greener is routine.*
- *You are committed to seeking a better way.*

Here's a quick overview of the five steps:

Step 1: Get Ready helps you lay the groundwork for success.

Step 2: Get Started helps you decide how green you want your business to be, select the best approach to get there, and assess the impact your business has on the environment. The Emerging Issues and Motivations Charts will help identify issues and motivators that influence these choices, and the Environmental Impact Assessment Chart captures your business' impacts on the environment.

Step 3: Set Goals helps you choose your greening goals and identify the actions to achieve them. Use the Goals Charts to help identify and prioritise goals.

Step 4: Go Green presents a discussion on what to keep in mind as you move forward.

Step 5: Ensure Continual Improvement discusses how to make sure your company continues to reduce its environmental impact and flourish at the same time. This final step includes ideas for measuring progress and updating goals.

EXPLAINER

Five steps to sustainability

No organisation achieves this in a single leap. Organisations that have systematically increased their sustainability describe a journey with five steps:

1

Unaware: The organisation is at risk, but people in it are not aware of this and not thinking about change.

2

Aware: People become aware that practice is leading to risks for the organisation and want to make changes but may not know how to and need help.

3

Making changes: People in the organisation start to take action and put in place new initiatives to improve key areas, such as investing in new skills.

4

Delivering: New practices are established where needed and things are mostly good enough. Risk analysis becomes important in managing uncertainty and allowing further growth.

5

Strong or excellent: Organisations become strong; they consistently support and delivery their mission, and may lead their field through good practice and innovation.

Step 1: Get Ready

Step 1 will help you:

• Assess your compliance.

• Engage your employees.

• Find support.

• Build your environmental knowledge.

• Plan appropriately.

GREEN·STEPS

TO EMPLOYEE ENGAGEMENT

RESEARCH
& PLANNING •

TRAINING &
DEVELOPMENT •

CULTURE &
BEHAVIOUR CHANGE •

MEASUREMENT
& EVALUATION •

Step 1: Get Ready

Assess Your Compliance

Your first step would be to identify and meet any regulatory requirements. How embarrassing would it be to say you are a green company and then be hit with an environmental violation? Knowing your regulatory requirements can also help you identify your environmental impact and set goals that reduce the impact and regulatory liability.

Engage Your Employees

Employee buy-in is critical for success. It is your employees who will be responsible for implementing more sustainable practices. Sustainability may require a cultural shift for your company and that can only happen with the support of your employees. Share your vision of what you want your business to become with your employees, involve them upfront, and ask for suggestions on how to green their activities.

Employees may have great ideas on how to reduce environmental impacts and implement your vision. They may recognize; where waste and inefficiencies occur better than upper management. For instance, the employees responsible for waste are probably the best source for ideas on establishing a recycling programme. You may find that some of your employees are already familiar with greening strategies and even practice them at home or have experience from a previous job.

There are many ways to encourage employee participation. Depending on the size of your business, consider creating a green team to head up sustainability initiatives. Provide rewards for good ideas and incentives for environmental behaviour. Perhaps most important, as the owner or manager, it is vital that you "walk the talk" and demonstrate green behaviour as an example to your employees.

Find Support

There are many government and NGO sustainable business organisations that can provide information on environmental practices, or join a network such as the **Big Green Book: Small Business Environmental Network**, (www.biggreenbook.com) and create a network of green product and service providers. Consider partnering with other small businesses that are going green and support each other with discounts and advertising. Environmental committees and workgroups in trade associations and other business organisations can also be helpful. Many local and government regulatory agencies have initiatives to help small businesses go green.

Build Your Knowledge

Being familiar with environmental issues will help you understand the environmental impact of your businesses and make better decisions for the future. You can start with the resources in this guide and then build your knowledge by reading some of the many books, articles, and web sites on environmental issues. Your interests may range from environmental philosophy to technical information to finding out more about business and the environment. The more informed you are, the easier it is to develop a successful strategy and stay motivated.

Plan Appropriately.

Careful planning, as with any intelligent business decision, can help you gain maximum success. If your employees don't share your vision or if you decide to roll out your greening plan during your busiest time of the year, it's going to be difficult to make progress. Be sure to allocate sufficient resources to ensure success and include greening initiatives in your budget planning.

Step 2: Get Started

This step includes several forms that will help you plan strategically.

Define Your Green Vision

A clearly defined vision of what you want your business to become will help you set goals, motivate employees, and gain support from customers. What does sustainability mean to you? What does an environmentally-friendly version of your business look like? You may not know the answers to these questions yet, but Step 2 will help your sustainable business vision become a little clearer.

Step 2: Get Started

Step 2 will help you:

- Create a long-term vision of your sustainable business.

- Choose your approach to greening.

- Identify the environmental impacts of your business.

Our vision is to pioneer a green business model that blends profit with environmental and social benefit, whilst delivering outstanding construction services.

(Sample environmental sustainabilty vision statement)

Environmental Sustainability Ruler

Look at the Environmental Sustainability Ruler that follows and think about where you want to position your business? Do you want to pollute less and use fewer resources than companies in the same sector? This will make you a greener than average company. Maybe you want to be truly sustainable and move towards using only renewable resources, producing zero waste, and advocating for greening your community?

Use the Environmental Sustainability Ruler to help guide your vision.

Environmental Sustainability Ruler

Environmental Sustainability Performance

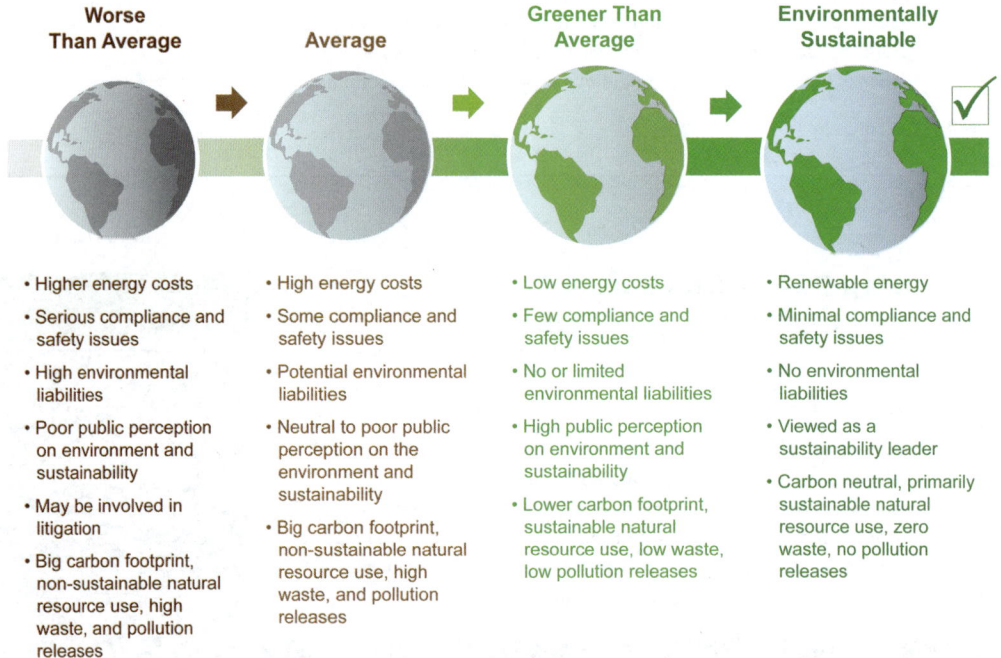

Worse Than Average	Average	Greener Than Average	Environmentally Sustainable
• Higher energy costs	• High energy costs	• Low energy costs	• Renewable energy
• Serious compliance and safety issues	• Some compliance and safety issues	• Few compliance and safety issues	• Minimal compliance and safety issues
• High environmental liabilities	• Potential environmental liabilities	• No or limited environmental liabilities	• No environmental liabilities
• Poor public perception on environment and sustainability	• Neutral to poor public perception on the environment and sustainability	• High public perception on environment and sustainability	• Viewed as a sustainability leader
• May be involved in litigation	• Big carbon footprint, non-sustainable natural resource use, high waste, and pollution releases	• Lower carbon footprint, sustainable natural resource use, low waste, low pollution releases	• Carbon neutral, primarily sustainable natural resource use, zero waste, no pollution releases
• Big carbon footprint, non-sustainable natural resource use, high waste, and pollution releases			

As you define your vision consider how outside environmental issues, such as regulatory changes, will affect your business. For instance, is your local authority getting serious about enforcing discharge water rules? Also, think about marketplace trends. Are your customers interested in greener companies or are your corporate clients looking to green their supply chain? Awareness of these issues will better inform your greening decisions. The Environmental and Regulatory Issues Chart that follows will help you identify relevant outside issues.

Example Environmental and Regulatory Issues Chart

A Small Business might fill the chart out as follows:

Environmental and Regulatory Issues	Potential Impact on Your Company	Positive or Negative	Level of Concern / Likelihood	Time Period
Climate Change	Not sure, depends on regulations	Don't know	Low / high	Short for regulations; long term for environmental. changes
High Energy Prices	Higher costs	Negative	Medium / medium	Not sure
New Regulations GHG (Green House Gas Regulations)	PERC phase out would require new machines / approaches	Negative. – High initial cost. Positive – Levels playing field reduces environmental. liability, compliance & safety issues	High / not sure	Need to find out more about possible local council or governement regulations and timing. Research alternatives
Market Pressures	Greener consumers	Depends on our response	High / medium	Current? Need to research trends & look at response of competition

Here is a chart for you to complete:

Environmental and Regulatory Issues Chart

Tick When Task Completed ✓

Environmental and Regulatory Issues	Potential Impact on Your Company	Positive or Negative	Level of Concern/ Likelihood	Time Period
Climate Change				
High Energy Prices				
New Regulations GHG				
Market Pressures				

Now consider your motivations. What are the top reasons you want to go green? Knowing what is driving your efforts will help you select goals, set priorities and communicate your vision. Most importantly perhaps, understanding your underlying motivations will help you know when you have achieved your goals. Use the Motivations Chart on the next page to identify your most important motivators and the level of their importance.

Tick When Task Completed

Motivators for Going Green	Importance (low, medium, high)
Personal convictions	
Increased profit	
Image	
Longevity of company	
Customer demand	
Employee satisfaction	
Add value to the community	
Desire to be a leader	
Expand customer base	
Keep up with the competition	
Inspire innovation	
Cost of compliance	
Environmental constraints e.g. water shortages, raw materials etc.	
Energy costs	
Regulatory concerns	
Other	
Other	
Notes	

After listing outside environmental issues and identifying motivators, go back to the Environmental Sustainability Ruler to see if you want to adjust your desired location on the bar. Then fill out the final Putting It All Together Chart that follows to summarise your objectives, outside environmental issues, and motivators. If you want to formalise your vision, use this chart to help write an environmental commitment statement or sustainability policy. You can refer back to this Chart when setting specific goals and actions.

Tick When Task Completed

Vision (where you want to be on the Environmental Performance Ruler)	
Top Environmental and Regulatory Issues of Concern *(in order of priority)*	
Motivators with highest importance	
Write a sentence or two describing your vision of sustainability and long-term objectives for the business.	
Approach	Formal EMS (ISO 14001 style) Other formal approach _____ Greening Guide steps (this publication) Ad hoc Other _____

EMAS -

The European
Eco-Management
and Audit System

EMAS

Key elements of EMAS

EMAS' distinctive key elements are performance, credibility and transparency:

Performance

Carrying out annual updates of environmental policy targets and actions to implement and evaluate these targets

Transparency

Environmental statements provide public information about the environmental performance of the organisation

Credibility

Third party verification by independent auditors guarantees the value of both actions taken and disclosed information

EMAS and ISO 14001

The European Commission has recognised that ISO 14001 can provide a stepping stone for EMAS. The EN ISO 14001: 2004 environmental management system requirements are an integral part of EMAS III (Annex II of EMAS III).

However, EMAS takes into account additional elements to support organisations in continually and significantly improving their environmental performance.

EMAS

+ Employee involvement

+ Public reporting through EMAS environmental statement

ISO / EN ISO 14001

+ Registration by public authority

+ Legal compliance

+ Performance Improvement checked by environmental verifiers

(Adapted from European Union EMAS Documents)

You should now have a good idea of where you want to see your company in the long term. You should also, by now, recognise the environmental issues that are likely to affect your company, and the internal values driving your efforts to improve sustainability.

Choose Your Approach

A successful approach to greening can be simple or complex. Larger organisations may benefit from a structured approach, while a smaller company can make major improvements with informal policies or an ad hoc style. There are many approaches in between. What is important is to select the approach that will help you reach your long-term objectives.

The **Environmental Management System (EMS)** is a widely used approach that provides a formalised structure for planning and implementing a comprehensive environmental management programme. Many companies, particularly large multi-nationals, certify their EMS with the International Organisation for Standardisation (ISO). Certification provides credibility, and some companies require their suppliers to be ISO14001 certified. For more information on EMS and ISO14001 *visit www.iso.org* (see local advisors in Directory listings at rear of book). An EMS, even an ISO-certified EMS, does not automatically make your company green or sustainable. It is just a tool to help you get there.

There are other formalised approaches to greening which could also be a part of another management approach such as Lean-a business methodology that streamlines manufacturing to eliminate waste and reduce cost. You may prefer a less formal approach. The steps in this guide provide the same focus on strategic planning and continual improvement as an EMS, but are simpler and less formal. If you decide to go with a formal EMS, you can still use the steps presented here to help identify your impacts, objectives and targets.

Assess Your Impact

Once you know where you want to go, it's then important to understand what impacts your business has on the environment so you can identify the actions to take which have the greatest benefit for the environment. Don't be intimidated by this exercise. Nobody knows your business as well as you, and you probably already have a good understanding of your largest impacts. Environmental permits or regulations that apply to your business usually indicate areas already having an environmental impact. For example, an air permit means that you are releasing air pollution.

Use the Environmental Impact Assessment Chart on page18 to identify the overall environmental impacts of your business. You can then assess and evaluate the relative contributions that all your business activities have in a positive or negative way on the environment.

Environmental Impact Assessment Chart Instructions

This Chart will help you identify the specific environmental impacts of your company. It already includes information on impacts for common business functions. You need to customise it to reflect your company's unique situation.

The individual columns are described below.

1. Activity Area:

The Chart is organised by functional area-transportation, office, warehouse, manufacturing, business processes, and building and grounds. Business process refers to non-manufacturing processes that are specific to your business like food preparation in a restaurant, the working area of a garage, or a retail store's sales operations. You will need to customise the rows under Business Process to fit your business.

2. Environmental Impacts:

This column captures how each activity area can impact the environment. Air and water pollution, waste, toxins, habitat loss, use of natural resources, and Green House Gases (GHG) are typical environmental impacts. Impacts can be direct, such as emissions from the exhaust of your delivery van or indirect, such as GHG emissions from the power plant that produces your electricity or toxins released during the manufacturing of the bleached white paper you purchase.

3. Impacts of Your Company:

Describe, or if possible quantify, each activity's impact at your company. For example, under Paper use, list the main uses for paper in your company and how much you use. You might enter "printing reports and invoices, two reams a day." Alternatively, under Delivery services, you might record "two LPG-powered company vans that drive about 100 miles a week with an average mileage of 20 miles per gallon (MPG)." Permits or other regulatory require-ments will tell you about some of these impacts. If possible, include costs. This information will help you set and evaluate goals so be as detailed as possible.

4. Impact Contribution:

What is the relative contribution of each activity area to the overall environmental impact of your company? You may want to have a short description for the contribution and then rate it as: very low, low, medium, high or very high. Consider factors such as:

Environmental Impacts
quick reference

Air Pollution: The release of harmful matter like particulates, and gases like sulphur dioxide, nitrogen oxides, carbon monoxide, and volatile organic compounds into the air. Ozone, a harmful air pollutant, is created by sunlight interacting with other air pollutants.

Erosion: The wearing away of soil. The increased flow of stormwater from impervious surfaces like rooftops and pavement erodes land, scours stream banks, adds silt that carries contaminants to water bodies and degrades habitat.

GHG Emissions: The release of heat-trapping Green House Gases (GHGs) such as carbon dioxide, methane, and nitrous oxide into the air. Greenhouse gases keep the earth warm, but increased concentrations contribute to climate change.

Water Pollution: Sewage, fertilisers, pesticides, oil, silt, and other pollutants that are discharged, spilled or washed into water, including contaminants from air pollution that settle onto land and are washed into water bodies.

Habitat Loss: Degradation and loss of the natural conditions that animals and plants need to survive. Caused by activities such as; development, deforesta-tion, and contamination from stormwater runoff and other pollution. It can occur directly from activities like road building, or indirectly, for example contamination from vehicle exhausts.

Toxins: Chemicals which pose a severe health risk such as chlorine, formaldehyde, and dioxins. Toxins can be poisonous, cause cancer, and harm reproductive systems, and may be present in pollution, manufacturing by-products, and chemical products like cleaning solvents.

Resource Use: Using, extracting or harvesting natural and manufactured resources can deplete ecosystems and destroy habitat. Associated activities such as transportation and processing can cause air and water pollution. Excessive extraction of water from lakes and rivers, or aquifers can damage habitats by drying wetlands, creating low flow rivers, and stopping natural springs.

Hazardous Waste: Waste that is considered toxic or flammable. Because it is strictly regulated, there are formal regulatory definitions of hazardous waste.

Waste Disposal: Removing and eliminating discarded materials. Disposal of non-toxic waste material has environmental impacts from transportation, landfill space requirements and leaching, or incineration.

Energy Use: The production and use of energy from fossil fuels like coal and petroleum creates air pollution (carbon monoxide, carbon dioxide, and toxins like mercury and benzene) and hazardous solid waste (from coal) and destroys habitats.

Volume or size: (e.g., amount of waste generated, or number of miles driven by company vehicles).

1. Toxicity (a very hazardous chemical versus a non-hazardous chemical).

2. Direct releases to the environment (e.g., delivery van exhaust, releases of an ozone depleting substance, or discharge of industrial wastewater to the sewer).

3. The potential for harm, either to employees or the environment (the high possibility of petrol spills from refuelling a lawn mower, or asthma from air pollution from diesel lorries).

4. Indirect harm to the environment (air pollution from the generation of electricity or the loss of habitat from road building).

5. Frequency of an activity (e.g., pesticide applications probably occur infrequently, business travel may occur frequently, and heating, ventilation, and air conditioning (HVAC) use occurs very frequently).

Tick When Task Completed

Environmental Impact Assessment Chart

1. Activity Area	2. Environmental Impacts	3. Impacts of your company	4. Impact Contribution
TRANSPORTATION			
Employee Commuting	Air pollution		
	Energy use		
	GHG emissions		
	Habitat loss		
	Water pollution		
Business Travel	Air pollution		
	Energy use		
	GHG emissions		
	Habitat loss		
	Water pollution		
Shipping / Receiving	Air pollution		
	Energy use		
	GHG emissions		
	Habitat loss		
	Water pollution		
Delivery Services / Fleets	Air pollution		
	Energy use		
	GHG emissions		
	Habitat loss		
	Water pollution		

notes

Environmental
Impact
Assessment

Environmental Impact Assessment Chart

Tick When Task Completed ✓

1. Activity Area	2. Environmental Impacts	3. Impacts of Your Company	4. Impact Contribution
OFFICE AREA			
Paper use	Air pollution		
	GHG emissions		
	Habitat loss		
	Resource use		
	Toxins		
	Waste disposal		
	Water pollution		
	Water use		
Solid waste	Air pollution		
	Energy use		
	GHG emissions		
	Waste disposal		
	Water pollution		
Lighting	Air pollution		
	Energy use		
	GHG emissions		
	Habitat loss		
	Toxins		
Heating, Ventilation & Air Conditioning (HVAC)	Air pollution		
	Energy use		
	GHG emissions		
	Waste disposal		
	Water Use		

notes

Tick When Task Completed   **Environmental Impact Assessment Chart**

1. Activity Area	2. Environmental Impacts		3. Impacts of Your Company	4. Impact Contribution
OFFICE AREA				
Other equipment (copiers, computers, etc.)	Air pollution			
	Energy use			
	GHG emissions			
	Habitat loss			
	Toxins			
	Water pollution			
Water use	Habitat loss			
	Resource use			
	Water pollution			
Purchasing	Air pollution			
	Resource use			
	Toxins			
	Waste disposal			
	Water pollution			
Cleaning	Air pollution			
	Resource use			
	Toxins			
	Waste disposal			
	Water pollution			
	Water Use			

notes

Environmental
Impact
Assessment

Environmental Impact Assessment Chart

Tick When Task Completed ✓

1. Activity Area	2. Environmental Impacts	3. Impacts of Your Company	4. Impact Contribution
MANUFACTURING			
Paper Use	Air pollution		
	GHG emissions		
	Habitat loss		
	Resource use		
	Toxins		
	Waste disposal		
	Water pollution		
	Water use		
Solid Waste	Air pollution		
	Energy use		
	GHG emissions		
	Waste disposal		
	Water pollution		
Lighting	Air pollution		
	Energy use		
	GHG emissions		
	Habitat loss		
	Toxins		
Heating, Ventilation & Air Conditioning (HVAC)	Air pollution		
	Energy use		
	GHG emissions		
	Toxins		
	Waste disposal		
	Water use		

Environmental
Impact
Assessment

notes

✓ Tick When Task Completed   **Environmental Impact Assessment Chart**

1. Activity Area	2. Environmental Impacts	3. Impacts of Your Company	4. Impact Contribution
MANUFACTURING			
Raw Materials	Air pollution		
	Energy use		
	GHG emissions		
	Habitat loss		
	Toxins		
	Water pollution		
Water Use	Habitat loss		
	Resource use		
	Water pollution		
Hazardous Waste	Air pollution		
	Persistent organic pollutants (POPs)		
	Endocrine disrupting chemicals (EDCs)		
	Waste disposal		
	Water pollution		
Releases	Air pollution		
	Accidental spills		
	Toxins		
	Waste disposal		
	Water pollution		
	Water use		

Environmental

Impact

Assessment

Environmental Impact Assessment Chart

Tick When Task Completed ✓

1. Activity Area	2. Environmental Impacts	3. Impacts of Your Company	4. Impact Contribution
BUSINESS PROCESS			
Meetings	Energy use		
	GHG emissions		
	Resource use		
	Waste disposal		
Other			
1. Activity Area	**2. Environmental Impacts**	**3. Impacts of Your Company**	**4. Impact Contribution**
BUILDINGS & GROUNDS			
Water Use	Habitat loss		
	Resource use		
	Waste disposal		
Mowing, Leaf Blowing, etc.	Air pollution		
	Energy use		
	GHG emissions		
Storm (Rain) Water Runoff – Roof	Erosion		
	Habitat loss		
	Water pollution		
Storm (Rain) Water Runoff – Paved Areas	Erosion		
	Habitat loss		
	Water pollution		
Pest control	Habitat loss		
	Water Pollution		
	Toxins		

Goal Setting

Specific

Measurable

Achievable

Relevant

Time-based

Step 3: Set Goals

Step 3 will help you:

- Identify SMART goals.
- Select and prioritise goals that will help you reach your objectives.
- Define responsibilities.

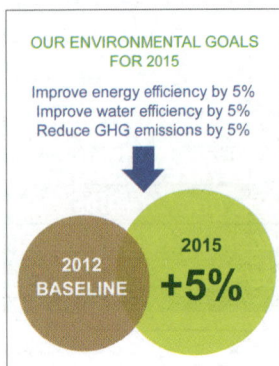

OUR ENVIRONMENTAL GOALS FOR 2015

Improve energy efficiency by 5%
Improve water efficiency by 5%
Reduce GHG emissions by 5%

2012 BASELINE

2015 +5%

Example of Goal Setting

In the introduction of each topic area in **Section 3: Opportunities**, there is also an overview of common environmental impacts from business practices.

The **UK government** and the **European Union** have developed numerous environmental regulations to ensure that the most significant environmental impacts are monitored, controlled and minimised. If any of your business activities require a permit, these activities most likely have a significant impact on the environment. Explore the Environment Agency's online compliance assistance resources for small businesses at *www.environment-agency.gov.uk* to better understand the regulations that affect your industry, to make sure you are not violating any regulations, and to identify impacts from your business. You can also check with your local authority regulatory agency or trade association. Some voluntary environmental organisations also provide tools and information to help identify environmental impacts.

With a better understanding of the impacts of your business on the environment, you may wish to review the Charts from **Step. 2 Get started**; to see if you want to make any changes to your green vision.

Step 3: Set Goals

A clear set of goals can turn the vision you developed in **Step 2** into reality. The right goals will help determine the future direction of your company, and motivate your employees. So how do you choose the right goals?

For starters, make sure your goals are **SMART: specific, measurable, achievable, relevant,** and **time-based**.

Specific: Perhaps you envision a carbon balanced company. This is a specific long-term goal. To reach it, you will also need to set specific short-term goals. An initial short-term goal could be to measure your Green House Gas emissions to determine a starting point, and a subsequent goal might be to reduce the company's carbon footprint by 10% a year.

Measurable: If you can't measure your goal, it is hard to know when it has been reached or how to evaluate your efforts. Consider the difference between a goal to be a green company and a goal to use 100% renewable energy. Without a precise definition, it is hard to measure "greenness," but the source of your energy is easy to measure.

Achievable: your goals need to be ambitious enough to make a difference but not impossible to achieve. The right balance will motivate your employees without discouraging them. You may want to be a zero-emissions company within one year, but it is probably impractical. A more realistic goal is to cut emissions by 20% in the first year with zero-emissions as a long-term goal.

Relevant: your goals need to relate to what you are trying to achieve. Make sure that your goals will meaningfully reduce your environmental impact and align with your vision.

Time-based: Goals need to have a defined timeframe. A deadline provides incentive to take action and move forward. Choose realistic timelines for your goals, and include milestones and periodic assessments to measure your progress and stay motivated.

Select and Prioritise Goals

1. Review Your Long-term Business Objectives

Where do you want your business to be in five or ten years? Before deciding on your goals, identify long-term business objectives to ensure that your goals will help you achieve your vision.

Review the *'Putting It All Together'* Chart from **Step 2** and then write several long-term objectives in the space provided below. Be sure the objectives are specific and clear enough for others to understand.

Long-term Business Objectives

2. List Goals and Activities

Taking your long-term objectives into account, list all the environmental and sustainability goals you can think of on a separate piece of paper, you will prioritise the goals in the next step. You may want to first read through **Section 3, Opportunities** for ideas. Also discuss the goals with your employees and review them against the **SMART** list to make sure you have goals that will take you where you want to be.

Once you have identified goals, list the activities needed to reach the goal. The **Environmental Impact Assessment Chart** from **Step 2** can help with this. For example, if your goal is to reduce electricity use by 25%, you can use the Chart to identify where you can get that saving from lighting, changing a business process to use less energy, or replacing old inefficient appliances.

> **"A goal** that is **not written** is not a goal. It only becomes **real** when you **write** it down."

Prioritise Key Goals

Low	Medium	High
Important to a few	Important to some	Important to most

BENEFIT AXIS

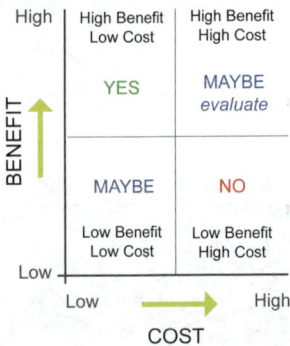

High

BENEFIT →

High Benefit Low Cost	High Benefit High Cost
YES	**MAYBE** *evaluate*
MAYBE	**NO**
Low Benefit Low Cost	Low Benefit High Cost

Low

Low   High

COST

3. Prioritise

After listing environmental sustainability goals and activities, focus on the ones that will help achieve your vision for the future, that are based on your most significant environmental impacts, and that will make the most sense for your business. Choose the goals that will address the greatest impacts (see impacts from the *Environmental Impact Assessment Chart*) and where you can make the biggest strides.

For example;

1. Do you run a retail store with piles of cardboard packing boxes leftover after a delivery arrives? Your goals may include working with suppliers to find alternatives to cardboard packing boxes, such as reusable wooden crates, and asking suppliers to minimise empty lorry journeys and transportation of empty crates.

2. Is your dry cleaning store using toxic chemicals? Your goals may include exploring alternative options to become a green cleaner or minimise the amount used.

3. Does your restaurant throw away large amounts of food waste daily? Your goals may include donating or composting food waste.

Like any business decision, you need to consider the costs and benefits of your goals – financially and environmentally. Evaluate your goals based on feasibility, payback period, financial return on investment, and social return on investment. Think about how much money you are willing to invest in sustainability measures. What changes you can afford to make? What effort that will be required from your employees? While it may not be easy to put an exact monetary value on environmental or sustainability benefits, it might help to think about prioritising goals in terms of the opposite grid:

You can use the **'Benefit Axis'** to consider the benefits to your company and to the environment. Obviously, a project that is low cost and high benefit to your company or to the environment is the project to choose. But what about a project that is high cost, has a high benefit for the environment but a lower benefit for the company? This project may take more thought before making a decision but don't automatically dismiss a goal because of the initial cost. Be sure to consider intangible benefits like customer perceptions and employee pride first. Analyse the costs over time and factor in all the components, including the intangibles, before making a final decision.

When setting priorities, consider which of the possible goals:

• Will make you the most competitive.

• Includes low-hanging fruit, like reducing or recycling office paper, which is important and easy.

• Will have the biggest positive impact on the environment or on your bottom line, like installing an on-site wind turbine.

• Contributes to the growth or longevity of your business.

• Has other benefit's such as the reduction of toxins, that also improves worker safety and reduces compliance issues.

• Relate to your vision and long-term objectives.

Environmental

Goals

Based on your priorities, select the goals that you want to focus on and enter them in the Environmental Goals chart below.

Environmental Goals Chart

Goal 1

Tick When Task Completed

Timeframe	Who	Metric

Activities for Goal 1	Timeframe	Who	Metric
1			
2			
3			
4			
5			

Goal 2

Tick When Task Completed

Timeframe	Who	Metric

Activities for Goal 2	Timeframe	Who	Metric
1			
2			
3			
4			
5			

Environmental
Goals

notes

Environmental Goals Chart

Tick When Task Completed

Goal 3

Timeframe	Who	Metric

Activities for Goal 3	Timeframe	Who	Metric
1			
2			
3			
4			
5			

Tick When Task Completed

Goal 4

Timeframe	Who	Metric

Activities for Goal 4	Timeframe	Who	Metric
1			
2			
3			
4			
5			

notes

Environmental
Goals

Environmental Goals Chart

Goal 5

Timeframe	Who	Metric

Activities for Goal 5	Timeframe	Who	Metric
1			
2			
3			
4			
5			

Plan Implementation

Once you know your goals, think about the activities that are needed to achieve these goals.

Then enter the activities into the **Environmental Goal Chart**. The chart also has space for the timeframe / milestones for each activity, the person who will be responsible for implementation, and how it will be measured.

Clearly defining this information will help ensure that your goals are achieved. Identifying employee responsibilities for implementing the actions are particularly important.

Consider also including environmental performances in employee appraisals. Employees are more likely to make environmental sustainability actions a priority if senior and middle management makes it a priority and if performance reviews communicate and define them clearly.

Step 4: Go Green

Step 4 will help you:

- Implement your greening strategy.

STOP WASTE

SAVE ENERGY

Go green

SAVE MONEY

Step 4: Go Green

Turn Your Strategy into Action

At this point, you are ready to turn your greening strategy into action!

It's your business, and you and your employees know best how to make a strategy work. **Steps 2** and **3** have helped you develop a vision and a plan. Now you just have to bring that plan into life!

Check to make sure your company goals are clearly translated into specific activities, that the activities are reasonable, and that each employee understands their responsibilities. Employees should also understand the company's vision for being environmentally sustainable, be aware of the company's greening goals, and should be assigned responsibility for specific goals.

Leadership and communication is the key to the success of any strategy. If greening your business means major changes to the company culture, much of your success depends on managerial skill. As you know, managers have to communicate effectively, *"walk the talk,"* and set a positive example.

It is important to reinforce responsibilities and green thinking on a regular basis. Educate your employees on why greening is important; e-mail relevant online articles, leave environmental magazines in the lunchroom, and talk about the underlying issues. Send out regular e-mails or post signs reminding your team of the company's green goals and vision for environmental sustainability. It is important to communicate progress towards goals so everyone can see how their actions make a difference and turn their actions on environmental sustainability into profitability.

Motivate your employees. Remind them that for the company's environmental sustainability goals to succeed it relies on teamwork. Recognise product performance and thank employees for their efforts. Consider friendly competitions between offices, departments or different employee groups. Maybe the group that reduces energy the most or uses the least paper wins a lunch out or cinema tickets.

As you move forward, remember to stay focused on the results. Step 5 will help you measure your progress and create a system for continual improvement.

Step 5: Ensure Continual Improvement

Sustainability is an on-going commitment to reduce environmental impacts for the benefit of future generations. The goal of **Step 5** is to help your company continue to make progress towards sustainability. This step will give you strategies for keeping your commitment going and making your company greener every year.

Measure Progress

Step 4 helped put your greening strategy into place. **Step 5** checks to see if the strategy is working. Product measures will tell you if you're moving along the Environmental Sustainability Ruler in the right direction and are on track to reach your goals. Measures will also help you evaluate your efforts so that you can keep doing what works and change what is not effective. Seeing results will also help motivate you and your employees.

There are different approaches to measurement. If you plan to participate in a programme that requires reporting to an external organisation, it is important to have detailed information and reliable metrics. If you don't plan on external reporting, you will still want to know how you are doing; you just don't need to be as rigorous.

In selecting measures, focus on the outcomes of your initiatives, not just your activities. If you have started a recycling programme, measure the increase in materials recycled rather than number of recycling bins. If energy efficiency is your focus, track the change in kilowatt-hours rather than incandescent light bulbs replaced.

Stick to the milestones for activities you identified along with your goals in **Step 3**. By tracking progress along the way, you can make changes to correct your course early on. This is particularly important for more ambitious goals such as reducing Green House Gas (GHG) emissions.

By breaking down a large goal into manageable pieces, you can periodically measure your progress, assess what's working and what's not, and then make the necessary adjustments.

Step 5: Ensure Continual Improvement

Step 5 will help you:

- Measure progress.
- Develop a strategy for updating your goals.
- Become more sustainable over time.

Continual Improvement

quick reference

"If you don't know where you are trying to go, the best map in the world won't help you much."

Plan

Identify aspects and impacts by implementing goals and objectives.

Do

Implement; including training and operational control measures.

Check

Assess the measurements and report results to decision makers.

Act

Decide on changes needed to improve process.

Communication

Communications top-down and bottom-up are important for keeping momentum and ensuring continual improvement. It is important to get feedback from your employees. Ask them about the impact of new environmental initiatives on their day-to-day work, whether new initiatives are burdensome and if "green thinking" is being integrated into their daily routine.

Asking for this information and providing employees with feedback on their environmental performance also communicates management's interest and commitment to sustainability. 'Communicating your Efforts' in Section 3 provides more ideas on communication.

Update Goals and Activities

Periodically re-evaluate your goals and activities. If goals are being met or exceeded, consider setting more stringent goals (and don't forget to recognise your employee's efforts for getting you there). If your team is not meeting the stated goals, try to determine the root cause. It may be that your implementation strategy is not clear, staff responsibilities need to be redefined, or perhaps the goals themselves are not realistic.

Over time, greening activities should become part of everyday work responsibilities. When this integration occurs, greening activities should be included in your Best Management Practices (BMPs) and standard operating procedures or work instructions. You can then move on to create new greening activities.

Moving Forward

Leadership and management support will remain crucial to the on-going success of your environmental sustainability initiatives. Continue to educate yourself and your employees about the latest thinking on environmental and sustainability issues. Revisit your vision at least annually, and update your goals as your business grows or changes. Encourage and empower your employees to always look for environmental ways to accomplish their jobs. Join voluntary programmes to develop and strengthen your greening efforts. Celebrate your efforts; plan an Earth Day event at your business or how about getting involved in local events within your community.

Remember to include greening in all decisions and try to anticipate the environmental or sustainable impact of any new activities or decisions. Continual improvement means being proactive, not reactive.

Periodically refer back to Steps 1 and 2 and ask:

- *Have we learned more?*
- *Has our vision changed?*
- *Are we satisfied with our progress along the Environmental Sustainability Ruler?*
- *Are we celebrating our greening successes?*

opportunities

Going green: Resource Efficiency

Going green: Resource Efficiency; your guide for the journey

A step-by-step approach to environmental sustainability cost saving.

This section describes the opportunities available for improving environmental and sustainable performance by area of impact through resource efficiency. Multiple options are presented, allowing you to determine how ambitious you want to be based on your resources and your unique business. Each topic area is arranged as follows:

• **The Issue:** an introduction to the impacts of business on the environment.

• **Action Plan:** a description of the options and opportunities to eliminate or reduce the environmental impacts of your business.

• **Resources:** select online resources.

Every business regardless of size or type has an environmental impact. We all use natural resources such as paper, water and energy, and we all generate waste. These activities have a negative impact on our environment but reducing this impact is often very easy, with no negative impacts to productivity or quality of life.

What is resource efficiency?
How can I use my resources smarter?
How will it help me?

By effectively managing your resources smarter and preventing and reducing waste you can:

• Save your business money

• Reduce energy consumption

• Enhance environmental performance

• Reduce operating costs

• Comply with legal obligations

• Improve the image of your business

• Review how your business waste can produce some quick wins.

Why not get going today by following some of the simple steps outlined in the following pages of the resourceSmart sme toolkit ?

Opportunities Aplenty Through Resource Efficiency & Smarter Usage!

As green thinking becomes part of your company culture, you and your employees will begin to recognise countless opportunities to improve your business' environmental performance.

A good place to start taking advantage of the numerous opportunities available to you is to start with some simple measures and consider how your business manages waste, purchasing, water, energy, and transportation.

resource**Smart**
sme toolkit

Decision-making help for everyday choices at **WORK**

1 **Ws** Waste	2 **PCh** Purchasing	3 **Wa** Water	4 **En** Energy	5 **Tran** Transport	6 **Ben** Benefits

toolkit**contents**

be resource**Smart**
reduce costs
maximise your profits

Resource Smart is 'exactly what it says on the tin' – a more resource efficient and smarter use of your resources.

With prices of energy and resources rising, in competitive markets resource efficiency makes smart sense. It leads to lower costs and better profitable opportunities.

chapter one

resource**Smart:** waste

Waste Prevention, Reduction, and Recycling

Ws
Waste

The business benefits of managing your waste are numerous and varied. As well as improving your 'green credentials', managing your waste will also increase your efficiency and save you money and resources. The key reasons for re-thinking your company's waste policy include:

Fulfilling environmental responsibilities

Managing your waste smartly will allow you first and foremost to meet your environmental responsibilities. Cutting the amount of waste you send to landfill and reducing the quantities of raw materials you use will contribute to your environmental and sustainability goals and enable you to promote a good environmental image.

Increased profitability

Reducing the amount you spend on waste will have a significant effect on the bottom line of your projects. With increases in the aggregates levy on the use of virgin materials and the ongoing rise of landfill taxes (expected to nearly treble from £14 per tonne to £35 per tonne over the next decade), the economic savings to be made from good waste management are significant.

ACTION PLAN

Eliminate waste

Avoid creating waste in the first place this is the most cost effective approach.
Recycling or treating waste costs

you money but dumping or discharging it costs even more!

Remember, waste is not just what is discarded into a bin or skip. When you consider the raw materials wasted, and the cost of processing or wasted labour, the real cost of waste is often 5 to 20 times the cost of its disposal.

A manufacturer looking to take action on being green for the first time can result in much improved resource efficiency.

Through the effective use of raw materials, it is possible to save as much as £1000 per year, per employee, from taking such steps but many businesses continue to throw away profit in the form of avoidable waste.

The following sections in this guide will help you work out your priority areas by following the waste hierarchy.

The good news is that such significant savings do not require massive effort, do not cost much money and give pay backs in months, not years. For example, simply swapping inefficient bulbs for more efficient versions can cut electricity consumption by 50%.

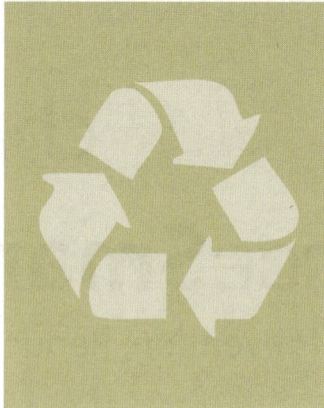

Ws
1
Waste

Reaping the rewards:

The 3 Rs are concerned with better resource efficiency in accordance with the following principles:

Reduce

This is where it all starts: If we reduce the amount we buy, whether It's energy, food or products, we will reduce the amount we end up wasting and throwing away. In the United Kingdom alone, the average office worker spends over £400 a year on food that is thrown away uneaten because items are bought, not eaten and left to go off.

Re-use

Use items as many times as possible, invest in reusable, rechargeable or refillable products which may involve an initial expense, but this is paid back over time. Even finding a secondary use for things is helpful, so use your head and think inventively.

Recycle

There are both environmental and economic imperatives for recycling still serviceable items, or items which are stripped down to recover their component parts and materials, which are themselves'

valuable raw materials. Recycle what you can, after you have re-used it.

The final stage in this process, which completes the 3 Rs 'loop', is the specification and use of materials with higher recycled content on future projects to further reduce the demand on natural resources.

Dispose Responsibly

There will always be some items or materials that can't be recycled or reused, when this occurs ensure that you dispose of what's left in a responsible way, and that avoids any harm to the environment.

Take stock

We need to start rethinking our attitudes to buying and to wasting all our vital resources and to start considering where all this waste goes to!

As you work through the action plan, note down the amount of raw materials you consume and waste you produce, so you can track the opportunities to improve and see how much you have saved. Paper and other office wastes are often good places to start, particularly if

your office is a large part of your business.

Do it!

Make sure that everyone understands what you want to do and why! Make sure they are on-board with your plan, before moving on to more complex changes.

Don't forget

Put posters up as a reminder to follow good practice.

Get the backup you need

If at any time you need assistance to work out the best way forward or for help with any waste issue, there are a number of waste management and recycling companies listed in the resource directory which provide help in dealing with all types of waste streams.

Celebrate your successes

Keep track of your success and check the progress you have made, perhaps six months and a year after you start. There is nothing like seeing the savings you have made to justify your efforts and to encourage you to move forward confidently.

PAPER

Almost all businesses use paper. Despite talk of the paperless office, paper consumption continues to grow by about 20% a year. By implementing some of these easy actions you can start making small savings that will soon add up:

Only use what you need

- Only print and photocopy where necessary.
- If you have to print, or photocopy, use both sides of the paper.

Stop unwanted faxes

- Set up fax machines so they don't print unnecessary header or report sheets.
- Register with the Fax Preference Service to stop junk faxes at: www.fpsonline.org.uk, or telephone: 020 72913330.

No more junk mail

- Cancel unwanted publications.
- Register with the Mail Preference Service at: www.mpsonline.org.uk, or telephone: 020 72913310 to stop junk mail.

Re-use paper

Paper that has only been printed on one side makes great scrap paper pads for notes and can be used to print draft documents.

Use recycled paper

- Ask your supplier if they stock locally produced, recycled paper. Paper can be recycled up to 5 times, reducing the environmental impact of paper production.

(*Make sure service and maintenance warranties are not adversely affected by using recycled paper. There is no valid reason why they should be.*)

Re-use envelopes

- This is often possible, especially for internal use in your business.

Recycle

- This is often cheaper than paying to have waste disposed of. Check the Big Green Book online directory (www.biggreenbook.com) and listings in the rear section of this directory for details of paper recycling companies in your area.
- Make paper recycling bins widely available and label them clearly. Let staff know where they are and what can be put in them.

A best practice office can use as little as seven reams of paper per person per year. How many do you use?

Recycling

is an excellent way of saving energy and conserving the environment.

Did you know that?

- 70% less energy is required to recycle paper compared with making it from raw materials.
- Recycled paper produces 73% less air pollution than if it was made from raw materials.
- 12.5 million tonnes of paper and cardboard are used annually in the UK.
- The average person in the UK gets through 38kg of newspapers per year.
- It takes 24 trees to make 1 tonne of newspaper.

Ws
¹
Waste

IN THE OFFICE

As well as paper, there are many opportunities to reduce waste and save money in the office:

Buy recycled cartridges

- High quality re-manufactured toner cartridges are available with the same performance as new ones, at a lower price.

Return cartridges

- Return your toner cartridges for re-manufacture. This can be done by pre-paid envelope through specialist companies. This is free and often schemes pay you or donate money to charity.

Mobile phones and their batteries

- Can be returned for recycling. Again, often schemes either pay you, or donate money to charity.

Coffee time

- Avoid buying disposable cups and catering products like sugar sachets and paper plates.

Renovate furniture

This can save up to 50% of the cost of new products.

Or buy second-hand

Again, much cheaper than new, and benefits the environment.

BUY WHAT YOU NEED

What you buy has a strong effect on how much waste you produce. Before you buy any product ask yourself the following:

Necessary

- Do I need to buy it?

Quantity

- Am I buying more than I need?

Re-cycled

- Is it made from recycled materials?
- Can it be recycled?

Packaging

- Is it heavily packaged?
- Can the packaging be recycled?

Re-use

- Can it be re-used?

Ws

Waste

ELIMINATE PACKAGING

Ask yourself? whether packaging is essential or an excuse to avoid taking responsibility. By educating your workforce to handle items properly, you may be able to send products unwrapped, thereby getting rid of excessive packaging waste.

Alternatively consider different types of packaging such as heavy duty or permanent packaging which can be reused – you may wish to specify to your suppliers that they implement reusable packaging systems such as returnable pallets and crates.

Common Types of Packaging Waste

Most companies dispose of packaging waste, from boxes, bottles, and milk cartons, food wrappers to pallets, oil drums and paint tins.

Waste Packaging: Paying Out or Cashing In

Packaging waste is usually generated in two ways;

• As a result of the production process; and/or

• As product or transit packaging

coming in with the supply of resources.

This waste will cost you or your company money and has a negative impact on the environment. Remember most companies have to comply with packaging regulations.

If packaging becomes waste, the cost will be affected by the following:

• The increasing price of transport, treatment and disposal of waste to landfill;

• The price of lost resources;

• The cost of staffing; and/or

• The price of compliance for packaging waste.

Sound waste management will help you to comply with regulations and also may improve your company's public image:

• Stakeholders increasingly demand sound environmental practices;

• Company image affects employee morale and shareholder perception;

• Environmental performance impacts on risk assessment and insurance issues.

PACKAGING TIPS

As a user of packaging:

Less packaging

• Speak to your supplier to see if they can supply products with less packaging, whilst maintaining the integrity of the products.

Re-usable/returnable packaging

• Ask your suppliers to use re-usable packaging where possible.

Don't damage the packaging

• Avoid contaminating packaging with other materials, such as glue, so the packaging can be recycled more easily.

Re-use

• Re-use materials such as bubble wrap, boxes, pallets and crates for regular deliveries.

If you produce packaging or packaged products:

Use smart design

• Minimise the use of materials in the packaging, whilst still protecting your products.

• Try to design packaging so that the components can be easily segregated for re-use or recycling.

Ws
Waste
1

HAZARDOUS WASTE

Under UK law, hazardous waste is any waste that is defined as hazardous by the European Hazardous Waste Directive. These wastes have hazardous properties that may make it harmful to human health or the environment.

Examples of wastes classed as hazardous waste include:

• Asbestos;

• Lead-acid batteries;

• Electrical equipment containing hazardous components, such as cathode ray tubes (e.g. televisions);

• Oily sludge's;

• Solvents;

• Fluorescent light tubes;

• Chemical wastes;

• Pesticides.

How much Hazardous Waste is produced in The UK?

In the UK, some 4.6 million tonnes of hazardous waste is produced each year. Around 39% of the hazardous waste that is produced in England and Wales is sent to landfill, in Scotland it is around 32% sent to landfill with any of the remaining waste being recycled, treated or incinerated.

Why Minimise Hazardous Waste?

By minimising the amount of special waste you produce, you will:

• pay less for waste disposal;

• be better able to comply with environmental legislation and avoid costly fines;

• improve your company's public image by reducing its impact on the environment.

Hazardous waste that is properly managed and disposed of in accordance with the law poses a small risk to the environment; it only becomes harmful if it is managed badly or disposed of illegally.

Because of the extra hazardous risks that special waste poses to human health and the environment, strict laws control how it is managed.

Recycling Hazardous Waste

Some hazardous waste, such as solvents, oils and metals, can be re-used, recovered or recycled, while other types of waste may be incinerated. For example, waste mineral oil can be burned as fuel, but it is better for the environment if it is recycled.

Be aware that a waste management licence or suitable exemption may be required to treat or recycle hazardous wastes.

WASTE DUTY OF CARE

Waste materials produced as part of your business or within your workplace are regulated by law. As a business, you have a duty to ensure that any waste you produce is handled safely and in accordance with the law.

You must make sure that anyone that you pass your waste on to, such as a waste contractor, scrap metal merchant, recycler, local council or skip Hire Company, is authorised to take it. If you do not, and your waste is disposed of illegally, you could be held responsible.

The Duty of Care has no time limit, and extends until the waste has been either finally and properly disposed of, or fully recovered.

chapter two

resource**Smart:** purchase

Environmentally Preferable Purchasing of Products & Services

PCh
Purchasing

'Green purchasing' or 'sustainable procurement' is about considering environmental, economic, ethical and social factors when making a purchasing decision. It is about looking at what the product is made of, where it has come from and who has made it. Ultimately the aim is to minimise the environmental and social impacts of the purchases that we make.

PURCHASING

There are many environmental or sustainability aspects that should be considered when establishing specifications for purchasing products or services. The list below identifies key issues and questions to be addressed for each.

Traditionally purchasing considerations went no further than the initial purchase price. Today we know that this initial outlay may not be the largest expense. The cost of energy and water are likely to rise significantly over the coming decades, as resource scarcity and environmental controls on utility companies increase. Cost savings that might seem marginal at today's prices could well increase considerably.

ACTION PLAN

Departmental Green Procurement Objectives

What specific green procurement objectives have been established by the purchasing department? The Policy on Green Procurement requires the individual buyer, departments and agencies to set and monitor targets for green procurement through the annual Report on Plans and Priorities, and Performance Reports.

3R's Considerations

- Reduce: Is there a need for the purchase? Are there other options to reduce consumption? Can demand for the item be aggregated amongst multiple users, to achieve better asset utilisation or minimise shipping? Rather than buying a product, can services be used to meet the need?

- Reuse: Can a second-hand or used item meet the requirement? When re-using items, consider costs of refurbishing and maintenance. Is the product being purchased reusable? Can it be economically repaired or upgraded to extend its life?

- Recycle: Can the item be recycled at end of life? Do programmes exist for recycling in local facilities? Is the product designed for easy dismantling for recycling?

2
PCh
Purchasing

Environmental Performance Benchmark

- Have studies of the environmental attributes of these products or services been completed?

- Are environmental performance labels available for the products or services? Have the products or services been certified by an environmental performance label? (e.g. Eco-Label)

- Are other environmental standards available for the products or services? Do the products or services meet those standards?

Performance Testing

- Is it possible to verify the performance of products or services prior to purchase?

- Do the products or services meet the required performance specifications?

Recycled Content and Renewable Resources

- Does the product include recycled content?

- What percentage of recycled materials does the product contain?

- What type of recycled materials does the product contain? Pre-consumer or post-consumer recycled content?

- Does the product contain reconditioned parts?

- Is the product made from rapidly renewable materials? Rapidly renewable materials are defined as materials that are renewable from natural sources within a ten year cycle (e.g. bamboo, kenaf, wool).

Resource and Energy Efficiency

- Do the products or services make efficient use of resources and energy throughout their life cycle? Are they made with sustainably managed resources or processes that are resource-efficient?

- What is the environmental operating costs such as energy or water consumed by the products or services over their life? Do they consume less resources or energy, relative to their competitors?

- Does the product have any energy, water or fuel saving features (e.g. Power-down mode,

low-flush toilets and programmable thermostats)?

- Are there clear instructions as to how to use the product in the most efficient way?

Hazardous Materials

- Does the product require Material Safety Data Sheets (MSDS)?

- Do the suppliers offer a non-hazardous equivalent for this product?

Ozone-Depleting Substances

Fluorinated greenhouse gases (F gases) are powerful greenhouse gases that contribute to global warming if released into the atmosphere. Their effect can be much greater than carbon dioxide. Hydrofluorocarbons (HFCs), Perfluorocarbons (PFCs) and Sulphur Hexafluoride ($SF6$) are all types of F gas.

HFCs are the most common type of F gases and are mainly used as the refrigerant in air conditioning and commercial refrigeration systems. F gases are also used in other areas such as fire protection systems, solvents, high voltage switchgear,

types of aerosols and in specialised industrial processes.

F gases form part of the Kyoto Protocol's 'basket' of greenhouse gases. Action to contain, prevent and reduce emissions of F gases is being taken by the EU as part of its obligations under the Kyoto Protocol. The UK and the EU are signatories to the protocol and the UK is therefore committed to reducing its emissions

The EU framework has been fully implemented in Great Britain by the Fluorinated Greenhouse Gases Regulations 2009 (FGG Regulations 2009). Northern Ireland has its own similar regulations.

Helpdesk

From 1 April 2012 F-Gas Support services are being delivered by Defra: please send your queries to defra.helpline@defra.gsi.gov.uk.

Air Quality

- Does the product release volatile organic compounds (VOCs)? Is there a suitable replacement that releases fewer VOCs?

- Does the product release any other criteria air contaminant or air pollutant emissions? Is there a suitable replacement that generates lower emissions?

Packaging

- Is the packaging necessary? Can it be eliminated or reduced through bulk packaging?

- Is the packaging reusable? Does it contain reusable parts?

- Is the packaging recyclable? Does it contain recycled materials?

- Is the packaging made from rapidly renewable materials?

- Will the suppliers remove the packaging from the site following installation?

Durability and Useful Life

- Is the product durable? What is the expected useful lifespan of the product?

- Is the product reusable or does it contain reusable parts?

- Is the product designed for easy dismantling for reconditioning and reuse?

- How long is the warranty? Should an extended warranty be purchased to increase life span?

- Is it economical to repair or upgrade the product?

- Is the product designed for easy maintenance, repair and/or upgrade?

- Are maintenance and replacement parts readily available and reasonably priced?

Look for products that are

CO$_2$ neutral and Reduce Your Carbon Footprint

2 PCh
Purchasing

Recycling

• Is the product recyclable?

• Do appropriate local facilities exist for recycling?

• Is the product designed for easy dismantling for recycling?

• Does the product include a return for recycling policy?

• Will consumables (such as toner cartridges) be accepted for recycling?

Disposal and Waste

• What is the quantity of waste generated by the products or services during its life time? Do the products or services generate less waste than its competitors?

• During the project, will all wastes be source separated on site and recycled?

• Are there local recyclers that can be used for waste management?

• What is the cost of disposal arrangements?

• Where hazardous waste is involved, can a certified recycler be engaged to reclaim or recycle material?

Indirect Costs

• What indirect costs are associated with the products or services (e.g. less energy efficient IT equipment will produce more heat, causing the building's air conditioning system to work harder and further increase electricity costs)?

• Do administrative costs, such as complying with Workplace Hazardous Materials Information System, apply?

Environmental Attributes of the Suppliers

• Do the suppliers have a certification or registration (e.g. ISO 14001 registration)?

• Do the suppliers have an Environmental Management System (EMS) or environmental policy in place?

• Do the suppliers engage in voluntary environmental initiatives (e.g. Carbon offsetting)?

chapter three

resource**Smart:** water

Protection, Conservation and Re-use

Wa ³
Water

Being more water efficient and cutting down on the water your business consumes can save you money. It's as simple as that.

Water supply and waste water disposal cost your business money.

Managing your company's water usage effectively is one of the easiest ways to reduce costs.

Good housekeeping is often all that is required to achieve substantial savings - you do not need to spend a great deal of time or money. The more water you use, the greater the potential for savings.

This chapter helps you work out an action plan, checking where you are using your water, and then giving you ideas to help you make real savings.

ACTION PLAN

The first steps are to determine the amount of water used and waste water produced by your business during the last 12 months and how much this costs. Check your invoices from your regional water and wastewater service supplier. It is important to know how much water you use, so you can maximise your savings by taking the most appropriate action.

Meter it

If you have a water meter, check your meter readings and make sure they agree with the bill - do not pay for someone else's mistake. Regular monthly meter readings will show a pattern of your water usage.

Your water and wastewater service supplier can assess whether your meter is the appropriate size for your company's current water usage and needs.

If this assessment shows that you could reduce the size of the meter, your business could qualify for a reduction in the fixed element of the meter charges. If you don't have a water meter, your supplier will help you assess whether installing a meter would be a viable option to reduce your company's water and waste water charges. If you don't have a water meter and cannot get one, you should still estimate water use - this will help you work out where to focus your water saving efforts.

Waste water

You should also establish the amount of waste water discharged by your business in the same period. This figure is usually estimated on your water bill, although if you have a water meter fitted then this will provide an exact charge on your bill relating to the volume of water your business uses.

You can check this data is accurate by comparing the consumption and discharge volumes. Remember, the volume of discharge may not exactly mirror the consumption volume as it is necessary to take account of the volume of water used in business process or production, or from additional rainfall or contaminant.

Certain types of business may receive a non-return to sewer allowance on their waste water charge. Again, your water supplier can provide assistance in determining the right non-return to sewer allowance

Conduct water walk rounds

See where, how and when water is being used by your business.

Meter it to check it

Leaks in visible pipes are obvious, but leaks in hidden sections (including sections underground) can go undetected for years. Monitoring your water meter by noting meter readings regularly, will help show up leaks.

These will be detected as sudden jumps in consumption assuming no great changes in demand have

been instigated. Do you use water at weekends? Again this emphasises how important a water meter is – if you think that you don't, check your meter to make sure. If you have processes that use large amounts of water, consider installing sub meters – they will help you target reductions for particular processes.

Focus on the major water users first

Estimate the amount of water used in different activities to identify where you need to focus on. If your total estimates of water consumption are much less than your overall total consumption as indicated by your bills, you may have missed a major water use.

Follow the water saving hierarchy to help you save money.

Having determined the main uses of water, focus your attention on these; identify the most appropriate ways of minimising water consumption in each area/ activity of your business. In order of priority:

• Stop leaks and spills (and ensure

that your pipes are well insulated to protect against frost damage). Dripping taps and leaking pipes can cost a lot of money.

• Eliminate unnecessary water use. Is the process or activity really necessary? Does it make the most sense to use water, or is there a more cost effective alternative?

• Reduce water use. Could water be used more efficiently? Is there an alternative process or activity that would be better?

• Re-cycle the water. Can the water be recycled for use elsewhere? (e.g. Flushing toilets).

Water

IN THE OFFICE

You may be spending considerably more on water for your office than you need to. Save water by:

Toilets

• Using a cistern volume reducer. These small bags of water are inserted into toilet cisterns and save water with every flush. (Note these should not be used with dual flush systems.)

Approximate cost £3 to £5 per cistern.

• For men's toilets, consider installing a flush control system – these are now fitted as standard in new commercial buildings.

Approximate cost £150 per controller.

Taps

• Stop dripping taps – they waste a lot of water. Often fitting a new washer is all that is needed. Keep a stock of washers – they only cost a few pence.

• Forgotten to turn off a tap? Most building suppliers stock self closing taps, which slowly close if abandoned. They often fit existing tap bodies, so you needn't disturb the pipe work.

Approximate cost £20 each.

• Many taps give an unnecessarily high flow after only a quarter turn – a flow restrictor reduces this.

Approximate cost £3 each.

Sinks

• Make sure plugs are available for washing hands, dishes or food.

• If you need a certain depth of water to wash something small, but only have a very large sink, use a bowl.

Dish wash efficiently

• Only use the dishwasher when you have a full load.

Showers

• Consider switching to low flow, high velocity showers which use less water than standard power showers.

FACTORY / WORKSHOP / TRANSPORT

There are many opportunities to save water here:

Cleaning

• Scrapers, squeegees and brushes can often reduce the time and water needed to clean an area. They can also reduce the amount of solid waste that is flushed down your drain, and so reduce the volume of effluent you discharge.

Rinsing

• It is often more water efficient to rinse a product in stages (e.g. in a series of tanks). You can rinse the product in the dirtiest water first, and then in progressively cleaner water. At the same time, move the water gradually from the last rinse to the first rinse.

Shut it off!

• Items that don't need water continuously can be isolated with a simple switch, preventing water running continuously down the drain. Another way to do this is to fit trigger nozzles to all hoses.

Approximate cost £50 each.

Re-use it

Careful examination of the quality and availability of used water, together with an understanding of your water requirements, may

3 Wa
Water

Re-use it - *Cont...*

suggest opportunities for re-use, such as first wash down of floors and containers. If there is a large amount of water, it may be worth treating it to enable re-use.

BOILERS

Check it

• Regularly check your boiler and associated system for leaks. Water supplied to boilers often has to be treated, e.g. softened. This adds value to the water (£2 to £3/m3) so there is an added incentive to reduce leaks and losses.

Maintenance matters

• Make sure your boiler system is well maintained and serviced regularly. As well as reducing the chance of leaks, it will save you energy. Free help and advice is available from the Energy Saving Trust Helpline on 0300 123 1234. .

chapter four

resource**Smart**: energy

Energy Efficiency, Conservation and Renewables

4 En Energy

'The Most Sustainable Energy is Energy Saved',

Being Energy smart will put results on a businesses bottom line.

As the cost of energy increases, energy efficiency will become increasingly more important to businesses.

There is a lot of information now available to businesses, including useful hints, tips, and case studies, to provide ideas on how your business can become more energy efficient, and therefore save money.

Many of the energy efficiency options available to business have a short payback period. The payback period is the period of time required to 'pay back' the upfront cost associated with available options. The upfront cost is often recouped through reductions in costs associated with savings in energy use over time.

Most businesses could use less energy and make significant savings by a few simple actions, this chapter will help you get started.

It focuses on areas where small businesses use most of their energy:

- **Heating**
- **Lighting**
- **Office equipment**
- **Compressed air**
- **Motors, drives, fans and pumps**

ACTION PLAN

Before working out where to look for savings you need to know how much energy your business is currently using.

Check your meters

Regularly check how much electricity and gas you are using. Monitoring helps you assess your improvements and enable you to check that you are being billed correctly.

Tariffs and bills

Check your bills. Even the largest providers can make errors on your bill - don't pay for their mistakes. Check to make sure your bills relate to what you use, rather than an estimate.

Conduct energy walk rounds

It is important to vary the times of your walk around, as energy use varies during the day and at weekends. See where and when energy is being used by your business. Use the opportunities listed in this chapter as a suggested tick list.

4 En
Energy

HEATING

Heating can be a significant part of your energy bill. There are often opportunities for savings:

Too hot

- The maximum recommended heating level is 19°C. For each extra 1°C, costs rise by 8%. This can be as much as £200 a year for a small office.

Use thermostats properly

- Set thermostats and radiator valves correctly and check they are in a sensible location – not somewhere too draughty or unusually hot or cold.

Obstructed radiators

- Blocking radiators with furniture reduces their output and takes longer to warm up the room.

Stop draughts

- They are uncomfortable, and they waste energy – draught-proof windows and doors.

Unwanted heating

- Un-insulated pipe work wastes heat and therefore energy. Where you are attempting to cool an area, this can mean cooling

systems need to work harder to compensate, wasting more energy.

Heating and air conditioning

- If heating and air conditioning units run at the same time, they waste lots of energy - and therefore lots of your money!

Portable heating

- Portable electric heaters are expensive to run, so should only be used as a last resort - add a timer to switch them off automatically.

Service your boiler system

- Heating costs can increase by 30% or more if the boiler is poorly maintained. Remember to regularly check your system for leaks too.

Unnecessary heating

- Reduce the heating in areas, such as store rooms, which need less heat. If your heating is timed, make sure it corresponds to when the building is occupied.

- Don't heat an empty building when you are on holiday – reduce the thermostat temperature to frost protection mode.

Open windows

- Opening windows or doors if the heating is on wastes money. Turn down the heating instead.

IN THE OFFICE

You may be spending considerably more on electricity for your office equipment than it cost to buy originally!

Do you have a computer? Save energy by:

Switching off at night and weekends

- This cuts running costs by 75%. For 3 computers and monitors this can cut costs from approximately £180 a year to less than £50.

Turning the monitor off

- If you switch the monitor off when it is not being used (e.g. lunchtime) and activate standby options, energy consumption can be cut by 90% a year. Forget a screensaver - most don't save energy, only the screen phosphors.

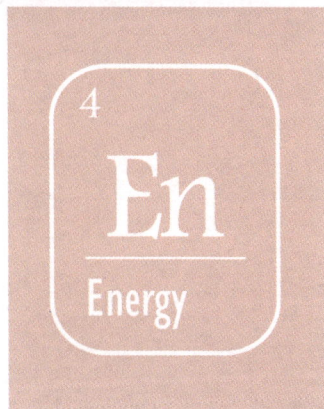

4

En
Energy

LIGHTING

Lighting can account for 50% of the money spent in an office on electricity.

The following tips can help you cut costs:

Why light empty rooms?

- Encourage staff to turn off lights when they leave a room and when they go home at the end of the day.
- Do not light unused, locked, areas.

Switch off

- A fluorescent tube uses over 500 times more energy in 15 minutes than it takes to restart it – switch it off if it's not needed.
- Have you got enough light switches? Consider installing pull-cord switches to enable improved control of individual light fittings or groups of fittings.

Approximate cost £15 per switch.

Too bright

- You may be able to reduce lighting in places such as corridors. One way to do this is to remove tubes from alternate fluorescent fittings.

Don't block the light

- People often prefer to work in natural light.
- Make sure windows and skylights are cleaned at least once a year.
- Clean light fittings once a year too.

High ceiling

- High pressure discharge lighting is more efficient than most fluorescent systems and saves money.

Outside lighting

- You only need outside lighting when it is dark. Even then, you may not need it throughout the night – fit time clocks with photocells to cut costs, or fit movement sensors for security lighting.

Approximate cost £60 per photocell.

Light bulbs

Energy saving light bulbs use different technology that enable them to produce a highly efficient and compact light using a fraction of the energy.

By making a smarter choice of light bulbs you can reduce your energy bills considerably!

- Slim line (26 mm) fluorescent tubes use 8% less electricity and are cheaper than the older 38mm tubes.
- Installing high frequency fluorescent lighting eliminates hum and flicker, and can reduce electricity consumption of between 30% to 60% when compared to conventional incandescent bulbs.
- Replace tungsten bulbs with compact fluorescent lamps – as well as saving energy they have a longer life.

WATCH THE LIGHTS

Myth:
Turning fluorescent lights on and off uses more energy than leaving them on.

Truth:
A fluorescent tube uses 500 times more energy if left on for 15 minutes than the energy required to restart it!

Fact:
Energy saving light bulbs use only a quarter of the energy of normal light bulbs and last up to eight times longer.

4
En
Energy

IN THE OFFICE

Do you have a photocopier?

Switch it off at night

Leaving a photocopier on overnight uses enough energy to print over 5000 - A4 copies.

Locate it wisely

- Try to put it in a naturally ventilated area - this will avoid air conditioning having to work hard to compensate for the heat from the machine.

- Remember health and safety - photocopiers should not be closer than 3 metres from anyone's desk. Switching off other office machinery (such as laser printers) overnight can also reduce their energy consumption by 75%. Similarly, vending machines and water coolers can be switched off at evenings and weekends.

COMPRESSED AIR

Compressed air is very expensive to produce -10 times more than electricity!

Stop the leaks!

- Leaks are responsible for the biggest energy losses - a leak the size of a match head uses 1 kWh of compressor power.

- It is important to spot and repair all leaks immediately – This can lead to big savings.

- It is easiest to check for leaks during periods when there is no demand for air. During quiet periods listen for obvious leaks and repair immediately.

- Smaller leaks can be detected using a soap-water solution.

- Check all joints, connectors and other fittings.

- Schedule a quarterly test programme.

- Unused pipe work should be isolated to reduce the risk of leaks.

Operating pressure

- If you can lower the operating pressure you can save energy – a reduction of 1 bar (15 psi) will save around 7% of the energy.

Air supply

- Efficiency improves if the intake air is cool - reducing the intake temperature by 4°C increases efficiency by 1%.

Alternatives

- If you are using compressed air to clean machinery, could you use a brush instead?

- Could the job be done directly using electricity?

MACHINERY – E.G. MOTORS, DRIVES, FANS OR PUMPS

Only run it if you need to. Even if there is no load, a motor can still use as much as 40% of the full load power.

- Turn off machinery that is idling and switch it off during lunch breaks if it is not needed.

Maintenance matters

- A badly maintained system costs more to run.

Higher efficiency motors

- These now cost the same as standard efficiency motors.

- Installing a higher efficiency motor could mean payback of the purchase price in less than 3 months of operation.

Remember, more detailed help and advice is available from the organisations listed in the Resource Directory in Part 3 of this handbook.

resource**Smart**: transport

Alternative Options and Vehicles

Whether you run just two vehicles or dozens of cars and vans, transport costs can represent a significant financial burden to your business.

And if your fleet of vehicles is not well run, excess running costs can be up to 35%, hitting the bottom line.

Not only can your choice of vehicles and the way in which you use them be a source of savings, but so too can the fuel they use. Cleaner fuels can save you up to a third of your fuel bills, cut your road tax and reduce company car tax…

…And that's only half the story. Road transport accounts for 22% of the CO_2 emissions in the UK and is one of the main contributors to poor air quality.

Showing your commitment to the environment and the health of the local community by improving your company's environmental credentials can also be good for customer relations, ensuring your fleet never costs you dear in terms of your reputation or repeat business.

ACTION PLAN

Identifying the issues

Before you can start saving money, you need to assess the actual performance of your fleet. Identify the number and type of vehicles used, mileage patterns, overall costs and fuel consumption. Improvements can then be measured against this baseline.

Workplace travel plans

Making it work

Successful travel plans need wide support to succeed. They need to be seen to be fair, be backed by concrete support for change from the company, and be clearly communicated, including listening and responding to concerns.

The Department for Transport (DfT) recommends setting up a working party or steering group to make sure the travel plan gets the right input and support across the organisation.

This could be a Joint Environment Committee or an individual, but either way it would need to involve the facilities manager, personnel manager, union rep, fleet manager, communications manager and managers of any departments whose work generates business mileage.

Employers need to determine which transport alternatives workers could be prepared to use. Gathering the right data is vital to support this, such as:

• site audit

• staff discussion group

5

Tran
Transport

- local transport information
- relevant resources, such as car sharing databases
- staff travel survey
- business travel data
- mapping where staff live.

Negotiating for change

Travel plans can enable a company to reduce the impact of travel and transport on the environment, while also bringing direct benefits to employers and to staff. Travel plans based on best practice have the potential to address real problems faced by individuals in travelling to work.

These are:

1. **Lost time:** absorbed in traffic jams, where no other activity can be pursued.
2. **Costs:** especially for low-paid workers.
3. **Safety:** on roads; using/waiting for public transport; and walking.
4. **Stress:** induced by congestion, mechanical failures, and poor driving conditions.
5. **Health impacts:** from emissions and from inadequate physical exercise.

Travel plans will work best when workers know that their concerns are being listened to, and if the plan does not give privileges to more senior staff.

Discussions and publicity about the plan should answer the questions "what's in it for me?" by setting out the benefits to individual members of staff, including:

- fairer systems, with financial or other incentives for sustainable travel available to all staff, including those without access to a car
- assured parking for those with most need to access a vehicle
- a less stressful options for travel to work,
- opportunities to build healthy exercise into daily life
- reduced journey times to work
- reduced travel costs, or even eliminating the need to run a car

Travel for work

Travel may also be an essential part of a worker's job. In this case there are many things that can be done to reduce the environmental impacts of travel, such as switching fleets to 'greener' vehicles, for example smaller, electric or hybrid vehicles.

(see the Energy Saving Trusts website at: www.est.org.uk/fleet for additional advice).

- Give training to drivers on 'greener' driving techniques.
- Make sure any essential car user allowance rewards those using energy-efficient cars.
- Promote the use of public transport, cycling and walking where this is an option.
- Promote the use of train travel rather than flying for short-haul business trips.

Reducing unnecessary meetings through telephone and video conferencing can reduce long hours as well as travel emissions.

If your meeting or event is necessary, check out ways of reducing its impact, and ensure travel directions to your workplace give public transport directions.

Green staffs travel plans – bargaining checklist

1. Do your research to make sure you're not outmanoeuvred and can take the initiative on negotiations if necessary.

2. Raise awareness among members about the more beneficial kinds of Green Staff Travel Plan packages that can be achieved and the reasons why reducing car use is important.

3. Where there is a proposed change to one aspect of travel-related terms and conditions (for example, car parking fees), this is an opportunity to argue for a coherent, well-developed travel plan, rather than piecemeal measures introduced under the guise of 'green' policy.

4. Where employers are initiating a travel plan, seek to involve everyone through its development.

5. Make sure you get clear agreement on terms of reference at the start of travel plan negotiations, which assure staff that the aim is to produce a travel plan with benefits to workers as well as to employers and the environment.

6. As an employer understand that if you want to have a real impact on car use, the most effective measures will include financial incentives.

7. Make sure you have all the relevant data resulting from staff travel surveys to put plans in place.

8. Remember that this is a great opportunity to raise your companies' profile in the local community.

Did you Know...?

The benefits of car sharing can really be put into perspective when you consider that every day there are 10 million empty seats on Britain's roads.

Save Cash!

On average, daily car sharing for one year can save commuters around £1,000

5

Tran

Transport

10 Tips for Green Fleet Management

There are a lot of ways for making your fleet greener. Not only is this better for the environment, but green fleet management is cost effective for you as a business.

It's all about the bigger picture for businesses today; commitment to your social and environmental impact is more important than ever. Through greener fleet managment, you can be kinder to the whole environment, earn brownie points for "doing your bit" and make savings that ultimately improve your bottom line.

The following are our top ten tips to a greener way of managing your business fleet.

1. Promote cars with low CO2 emissions to reduce employee car insurance.

2. Evaluate alternative fuel cars to see if they might benefit your fleet.

3. Ensure vehicles are regularly serviced – poorly maintained vehicles have higher toxic emissions and fuel consumption.

4. Identify opportunities to reduce mileage by recording & analysing business travel.

5. Record & analyse individual fuel consumption to encourage fuel efficient driving.

6. Promote safe, economic & environmentally-friendly driver training.

7. Ensure mileage reimbursement rates are environmentally sensitive and do not encourage drivers to make excessive journeys.

8. Provide access to web sites and route planners to minimise vehicle mileage.

9. Promote satellite navigation & telematics to help drivers avoid congestion and use the most efficient route to reach their destination.

10. Review arrangements for tele/video conferencing as an alternative to business travel.

chapter four

resource**Smart**: benefits

Making the business case for action

Environmental Benefits

The Carbon Trust estimates that most businesses could easily save 20% of their energy costs through simple, low-cost measures.

There are many persuasive arguments you can use when negotiating for environmental changes at work.

As described in the previous sections with tips on specific areas, like heating, waste or transport.

When you go to meet management or employees it is important that you are well prepared about the environmental issues affecting your business.

Benefits to employers

Employers and employees who recognise that improving their energy efficiency and environmental impact is an investment for the future, not just a cost, will benefit in a number of ways.

Reduce overheads

Increasing energy efficiency will impact positively on energy costs, consumables, waste management and disposal, water bills, hardware, and transport bills.

The UK Department for Business Innovation and Skills (BIS) has recently found a "strong and significant relationship between energy efficiency and labour productivity".

The most economically productive firms are also those that are most energy efficient.

Increase sales

Customers, other businesses in the supply chain, and government all prefer companies with a clean, green record.

The top priority for companies over the next few years should be the environment (*Annual Mori poll of public attitudes to Corporate Social Responsibility, October 2011*).

Reduce insurance premiums

In sensitive sectors, such as the chemical and pharmaceutical industries, insurance companies now require environmental audits to be carried out before they will provide insurance cover. This trend is spreading to other parts of industry as environmental pressures, including the threat of legal action, intensify.

Attract green investment

Increasing numbers of investors invest only in businesses that have environmental, sustainability and corporate responsibility policies, whether for purely ethical reasons, or for financial reasons. Fund managers are coming under increasing pressure from lobby

Ben

Benefits

groups and the people whose money they manage.

Almost 80% of the FTSE 100 companies have identified climate change as a business risk, according to the Carbon Neutral Company

Attract government subsidies and reduce taxes paid

Taxes

Workplaces that reduce their environmental impact can save tax in a variety of ways. These taxes are designed to incentivise improvements by accounting for the 'external' costs to the environment of certain activities. The main ones are:

1. The Climate Change Levy, a tax on non-domestic energy users; there is a variety of exemptions based on industries adopting good environmental practice, and revenue is also returned through lower national insurance contributions and support from the Carbon Trust

2. Fuel duty, vehicle excise duty, and air passenger duty

3. The Landfill Tax

4. Enhanced Capital Allowances (ECAs), which allow businesses to invest in energy and water efficient technology and write off the cost against taxable profits – see www.eca.gov.net.

Subsidies and grants

There is a range of incentives available for organisations interested in installing energy-efficient equipment, buying renewable energy generation (including combined heat and power – CHP), and other environmental measures. These include:

Small and medium-sized enterprises (fewer than 250 employees) may also be eligible for an interest free energy efficiency loan of between £5,000 and £100,000, repayable over a period of up to four years. See www.carbontrust.co.uk for more details.

If you work in the public or voluntary sector, your organisation might also be eligible for funding from the "partnership for renewables" and grants of up to £1 million from the Government's Low Low Carbon Buildings Scheme.

See the website on www.pfr.co.uk

Please note that schemes, grants and subsidies are all prone to change and that new ones are constantly being added. Check the Carbon Trust, HMC and BIS websites for all the latest information. Employers can get advice on energy saving and find out about various local, national and international funds that might be available to their particular sector by contacting relevant government agencies.

Try the ones listed below to help you get started:

1. The Carbon Trust (energy) is a world-leading organisation helping businesses, governments and the public sector to accelerate the move to a low carbon economy through carbon reduction, energy-saving strategies and commercialising low carbon technologies.

2. WRAP (waste) works in England, Scotland, Wales and Northern Ireland to help businesses, local authorities, communities and individuals reap the benefits of reducing waste, developing sustainable products

**ENVIRONMENTAL
SUSTAINABILITY
= PROFITABILITY**

6

Ben

Benefits

and using resources in an efficient way.

3. Waterwise (water) is focused on decreasing water consumption in the UK at work and in the home as well as building the evidence base for large scale water efficiency. They are the leading authorities on water efficiency in the UK.

4. Energy Saving Trust (transport) gives impartial, accurate and authoritative advice on how to reduce carbon emissions and become more sustainable, as well as to help people to save money on their energy bills.

For other environmental information and advice go to:

5. The Department for Energy and Climate Change (DECC) to find out about issues relating to: Energy, Green Deal, Renewable Heat Incentive, ECO etc.

6. The Environment Agency (EA) to find out about issues relating to: Pollution, Hazardous waste, Flooding and Wildlife. The agency is the environmental regulator for England and Wales and responsible for improving and protecting the environment.

7. The Scottish Environment Protection Agency (SEPA) to find out

about issues relating to: Pollution, Hazardous waste, Flooding and Wildlife. The agency is Scotland's environmental regulator and responsible for improving and protecting the environment.

Emissions trading

The EU ETS is the largest multi-country, multi-sector greenhouse gas emissions trading system in the world. It includes around 11,000 installations (excluding aviation) accounting for about 45% of EU carbon dioxide (CO2) emissions.

Heavy industrial employers can sell spare emissions permits if they improve energy efficiency, through the EU Emissions Trading Scheme (EU ETS). Since 2010 emissions trading was extended to include large service sector employers. In the future, as permits reduce and the price of carbon increases, these permits are likely to operate more like a tax. In 2007 the Stern Review estimated the true cost of the environmental damage of a tonne of carbon at £58 *($85)*, though current carbon prices are considerably lower than this.

Small Businesses are Going Green

70%

of small businesses anticipate going green in the next two years.

61%

of small businesses are actively trying to go greener.

56%

of small businesses go to exhibitions to learn about green products.

do your part, be resource**Smart:**

6

Ben
Benefits

Gain certification

Well-established voluntary accreditation schemes like EMAS, ISO14001 and EEAS can help a company demonstrate its environmental commitments. There are also awards and prizes for organisations that go the extra mile on environmental issues.

Improve staff retention, morale and productivity

A feel-good factor in the workplace and a more comfortable working environment that staff has some control over will attract employees. Employees want to work for clean, safe, caring and innovative companies, and potential recruits are starting to question companies' environmental performance.

Improve the value of the workplace building

More than 75% of respondents to a recent carbon trust survey said they were willing to pay more to occupy premises that were built to high environmental standards and energy efficient.

Comply with legislation and prepare for new laws

UK and European law lays down a framework of regulations that affect business, based on the principles that:

• Preventative action should be taken

• Environmental problems should be corrected at their source.

• The polluter should pay for environmental damage.

UK & EU Directives and Regulations cover water quality, waste disposal, industrial air pollution, vehicle emissions, pollution from large combustion plants, environmental impact, and access to environmental information, liability for damage caused by waste, environmental audits, and landfill waste. In the UK these measures are enshrined in the Environmental Protection Act 1990 and a variety of other laws – 751 laws and growing, according to the Environment Agency in 2010!

Don't forget to:

• Include sustainability in all of your decisions and actions.

• Communicate your efforts.

• Be a leader in your industry and community.

• Always strive for improvement.

Conclusion

Be thoughtful in whatever your choices are. Whether it is having a greener office space, or even choosing what kind of shoes to buy. We hope this handbook inspires the creative spirit in you to consider how even your everyday decisions affect life on the planet. No single thing you do will in itself make a large effect one way or the other, but there are millions of people in this country alone that cumulatively can make a difference.

The process of becoming environmentally sustainable may not always be easy or the decisions clear, but your efforts are important. You will give consumers a greener option and lead other businesses towards green ideas. As the toolkit in this handbook shows, environmental sustainability can also make your business more profitable and secure and if you are surrounded in an environmentally responsible work environment, and make green choices in how you work there, it becomes more natural to extend the way you work into the way you live, which follows in the toolkit for the Home in the next section.

Good luck on your efforts to make your business green and more environmentally sustainable.

appendix A

Green Speak - eco jargon

Green Speak

Don't get daunted by eco-jargon any more.

This glossary of 'Green' lexicon will put words and technical terms into context and help you understand all things from a Green Perspective.

Air Pollution
Contaminants or substances in the air that interfere with human health or produce other harmful environmental effects.

Alternative Energy
Usually environmentally friendly, this is energy from uncommon sources such as wind power or solar energy, not fossil fuels.

Anaerobic Digestion
A naturally occurring process of decomposition and decay, where organic matter is broken down to a simpler chemical component under anaerobic conditions (without oxygen).

Bio-degradable Municipal Waste (BMW)
Waste that can be degraded, commonly known as rubbish, garbage and trash.

Bio-diesel
The bio-fuel substitute for diesel. It derives from oilseed based crops – mainly oilseed rape (OSR) in the UK, and palm oil in South East Asia.

Bio-diversity
Bio-diversity refers to the essential variety on our planet, including all organisms and species and their individual genetic variations and how they assemble themselves into harmonised biomes and ecosystems.

Bio-ethanol
The bio-fuel substitute for petrol. It derives from cereal based crops – mainly wheat in the UK, and maize (corn), soya beans and sugarcane in the US and South America.

Bio-mass
Bio-mass is a biological material that is derived from either living or recently living organisms and can be used as a renewable energy source. Bio-mass materials can come from many plant or animal origins such as wood, agricultural crops, food waste, alcohol fuels and many more.

Bio-gas
The bio-fuel substitute for natural gas. It derives from organic waste materials including animal waste and waste generated from municipal, commercial and industrial sources through the process of anaerobic digestion.

Black Water, Brown Water, Foul Water, or Sewage
Term used to describe water containing human effluent.

Blue Water
Refers to surface and ground water.

Cap and Trade
A cap being placed on the total amount of allowable emissions, the distribution of this total between polluters, and the creation of a marketplace where owners of the permits can trade with each other.

Carbon
An element in fossil fuels, and in carbon dioxide. Often used as shorthand for both of these, but when talking about measurements, it is important to be clear whether these are expressed in tonnes of CO_2, or of carbon (1 tonne carbon = 3.67 tonnes CO_2)

Carbon Audit
A way of measuring the CO_2 emissions of an organisation, sometimes only from direct energy use (e.g. energy bills, fossil fuel use), often including emissions from transport, and sometimes from indirect sources like purchasing of supplies.

Carbon Capture and Storage (CCS)
The process of capturing carbon that is emitted from energy production and diverting it into ground storage areas, to reduce the amount of CO_2 emitted into the atmosphere.

Carbon Dioxide Equivalents (CO2e)
The internationally recognised way of expressing the amount of global warming of a particular greenhouse gas in terms of the amount of CO_2 required to achieve the same warming effect over 100 years.

Carbon Footprint
The total emissions of greenhouse gases (in carbon equivalents) from whichever source is being measured – be it at an individual, organisation or product level.

Carbon Labelling
Used to measure for the consumers the amount of embedded carbon there is in the product.

Carbon Neutral
Through carbon offsetting a organisation or individual are counterbalancing the emissions they produce to make themselves carbon neutral.

Carbon Offsetting
The process of reducing greenhouse gas emissions by purchasing credits from others through emissions reductions projects, or carbon trading schemes. The term often refers to voluntary acts, arranged by a commercial carbon offset provider.

Carbon Reduction Commitment
Is a scheme, that will apply mandatory emissions trading to cut carbon emissions from large commercial and public sector organisations.

7
GS
Green Speak

Carbon Sink
An absorber of carbon dioxide; oceans and forests are natural carbon sinks.

Carbon Zero
This is to reduce all carbon emission to zero by good practice, not including offsetting.

Clean Development Mechanism (CDM)
UN regulated scheme that allows countries with an emission-reduction or emission-limitation commitment under the Kyoto Protocol to implement an emission-reduction project in developing countries.

Climate Change
Long-term trends in the average climate, including temperature and rainfall patterns. The IPCC has stated clearly that climate change is primarily caused by human activity.

Climate Change Agreement
An agreement between the Government and a business user, whereby a reduced rate of the Climate Change Levy Is payable in return for a commitment by the user to achieve certain predeter-mined targets.

Climate Change Levy (CCL)
A Government levy on carbon-based fuels to promote energy efficiency. Businesses that use renewable energy can therefore get a reduction or exemption from the CCL. There are also discounts of 80% for some sectors with heavy energy use.

Combined Heat and Power (CHP)
Using the waste heat which is a by - product of energy production to heat space.

Corporate Social Responsibility (CSR)
A businesses plan to reduce its impact on environmental, social and political issues.

Cradle to Grave
The life of a product, from creation to end use.

Cradle to Cradle
Using an end use product for the source of a new product.

Day-lighting
The use of natural light to supplement or replace artificial lighting.

Decentralised Energy (DE)
Producing energy on a local scale away from the conventional large scale power against internationally agreed Fairtrade standards.

Deforestation
The term deforestation refers to the permanent, long-term conversion of an intact forest into land used for another purpose. Forests are being cleared through burning to use the land for grazing animals or growing crops, or the wood for fuel, a major contributor to carbon dioxide emissions.

Ecological Footprint
Measures how much area of natural resources human population requires to produce the products it consumes and to absorb its wastes under prevailing technology.

EEAS
Energy Efficiency Accreditation Scheme. A UK environmental management system focusing on energy use, now managed by the Carbon Trust.

Effluent
Effluent is the liquid discharged from any source. Effluents can originate from municipalities, industries, farms, ships, parking lots etc. Effluent does not always contain contaminants, in the strictest sense it could be just pure water.

EMAS
The European Community Eco-management and Audit Scheme (EMAS), which is based on the EMAS Regulation (EC) No 1221/2009 is a voluntary environmental management system (EMS) for organisations operating in or outside the European Union. EMAS has been designed for companies and organisations of the public and private sectors to help manage their environmental impacts.

Embedded Carbon
The term used to describe the way in which the carbon footprint of any product, as measured by a full lifecycle assessment from 'cradle to grave', can be represented in terms of kg of CO_2 per kg of product.

Embedded Water, Virtual Water, Embodied Water or Shadow Water
The amount of water that is used to produce a product, from the start to finish. It includes all the water that has been used throughout the whole production of a product.

Emissions Cap
A limit placed on companies regarding the amount of greenhouse gases it can emit.

Emissions
In the industrial context, emissions are the gases, liquids and solid matter given off by, among other things, factories and motor vehicles, often used to refer to substances discharged into the air.

Emissions
In climate change terms, the release of a greenhouse gas like CO_2 into the atmosphere.

Emissions Trading
A system that allows countries or businesses that have committed to CO_2 reduction targets to 'buy' or 'sell' emissions permits among themselves, in theory allowing participants to reduce emissions where it is most cost-effective to do so.

Energy Audit
A programme carried out by a utility company in which an auditor inspects a home and suggests ways energy can be saved.

Energy Efficiency
Using less energy to perform the same function.

Environmental Management System (EMS)
A voluntary system designed to continually improve the organisation's environmental performance. Examples include EMAS, ISO14001, and EEAS.

Ethical Consumerism
The purchasing of products that do not harm or exploit the workers that help produce a product and to minimise the impact on the environment.

Ethical Investment or Socially Responsible Investment (SRI)
Money that is directed towards activities which have a positive social and/or ecological impact.

FAIRTRADE Mark
Is a label that appears on UK products as a guarantee that they have been certified against internationally agreed Fairtrade standards.

Forest Stewardship Council (FSC)

Is an independent, non-governmental, not-for-profit organisation setup to respond to concerns over global deforestation. It provides internationally recognised standard setting, trademark assurance and accreditation services for companies, organisations and communities interested in responsible forestry. See Forest Stewardship Council

Gigawatts Hour

One gigawatts hour is equal to 1,000 megawatt hours.

Global Warming

Is most often used to refer to the greenhouse gas effect caused by human activities.

Green

A term that is widely used to describe a product or service designed in an environmentally sensitive manner.

Green Design

A design, usually architectural, which conforms to environmentally sound principles of building, material and energy use. A green building, for example, might make use of solar panels, skylights, and recycled building materials.

Greenhouse Effect

Gases produced naturally and by human activities that have contributed to the warming of the planet, know as Global warming, by trapping the sun's rays.

Greenwash

The term used to describe a positive public relations act that has unsound environmental benefits.

Grey Water

Polluted water that is associated with the production of goods and services, it is calculated as the volume of water that is required to dilute pollutants to such an extent that the quality of the water remains above agreed water quality standards.

Ground Source Heat Pumps

Use energy stored in the ground, which can provide heating for buildings.

HSE

The Health and Safety Executive – the Government body responsible for enforcing, encouraging and regulating workplace health, safety and welfare.

HVAC

Heating, ventilation and cooling.

Hybrid Vehicle

A hybrid vehicle combines two or more sources of power to be able to function. The most common hybrid engine uses traditional internal combustion engine with an electric motor; this is a hybrid electric vehicle (HEV).

Hydroelectric Power

Electricity produced by the power of water (often held in dams) driving turbines.

Incineration (direct combustion)

The controlled burning of municipal solid waste to reduce waste volume and to produce energy - Energy Recovery and Disposal.

Intergovernmental Panel on Climate Change (IPPC)

Is a scientific intergovernmental body set up by the World Meteorological Organization (WMO) and by the United Nations Environment Programme (UNEP). (Source: IPCC)

ISO14001

An international environmental management system and standard.

Kyoto Protocol

Is an international agreement linked to the United Nations Framework Convention on Climate Change. The major feature of the Kyoto Protocol is that it sets binding targets for 37 industrialised countries and the European community for reducing greenhouse gas (GHG) emissions.

Landfill

A method of disposal of rubbish, by burying it underground

Life Cycle Assessment

An assessment of the environmental impacts of a work process or product through its manufacture, use and disposal.

Micro-generation or micro-energy

The production of energy on a small scale, e.g. wind turbine, solar panels.

Mobius Loop

The Mobius Loop recycle symbol has no specific meaning but is generally understood to signify the interlocking steps of recycling: reuse, reduce, recycle.

Negative Screening

Identifying companies that partake in 'bad' practises, such as arms dealing and cigarette production.

Oilseed Rape (OSR)

Raw material for Bio-diesel.

Organic

Organic as an agricultural practice is one that is more environmentally sus-

tainable and adheres to set standards as defined by certain governing bodies.

Rainwater Harvesting

The collection and use of rain which falls on buildings and would otherwise go straight to the drainage system.

Recycling

Using a material again rather than throwing it away. Through the process of recycling, valuable materials such as plastics, cardboard, paper, and metal are processed into new products.

Renewable Energy

Renewable energy is energy that can be infinitely replenished as it comes from natural resources such as geothermal heat, wind, tides, sunlight, etc.

Solar Panels

Cover two areas of generation:
1) Solar thermal or solar water heating panels which are used to heat water.
2) Solar electric which is used to produce electricity also know as photovoltaic (PV) systems, solar cells that convert light into electricity.

Sustainability

In its simplest form, sustainability is the idea of being able to accomplish current goals without compromising the ability of future generations to do the same.

Volatile Organic Compounds (VOC)

Are organic chemical compounds that are highly evaporative and can produce noxious fumes.

Waste Management

The concept of waste management involves the collection, removal, processing, and disposal of materials considered waste.

Water Footprint

The total volume of freshwater that is used to produce goods and services consumed by an individual, community, nation or planet.

Water Scarcity

When annual availability of renewable fresh water is 1,000 cubic metres or less per person in the population.

Wind Power

Energy generated from large propellers that when spun by the wind, drive turbines that power generators and create electricity.

Zero Carbon:

Workplaces or homes that use no fossil fuels, only renewable sources of energy. Compare carbon neutral.

Identifying opportunities for green growth

Complete the checklist below to understand how much progress you have already made and how ready your business is to capitalise on green growth. Answer the questions by inserting a single point score in each of the rows. At the end calculate your total score.

A high score means that you have lots to shout about, while a low score means there are lots of opportunities you can take advantage of.

Energy and carbon reduction	Yes = (3 points)	Partially = (1 point)	Add to Plan = (0 point)
We collect our energy consumption data	☐	☐	☐
We set targets on our energy consumption	☐	☐	☐
We have introduced low / no-cost energy efficiency measures	☐	☐	☐
We have invested in energy efficiency projects / measures	☐	☐	☐
We have measured a reduction in our energy consumption	☐	☐	☐
We report our energy consumption	☐	☐	☐
We use on-site renewable energy sources	☐	☐	☐
We have engaged our employees in our energy strategy	☐	☐	☐
We have achieved the Carbon Reduction Standard	☐	☐	☐
We communicate our energy efficiency commitments to our staff and customers	☐	☐	☐
We have redesigned our products and services to reduce their impact on the environment	☐	☐	☐
Managing waste and water			
We measure our waste and set targets for reduction	☐	☐	☐
We have achieved cost savings through reduction in waste	☐	☐	☐
We have installed water saving devices in our premises	☐	☐	☐
We have re-designed processes to save water	☐	☐	☐
We have trained our staff to treat water as a scarce resource	☐	☐	☐
We communicate our sustainability commitments to our customers	☐	☐	☐
We have implemented a management system or won an environmental award	☐	☐	☐
We use Eco Labelling/Carbon Labelling	☐	☐	☐
We advertise our 'green credentials' in trade press, website or newsletter	☐	☐	☐

Results	Total Points	+	=
36 - 60 points	You have a well established carbon management programme. Your company performs very well in some areas, but there is always room for improvement. Please review this guide to find relevant advice.		
20 - 35 points	You have made some good progress. Familiarise yourself with this guide and contact us to find ways of expanding on your green growth.		
0 - 19 points	There is much to do, but also lots of opportunity to capitalise on green growth in your company. Please review this guide in detail and contact us so that we can support you in developing your green growth strategy.		

7
Env
Environmental

8
Sus
Sustainability

Environmental
Sustainablity *Policy*
Sample Checklists & Policy

B

20
Pol
Policy

Environmental Sustainability Policy

Date of policy: DD / MM / YYYY

Insert company name

[*Insert company name*] recognises that sound business management must take into account the effects of its business on the environment and we are committed to conducting our business in an environmentally sustainable manner. We accept that we have a responsibility for the environment and sustainability, which should be influenced, incorporated and promoted within our operations and the services we provide.

We have a system in place which manages the environmental and sustainable impacts associated with our operations and services we provide. Senior management is fully committed to this policy and supports this commitment by:

• [*Insert company name*] its directors and employees at all times complying with all applicable laws and regulations relating to the environment and sustainable development.

• Our senior management being responsible for ensuring compliance with this policy, including the establishment of programmes and reporting requirements.

• Developing, maintaining and implement policies, procedures and management systems to assess and monitor, on a continuous basis, the environmental impact of our operations.

• Setting targets annually in order to achieve continuous improvement.

• Providing sufficient resources and appropriate training to manage our impacts effectively.

• Incorporating in our environmental practices the best available technology that is economically available.

• Minimising the use of all materials, energy, travel, water and waste and not using any materials derived from endangered species.

• Specifically targeting reductions in our carbon emissions associated with energy consumption, purchasing and business travel [*either domestic and/or overseas.*]

[Select the most appropriate]

• **[Large firms]** Our Environmental Management System (EMS) will comply with recognised environmental standards including the International Standard ISO 14001:2004 and will be externally audited

or

• **[Smaller firms]** Our Environmental Management System (EMS) will comply with recognised standards including BS:8555 and will be externally audited

or

• We are currently working towards achieving a recognised environmental management system that complies with the International Standard ISO 14001:2004 or BS: 8555.

We look to our employees' support and professionalism in making this policy truly effective on behalf of [*insert company name*].

Signed: *Managing Director*
....

Date: DD / MM / YYYY

B

ENERGY visual inspection
Sample Checklists & Policy

ENERGY visual inspection: What do I need to look for?

Undertaking a simple visual inspection of your site will help to easily identify sources of energy wastage.
Use this Checklist or Photocopy it; then mark off the items as you move around your workplace.

NB > Inspections are most useful when undertaken on a typical working day during business hours.

Date of Inspection: DD / MM / YYYY	*Circle*
1. Are there any lights left on in unused or occasionally used areas (i.e. toilets, storerooms, kitchens)? **What can you do right now?** Place switch off signage by light switches. Investigate installing light timers or movement sensors.	*Yes / No*
2. Are lights left on in naturally lit areas? **What can you do right now?** Place switch off signage by light switches. Investigate installing light timers or movement sensors.	*Yes / No*
3. Are any appliances or other equipment left on when not in use (i.e. nights / weekends)? **What can you do right now?** Place switch off signage by light switches, electrical appliances and equipment. Investigate installing light timers or movement sensors. Assign a person to check before they leave each day.	*Yes / No*
4. Are heating and cooling temperatures set for optimum efficiency (i.e. 18°- 20°degrees in winter, 25°- 26°degrees in summer)? **What can you do right now?** Reset to optimum temperature range. Encourage and remind people to dress appropriately.	*Yes / No*
5. Are heating /cooling systems turned off when staff and customers are not present (i.e. nights / weekends)? **What can you do right now?** Assign a person to check before they leave each day. Investigate installing timers.	*Yes / No*
6. Are doors and windows open or closed when heating or cooling is on? **What can you do right now?** Install self closing door hinges. Set heating and cooling thermostat to recommended range (i.e. 18°- 20° degrees in winter and 25°- 26° degrees in summer).	*Yes / No*
7. Are staff members aware of the importance of saving energy? **What can you do right now?** Place switch-off signage by light switches, electrical appliances and equipment. Use internal newsletters to share information. Start the conversation.	*Yes / No*

ecoSmart
home-owner toolkit

Decision-making help for everyday choices at **HOME**

Utilities **Transport** **Shopping** **Waste** **Health** **Participate**

toolkit**contents**

be ecoSmart
reduce costs and live a healthier lifestyle

Being environmentally responsible and sustainably smart doesn't mean you need to live a reduced lifestyle. Living a smarter greener lifestyle provides eco**Smart** options that offer long-term benefits. Your home will benefit from lower energy and water bills, a warmer house in winter, a cooler house in summer, increased resource efficiency and a healthier home for your family.

Congratulations on Re-thinking Your Home!

Your home is one of over 26 million households in the United Kingdom.

Every sustainable action - small or large - in one of these homes, if repeated everywhere, could be a powerful change-maker for a more economical and environmentally sustainable future.

While governments talk about sustainable housing; thousands of individuals are creating healthy, comfortable and affordable spaces to call 'home', while also turning their homes into low-carbon, money saving exemplars.

Together with your family, neighbours and others across the UK, you can also lead the change towards a more environmentally sustainable future – starting right in your very own home.

The word 'sustainability' has recently become part of everyday language. It has been used to describe everything from energy efficiency projects to recycling your tin cans.

But what does it really mean? In 1987, the United Nations World Commission on Environment and Development defined sustainability as:

"meeting the needs of the present generations without compromising the ability of future generations to meet their needs."

In other words making sure that there is still plenty left in the bank for others to enjoy and use productively.

Therefore this second part of the Environmental and Sustainability Handbooks'- toolkits is designed to help you put this big picture concept into practice by giving you a simple starting point for making decisions in your home that will improve health, increase efficiency, save you money, and make your community a better place to live. While leaving the planet with something in the bank for all the children and their grandchildren's children to also enjoy and make use of in the future.

Congratulations on Re-thinking Your Home!

Firstly, imagine all of the natural resources your house requires: water, energy, food, building materials, and methods to transport yourself and your belongings.

By changing the way you make household decisions you can contribute to increased environmental sustainability. In turn, you will see direct benefits to your family, your community, the planet and your bank balance...
...Your choices make a difference.

For example, by choosing to paint a room with non-toxic and eco-certified materials (such as *Volatile Organic Compound* (**V.O.C.**) free paints), you're doing much more than changing the room's colour. You are also reducing your families, exposure to potentially toxic chemicals while supporting an emerging industry that values social and environmental, as well as economic, benefits.

Many of the ideas in this Home-toolkit section are taken from examples of Britons who have already made changes in their homes, and who have made a positive impact in their own communities. **Their actions and successes show how you can begin to make these changes.**

This **Environmental & Sustainability:** *Home Toolkit* section of the handbook, will provide you with the means you need to understand and talk about the sustainability challenge. It will also offer some suggestions to help you think through everyday household decisions while providing tips to be implemented room-by-room in your home.

In the following pages you will also find resources to look deeper into the issues that matter to you, and your family, most. The helpful checklist at the end of the Home-toolkit section will help you to start making changes and to track your own actions and successes.

For those ready for an extra challenge, you will also learn about the benefits of green home renovation projects and how to transform simple tips into a way of enriching your wellbeing and the whole community around you.

Did you know?

The benefits of Environmental Sustainability in the Home:

- Save money over both the short and long-term by making your home more energy-efficient
- Increase the resale value of your home
- Enjoy greater comfort in your home as you create a healthier, more efficient space
- Contribute to the preservation of the UK's biodiversity by minimising your impact
- Help slow or reduce the effects of climate change
- Help Britain strengthen its leadership position by moving the UK towards a sustainable future, one that supports social well-being, ecological health, and economic vitality

The Big Picture:

Environmental | Sustainability

Environmental Sustainability is about inventing the future we want to live in. The choices individuals make at home, and as part of a larger community, affect news headlines every day; stories about climate change, water scarcity, housing shortages, contaminated food and air pollution. These stories are elements of a bigger picture that is unfolding.

For example; impacts on the UK's environment, are increasing through:

- **Land development**
- **Water consumption**
- **Population growth**
- **Demand for housing**

Which is reducing our:

- **Fish stocks**
- **Bio-diversity**
- **Woodlands**
- **Freshwater**
- **Air quality**

If we draw the current situation, it looks like a funnel:

Declining natural resources and services

Increasing demand for natural resources and their services

Imagine what will happen if these two trends converge?

The arrows represent increasing pressures on us. These pressures include, for example, growing demand for resources and ecosystem services (such as water filtration, flood control, climate regulation and soil stabilisation) and the declining capacity of the earth to provide those resources and services. It also includes the social tensions resulting from inequality and human rights abuse.

These pressures continue to grow over time. Right now, much of the UK's economic growth reduces the amount of pure water, farmland, clean air, woodlands and natural diversity for present and future generations.

Practicing environmentally sustainable solutions means joining together as a community to maintain economic prosperity without degrading the environment, our health, education or cultural integrity.

Becoming environmentally sustainable challenges us to live our lives making decisions today that do not compromise the opportunity for future generations to enjoy a rich quality of life in the future.

United Kingdom's bold move
Energy Act 2011 (18th October)

The Energy Act 2011 includes provisions for the new 'Green Deal', which intends to reduce carbon emissions, cost effectively, by revolutionising the energy efficiency of British properties.

Green Deal

The new innovative Green Deal financing mechanism enables the provision of fixed energy efficiency measures and improvements of households and non-domestic properties, funded by a charge on energy bills that avoids the need for consumers to pay upfront costs.

The Green Deal is a solution to the problems resulting from the current lack of investment in energy saving measures in homes and non-domestic buildings; many properties have poor energy efficiency ratings. This is despite the fact that investment in such measures can produce savings on future energy bills. The Green Deal aims to provide finance to fund fixed improvements which will provide savings for the bill payer (and future bill payers).

Green Deal for Home Owners

The Government is aiming the Green Deal squarely at homeowners and retro fitting as many older type properties as is possible. The biggest winners are going to be the older style properties built prior to the 1920's. There is a limit of £10,000 for domestic home owners at present.

Homeowners will be able to install the following types of green measures:

• *Wall insulation* (both solid and cavity walls will be covered.)
• *Loft insulation*
• *Double glazing*
• *Door insulation*
• *Smart meters*

The above measures are aimed at reducing demand on your energy; once these have been installed it will cost you less to heat your home thus cutting your energy bill.

The other types of measures that will be covered by the Green Deal are 'energy in' measures, these will include:

• *Solar power*: both Thermal and Photo Voltaic panels
• *Air and ground source heat pumps*
• *Biomass boilers*

Because these types of technology use less power to heat your water and home, the idea is that you will be cutting your energy bill in the long term.

Each property will have to be rigorously inspected by a Green Deal accredited advisor to see which measures will return the best results. The Green Deal for homes will enable up to 26 million homes to be upgraded over the next 25 years.

GREEN DEAL APPROVED

For further information check out the Department of Energy and Climate Change website:
www.decc.gov.uk/en/content/cms/tackling/green_deal/green_deal.aspx

4 Key Causes of Un-Sustainability

There is a consensus between international scientists, NGO's, businesses, the UN and Government bodies, that there are four key causes by which we compromise the ability of future generations to meet their needs.

These are the basic ways in which we are un-sustainable.

1 We mine and excavate the earth's crust for items such as heavy metals and fossil fuels and allow it to build up in natural systems (air, water, land, plants & animals) faster than nature can cope.

2 We create and use synthetic or persistent compounds and chemicals (such as pesticides for plants and fire retardants in carpets) that build up in natural systems faster than nature can cope.

3 We continuously damage natural systems and the free services they provide (such as climate regulation and water filtration) by physical means at a rate faster than nature can regenerate (for example, over-harvesting forests and draining wetlands).

And...

4 We create and live in societies in which many people cannot meet their basic needs (for example, food, meaningful employment or affordable housing).

Hundreds of leading public and private organisations around the world are now using these four root causes of un-sustainability to help them make strategic decisions from an environmentally sustainable perspective to help reduce financial risk and support eco-innovation.

As Individuals we can also incorporate these principles into how we live a more environmentally sustainable lifestyle at home.

The remainder of this Home-toolkit section will give you tips to help you do just that.

Everyday Decisions

Achieving environmental sustainability means living within the earth's ability to support us indefinitely.

If environmental sustainability is about meeting our collective needs and living within natural limits, *how do you know if your personal decisions are helping to achieve that? What does 'success' look like for you in your home?*

For most people, the ideal green home is probably:

• Healthy to live in

• Comfortable and attractive

• Within easy access of work, shopping and play

• Affordable to operate and maintain

• Connected to a thriving neighbourhood and community

• Efficient in how it uses energy, water, materials and space

To achieve our ideal green home, it helps to know how our decisions relate to the root causes of un-sustainability, and what opportunities there are to make more environmentally sustainable choices.

The tools and tips that follow address the six categories to the right and will help you make environmentally sustainable choices at home a reality.

 **Categories**

 **Utilities**

 **Transportation**

 **Shopping**

 **Waste**

 **Health & Wellbeing**

 **Participation**

Utilities

Utilities are basic services such as water, electricity and gas, or anything that fuels, heats and cools your home.

Relationship to four root causes:

Production of utilities often contributes to overloading the atmosphere with greenhouse gases (GHG) from burning materials we dig out of the earth, as in the case of coal and natural gas used for heating homes and generating electricity. This can lead to a progressive physical impact on natural systems.

These are root causes of un-sustainability.

Opportunity:

Use less and save money. There are simple conservation methods and devices that can help you get started. Investing in the energy efficiency of your home has high returns.

Ask yourself

Can I reduce my use of this utility?

When you conserve the amount of water, gas or electricity you use, you reduce the impacts associated with its production and delivery. For example, burning less fossil fuel will introduce fewer poisonous compounds into the environment and particulates into our air. Reducing your use of water can be as simple as choosing to sweep your driveway rather than power-washing it.

Can I get the same utility service another way?

Some of the services associated with utilities - ***particularly electricity*** - can be supplied from renewable resources such as solar, geothermal, or wind. Check out whether your energy provider offers a green tariff linked to renewables.

Can I be more efficient in the way I use my utilities?

There are simple, inexpensive devices such as tap aerators and low-flow showerheads to help you reduce water usage. In many homes a £500 investment in wall insulation can result in savings of up to £300 a year on your energy bills.

The resulting £500 investment can be paid off in energy savings and reduced energy bills in under three years, all the while increasing the comfort of your home, *'in some cases if you are of pension age or on certain benefits cavity wall/loft insulation costs can be reduced or even available free of charge'*.

Transport

Transport

Ask yourself

Can I stay closer to home?

Can you find the products or services you need nearby? Visit your local businesses to see what's available. What you need is probably closer than you think. Plan your journeys with an eye on efficiency and make one trip instead of several.

Do I have to drive?

If you must go, can you get there without driving? Give yourself enough time to walk or cycle, and check out your local transport bus-schedule on-line. It will save you worrying about where to park and save you money too. If you have to drive then how about carpooling, more people per litre of fossil fuel used means greater efficiency for you and fewer emissions. In some areas you can also enjoy the benefits of the carpool lane!

Do I really need to go?

Sounds obvious, but it's a question worth asking. We're used to jumping into our cars and going somewhere at the drop of a hat. Next time, before you put the keys in the ignition, consider if you need to go at all.

Transport includes all of the ways you move yourself and your belongings from place to place. It could be by foot, bicycle, car, train, boat or plane.

When thinking about transportation, consider the location of your home relative to public transport, green space, places of recreation, work and shopping - all of which will impact on your quality of life.

Relationship to the four root causes:

Many modes of transportation depend on the burning of fossil fuels, meaning mobility is related to materials we dig from the earth's crust. Our impact is magnified by the continual build-up of compounds that natural systems struggle to cope with - like sulphur dioxide and nitrous oxides. Directly and indirectly they can harm natural systems and affect human health.

Opportunity:

Cycle instead of driving. If cycling is not an option, why not carpool or use public-transport? Walking and cycling will reduce your monthly fuel bills and keep you healthy through regular exercise.

Shopping

Shopping refers to anything we buy, from food to furniture, clothes to toothpaste.

Relationship to the four root causes:

What we buy is made from materials extracted from the earth's crust, and synthetic compounds that we create from these materials. These can build up in natural systems faster than the natural world can reclaim them. In addition to the resources needed to make products, think about the wages and working conditions of workers producing them.

Opportunity:

Choose what you buy carefully. Reading labels and claims will help you vote with your purse or wallet, reduce your environmental footprint, and support workers' rights to healthy and safe working conditions at home and abroad.

Ask yourself

Do I really need it?

An obvious but rarely asked question. Does it need to be new? Can you rent, share or borrow? The most environmentally sustainable choice is buying only what you need!

How or where was it produced?

Look for a label, a tag or ask the seller. Support your local economy when possible.

Is it durable?

Knowing about the materials and their lifespan is a key component to the durability of any product. Ask yourself how long the product will be useful to you and, if not needed anymore, can it be recycled. This is often where cost and durability come head-to-head.

What am I supporting by making this purchase?

Every time we use our purse or wallets, we are voting with our monetary power. Does this company share your values? Have they made a commitment to being more environmentally sustainable? If you don't know, do some research to find out.

What can I do when it's no longer needed?

Some companies practice cradle-to-cradle, taking the whole lifecycle of the product into consideration and alleviating the stress on our landfills. If they don't, ask yourself: how can the product be safely reused, recycled or disposed of? Does the company or manufacturer supply replacement parts, a recycling or take-back programme?

Ask yourself

Can I reuse or repair this?

Save time and money by simply reusing something you already own. Can you repair what you already have and stop something from entering the waste stream?

Is my rubbish someone else's treasure?

Bartering, swapping or garage and car-boot sales are an easy place to start. You can also drop off items at your local thrift store, donate to local charities or access a host of on-line trade, swap and sell communities.

Can I recycle this?

From mobile phones to batteries to paint, many goods can be recycled nowadays. If you can't repair, reuse or sell something, it's likely it can be recyclable – and will create value as your waste becomes something new. Find a depot or drop-off centre near you. Also, look to see if the product or packaging is recyclable or made of recycled materials before you buy.

Do I have to throw this out?

Composting is a perfect example of how to keep organics out of the traditional waste stream. Whether you have a big garden or a small balcony, everyone can compost. Diverting organics from the landfill reduces greenhouse gas emissions associated with decomposing waste. And if you've ever bought a bag of soil, you'll wish you started this money saving venture a lot sooner!

Waste

Waste is everything you throw away. It can come from things you buy and don't use (such as packaging), but it can also be energy in-efficiencies (for example, heat loss through gaps and cracks around your home).

Relationship to the four root causes:

Landfills are being filled up and there is less space available to handle our waste. This contributes to a root cause of un-sustainability because natural systems are degraded when we create new land-fills.

Once waste arrives at the landfill, we also risk leaching harmful chemicals and compounds into the land, air and water.

Opportunity:

There is no such thing as waste in natural systems. It's a term that's only relevant in human systems. Mimicking nature as much as possible is a first step to reducing the amount of waste we create.

Reducing our overall consumption is obvious, but we can also reuse, reclaim or repurpose many items before we even get to recycling!

Health

Health refers to the mental, physical and emotional wellbeing of you, your family, neighbours and even perfect strangers. Increasingly, people understand that the health of our environment and our personal health are closely linked.

Relationship to the four root causes:

When the balance of the earth's systems is compromised - by digging up, dumping into or degrading the environment - your own well-being is affected. It might directly impact your health. For example, a decline in air quality can lead to a rise in asthma. Your health and well-being can also be impacted when you feel unsafe, undervalued or disconnected from your community.

Opportunity:

Maximise the health benefits of the space you call home. For example, use non-toxic products to create a healthy home environment. By maximising natural lighting you'll make your home more enjoyable and save on energy costs. Give back to your community to help create a vibrant, flourishing neighbourhood that everyone can enjoy.

Ask yourself

How does this affect my health?

A huge number of products on the market today contain chemicals that are either harmful to human health or have never been tested for human safety.

Become a savvy label reader and choose safer, non-toxic alternatives. You may even consider simple, safe and cost effective ways to make your own home cleaning solutions.

How healthy and comfortable is my home?

Maintaining a healthy home means looking at how each part affects the whole.

For example, ventilate your home to maximise air flow and control humidity, and reduce exposure to toxins or allergens such as mould.

(**See** - *"seeing your house as a system"* section.)

See pages 103 / 104 for some information on the many different Environmental or Sustainability Labels for the Home. You'll find a list of labels that will help you identify safer, healthier and greener products.

Ask yourself

Who needs to know about this?

It's likely that not just you or your family has encountered a specific hurdle. Start with a group you feel most comfortable talking to; maybe that's your local sports club, local businesses, school or a few neighbours. Bring your message of hope, inspiration and urgency to people on your list, starting with the most approachable and working to the most influential.

How can I share?

Connecting with members of your local community can be fulfilling and educational! How you choose to get involved depends entirely on you. Think about your skills and your passion – public speaking, writing, working with your hands, making music, teaching, etc. – and how you can incorporate that activity into a way of giving back into the local community.

With the background on this and the previous pages and with the tips that follow, you can now take the first steps to change the decisions you make at home from a more environmentally sustainable point-of-view.

Participate

Participation is your involvement in your local community. It could be with your neighbours, co-workers, community groups, or even a local politician? Or it could be getting your children involved as well as local schools?

Relationship to four root causes:

Getting involved in your local community and sharing knowledge with others is important.

Helping others understand and overcome the root causes of un--sustainability by showing them ways to make better decisions, or together tackling barriers, will create a ripple effect throughout your local community and beyond.

Opportunity:

There are infinite ways of getting involved in your local community. Maybe you prefer to start small with a few friends around the kitchen table.

Or go big by organising a community-wide event. Whatever you do, remember to have fun and share your enthusiasm with others?

Whole House

How can I share?

Seal that leak:

Draughts account for a smaller percentage of heat loss from our homes but they cause the greatest discomfort and encourage us to turn up the heating.

If you combined all the "heat leaks" in an average British home, you would find a hole the size of a football! Draught excluders and caulking of doors and windows can reduce heating bills by a whopping 25%.

This investment will pay off faster than almost any other home improvement, even if your house is already well insulated. Check out more at:

http://energy.gov/energysaver/articles/weatherstripping/

Can I reduce my use of this utility?

Save money, save energy:

Programmable thermostats cost between £50 and £100; and only take around 20 minutes to install.

(**See** *Resource Directory for Local Tradesmen*)

You stand to save 10% or more on home heating costs. While your home is occupied set the thermostat between 19- 21°C. You can also experiment by reducing the temperature depending on the season and your own family's comfort level.

Do I have to drive?

Hail a hybrid:

If you need a taxi, don't call any old company. Opt for a company that has a fleet of hybrid taxis if you have the choice. You'll be saving fuel, resulting in lower emissions.

Hybrid taxis are popping up all over the place, in part spurred by government programmes that offer discount licensing on the cleaner models. So if you call to request a car, ask if a hybrid is available (that will also signal to companies that there's a demand). You can also rent hybrids or how about joining a car co-op that has them.

What am I supporting by making this purchase?

Invest green, invest ethically:

Most people don't know where their money is going when they invest or deposit it. So make sure the institution you're banking with is making investments that combine financial objectives with concern for social, environmental and ethical issues.

Green and ethical investment offers a means by which we as consumers can advance positive social and environmental goals while achieving financial returns.

High street banks with an ethical mandate are limited in the UK but many banks have adopted ethical policies in some areas of business. Ask your bank or financial advisors about ethical investment options.

See the free buyers' guide for an independent rating on: ***www.ethicalconsumer.org***

Did you know?

According to the 2011 National Statistics report on UK emissions statistics, UK households were responsible for 15% of the nation's 456.3 million tonnes output of greenhouse gas emissions in 2010. "Fuel-guzzling SUV's get a lot of blame for creating pollution and causing climate change, and rightly so. But the average home in Britain and other parts of the industrialised world actually causes more than twice the greenhouse gas emissions of the average vehicle."

Source: decc.gov.uk

Whole House

How does this product affect my health?

Steer clear of these furnishing features:

• Flame retardants: the most common being Polybrominated diphenyl ethers or PBDEs.

They are synthetic chemicals that persist in the environment, having appeared in food, household dust, and human breast milk. PBDEs are known as neurotoxins and have been linked to birth defects and reproductive damage.

• Stain and stick resistant materials: contain Perfluorinated chemicals (PFCs).

PFCs are extremely persistent. Researchers are finding serious health concerns about PFCs, including increased risk of cancer and as a hormone disrupter known to cause birth defects and developmental problems.

• Dust mite free: will contain a miticide, a man made chemical to kill dust mites and is considered to be a neurotoxin.

How healthy and comfortable is my home?

Take a deep breath:

Britons typically spend an average of 90% of their time indoors. Indoor air quality has been shown to cause and / or exacerbate a wide array of health effects like allergies, asthma, respiratory infections etc, which is due to a cocktail of various toxins present at any time.

We need clean air inside and out so bring in the green; certain indoor plants have proven to be positively beneficial and will add colour and vitality, as well as clean and purify naturally the air in your home.

Do I really need this product?

Fine furnishings:

Instead of spending money on new furniture think of how you could reuse existing furniture that you were considering getting rid of.

Refurbish existing furniture or buy second hand to keep waste out of the landfill. When buying new, look for locally produced items or those made from recycled materials. An added bonus is when the materials are recyclable themselves.

Check out!

The Furniture Re-use Network (FRN) is a charitable organisation of 400 furniture and appliance re-use and recycling organisations in the UK that collect a wide range of household items to pass onto people in need.

The FRN promotes the re-use of unwanted furniture and household effects for the alleviation of need, hardship, distress and poverty.

•   2 million items per year are re-used and passed onto low income families.

•   85,000 tonnes of waste are diverted from landfill.

•   3000 people are working in the UK to collect and deliver furniture and appliances.

•   Check them out and where to find your nearest centre at www.frn.org.uk

Kitchen

Do I have to throw this out?

Black Gold:

Your kitchen waste is about 40% organic wastes. Compost your kitchen peelings and keep all that waste out of the landfill. Turn it into rich garden compost for growing your own vegetables or herbs.

Bag it:

Reusable shopping bags cut down on your need to use petroleum-based plastic bags from the supermarket or local store.

Keep a spare bag in the car and one at the office. In Wales ALL carrier bags are charged for; no matter how much you spend or how big the item is. At home try using fewer bags, lining only one waste bin with a compostable or biodegradable bag.

Buy bulk:

It's cheaper and uses less packaging.

The tap is where it's at:

In the UK alone, around 15 million plastic bottled drinks were sold a day in 2011 *(source: defra.co.uk).*

Avoiding bottled water will reduce health risks from chemicals that leach out of plastics, keep bottles out of the landfill and save you money. Instead, put a filter on your tap or in your fridge.

Can I reduce my use of this utility?

Ice cold:

Set your refrigerator and freezer to the most efficient temperatures: refrigerator from 2°C to 3°C (35°F to 37°F) and freezer to -15°C (5°F). Maintain stand-alone freezers at -18°C (0°F).

You can use a thermometer to check temperatures and adjust settings as needed. ***Remember*** to regularly vacuum the cooling coils at the back of your older refrigerator to maintain performance.

Load it up:

Run your dishwasher full. Let dishes air-dry or use the economy setting. Don't waste water prewashing or rinsing; most dishwashers are up for the challenge.

Leaking taps:

A dripping tap could waste up to 5,500 litres of water a year and cost up to £18 a year if you're on a water meter.

Did you know?

Food Packaging Waste: The global food packaging industry is worth billions, but did you realise that up to 50% of the price of food we buy can be down to its packaging costs?

The more we buy, the more we eat, and the more packaging we throw away - and so the financial and environmental costs to our world keep on increasing.

Kitchen

Can I be more efficient in the way I use my utilities?

Be an A-rated Energy Star:

All new appliances must show their energy rating between A and G. The difference in the annual energy consumption can make a dramatic difference to the annual running costs.

Look for the Energy Efficiency sticker (on products from dishwashers to cookers).

These products must meet or exceed technical specifications that ensure they are among the most energy efficient on the market. For more, visit *www.energysavingtrust.org.uk/Electrical/Energy-Saving-Trust-Recommended-products*

How can I share?

Promote the low-hanging fruit:

Let your friends and neighbours know about the easiest things they can do to start on the path of environmental sustainability at home, such as reducing waste and implementing energy-saving measures.

For example, once you start composting; share those skills with someone you know. Help them get started and show how easy it really is. *Get your children and their friends involved!*

How or where was this item produced?

Fresh is best:

Join a local food co-operative or veg box scheme in your neighbourhood that supplies organically grown vegetables, seasonal fruit & veg boxes, organic meat and more.

Eating foods in season guarantees they're packed with flavour and high in vitamins and minerals. Buying locally produced food is good for the UK's local rural economies. It also reduces packaging, fossil fuel use for transport, and you'll know where it came from.

How will this affect my health?

Sticky business:

The toxic particles and gases emitted from conventional stovetop cookware made of Teflon and other non-stick coatings can stay in the body forever.

Applied to everything from frying pans to pizza boxes to microwave popcorn bags, exposure to these dangerous toxins should be avoided altogether.

Use alternative cookware made of stainless steel, cast-iron or a non-PFOA non-stick coating.

Check Out!

Use Local Foods Finder to find Farmers' Markets, Farm Shops and Pick Your Own in your local community on *www.localfoods.org.uk*

Farmers' markets operate in every corner of the United Kingdom. Find one near you at *www.local-farmers-markets.co.uk*

National Farmer' Retail & Markets Association is a co-operative of Farmers and Producers selling on a local scale. Check them out at *www.farma.org.uk*

Bedroom

How does this affect my health?

Sleep well:

Because mattresses and pillows in the UK have to meet certain fire resistance standards, they will all contain chemicals to some extent. To minimise their effect, buy bedding with a flame retardant inner lining.

Then buy a natural fleece as an under blanket - wool is naturally flame-proof.

Most mattresses are made using synthetic materials originating from petrochemical derivatives called flexible polyurethane foam.

Pillows and mattresses made from polyurethane, and duvets filled with polyester, can all emit chemical vapours; look for natural alternatives.

In the UK, avoid purchasing crease resistant or 'easy care' cotton sheets, night clothing and curtains. They are likely to have been treated with a form of formaldehyde, a Volatile Organic Compound (VOC) that can irritate the skin and will never wash out of the fabric, so it could irritate you for life.

How or where was this item produced?

Go organic:

Choose organic cotton bedding and clothing. Conventional cotton growers use about 25% of the world's insecticides and more than 10% of the pesticides. Many farmers who work on cotton plantations in the developing world face health risks associated with over, and on-going, exposure to agrochemicals.

Once it is harvested, cotton is also bleached, treated and dyed, adding to the chemicals contained in its fibres.

Can I reuse or repair this?

Good as new:

Remember those trousers that popped a button or a favourite shirt with an indelible stain; then why not fix-them-up and you'll have a whole new wardrobe you probably forgot about?

Did you know?

Mothballs

Mothballs are made of either Naphthalene or Paradichlorobenzene.
Both of these substances are toxic and have been associated with cancers.

Good Option:

• We are not aware of any non-toxic commercial product to keep moths away from clothes.

Best:

• Store woollens with cedar blocks or in cedar chests, or in a gauze bag containing cedar chips.
• Clothes can also be stored with 2 handfuls each of dried lavender and rosemary, plus 15ml each of fresh cloves and dried lemon peel.
• If you suspect your clothes have been infested with moths, place them in a plastic bag in the freezer for several days. This will kill all moths and moth eggs (please thaw out before wearing!)

Bedroom

How can I share?

Swap it up:

If you're weary of your garments, call some friends and organise a clothes swap. Your old is their new. If you haven't done so already, how about trying out one of the many vintage clothes stores appearing on our high streets for your next shopping trip.

Find clothes that are unique, relatively affordable and environmentally sustainable from a re-use point of view. Vintage can, admittedly, be a very nice word for 'second hand'. That doesn't mean, however, that vintage clothing is inferior to clothing you could buy on the high street today, check it out for yourself.

Can I be more efficient in the way I use my utilities?

Sweet dreams:

Before bed, turn down your thermostat to about 15°C. The same rule can apply when you leave the house. You will save 10 to 15% on your total energy bill.

Did you know?

"In the UK, there are over 30,000 chemicals registered for production and use, and the majority have not been tested for their impacts on human health, wildlife or the environment.

Even chemicals that are known to cause cancer and other health problems are permitted for use by industry and in consumer products. Each year, an increasing volume of toxic chemicals is released into the UK's environment."

The safety of chemicals is regulated through EU-wide legislation and regulation of chemical safety.

The UK follows the EU regulatory framework: REACH (Registration, Evaluation and Authorisation of Chemicals) Under the new REACH regulation the EU is currently implementing to harmonise the safety assessment of these chemicals, 'existing' and 'new' chemicals (i.e. those marketed after new test guidelines were introduced in 1981) are subject to the same scrutiny in terms of safety and risks to human health and the environment.

Living & Dining Room

How does this affect my health?

Bust that dust:

Most electronics contain flame retardants or PBDEs. Toxic dust is then sloughed off your TV or stereo, making its way into your indoor air. Dust regularly with a damp cloth.

When making a new purchase, buy from companies who no longer use PBDEs. Greenpeace created an online guide to greener electronics at **www.greenpeace.org/international/campaigns/toxics/electronics**

Recycle old electronics or e-waste to keep hazardous compounds out of our water and landfills.

Play it safe. Toy recalls have you worried? Check out *Healthystuff.org*. They are the Consumer Guide to toxic chemicals in toys. They rank toys and list chemicals of concern. They have tested plastic and wood toys for lead, polyvinyl chloride and other harmful chemicals. Last year, 20% of the 1,500 toys they tested contained lead. Children's play jewellery ranked the highest.

Choose toys made of natural materials like wood or organic cotton or wool.

How or where was this item produced?

Magic carpets:

Before you buy a new rug or runner, find out where it was made.

Ask your furniture retailer under what conditions your carpets were produced, and consider buying floor coverings from suppliers that can prove safe and equitable working conditions for their workers.

Did you know?

Electronic waste is the source of 70% of heavy metals (such as lead, arsenic, copper and nickel) found in our nation's landfills.

If you feel you must upgrade your mobile phone, ask your service provider how you can properly dispose of your old phone.

Living & Dining Room

Can I recycle this?

Close the loop:

Electronics contain dangerous materials such as lead and mercury. Recycle your old televisions, computer monitors, and mobile phones to keep hazardous compounds and chemicals out of landfill and ground water.

Most retailers offer battery recycling programmes, as do all the major supermarkets and DIY stores. If in doubt, ask wherever you buy batteries and electronics.

Can I reduce my use of this utility?

Phantom power is scary:

Your electronics – TV, VCR, DVD, etc. – use power even when you turn them off.

Unplug to save money and energy. Use a power bar to make it easier; you'll only need to flip a single switch!

Can I reduce my use of this utility?

Screen savers do not save energy:

In fact, they consume almost as much energy as a computer in use (most power consumption comes from the monitor).

Turn off your computer monitor to save more money and energy.

Check it out!

Most of us don't know what to do with our old IT when we are finished with it. Re-use, reduce, recycle is the green mantra but how do schools, businesses, or individuals manage this? Consider Computers 4 Africa when you change your computer, a UK charity which sends refurbished computer equipment out to Africa and provides a simple solution to your WEEE problem.

To date, Computers 4 Africa has sent over 6000 PCs to countries all across Africa.

They will collect unwanted PC's, and then refurbish and data-wipe them before sending them out to schools, colleges and projects. They are looking for; Working PCs, Monitors, Mice, Keyboards, Laptops, Power leads, Laser Printers, Scanners and Projectors.

Full details of the minimum specifications can be found on their website at: *www.computers4africa.org.uk*

Bathroom

How or where was this item produced?

Behind the label:

Choose 'Post Consumer Waste' (PCW) recycled toilet and tissue paper.

So, is the answer for eco-warriors everywhere to buy recycled toilet tissue wherever possible?

As with so many eco-dilemmas where we aim to buy something to make a difference, the answer is only a qualified **'yes'.**

Does recycled paper save trees? *Yes*

- and given that each of us across Europe uses 13kg of toilet tissue per year, equivalent to around 22 billion rolls Europe-wide, recycled toilet tissue has the potential to save a lot of trees.

Does it reduce energy consumption? *Yes.*

Producing recycled paper involves between 28 to 70% less energy consumption than making virgin paper, and uses less water.

How healthy and comfortable is my home?

Body scrub:

Many beauty products contain ingredients that are toxic. The amount is minute, but over a number of years they accumulate and can cause health problems.

A healthier choice is to buy the natural and organic toiletries and cosmetics sold alongside the chemical-based products - or try making your own. Place equal amounts of bran and crushed oats (porridge oats) in a muslin bag and use this to clean yourself under the shower. Oats and bran are natural cleaners and provide good exfoliation.

How does this affect my health?

Go natural:

Avoid beauty products with Parabens (a class of chemicals used as preservatives), Phthalates (Industrial chemicals used as plasticisers), Triclosan (used as an antibacterial and antifungal agent), and synthetic dyes.

Each day we smear and spray ourselves with personal care concoctions that contain potentially harmful chemicals, some of which have been linked to cancer, birth defects, learning disabilities and other major health problems. Greenpeace (*greenpeace.org.uk*) and the Women's Environmental Network at (*www.wen.org.uk*), both provide useful lists of products to avoid as well as listing companies with good track records.

Did you know?

The average person uses 9-12 personal care products each day.

This translates to about 126 different chemical compounds, some of which are not regulated.

As a mostly self-regulated industry, the companies, not the Health and Safety Executive, perform the health and safety testing before the products hit the shelves.

Bathroom

Can I be more efficient in the way I use my utilities?

Stem the flow:

Install low-flow toilets and taps. A tap aerator alone can save up to 10 litres of water per minute. Water-efficient showerheads conserve energy without changing water pressure.

During a 6-minute shower you could save as much as 108 litres of water. The amount of energy required to treat, deliver and then re-treat (as sewage) one cubic metre of your toilet water produces one kilogram of carbon dioxide.

A low-flow toilet will reduce the amount of water you use and, indirectly, greenhouse gas (GHG) emissions.

Can I reduce my use of this utility?

Wrap it up:

Save money by insulating your hot water tank and set the thermostat lower. Every 5.5°C reduction saves up to 13% on your water heating costs.

Do I have to throw this out?

Safe disposal:

Unused or expired prescription medication that gets flushed down the toilet will eventually find its way into streams and rivers (aka, our drinking water).

Take old meds back to your local pharmacy for safe disposal. Not only are you eliminating the risk of an accidental poisoning in your home, but you're also playing a role in keeping our oceans and landfills free of pollution.

Check out!

Read the labels; those named 'green' or 'natural' and even 'organic' can be misleading. Under present rules only 1% of ingredients need to be from an organic source for the product to qualify.

Look for the Soil Association logo this is the only accreditation guaranteeing that 95% of a product's ingredients, excluding water, are derived from an organic source.

Laundry Room

How does this affect my health?

Clean yet green:

Conventional laundry detergents are full of ingredients like petro-chemicals, powdered enzymes, optical brighteners, synthetic dyes and fragrance.

Look for biodegradable, fragrance-free, and non-toxic detergents that clearly list all ingredients, and use chlorine-free bleach.

There are greener alternatives: brands such as Ecover and Method are widely available, and there are lots of household products already in your cupboards that will do the cleaning just as well.

Can I be more efficient in the way I use my utilities?

Keep it cool:

Up to 90% of the energy you use to wash clothes comes from heating the water. Wash all fabrics in cold water – they will keep their colour longer and you'll notice the savings on your next utility bill.

Did you know?

Fumes from slightly damp dry cleaning can contribute to indoor air pollution. Toxic chemicals like Perchloroethylene, a carcinogen and respiratory irritant, evaporate from clothing into your home. If you must use conventional dry cleaning, remove the plastic bag and hang clothes outside to speed up the evaporation of solvents.

Avoid buying clothes that need to be dry-cleaned or look for dry cleaners using greener alternatives such as: www.johnsoncleaners.com that have over 150 GreenEarth cleaners across the UK.

Laundry Room

How healthy and comfortable is my home?

Whiter than white:

Supermarket shelves are positively groaning under the weight of cleaning products for our laundry. We also demand a lot from our washing powder. 'Whiter than white', 'spring fresh' and 'soft enough for babies' are all claims used to sell us laundry powders and liquids and manufacturers would have us believe that they are both essential and super-efficient for keeping our laundry clean.

In reality, the vast majority of commercially produced cleaning products contain harmful chemicals that will end up in our homes, or going down the drain and into our rivers, lakes and oceans.

How can I reduce my use of this utility?

Hang out:

Line-dry clothes – outdoors, or indoors on a clothes horse or washing line, whenever possible.

If you must use a tumble dryer - one of the most energy-hungry domestic appliances, make sure all items are well spun beforehand.

Line-drying laundry can save the average household about £70 per year in energy costs.

Did you know?

Coloured clothes rarely, if ever, needed to be washed at anything higher than 40°C.

A wash at 60°C uses more than 30% more energy than washing at 40°C and will fade the colours in clothes faster too.

White-wash settings use much more energy and water than other settings. Most whites wash well at 40°C, especially if soaked in a sink or bath in advance.

Garage

Is my rubbish someone else's treasure?

Reduce, reuse and recycle:

Use recycled building materials for your next renovations. Find stone, tiles, bricks, flooring, and more at salvage yards and junkyards.

Add personality and value to your home, help create a market for recycled goods, and encourage others to recycle too.

If you have unwanted items - don't bin it! Recycle it!

Take a look at:
www.recycle.co.uk or *uk.freecycle.org*
and lessen your impact on the environment.

Can I reduce my use of this utility?

Retire that second fridge:

Refrigerators are one of the top energy-hungry appliances in the home. Parting with that full size 15-year-old fridge could save you around £120 a year and prevent about 240 kilograms of greenhouse gas emissions.

How does this affect my health?

Don't inhale:

Wood dust from treated or composite wood products can contain hazardous chemicals that are harmful to your health. Make sure your garage or workshops are well ventilated, and wear a mask or use tools with integrated dust collection systems.

Open windows or the garage door and vacuum sawdust as you go. Additionally, all paints, solvents and other chemicals stored in your garage need to be in tightly sealed containers.

Did you know?

- If Britons stopped idling in their car for just three minutes a day, over a year we would collectively save 630 million litres of fuel and 6.3 billion kilograms of Green House Gas emissions.

- Collectively recycling all our drinks cans would stop new materials from being mined and processed. Recycling would contribute to reducing 126,000 tons of CO_2 equivalent in the UK's atmosphere, the equivalent of taking 27,000 cars off Britain's roads for a year.

Or enough energy to power 41,000 UK homes for a year.

Source: WRAP (Waste Resource and Recovery Programme)

Garage

What can I do when it's no longer needed?

Give it away now:

Most of us have too much stuff. Things which need to be dusted, stuff that needs fixing and things that clog up our garages and sheds.

Make someone in your community happy by posting items you no longer need and bartering online at:
uk.freecycle.org or www.freegive.co.uk or www.snaffleup.co.uk

Do I have to drive?

Drive green:

Instead of arriving at work harried and stressed out from driving, consider carpooling. You'll save money, arrive more relaxed, and reduce your personal greenhouse gas emissions.

Register with a carpool near you or start one with your co-workers and neighbours who share a similar commute.
Check out: www.carpooling.co.uk or www.carshare.liftshare.com or www.nationalcarshare.co.uk

Can I recycle this?

Wheel them in:

Tyres are recyclable and not just into other tyres. Recycling specialist retailers have a huge selection of really useful items made from your used or damaged car tyres, ranging from pens, notebooks and mouse mats to window boxes and planters, belts and sandals. If you've got a spare tyre or two, you can recycle it yourself in a number of ways.

For example; turn it into a swing if you've got a tree big enough, or a flowerbed: stack them on top of each other, fill with soil and use them to grow potatoes.

Have you thought of?

Washing your car on the grass? This will give the lawn a drink and the soil will help break down any impurities in the water to prevent them from getting into storm drains and local water courses.

Garden

Do I have to throw this out?

Compost it:

Over 30% of the average household's kitchen waste can be composted which makes a nutrient-rich fertiliser that helps soil retain its moisture. Not only will there be fewer truck loads going to the landfill but your plants will love it. You'll also save money by avoiding chemical fertilisers which can end up in our drinking water.

How can I share?

Pay it forward:

If you have a large garden which you can't manage yourself anymore why not share your garden with someone who would like to turn it into a vegetable garden. Then you can divvy up the fruits of your shared labour.

Can I reduce my use of this utility?

Plant green, Save green:

Deciduous trees shade windows in the summer while letting sun shine through in the winter.

Plant them on the west and east sides of your home. Coniferous trees can help ward off winter winds.

Plant them to fight off prevailing winds, often on the north side.

How or where was this item produced?

Hit the deck:

Always look out for the Forestry Stewardship Council (FSC) symbol on timber to be used as decking, and on wooden furniture to sit on it, to ensure it is sustainably sourced.

Use linseed oil instead of toxic wood preservatives to maintain your decking and wooden furniture.

Also check out 'plastic timber', made from recycled wood and plastic, as an alternative.

Did you know?

Watering the lawn and garden takes up almost 40% of total household water use during the summer, have you thought of:

Collecting Rainwater from your roof it is ideal for irrigating your garden and lawn.

All you need is to simply install a rain barrel or two for storage of the rainwater.

Garden

Garden

How does this affect my health?

Grow green:

Choose organic or non-toxic alternatives to pesticides.

Pesticides used to kill insects and weeds in your garden work a little too well: *they don't discriminate!*

They also expose us to a frightening list of health effects. Nature-friendly insecticidal soaps, biological controls such as nematodes and alternative gardening techniques can replace toxic chemical sprays.

Check your local gardening supply store for non-toxic alternatives, which are now widely available.

Can I be more efficient in the way I use my utilities?

Every Drop:

Save water by xeriscaping, a landscaping philosophy that considers water conservation.

You will use up to 50% less water and it helps native plants better adapt to their local area.

If you have a lawn, water in the evening and use a soaker hose instead of a sprinkler.

About half of the water used on lawns is lost to evaporation or run-off due to over-watering.

Building a rain garden is another technique.

Have you thought of?

Encouraging wildlife

Install any of the following: bat boxes, bumble-bee nests, nesting boxes for birds. Put out food (mealworms, nuts and seeds) and fresh water for birds.

Plant a patch of native wildflowers, such as Marsh Marigold, Purple Loosestrife and Creeping Jenny, to encourage insects, butterflies, dragonflies and bees.

Design your garden so that it is inviting to frogs, hedgehogs and even badgers. For good advice on creating a wildlife garden check out the; Royal Society of Wildlife Trusts at: *www.wildlifetrusts.org*

Make Your Next Renovation a Green One

It's not environmentally sustainable, or affordable, to retrofit and renovate your home over night just to take advantage of available green products and grants. However, when something finally does need replacing these ideas will keep you on your course towards environmental sustainability.

Focus on design and save money: The best way to ensure that your project is affordable is through good design. It is much less expensive and time-consuming to identify and remedy problems on paper than mid-stream in the construction stage. Just a few hours of a professional architect's time can save hundreds, or even thousands of pounds in construction change re-orders. Also, have your plans reviewed by a professional energy efficiency expert (find a local expert in the Directory at the rear of this book) to identify the design elements and products that can make your home as energy efficient as possible. When considering the design of your renovation, ask yourself how your decisions help reduce your contribution of the four root causes of un-sustainability. (For a reminder of the four root causes, see page 74.)

Downsize and upgrade: Smaller renovations disturb less land during site work, and use fewer materials and energy throughout the construction and the operation of the home.

This reduces the ecological footprint of your home, and reduces the damage to natural systems. The money you save can be spent on incorporating special features that will increase your home's overall efficiency, comfort, and beauty.

Integrate good ideas: Integrated building design means bringing together the entire renovation team at various stages of the project to share ideas and identify readily achievable green design goals. This can save both money and time on your project.

To help you prioritise, we've listed these renovation ideas in order of importance (or where the biggest impact will be felt):

1. **High performance building envelope:** By building with better windows, an air tight envelope, and better insulation, the size of the heating equipment needed for your home can be significantly reduced, not to mention your heating bills. The benefits of upgrading an older inefficient heating system cannot be underestimated. There are huge financial savings to be gained.

2. **When you're building, build passive:** Paying attention to solar orientation (where and when your home receives direct sun or is shaded) and natural airflow, known as

Check Out!

Living Roofs: Cities and towns place a great pressure on the environment. In a bid to counteract this impact, many people are installing a green or living roof. Vegetated roofs have been in use for a long time, from the hanging Gardens of Babylon to the turfed roof houses of Ireland and Scandinavia. Some cities, like Portland, Oregon, USA, are leading the way in green roofing.

Green Roof Installation: There are a number of companies specialising in the installation of living roofs; check them out on the internet (big green book & directory!!) But there are also numerous sites to help the competent DIY'er, too. You could make a start with the garden shed!

Make Your Next Renovation a Green One

passive solar design, can significantly reduce your need for more expensive mechanical heating systems. For example, strategically placing windows on south and west-facing walls can substantially reduce heating costs while reducing your requirement for artificial lighting fixtures, all of which will reduce negative environmental impacts.

3. **Bold and beautiful**. Any renovation will require purchasing materials. Use locally harvested and / or produced products made from renewable resources to reduce the distance these products have to travel and causing damage to natural systems. By selecting building materials and finishes that are durable and which require little maintenance, you will save money in the long run. It will also reduce the amount of materials sent to landfills.

Some examples include:

• **Carpets** are comfortable for the home environment; however they can act as a trap for dust particles, bacteria, and mould spores. New carpets can contain various chemicals used in the manufacturing process that will off-gas and become airborne, affecting your indoor air quality. For a healthier carpet, look for natural fibres like Wool, Sisal, coir, Jute and Seagrass.

• **Cork** is antimicrobial, resistant to mould and mildew and is a naturally environmentally sustainable resource. Cork flooring is now offered in many colours, and in both planks and tiles.

• **Bamboo** is a fast growing, renewable resource that is very hardwearing and dimensionally stable. Floors made from bamboo can be used in any area of the home where you might use a wooden floor. You can also find bamboo cabinetry as an alternative to pressed woods.

• **Linoleum / Marmoleum** is a natural product made from linseed oil, wood flour, rosin, jute and limestone. Because linoleum is a natural organic product, its performance is enhanced by time, as exposure to air serves to harden and increase its durability.

• **Finishes** should include natural alternatives. Look for natural oil/wax based finish for wood floors and interior woodwork. Use low-toxicity water-based caulking for caulking joints in wood, metal, masonry, tile and ducts. This caulking should only be applied to clean, dry surfaces. Keep in mind some products are better than others. Ask a professionals advice!

Remember, green renovations are good for you the environment and they will get you more bang for your money. Green buildings sell and rent for higher prices and attract buyers or tenants more quickly.

These are but a few of the many ways in which a green renovation can save you money, increase the net worth of your investment and help towards making your home a more environmentally sustainable place to dwell in.

Did you know?

Good wood

If you are buying new wood, make sure it has the FSC (Forestry Stewardship Council) logo. Its your guarantee that you are not contributing to global forest destruction or unethical displacement of forest communities.

Go to *www.fsc-uk.org*

Seeing your house as a system

A system is a set of parts forming a complex whole. For example, your body is a very sophisticated system of interconnected parts. Your heart pumps blood around your body, and exchanges oxygen for carbon dioxide with your lungs; your nerves run throughout your body enabling you to sense heat, cold, feel textures, pain and pleasure and so on.

Each part of your body plays an essential role in keeping you healthy.

Now think of your house as a system with interconnected parts:

- Building frame and its components (walls, heating system, windows)

- Inputs (energy, water, furniture)

- Outputs (waste, heat, gases, sewage)

- Activity inside the house (heating, cooking, eating, sleeping)

The envelope of your home is like your body's skin and skeleton. The equipment and appliances in your home are like the organs in your body. Your home's finishes are like the clothes you wear, and the services (such as water, gas and electricity) are like the food you eat. Just as your body needs sufficient nutrition, exercise and sleep to stay healthy, each part of your home needs to be integrated and functioning well in order for the whole system to be healthy.

For example, a house that performs well as a system featuring a tight, well-insulated building envelope, high quality windows, and passive solar strategies will allow you to downsize or even eliminate your home's heating and/or cooling equipment. Therefore, anytime you make changes to your home – and especially when doing renovations – it's important to think of your house as a system.

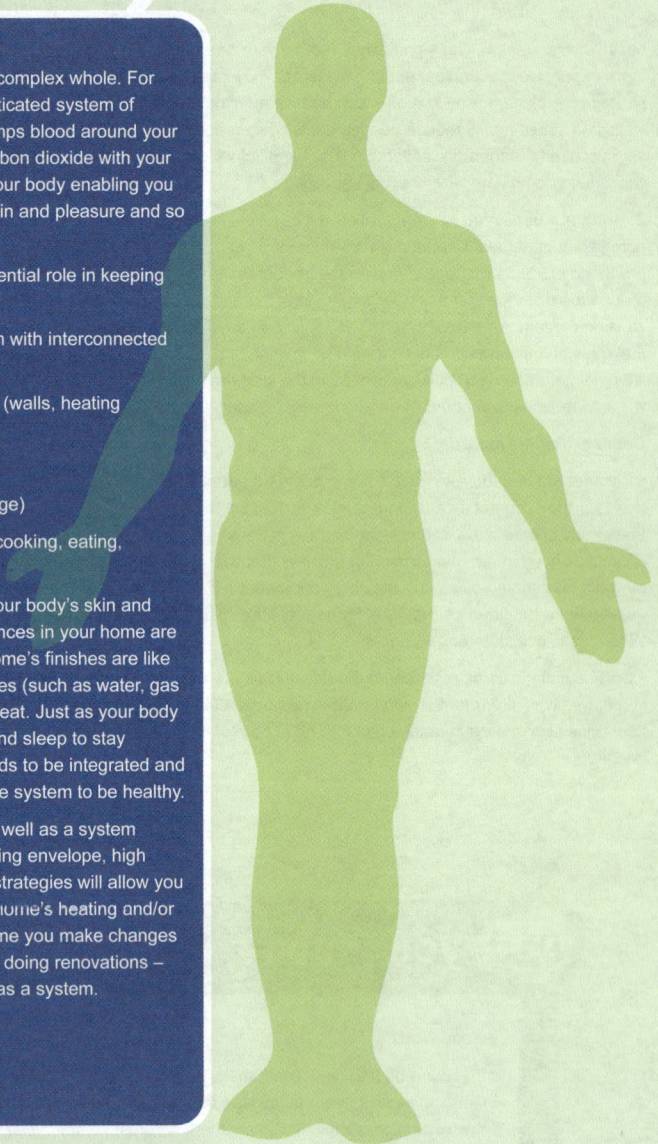

Going Deeper:
Changing the World around You

Times have changed and we understand, more than ever before, the importance individuals play in societal change. The environmental sustainability challenge we all face will not be met without unprecedented leadership. What the world needs now, more than ever, are role models, champions, and people who are willing to stand up and make a difference.

You do not have to be part of an organisation to inspire change in your community. You and other members of your household can change the world beyond your home one step at a time.

Individual choices

Start with what you love. These days we are inundated with information about how to go green. But where do you start? Any successful journey of change will begin with thinking about what you love.

Choose one issue to focus on. Starting with something you are passionate about (for example, cooking or cycling). Then when you encounter challenges, you will be more likely to see it through and find creative solutions. Remember that every positive step you take helps you to reduce, and eventually eliminate, contributions to the four root causes of un-sustainability.

Read, watch and listen. Once you have a focus, it is easier to grow the scope of what you know. Build on what you read and hear. This is where individuals' creativity can shine. For example, you could conduct an energy-use assessment of your house to see how greater efficiencies can be made, or research environmentally sustainable products and information on material recycling in a closed-loop approach. Think about how what you read, watch and hear relates to the four root causes of un-sustainability, and all the ways you can incorporate change towards environmental sustainability in your life.

Community Action

Be bold and spread the word. Current research shows the most trusted advisors in people's lives are not experts like scientists and politicians; they are people just like you. Share your experience with others, including the hurdles you have overcome. People will identify with others who share the same obstacles that they do. Modelling new behaviour alone is one of the most powerful ways to influence the behaviours of others.

Normalise behaviour. We are creating a 'new normal' for Britons – sustainable living is becoming a way of life. People often change only when they feel sufficient social pressure to do so. Recycling is a good example: Green boxes are an obvious social cue. Nobody wants to be labelled as the only person on the street without a green box. Also, one person bringing reusable shopping bags to the supermarket might be viewed as an eccentric. But when almost everyone is using them, you feel out of the loop without one. An important way to leverage the impact of your behaviour is to communicate how many people have already changed. Research shows people do not want to be behind the curve. Motivation comes from the perception that they are in the majority and not a laggard.

Did you know?

Do-it-yourself culture has us firmly in its thrall. It's a rare home that doesn't possess a toolkit, electric drill or work bench. However, for every TV makeover show, there is an equivalent show featuring DIY disasters and half finished jobs. According to the Department of Trade and Industry, each year 250,000 serious injuries and 70 deaths are caused through carelessness and lack of knowledge when undertaking DIY. It's also wasteful and polluting. An estimated 12-25% of the paint sold in the UK is never used, and many jobs use highly polluting, toxin-rich materials that pose risks to human health and the environment.

Going Deeper:
Changing the World around You

Policy Change

Influence the influencers. At the end of the day, we need to make it easy for people to live environmentally sustainable and remove the barriers to personal change.

The political sphere and the marketplace can either facilitate or impede environmentally sustainable behaviour.

As citizens and knowledgeable consumers, we need to communicate societal needs. First, be clear who you need to speak to: it could be a letter to your local Member of Parliament about an issue that affects all Britons, a call to your local councillor to rid your town or city of an ancient by-law prohibiting clothes-lines, or a chat with the owner of the local fruit and veg shop down the street to request if they could source local produce.

When thinking about how to approach decision-makers, traditional avenues like petitions, marches and town halls still exist, but they are definitely not the only way to influence policy. Making a phone call, scheduling a face-to-face coffee meeting or inviting a decision-maker to an event are other means to initiate policy change.

Keep the big picture in mind and think of how you can promote change on the ground.

> *"Each person, group or organisation working towards a different world may seem powerless and insignificant but all of them can add up to a force that can become irresistible."*
> *~David Suzuki~*

There are endless possibilities for specific actions to help move us all towards environmental sustainability.

Overall, remember how important it is to:

Become an environmental champion:

All it takes is passion and commitment. Find the issue you are most passionate about and get organised.

Advocate for sustainable change:

Write letters, make phone calls, run for political office, start a new business, take a risk.

Unleash the sustainability champion within you!

Go Green! Pledge

Join fellow homeowners and individuals who are pledging to take personal steps to build environmental sustainability into their everyday lives, which will have a collective impact in improving the quality of life for everyone.

Go Green! Pledge

Today I agree to embrace my responsibility to help improve the environment and develop a more sustainable outlook. I pledge to directly impact the Earth's Health by making environmentally and sustainably responsible choices every day.

My pledge is to…

Increase Resource Efficiency

- Turn off lights, computers, and electronics when not in use
- Use rechargeable batteries
- Set electronics to use energy saver features and replace incandescent lights
- Save water with low flow shower heads and other water saving products
- Purchase Energy Star or other types of energy rated products
- Use email instead of the mail
- Use both sides of paper when making copies
- Walk whenever possible
- Ride bikes or bike share
- Car pool or car share
- Re-think transportation methods and use public transit whenever possible

Choose to Re-Use

- Use reusable mugs (for coffee, tea, juice etc…)
- Use reusable jute or cotton bags instead of plastic
- Pack lunches in reusable food containers
- Buy products made from recycled materials

Choose to Re-Use Cont...

- Print drafts on the back side of used paper
- Make notepads from used paper
- Donate used equipment and furniture
- Compost organic materials

Recycle

- Recycle plastic, paper, glass, aluminium, and cardboard
- Recycle disposable batteries
- Recycle toner cartridges and replace with recycled cartridges
- Use paper made from recycled materials

Reduce harmful impacts on the environment

- Reduce pollution
- Reduce energy consumption
- Reduce waste
- Purchase products from companies that reduce pollution, waste, and energy consumption
- Adjust thermostats
- Wash clothes in cold water

Use Education as a Tool

- Learn more about being Green
- Apply green concepts at home and with members of my family
- Investigate new technologies and ways to help the environment
- Help your child's school, university or my local community organise events that teach others Green concepts and practices

From the above *Go Green Pledge* you can pick and choose whatever initiatives that best fit with what you can do. The most important thing is for everyone to commit to doing something to improve the environment in the communities in which they live, work, and play.

Above all else, being 'green' should not be viewed as a middle-class luxury, or as an ideal that can be set aside in periods of economic woe. If there is one thing we want you to take away from this handbook, it is that being 'green' does not need to be expensive or draconian while helping to secure a future for the planet.

Continuing the Journey

If you've done everything recommended in this handbook and completed the checklists at the back, congratulations! You have made some significant changes where you've probably already noticed financial savings and you may be feeling healthier too.

You may also be asking what more you can do?

Lots! The path to environmental sustainability is a long one. To help get you there, keep these things in mind as you make household decisions:

Remember that you are part of a system

Everything you do will impact something else. Try to imagine how your decision will affect other parts of the system, and take action understanding that your sphere of consequence will inevitably be larger than your action.

Think about your vision for an ideal home and lifestyle

Consider creating a vision for your household. Ask yourself, "If my household were totally sustainable, what would that look like?" Involve other people that live in your house to help you create this vision. Invite your neighbours to brainstorm together. Ideally, you won't contribute to the four root causes of un-sustainability at the beginning of this toolkit for the Home – but other than that, you can do whatever you want. Be creative!

Identify actions to move you towards your ideals

These actions can be anything that takes you towards your ideals of an environmentally sustainable household, in any or all of the six areas of shopping, transport, utilities, waste, health and participation.

To figure out which actions to take first, consider if they are:

• Moving you in the right direction

• Able to be developed further by acting as stepping stones for future actions

• A good return on investment.

The decisions you make in your home will affect the future of your local community, the region and the country as a whole.

You are not alone

There are thousands of people realising the excitement, financial savings, as well as improved health associated with moving their whole household towards environmental sustainability. Consider volunteering in your community to help build relationships and create groups to support each other in the transition towards environmental sustainability.

Celebrate your successes

Every change that you make with an eye to becoming more sustainable is reason to celebrate! Give yourself a pat on the back for your foresight in 'avoiding the walls of the funnel' as described at the beginning of the toolkit.

Continue to ask yourself, "what next?"

When you ask this question it will help you be clear about how the results of your decisions can be stepping stones towards taking other steps down the path to environmental sustainability.

Environmental Sustainability is about nothing less than deciding the future of our world. We all share the privilege and responsibility of making choices in our lives. It is up to each of us to create a future we can be proud of passing on to our children and future generations, while enjoying all the riches an environmentally sustainable lifestyle offers.

Environmental and Sustainability Labels for the Home

There are some key things to consider when selecting building products and household items to ensure validity of environmental sustainability claims made by manufacturers. Not forgetting budget and availability, you may want to ask yourself the following questions when choosing building materials and household products:

1. Is it manufactured in a socially and environmental manner?

2. Can it be re-used or recycled?

3. Is this product manufactured with renewable energy?

4. Is this product energy-efficient?

5. Is it durable? And last but not least,

6. Is it locally manufactured?

Consumers can avoid greenwashing by looking for products with widely accepted environmental standards. The following pages provide a list of the most common standard setting and certification organisations. For each label, consider which of the root causes the label alerts you to.

Learn more about each of the labels that follow.

Marine Stewardship Council (MSC) Logo

The MSC logo helps you identify fish to eat that have come from well-managed, sustainable sources. With fish stocks dwindling in many of the world's seas, this certification scheme gives threatened stocks a chance to recover.

Friend of the Sea Logo

Friend of the Sea is a certification logo and promotion of seafood from sustainable fisheries and sustainable aquaculture. It is the only certification scheme which, with the same logo, certifies both wild and farmed seafood.

Forest Stewardship Council (FSC) Logo

The FSC logo helps you spot wood and paper products that come from well-managed, sustainable forests; choosing products marked with this logo means you're not contributing to damaging threatened areas such as tropical rainforests.

Programme for the Endorsement of Forest Certification (PEFC) Logo

PEFC is an international non-profit, non-governmental organisation dedicated to promoting Sustainable Forest Management (SFM) through a unique global certification system. PEFC-certified timber is widely available in construction-grade strengths from an extensive network of merchants and suppliers with a huge variety of softwoods and hardwoods available, offering the widest choice of sustainable timber available to the construction sector.

Compostability Mark of European Bioplastics Logo

The Compostability Mark enables compostable products to be identified by a unique mark and channelled for recovery of their constituent materials in specially developed processes. The Compostability Mark thus conveys product information to waste-disposal plant operators and product image to consumers

Soil Association Logo

The Soil Association logo gives you the guarantee that not just the food was grown without pesticides but also that any animals involved in its production were treated humanely.

Leaf UK Logo

The Linking Environment and Farming (Leaf Marque) brings you food produced by farmers who are committed to improving the environment for the benefit of wildlife and the countryside. The mission of LEAF enables farming that enriches the environment and engages local communities. Everyone can be involved with LEAF; farmers, the food chain and the consumer.

Fair Trade Foundation Label

Fairtrade is an ethical trade system that puts people first. Fairtrade offers farmers and workers in developing countries a better deal, and the opportunity to improve their lives and invest in their future. Fairtrade gives consumers the opportunity to help reduce poverty and instigate change through everyday shopping.

Environmental and Sustainability Labels for the Home

Rainforest Alliance Certified Logo

The Rainforest Alliance Certified seal ensures that a product comes from a farm or forest operation that meets comprehensive standards that protect the environment and promote the rights and well-being of workers, their families and communities. Products that carry the green frog seal include coffee, tea, chocolate, fruit, ready to drink beverages and juices, flowers, paper and tissue products, furniture and more

Natureplus logo

Natureplus is an international label of quality for sustainable building and accommodation products, tested for health, environmental awareness and functionality. The label's primary aim is to provide consumers as well as architects, tradesmen, building companies and all those involved in construction, with a reliable orientation aid towards the best sustainable products which are environmentally safe and not posing any health risks

The Leaping Bunny Logo

Companies certified through the Coalition for Consumer Information on Cosmetics' (CCIC) Leaping Bunny Program make a voluntary pledge to eliminate animal testing from all stages of product development. The companies' ingredient suppliers make the same pledge and the result is a product guaranteed to be 100% free of new animal testing.

Natrue-Label

The Natrue-Label is a guarantee for cosmetic products. Their goal is to promote and protect natural natural beauty and skin care products. Any product with the Natrue label is intended to be as natural as possible, using natural and organic ingredients, soft manufacturing processes and environmentally sustainably practices.

The Carbon Trust Standard Logo

The Carbon Trust Standard is a certification mark of excellence, designed to recognise organisations for real carbon reduction. To qualify, organisations must measure, manage and genuinely reduce their carbon footprint and commit to reducing it year on year. Certification is valid for two years, after which, organisations must undergo recertification.

Energy Saving Trust Recommended Label

Energy saving products uses less energy and therefore has less of an environmental impact as well as being cheaper to run. The Energy Saving Recommended logo is a quick and easy way to spot the most energy efficient products on the market.

EU Eco Label

A voluntary scheme designed to encourage businesses to market products and services that are kinder to the environment and for European consumers - including public and private purchasers - to easily identify them.

EU Energy Label

By law, the European Community Energy Label must be displayed on all new household products displayed for sale, hire or hire-purchase. Household appliances offered for sale, hire or hire-purchase must be accompanied by a fiche and a label providing information relating to their consumption of energy (electrical or other) or of other essential resources. Products are generally rated from 'A' to 'G', with 'A' being the most efficient ('A+' and 'A++' for the most efficient fridges and freezers).

EU organic products label

This organic product label indicates that the product has been grown within sustainable cultivation systems. Foods may only be marked as "organic" if at least 95% of their agricultural ingredients are organic.

Water Efficiency Label

The Bathroom Manufacturers Association's Water Efficient Product Labelling Scheme lets you compare hundreds of products that meet the standards of water efficiency. If you're thinking of buying a new bath, shower, tap or toilet, look out for the distinctive blue label water-efficient product.

Blue Angel Logo

This is the oldest eco-label in the world and it covers some 10,000 products in some 80 product categories. The label specifies that the product focuses on one of four different protection goals: health, climate, water, and resources.

Nordic Ecolabel or "Swan"

The Nordic Ecolabel demonstrates that a product is a good environmental choice. The "Swan" symbol, as it is known in Nordic countries, is available for 65 product groups. The Swan checks that products fulfil certain criteria using methods such as samples from independent laboratories, certificates and control visits.

Environmental Sustainability at Home:
Checklist

Achieving environmental sustainability at home and lessening your environmental footprint won't happen overnight. This checklist is designed to help you track your progress against the tips provided earlier in the toolkit, but it is also a small way to celebrate your successes. Don't forget, although this particular list is static, you will continue to learn about ways of making your home more environmentally sustainable.

Utilities

Ask yourself:
Can I reduce my use of this utility?
Can I get the same utility service another way?
Can I be more efficient in the way I use my utilities?

☐ Get an energy audit
☐ Research possible grant and rebate programmes provincially and locally
☐ Install a programmable thermostat
☐ Draught-proof windows and doors by weather stripping
☐ Buy energy efficient electronics and appliances
☐ Set the refrigerator and freezer to the most efficient temperatures
☐ Use the smallest appliance
☐ Only run the dishwasher when full
☐ Insulate the hot water tank
☐ Set thermostat to a lower temperature when asleep or away from home
☐ Install low flow toilet(s)
☐ Install aerators to taps
☐ Plug electronics into power bars
☐ Unplug phantom power sucks
☐ Wash clothes in cold water and use the shortest cycle
☐ Hang clothes to dry
☐ Retire your second fridge
☐ Replace windows with the double pane variety
☐ Install automatic lighting controls
☐ Set up a rain barrel
☐ Research xeriscaping or rain gardening
☐ Switch from a sprinkler to a soaker hose
☐ Plant deciduous trees to provide shade in summer but allow sun through in the winter
☐ Other: _____

Environmental Sustainability at Home: Checklist

Transportation

Ask yourself:
Do I really need to go?
Can I go somewhere local?
Do I have to drive?

- ☐ Look into hybrid taxi and car rental options
- ☐ Check car-shares or car co-ops in the area
- ☐ Walk, bike, or take public transport to work or run errands
- ☐ Drive a fuel-efficient vehicle
- ☐ Turn off engine to stop idling
- ☐ Take at least one less flight a year
- ☐ Other: _____

Shopping

Ask yourself:
Do I really need this product?
How or where was this item produced?
Is it durable?
What am I supporting by making this purchase?

- ☐ Find a shop or outlet that sells local food
- ☐ Join a food co-op
- ☐ Purchase organic and sustainably raised meat, poultry and dairy products
- ☐ Find a Farmer's Market and visit
- ☐ Eat foods when they are in season
- ☐ Purchase fewer paper products and only 100% PCW toilet paper and tissue
- ☐ Buy organic cotton linens & clothing
- ☐ Purchase non-toxic flooring options
- ☐ Purchase products that are local, and made of recycled or rapidly renewable products
- ☐ Eat meat-free meals a couple of days a week
- ☐ Other: _____

Environmental Sustainability at Home:
Checklist

Health & Wellbeing

Ask yourself:
How does this affect my health?
How healthy and comfortable is my home?

- ☐ Clean with non-toxic and green cleaners
- ☐ Safely dispose of toxic home cleaning products (www.productcare.org)
- ☐ Avoid personal care products with parabens, phthalates (fragrance), triclosan and dyes
- ☐ Buy clothes without stain resistance, wrinkle free treatments and without flame retardants
- ☐ Dust to minimise PBDE laden dust
- ☐ Purchase the safest, non-toxic toys
- ☐ Use non-toxic, biodegradable laundry soap
- ☐ Do not use chlorine bleach
- ☐ Solve dampness issues in the basement
- ☐ Do not dry clean clothes with traditional PERC chemicals
- ☐ Hand wash "dry clean only" clothes and hang to dry
- ☐ Ventilate garage or workshop area, wear mask, vacuum dust
- ☐ Garden pesticide-free
- ☐ Use low or no-VOC paints and finishes
- ☐ Grow plants indoors
- ☐ Other: _____

Participation

Ask yourself:
Who needs to know about this?
How can I share?

- ☐ Hold a weather stripping party (what is this?)
- ☐ Host a clothes swap
- ☐ Start a carpool at work
- ☐ Grow a vegetable or herb garden & donate extras to those in need
- ☐ Teach a neighbour to compost
- ☐ Start a community garden
- ☐ Collect e-waste from neighbours and take them to the drop-off depot
- ☐ Let political representatives know where you stand
- ☐ Contact the media
- ☐ Other: _____

Environmental Sustainability at Home: Checklist

Waste

Ask yourself:
Can I reuse or repair this?
Is my rubbish someone else's treasure?
Can I recycle this?
Do I have to throw this out?

☐ **Start composting**
☐ **Use cloth bags**
☐ **Buy bulk to reduce packaging**
☐ **Drink tap water instead of buying bottled water**
☐ **Safely dispose of medications**
☐ **Sign up for Red Dot to get off junk mail**
☐ **Use safe, non-toxic homemade solutions to get stains out of clothing and fabrics**
☐ **Recycle everything possible, including electronics and any materials coming out of a home renovation (such as drywall or wood)**
☐ **Use recycled materials for the next renovation**
☐ **Recycle unused mobile phone(s)**
☐ **Recycle tyres**
☐ **Check out swap, barter or trade communities online**
☐ **Donate old cupboards, sinks, and toilets to Habitat for Humanity's Restore**
☐ **Dispose of hazardous pesticides, paints and flammables responsibly**
☐ **Other: _____**

Great work! Just remember that even when any of the checklists are complete, there is always more to do. Keep learning about new ways to make environmentally sustainable choices at home and share those ideas with your family, friends, and neighbours.

biggreenDEAL

Are you switched on to the Green Deal?

Get free impartial advice and helpful information about the new government scheme at:

www.**biggreendeal**.co.uk

Your Green Deal contacts source for authorised Green Deal Approved

Green Deal Advisors • Green Deal Installers
Green Deal Providers • Green Deal Suppliers
Green Deal Certifiers • Green Deal Training
& much, much more about
the Green Deal Scheme itself!

THE GREENDEAL

Energy-saving improvements for your home or business without having to pay all the costs up-front!

- NO UP-FRONT COST ON NEW BOILERS
- NO UP-FRONT COST ON LOFT INSULATION
- NO UP-FRONT COST ON CAVITY WALL INSULATION
- NO UP-FRONT COST ON SOLAR PANELS
- NO UP-FRONT COST ON DOUBLE GLAZING

plus many more energy saving options and improvements through the Green Deal Scheme.

What is the Green Deal? The idea is simple. The government's flagship energy saving plan aims to transform all UK homes into properties that are warmer and cheaper to run.

The scheme allows homeowners and businesses the opportunity to implement energy saving improvements, without having to pay all the costs up-front and to pay for some or all of the improvements over time through their energy bills. The Green Deal Plan is a new type of unsecured loan which is paid back through the electricity bill at the property.

The Green Deal covers more than 40 different energy saving measures such as modern heating systems and better home insulation. It also extends to micro-generation to capture your own energy. All of these improvements are expected to pay for themselves through reduced energy costs, the actual savings will depend on how much energy you use and any increase in future energy tariffs. The following pages provide a brief overview to introduce you to the Green Deal.

greendealcontents

The following pages provide a brief overview to the Green Deal.

- The Green Deal: An Introduction
- Green Deal Assessment
- A Guide to the Green Deal
- Energy Companies Obligation
- Green Deal Directory

The Green Deal: An Introduction

The Green Deal: A new way you can make energy-saving improvements to your home or business without having to pay all the costs up-front.

What is the Green Deal?

The Green Deal is designed to help householders and businesses increase the energy efficiency of properties and therefore reduce greenhouse gas emissions across the UK. The Green Deal will be offered by the private sector to enable homeowners and businesses to implement energy efficiency improvements. The scheme lets customers pay for some or all of the improvements over time through their energy bills. The Green Deal Plan will be a new type of unsecured loan, and interest will be charged on the loan. You will be liable for the loan whilst you are the electricity bill payer at the property. It is likely that savings will mainly be made on your heating bills (e.g. gas, oil or electricity). Your Green Deal repayments will all be added to your electricity bill (because everyone has one of these). There may be an upfront charge for an initial assessment, which must be carried out before the Green Deal Plan is agreed.

SOME OF THE ENERGY-SAVING IMPROVEMENTS YOU COULD MAKE.

1. Loft insulation

Heat rises and it may be leaking into your loft. Insulating your loft, or topping up your existing insulation, will keep heat inside your living spaces for longer

2. Create your own energy

Technologies like wind turbines and solar panels can capture energy and turn it into electricity or heat for your home.

3. Windows

Homes leak heat through their windows. By replacing your windows with double or triple glazed windows, or installing secondary glazing to your existing windows, you'll keep your home warmer and reduce outside noise.

7. Boilers

Older boilers tend to lose a lot of heat so they use a lot of energy.

High efficiency condensing boilers and air or ground source heat pumps recover a lot of heat so they use less energy.

4. Draught proofing

Gaps around doors, windows, loft hatches, fittings and pipe work are common sources of draughts. Sealing up the gaps will stop heat escaping your home.

6. External and internal solid wall insulation

Older homes usually have solid walls. Installing insulation on the inside or outside of the wall can dramatically reduce the heat that escapes your home.

5. Cavity wall insulation

Some homes have walls with a hollow space in the middle. Putting insulation in this space is quick and makes no mess because the work can be done from outside your home.

Get a Green Deal from January 2013. Start now with an assessment.

The Green Deal Assessment

By booking a Green Deal Assessment, you've made the first steps towards making energy-saving home improvements, like insulation, to make your home more comfortable.

Where to start

Before you can undertake any energy-saving improvements, you'll need a Green Deal Advisor to undertake an assessment of your property. Many different organisations including energy companies, DIY stores, and local trade's people – are authorised under the Green Deal Approved Quality Mark to do this.

For help finding an authorised Green Deal Advisor visit the **www.biggreendeal.co.uk** website.

When you book an assessment you may be asked if there are any accessibility issues, like access to your loft, and whether you can provide bills showing your recent energy use.

A Green Deal Advisor will visit your home, talk to you about your property and your energy use and help decide if you could benefit from Green Deal improvements.

To help ensure they provide an accurate assessment, your Advisor may ask:

• How many people live in your home?
• The types of appliances and heating used
• How often the heating system is used
• If you have any current energy-saving measures installed
• Whether you own or rent the property
• Whether your home is a listed building, in a conservation area, built before 1900 or constructed in a non-traditional way.

They will recommend improvements and indicate whether they are expected to pay for themselves through reduced energy costs. The actual energy savings will depend on how much energy you use and the future costs of energy, and the actual cost of the improvements will depend on the price quoted by Green Deal Providers. All of this information will be provided to you in a Green Deal Advice Report (GDAR).

Keep in mind that some Green Deal Advisors may charge for their service, it's best to check when you make an appointment.

1. Assessment

YOU ARE HERE!

A Green Deal Advisor will come to your home, talk to you about your energy use and see if you could benefit from making energy efficiency improvements to your home.

2. Recommendations

Your Advisor will recommend improvements that are appropriate for your property and indicate whether they are expected to pay for themselves through reduced energy bills.

3. Quotes

Green Deal Providers will discuss with you whether a Green Deal Plan is right for you and quote for the recommended improvements. You can get as many quotes as you like (minimum of 3 is recommended), and you don't have to choose all of the recommendations made to you.

4. Installation

Once you've agreed to a Green Deal Plan, your Provider will arrange for the improvements to be made to your home by a Green Deal Installer.

5. Repayments

You can now start to enjoy a more energy efficient home. Your Green Deal repayments will be automatically added to the electricity bill for the home.

A Guide To The Green Deal

Your Advisor should have also given you:

• An Energy Performance Certificate (EPC) showing the energy use of a typical household of your type, plus some suggestions for improvements.

• A Green Deal Advice Report (GDAR) showing how your household uses energy, plus some recommendations for reducing your energy use and the savings you can expect from the improvements.

Now you're ready to get some quotes from any of the Green Deal Providers.

Note: *During the assessment, the Green Deal Advisor will not be able to recommend specific products or providers, or offer any other goods or services, unless you have agreed to this beforehand.*

Choosing a Green Deal Provider

You are free to take the Green Deal Advice Report to any Green Deal Provider to obtain quotes for a Green Deal Plan, which will include interest on the loan. In general, you are encouraged to obtain a minimum of three quotes from any of the Green Deal Providers to decide which (if any) is best suited to your individual needs and circumstances.

Only Green Deal Providers can offer you a Green Deal Plan. The improvements will have to be recommended by a Green Deal Advisor and installed by a Green Deal Installer. Look out for the Green Deal Quality Mark. Only Green Deal Advisors, Providers and Installers can use it. This shows they meet Green Deal standards and are authorised to operate under the Green Deal Scheme.

Entering into a Green Deal Plan

A Green Deal Provider will give you a quote for the cost of the work, and provide key terms such as the rate of interest and the repayment amounts. Once you're happy with a quote from a Green Deal Provider, they will write up a Green Deal Plan. This is a contract between you and the provider – it outlines the repayments.

Green Deal Plans are regulated under the Consumer Credit Act 1974. This provides you with important rights and protections, including cooling off periods and rules around exit arrangements and early repayments.

How repayments are calculated

Repayments will be fixed at the outset and will include costs associated with the administration and provision of credit for the Green Deal Plan.

Repayment levels will be based on what a typical household like yours is expected to save on energy bills. The Green Deal is designed to try to save you at least as much money as you will have to repay (The Golden Rule). However the actual level of your savings will depend on how much energy you use (e.g. to heat your home) and the future cost of energy.

Caution: If you use less energy than a typical household you can, if you want, take out a Green Deal Plan based on the typical savings shown on the Energy Performance Certificate. However, if you do this, your repayments are likely to be higher than your savings and therefore your energy bills are likely to go up overall. Alternatively, you can discuss with your Green Deal Provider whether your repayments should be reduced, so that they are in line with the savings that your household is likely to make. Your Green Deal Provider will discuss this with you and obtain a written acknowledgement from you if you decide to go ahead with repayments based on a typical household's estimated savings.

Repayment

Your Green Deal repayments will be collected by your electricity supplier via your electricity bill and passed on to your Green Deal Provider. The bills will separately identify Green Deal instalments.

At least once per year, your Green Deal Provider will send you statements of your account, showing how much you have paid off and how much you have left to pay. You can also request a statement of account and a copy of the Green Deal Plan at any time from your Green Deal Provider.

You have the right to pay your Green Deal off early. Your Green Deal Provider may charge early repayment fees – you should check with them.

Moving on

Green Deal repayments are part of the electricity bill for the property. So the person responsible for paying the electricity

bill – usually the occupier – is responsible for making repayments for the improvements. If they move, the next electricity bill payer will take on the repayments.

An Energy Performance Certificate (EPC) (for England, Scotland and Wales), or the Recommendations Report attached to the EPC (for Scotland) will show if there is a Green Deal on a home. If there is, the certificate or report will show the improvements made, the repayment amounts and how long you will need to make repayments for. If you own the property or are the landlord, you will have to provide a copy of these documents to the next occupier and get their written acknowledgement of the Green Deal.

New bill payer of a property with an existing Green Deal Plan

If you are the new bill payer and believe the Green Deal Plan was not disclosed to you, you should dispute the charges with your Green Deal Provider within 90 days of first being notified. After 90 days you will not be able to dispute the charges and will be liable to make Green Deal repayments while occupying the property.

Switching electricity supply for a property with an existing Green Deal Plan

You will be able to switch electricity suppliers and continue with payment of the Green Deal Plan via your new electricity supplier, provided that the new supplier is participating in the Green Deal payment collection system. You should contact your electricity supplier for further information.

Green Deal sales – cold calling

If you display a "No Cold Caller" sticker at your home, or if you are approached by a salesperson and indicate that you do not wish to be contacted anymore, you can expect the caller to stop contacting you. This applies to face-to-face, phone and electronic communications. You can report complaints to the Oversight and Registration Body. Salespeople who offer a Green Deal Assessment are required to:

• Allow at least one day before they can conduct the assessment, unless you provide written consent to a same day assessment.

• Explain cooling-off periods, if they apply
• Tell you what products and services they intend to provide, including marketing of products not related to the Green Deal
• Tell you who they work for and if they have commercial links with other Green Deal participants and third parties
• Tell you if they receive commission from other Green Deal participants.

Useful contacts and information:

Extra Financial Assistance

Many householders in older properties and those on benefits or low incomes may qualify for extra financial assistance. Ask your Advisor or contact the:

Energy Saving Advice Service
ESAS telephone: 0300 123 1234
www.gov.uk/greendeal

Complaint handling procedures:

Green Deal Oversight and Registration Body
GDORB telephone: 0 207 090 1031
Complaints: GDORBComplaints@gemserv.com
Enquiries about the Oversight and Registration Body: GDORBhelpdesk@gemserv.com

If a complaint or enquiry about the Green Deal cannot be resolved by the Green Deal Provider, or supplier, consumers may have recourse to the relevant Ombudsman, depending on the complaint.

Energy Ombudsman Service/Green Deal Ombudsman and Investigation Service on 0330 440 1624 or 01925 530 263, visit: www.ombudsman-services.org or email: enquiries@os-energy.org

Financial Ombudsman Service on 0800 023 4567 or 0300 123 9 123, visit: www.financial-ombudsman.org.uk or email: complaint.info@financial-ombudsman.org.uk

When choosing: *Green Deal Advisors, Providers and Installers remember to look for the Green Deal Approved Quality Mark first. All organisations delivering the Green Deal scheme must be authorised to act under the Green Deal, do not consider anyone with out it!*

Energy Companies Obligation (ECO)

The Energy Companies Obligation (ECO) is a new programme designed to reduce Britain's energy consumption by funding home improvements worth around £1.3 billion every year.

The funding comes from big energy suppliers. It's delivered to customers either directly from the supplier or by organisations working together, who have made special arrangements, such as Green Deal Providers.

Where to start

Free impartial advice services are available. Who can help with:

- finding out if you may be eligible
- explaining the support available
- accessing the support
- more information about the Energy Companies Obligation.

Many householders in older properties and those on benefits or low incomes may qualify for extra financial assistance.

Call the Energy Saving Advice Service (England, Scotland and Wales) on 0300 123 1234 or visit www.gov.uk/greendeal to see if you're eligible.

	People on certain income related benefits		
Living in a private property	Living in social Housing within a rural community	People living in a low income community	People living in older properties
Cavity wall insulation Some homes have walls with a hollow space in the middle. Putting insulation in this space is quick and makes no mess because the work can be done from outside the home.	✓	✓	✓	✓
External or internal solid wall insulation Older homes usually have solid walls. Installing insulation on the inside or outside of the wall can dramatically reduce the heat that escapes your home.	✓	✓	✓	✓
Loft insulation Heat rises and it might be leaking into your loft. Insulating your loft, or topping up your existing insulation, will keep heat inside your living spaces for longer.	✓	✓	✓	✗
Heating improvements Improvements, like replacing your boiler with a high-efficiency boiler or updating your heating controls, can help you reduce the amount of energy used to keep your home warm.	✓	✗	✗	✗

big green DEAL Directory

The **Green Deal** Offers Energy Savings for Householders and Businesses across the UK.

Make Your Home or Business, a *Green Deal Greener!*

Make Your Energy Bill a *Green Deal Cheaper!*

Big Green Deal *Directory*

This printed directory is further supported through the Big Green Deal website which provides a neutral platform from which householders and businesses can find information on living sustainably. The site will also connect you to a whole array of Green Deal Approved suppliers, of products and services which support the Government's Green Deal initiative.

By creating awareness and take-up in this new area via the Big Green Deal website, we aim to increase the energy efficiency of British properties in the public and private sectors across the UK.

Due to the early stages the scheme is currently at, the website will be expanded and constantly updated with all the latest information so you can make the correct and informative decisions about how to best move forward and improve the energy efficiency of your property, save money and cut carbon pollution.

Go to: www.**biggreendeal**.co.uk for more information.

Your contacts source for:

- **Green Deal** *Advisors*
- **Green Deal** *Installers*
- **Green Deal** *Providers*
- **Green Deal** *Suppliers*
- **Green Deal** *Training*
- **Green Deal** *Certification*

Green Deal Advice Service

CV Energy Ltd
26 Saville Grove , Kenilworth
CV8 2PR **07714 749059**

D W A Surveyors Ltd
23 Stamford Park Road , Hale
Cheshire , WA15 9EL
0161 928 1903
dw@dwasurveyors.com
www.dwasurveyors.com
(see full page advert for more information)

Green Deal Advisor Association
7 Delaine Close , Bourne
PE10 9LP **01572 725530**

Central Counties Home Inspectors Ltd
27A Kingsbury , Aylesbury
HP20 2JA **01296 311891**

Work Work Ltd
Alperton House , Wembley
HA0 1EH **02089 027290**

ECO-Residential Ltd
413 Jewellery Business Centre , Birmingham
B18 6DA **08081 471874**

Ampere GDP
Pottington Business Park , Barnstaple
EX31 1QN **01271 323052**

Darren Evans Assessments Ltd
23 Horse Street , Chipping Sodbury
BS37 6DA **01454 317940**

Energy Friend
Thomas Wright Way , Sedgefield
TS21 3FD **08000 461972**

UK Green Deal Advisory Service Ltd
SOAR Works Enterprise Centre , Sheffield
Yorkshire , S5 9NU
0800 285 1517
info@ukgdas.co.uk
www.ukgdas.co.uk
(see full page advert for more information)

Mark Group Ltd
70 Boston Road , Leicester
LE4 1AW **0800 616302**

Infinity Energy Organisation Ltd
South Way , Wembley
HA9 0HB **08008 620004**

Green Deal Advice Service

We Greenerise
Turbine Business Centre , Worksop
Nottinghamshire , S81 8AP
0800 779 7002
hello@we-greenerise.com
www.we-greenerise.com
(see full page advert for more information)

Green ECO Grants Ltd
US7 Armstrong House , Robin Hood
DN9 3GA **07702 118500**

British Gas
Canal Street , Leeds
LS12 2UE **08001 072750**

Carbon Low Real Estate Ltd
Berefsord Way , Chesterfield
S41 9FG **01246 452982**

Evolve
Southwick Farm Barn , Southwick
PO17 6EF **08456 789667**

Green Deal Advisors

Property Certification Group
23 Ellerslie Avenue , Rainhill
L35 4QP **08432 898244**

SolarTech Ltd
Sterling Business Park , Buckingham
Buckinghamshire , MK18 1TH
0845 838 2477 or 07501466127
coral.blundell@solartech.org.uk
www.solartech.org.uk
(see full page advert for more information)

Solar King UK
Bahana Close , Haydock
WA11 9XN **08006 783757**

Solas Renewable Energy
41 Bonhill Road , Dumbarton
Dunbartonshire , G82 2DL
0800 616 203 or 01389 734414
craig@solas.biz
www.solas.biz
(see full page advert for more information)

Richard Irvin Sustainable Energy Ltd
Irvin House , Aberdeen
AB12 3LE **01224 367182**

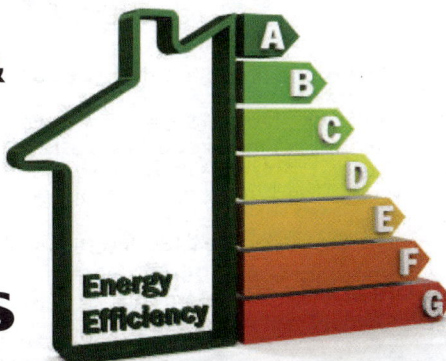

GREEN DEAL DIRECTORY

THE BIG **GREEN DEAL**

SOLAS

www.solas.biz

find us on

GREEN DEAL APPROVED

Saving homes and businesses energy and money for over 25 years

A different kind of

Green Deal

PROVIDER, ASSESSOR

and

INSTALLER

Comprehensive and effective home and business energy saving services

When you are looking for Green Deal help, choose Solas - as a social enterprise, we exist to help you, not to make a profit - you can trust us to deliver

GREEN DEAL DIRECTORY

THE BIG GREEN DEAL

The Homebuyers Friend Ltd

**RIGHT FROM
THE START**

**We are able to offer, Home surveys or Buyers Reports
Domestic Energy Assessments and Green Deal Advice**

Having recently qualified as a Green Deal Advisor, the starting point
for any Green Deal finance package, we can assure you of our total
impartiality, we are not tied to any providers and prefer to act alone
meaning the whole process is about you and your needs.

Whilst we are based in Oswestry, we have a network of
contacts throughout the whole of England & Wales.

Open 8am until 6pm 7 days a week, if you would like us to call you...
Please use the contact us page on our website

**www.thehomebuyersfriend.co.uk
E-mail address: info@thehomebuyersfriend.co.uk
Telephone numbers: 01691 658197** *(Office 8am to 6pm)*
Mobile: 07814 395001 *(Anytime)*

SAVA

FSB

*4 Arthur Street, Oswestry, Shropshire, SY11 1JP
Company No. UK 07405618 V.A.T No: 111 1297 64*

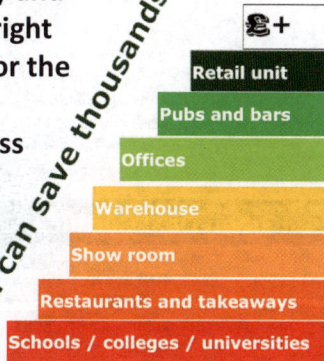

Green Deal Advisors

KnaufMarmorit
St Andrews House , Bristol
BS11 9DQ **01179 823870**

The Home Buyers Friend Ltd
4 Arthur Street , Oswestry
Shropshire , SY11 1JP
01691 658197   or   07814 395001
john@thehomebuyersfriend.co.uk
www.thehomebuyersfriend.co.uk
(see full page advert for more information)

Green Business Experts
69 Hungerdown ,
London , E4 6QJ
0844 272 0055 or 07988 939206
info@greenbusinessexperts.co.uk
www.greenbusinessexperts.co.uk
(see full page advert for more information)

J W Jones & Son
3-5 Bay View Road , Colwyn Bay
LL29 8DW **01492 531414**

NGPS Ltd
49 Evering Avenue , Poole
BH12 4JF **01202 736812**

Caroline de Mancha Stevens
6 Fortnum Place , Ilminster
TA19 0HT **01460 52309**

Altair Energy Ltd
North Caldeen Road , Coatsbridge
ML5 4EF **01236 702012**

ARAN Services Limited
Units 1-6 The Old Station , Bury St Edmunds
Suffolk , IP28 6NE
01284 812 577 or   0800 587 7795
info@aranservices.co.uk
www.aranservices.co.uk
(see half page advert for more information)

Green Deal Certification

Stroma LZC Ltd
Pioneer Business Park , Castleford
West Yorkshire , WF10 5QU
0845 6211111
lzc@stroma.com
www.stroma.com
(see half page advert for more information)

Green Deal Certification

NAPIT
Pleasley Vale Business Park , Mansfield
Nottinghamshire , NG19 8RL`
0845 543 0330
info@napit.org.uk
www.napit.org.uk
(see full page advert for more information)

BRE Global
Bucknalls Lane , Watford
WD25 9XX **08458 630014**

Blue Flame Certification
Whitfield Enterprise Centre , Stoke on Trent
ST6 8UW **08451 949031**

BSI Assurance Ltd
BSI Group , Milton Keynes
MK5 8PP **01908 814606**

NICEIC
Warwick House , Dunstable
LU5 5ZX **01582 539069**

ECMK Ltd
Presley Way , Milton Keynes
MK8 0ES **01908 560622**

CIBSE Certification Ltd
22 Balham Road , London
SW12 9BS **02086 755211**

Ocean Certification Ltd
192 Portland Road , Newcastle Upon Tyne
NE2 1DJ **01912 658225**

Certass Ltd
37 Carrick Street, Ayr
KA7 1NS **08450 948025**

British Board of Agrement
Bucknalls Lane , Watford
WD25 9BA **01923 665411**

FENSA Ltd
54 Ayres Street , London
Greater London , SE1 1EU
0207 645 3700
enquiries@fensa.org.uk
www.fensa.org.uk
(see full page advert for
Glass and Glazing Federation)

Green Deal Certification

ECA Certification Incorporating ELECSA
Mansfield Business Centre , Mansfield
Nottinghamshire , NG18 2AE
01623 683005
Sarah.Fry@eca.co.uk
www.elecsa.co.uk
(see half page advert for more information)

OFTEC (Oil Firing Technical Association)
Foxwood House , Ipswich
IP5 2QQ 08456 085080

Association of Plumbing & Heating Contractors (Certification) Ltd
12 The Pavilions , Solihull
B90 4SB 01217 115030

Elmhurst Energy Systems Ltd
16 St Johns Business Park , Lutterworth
Leicestershire , LE17 4HB
01455 883250
enquiries@elmhurstenergy.co.uk
www.elmhurstenergy.co.uk
(see half page advert for more information)

BM TRADA Certification Limited
Chiltern House , High Wycombe
HP14 4NP 01494 569821

Energy Saving Trust
112/2 Commercial Street ,
Edinburgh , EH6 6NF
0131 555 7900
greendealcert@est.org.uk
www.energysavingtrust.org.uk
(see full page advert for more information)

Green Deal Installers

Gemini Solar
Ty'n Y Weirglodd , Caernarfon
Gwynedd , LL55 4AX
01286 650701 or 07876 302484
info@geminisolar.co.uk
www.geminisolar.co.uk
(see full page advert for more information)

Green Deal Installers

SolarTech Ltd
Sterling Business Park , Buckingham
Buckinghamshire , MK18 1TH
0845 838 2477 or 07501466127
coral.blundell@solartech.org.uk
www.solartech.org.uk
(see full page advert for more information)

Richard Irvin Sustainable Energy Ltd
Irvin House , Aberdeen
Aberdeenshire , AB12 3LE
01224 367182 or 07768 230451
dave.mcgrath@richard-irvin.co.uk
www.richardirvinsustainableenergy.co.uk
(see full page advert for more information)

J W Jones & Son
3-5 Bay View Road , Colwyn Bay
LL29 8DW 01492 531414

Henson Heat Pumps & Renewables
19 Church Lane , Derby
DE7 6BB 07802 257796

ARAN Services Limited
Units 1-6 The Old Station , Bury St Edmunds
Suffolk , IP28 6NE
01284 812 577 or 0800 587 7795
info@aranservices.co.uk
www.aranservices.co.uk
(see half page advert for more information)

UK Solar Direct Ltd
Nuneaton Railway Station, Nuneaton
CV11 4BU 08450 178847

Forever Green Renewables Ltd
Middle Stanley Renewable Centre , Cheltenham
Gloucestershire , GL54 5HE
07794 303506
ben@forevergreen-energy.co.uk
www.forevergreen-energy.co.uk
(see half page advert for more information)

ThermaDetect
Lindley House , Camberley
GU15 3TS 01276 501703

Maven Services Ltd
Waterloo Farm Courtyard , Arlesley
SG15 6XP 08004 661006

PALM (Yorkshire) Ltd
23 Bescot Way , Shipley
BD18 1QA 08001 223363

A greener & better future

Energy efficient windows, doors and conservatories can make all the difference.

With fuel prices rising and the global drive to make the world a cleaner, greener place for future generations, fitting energy efficient glazing can save money, energy and the environment.

The Glass and Glazing Federation (GGF) is the main industry representative for companies who make, supply or fit, glass and glazing products in the UK. The GGF sets the standards for the industry and protects consumers, plus all GGF members carrying out Green Deal work are certified by FENSA, the GGF's subsidiary company.

Protecting Homeowners

If you use a GGF Member Company, your deposit will be covered by the GGF Deposit Indemnity Scheme and if you have a dispute with a GGF Member Company doing work in your home, our Conciliation Service is there to help resolve any issues free of charge.

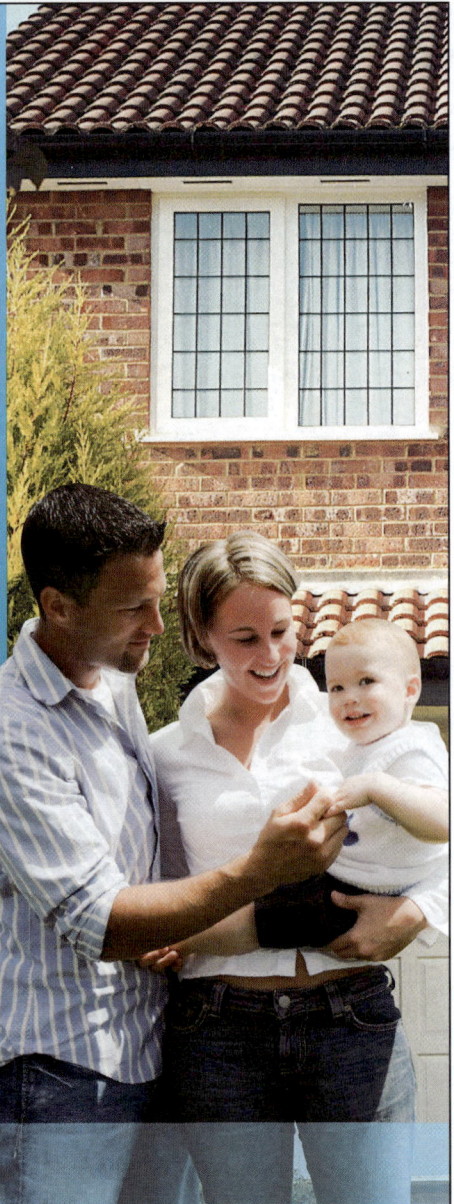

Choose from hundreds of GGF Member companies and get a quote now at www.ggf.org.uk

GGF

Glass and Glazing Federation

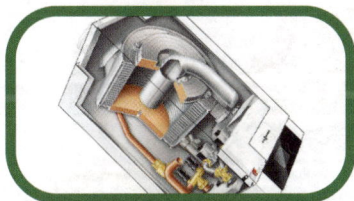

Green Deal Installers

Green Deal Initiative Ltd
10 Holbrook , Sheffield
S20 3FY **08006 442676**

Green Deal Solutions
150c Holland Street , Denton
Greater Manchester , M34 3GG
0844 477 0995
info@greendealsolutions.net
www.greendealsolutions.net

Raven Solar & Energy Solutions
54 Meliden Road , Prestatyn
LL19 9SE **01745 888000**

Absolute Insulation Ltd
Unit 20/21 Wanstead Road , Leicester
Leicestershire , LE3 1TR
0116 2313980
info@absoluteinsulation.co.uk
www.absoluteinsulation.co.uk
(see half page advert for more information)

Green Deal Installers

Pure Electrics/Pure Energy
Unit 6 Maesbury Road , Oswestry
SY10 8NH **01691 681051**

Life's Energy Ltd
127 Falsgrave Road , Scarborough
North Yorkshire , YO12 5EY
01723 371374
andy@lifesenergy.co.uk
www.lifesenergy.co.uk
(see full page advert for more information)

So Gecko Ltd
Upper Boat Business Park , Treforest
CF37 5BP **01443 888339**

Thextons Properties Ltd
Old Colonial , Birkenhead
Cheshire , CH41 1AY
0151 670 1122
mail@thextons.co.uk
www.thextons.co.uk
(see full page advert for more information)

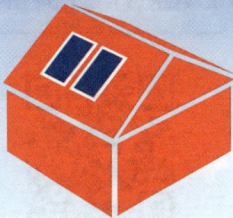

ENERGY INDEPENDENCE - THE JOURNEY BEGINS

There's more to Sustainable Energy

Energy price hike, up 9% again

Renewable Energy Solutions

Domestic P.V.

- 4kW PV array, grid tied inverter
- Benefit typically £775
- Payback typically 9 years
- 25 year PV panel warranty
- Canadian Solar & Other leading brands
- Feed in Tarrif rate to drop from 1st November

P.V. for Agriculture

- Farm building up to £24/m²/year benefit
- Set aside/barron ground up to £25,000 per acre, beats barley!

Office & Industry P.V.

- Save up to 118kg CO_2/year/m²
- Payback 7-8 years
- Staff discount schemes available
- Car Park Solutions
- Roof Space worth up to £30/m² per annum benefit

1 SOLAR PV

2 SOLAR THERMAL

3 AIR SOURCE HEAT PUMPS

4 COMBINED HEAT & POWER

5 FLUE HEAT RECOVERY

6 BIOMASS

7 GROUND SOURCE HEAT PUMPS

8 HEAT RECOVERY

HR01

Demand Reduction
- Voltage Optimisation
- LED Lighting
- Automatic Controls
- Thermal Insulation

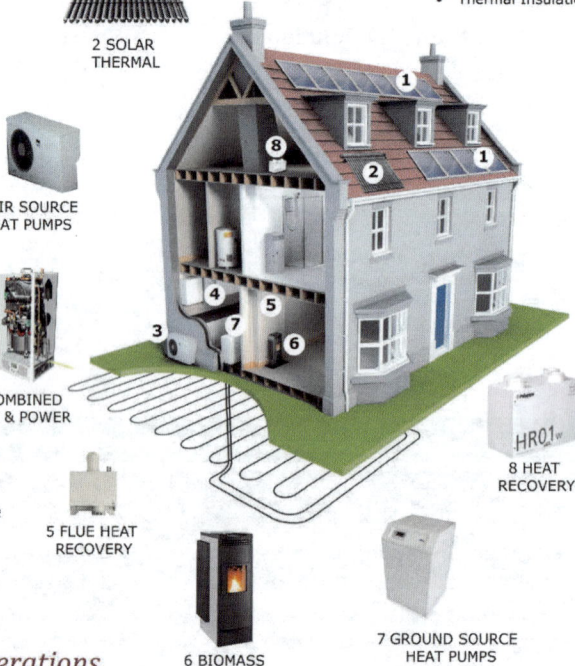

RICHARD IRVIN

A name trusted for generations
And for generations to come

INTEGRATED ENERGY SYSTEM

RICHARD IRVIN
SUSTAINABLE ENERGY

Irvin House
Hareness Road
Altens Industrial Estate
Aberdeen
AB12 3LE
T: 01224 367180
rise@richard-irvin.co.uk

Richard Irvin Services Group is a multi-discipline company offering

- Boiler Servicing, Upgrades
- Biomass boilers
- Domestic and Industrial CHP
- Solar Thermal Hot Water Systems
- Air and Ground Source Heating
- Energy Demand Reduction
- Full Property Insulation Services
- Wind Turbines 3kW-50kW
- Micro Hydro 1-50kW

www.richardirvinsustainableenergy.co.uk

TIME TO CONSIDER WINTER SERVICING

Life's Energy
Generate a Better Future
Energy Solutions
Add value to your property
General electrical, heating and plumbing work undertaken
Solar PV
Solar Thermal
Air & Ground Source Heat Pumps
Biomass
Heat Recovery Ventilation
Energy Efficient Gas Boilers
Contact Life's Energy for alternative solutions to Gas, Oil & Electric Boilers.
01723 371374
www.lifesenergy.co.uk

Green Deal Installers

Aire Valley Exteriors Ltd
Riverside Business Park , Baildon
BD17 7AD 01274 582260

Smart Solar PV Ltd
5 Astley Road , Bromsgrove
B60 2RS 01527 559199

Energy Connect UK Ltd
Woodgate Business Centre , Leicester
LE4 0AW 01162 425151

EverWarm Ltd
2F Inchmuir Road , Bathgate
West Lothian , EH48 2EP
0800 197 7755
enquiries@everwarmgroup.com
www.everwarmgroup.com
(see full page advert for more information)

NGPS Ltd
49 Evering Avenue , Poole
BH12 4JF 01202 736812

Green World Consultancy
22 Park Grove , Aberdere
CF44 8EL 01685 872533

Zenergy PV
385 Canal Road , Bradford
West Yorkshire , BD2 1AW
01274 535000
franco@greenshieldprotection.co.uk
www.zenergypvsolar.co.uk
(see full page advert for more information)

Gas Tech Wales Ltd
Unit 23 Cwm Small Business Centre , Ebbw Vale
Blaenau Gwent , NP23 7TB
01495 371321 or 07531 500104
info@gastechwales.co.uk
www.gastechwales.co.uk
(see full page advert for more information)

Alternative Energy Specialists Ltd
Folkestone Enterprise Centre, Folkestone
Kent , CT19 4RH
01303 297093 or 07816 937279
sales@alternativeenergyspecialists.co.uk
www.alternativeenergyspecialists.co.uk
(see full page advert for more information)

MIB Facades UK Ltd
Doddington Park Farm , Bridgemere
CW5 7PU 01270 520640

Green Deal Installers

ADS Electrical (Shropshire) Ltd
Home Farm Yockleton , Shrewsbury
SY5 9PZ 01743 821606

R. A. Brown Heating Services Ltd
Abbey Farm Commercial Park , Norwich
NR10 3AD 01603 898904

Radiant Heating Solutions Ltd
Hougham , Grantham
NG32 2HZ 01400 250572

CMS Enviro Systems Ltd
Caisteal Road , Glasgow
Scotland , G68 OFS
01324 841 398
info@cms-es.co.uk
www.cms-es.co.uk
(see full page advert for more information)

Power Pac Ltd
The Old Weaving Mill , Whitwick
LE67 5DH 08000 699607

BSW Building Services Ltd
Rock Lodge Vine Yard , Haywards Heath
RH17 7NG 01444 831138

De-A-Nay
121 Abery Hill Road , London
SE9 2HB 02088 504458

Renocon Ltd
Anchor Wharf , London
Greater London , E3 3QR
0207 538 5492 or 07904 507741
mike.threadgold@renoconltd.co.uk
www.renoconltd.co.uk

T & K Home Improvements Ltd
2-6 Huxley Close , Wellingborough
Northamptonshire , NN8 6AB
0800 622716
info@tkhi.co.uk
www.tkhi.co.uk
(see full page advert for more information)

Evesham Home Improvements Ltd
Willersey Business Park , Broadway
WR12 7RR 01386 853222

Solec Energy Solutions
Old Tetley Hall , Leeds
LS6 4DB 08455 193543

Zenergy JOIN THE SOLAR REVOLUTION
ADD VALUE TO YOUR PROPERTY
NATIONAL MCS AND GREEN DEAL APPROVED INSTALLERS OF ALL:
INSULATIONS
• Cavity Wall
• Loft and Roofs
RENEWABLES
• Solar PV
• Thermal
• Heat Pumps
HOME IMPROVEMENTS
• Glazing
• Doors
Call now on 08000 149 568
sales@zenergypv.com www.zenergypvsolar.co.uk
MCS ACCREDITED INSTALLERS
NAPIT
REA
TRUST MARK
Registered through: NAPIT
GREEN DEAL APPROVED

Green Deal Installers

Gas Tech (WALES)

Central Heating Specialists

Green Deal Approved
Central Heating Installations
Boiler Replacements
Boiler Servicing & Repairs
Underfloor Heating
Powerflushing
Free Quotations
All Work Guaranteed

GREEN DEAL APPROVED · GAS safe REGISTER · CORGI · OFTEC · NICEIC DOMESTIC INSTALLER

Tel: 01495 371321
info@gastechwales.co.uk
www.gastechwales.co.uk

The ideal Green Deal installer for energy efficient windows and doors.

CMS have an unparalleled track record of delivering energy saving measures within the private and social housing sectors. We work alongside some of the UK's largest local authorities, housing associations and utility providers and have consistently delivered market leading energy saving windows and doors to over 50,000 homes since our inception in 2006.

Product Excellence
- Manufacturers of Scotland's most energy efficient 'A' Rated, triple glazed, fully reinforced window - Source BFRC
- Full range of window and door styles to suit any property
- All products are Secured by Design approved
- All windows come with a 10 year insurance backed guarantee

Added Value Services
- All extracted windows are recycled into bi-products at our two dedicated recycling facilities in Scotland ensuring no waste goes to landfill
- Dedicated in-house CMS installation teams
- Service and maintenance plans available on all CMS installed products

CMS ENVIRO WINDOW SYSTEMS

CMS Enviro Systems Head Office
Castlecary, Cumbernauld, Glasgow G68 0FS
Tel: 01324 841 398 E: info@cms-es.co.uk
www.cms-es.co.uk

GREEN DEAL APPROVED
Installer*
Reg. No. BM11005
*Replacement glazing

Green Deal Installers

Cutter Solar Ltd
The Craft Workshop , Ross-On-Wye
HR9 6AA **01989 564680**

Northern Renewable Green Systems Ltd
98 Dale Grove , Leyburn
DL8 5GA **01969 622939**

Geefran Plastering Ltd
Billington Road Industrial Estate , Burnley
BB11 5UB **01282 459488**

NEXTGEN Energy
29 Vernon Walk , Tadworth
KT20 5QP **01737 360200**

British Gas
Canal Street , Leeds
LS12 2UE **08001 072750**

Energy and Environmental Consultants Ltd
28 Signhills Avenue , Cleethorpes
DN35 0BT **03331 234987**

Thomas Frederick Electrical Ltd
21 Mountfield Close , Meopham
DA13 0UJ **01732 823557**

Atlas Energy Installations Limited
16 Cleveland Drive , Rochdale
Lancashire , OL16 3HY
0800 014 7750 or 07972 771 254
info@atlas-energy.co.uk
www.atlas-energy.co.uk
(see full page advert for more information)

Wilts Electrical Contracting Limited
Porte Marsh Industrial Estate , Calne
Wiltshire , SN11 9PT
01249 812850
enquiries@weclimited.co.uk
www.weclimited.co.uk
(see full page advert for more information)

Solar Comfort Ltd
4 Lloyd Close , Hampton Magna
CV35 8SH **01926 419240**

Seddon Construction Ltd
Plodder Lane , Bolton
BL4 0NN **01204 570543**

Altair Energy Ltd
North Caldeen Road , Coatsbridge
ML5 4EF **01236 702012**

Green Deal Installers

Gentoo Group Ltd
Emperor House , Sunderland
SR3 3XR **0191 525 5971**

Green Deal Providers

Carillion
24 Birch Street , Wolverhampton
West Midlands , WV1 4HY
. 0800 917 5772
greendeal@carillionplc.com
www.carillionplc.com
(see full page advert for more information)

Gentoo Group Ltd
Emperor House , Sunderland
Tyne & Wear , SR3 3XR
0191 525 5971
luke.gallagher@gentoogreen.com
www.gentoogroup.com
(see half page advert for more information)

ARAN Services Limited
Units 1-6 The Old Station , Bury St Edmunds
Suffolk , IP28 6NE
01284 812 577 or   0800 587 7795
info@aranservices.co.uk
www.aranservices.co.uk
(see half page advert for more information)

Solar King UK
Bahana Close , Haydock
WA11 9XN **08006 783757**

SolarTech Ltd
Sterling Business Park , Buckingham
Buckinghamshire , MK18 1TH
0845 838 2477 or 07501466127
coral.blundell@solartech.org.uk
www.solartech.org.uk
(see full page advert for more information)

EDF Energy
40 Grosvenor Place , London
SW1X 7EN **08000 511905**

Inteb Sustainability Limited
Rural Busines Centre , Bilsborrow
PR3 0RY **01995 642308**

Green Deal Providers

Infinity Energy Organisation Ltd
Popin Business Centre , Wembley
Middlesex , HA9 0HB
0800 862 0004 or   0203 638 4030
info@infinityenergyorganisation.com
www.infinityenergyorganisation.com
(see half page advert for more information)

GHE Solar
Stags Grange Farm , Newbury
Berkshire , RG14 2TF
01635 202612
linda@ghesolar.co.uk
www.ghesolar.co.uk
(see full page advert for more information)

CarbonLow Real Estate Limited
23 The Bridge Business Centre , Chesterfield
S41 9FG 01246 452982

FITGAS Limited
76 Stephenson Way , Liverpool
L37 8EG 01704 832282

Climate Energy Ltd
Countrywide House , Witham
CM8 3UN 01376 531550

Wolseley UK
Spa Park , Leamington Spa
CV31 3HH 08701 622557

Local Energy
22 Upper Woburn Place , London
WC1H 0TB 02075 542800

Big Green Energy Ltd
Portland Industrial Estate , Bury
BL9 6EY 01617 641414

Mark Group Ltd
70 Boston Road , Leicester
LE4 1AW 08006 16302

Carrie Parisella
Fendale , Llandudno
LL30 2PY 01492 550126

Keepmoat Limited
The Waterfront , Doncaster
DN4 5PL 01302 346620

Network Green Deal Ltd
2 Lands End Way , Oakham
LE15 6RB 01572 725530

Grafton Merchanting GB
Gemini One , Oxford
OX4 2LL 01865 871700

Green Deal Providers

NPOWER Northern Limited
Acorn House , Worcester
WR4 9PF 08000 721740

ANESCO
Unit 10 Easter Park , Reading
RG7 2PQ 01189 702595

Insta Group
Insta House , Finchampstead
RG40 4PZ 01189 328811

British Gas
Canal Street , Leeds
LS12 2UE 08001 072750

Enact Energy
Tovaddon Energy Park , Tovaddon
.............08000 3904050

MEB Total Ltd
Fenton Trade Park , Stoke on Trent
ST4 2TE 08452 263233

GR33N Ltd
Unit 1 Enterprise Court , Doncaster
DN5 8AH 01302 875875

Green Deal Suppliers

Glass and Glazing Federation
54 Ayres Street , London
Greater London , SE1 1EU
0207 939 9101
info@ggf.org.uk
www.ggf.org.uk
(see full page advert for more information)

Solar King UK
Bahana Close , Haydock
WA11 9XN 08006 783757

Travis Perkins Plc
Lodge Way House , Northampton
Northamptonshire , NN5 7UG
01604 752 424
marketing@travisperkins.co.uk
www.travisperkins.co.uk
(see half page advert for more information)

Gentoo Group Ltd
Emperor House , Sunderland
SR3 3XR 01915 255971

Green Deal Providers

INFINITY ENERGY ORGANISATION

GREEN DEAL PROVIDORS
GREEN DEAL ASSESSORS

WEBSITE: www.infinityenergyorganisation.com
CONTACT: info@infinityenergyorganisation.com

WE AIM TO CREATE LOCAL JOBS FOR LOCAL PEOPLE

Green Deal Suppliers

Viessmann Limited
Hortonwood 30 , Telford
Shropshire , TF1 7YP
01952 675000
info-uk@viessmann.com
www.viessmann.co.uk
(see full page advert for more information)

EH Smith
Westhaven House , Solihull
West Midlands , B90 4NH
0121 378 5857
sustainable@ehsmith.co.uk
www.sustainablebuildingmaterials.co.uk
(see half page advert for more information)

Plumb Center
Wolseley UK , Leamington Spa
CV31 3HH 08701 622557

Green Deal Suppliers

Gradena Ltd
Beevor Street , Barnsley
South Yorkshire , S71 1HN
07799 635283
info@gradsol.com
www.gradsol.com
(see full page advert for more information)

Worcester Bosch Group
Cotswold Way , Wardon
Worcestershire , WR4 9SN
0844 892 9900
general-enquiries@ukbosch.uk
www.worcester-bosch.co.uk
(see full page advert for more information)

KnaufMarmorit
St Andrews House , Bristol
BS11 9DQ 01179 823870

GREEN DEAL DIRECTORY

Page 157

THE BIG GREEN DEAL

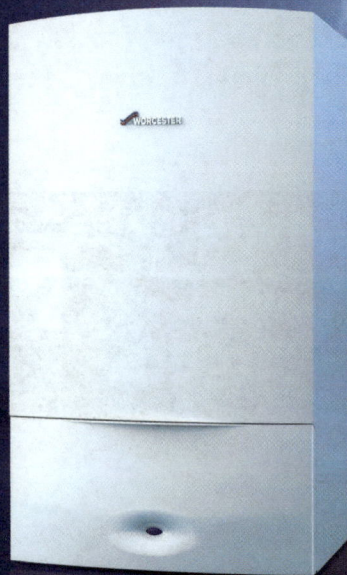

Green Deal Trainers

www.sevenoaksenergy.com

Winners of the Renewable Training Initiative Award 2012

Fully funded plumbing apprenticeships available with financial support for employer's

TRAINING OFFERED

Plumbing
Gas
Electrical
Solid Fuel (HETAS) Wet & Dry Systems
Renewables
Biomass
Photovoltaics
Solar Thermal
Heat Pumps
Rainwater Harvesting
Electrical

For more information or to book a course visit us at
www.sevenoaksenergy.com

We are accredited by City & Guilds, BPEC, LOGIC, NICEIC and HETAS.

DISCOUNTED COURSES IN FEBRUARY

Sevenoaks Energy Academy ltd
Units C1 & C2, Chaucer Business Park
Watery Lane, Kemsing, Sevenoaks, Kent, TN15 6YT
T: 01732 760077

Sevenoaks Energy Academy Ltd
"Training for a sustainable future"

Green Deal Trainers

Green Works
Unit 1 Bromford Central, Birmingham
West Midlands , B8 2SE
0121 328 9150
info@greenworks.co.uk
www.greenworks.co.uk
(see half page advert for more information)

Easy Green Deal
Viscount House , River Lane
Cheshire , CH4 8RH
0844 414 6041
enquiries@easy-mcs.com
www.easy-greendeal.com
(see half page advert for more information)

Sevenoaks Energy Ltd
Chaucer Business Park , Sevenoaks
Kent , TN15 6YT
01732 760077
richard.gould@sevenoaksenergy.com
www.sevenoaksenergy.com
(see half page advert for more information)

Green Deal Trainers

NAPIT
Pleasley Vale Business Park, Mansfield
NG19 8RL` **08455 430330**

PPL Training Limited
PPL House , Opus Avenue, York
Yorkshire , YO26 6BL
0845 260 0966
info@ppltraining.co.uk
www.ppltraining.co.uk/greendeal
(see half page advert for more information)

NICEIC
Warwick House , Dunstable
LU5 5ZX **01582 539069**

Elmhurst Energy Systems Ltd
16 St Johns Business Park , Lutterworth
LE17 4HB **01455 883250**

Green Deal Trainers

ppltraining Green Deal Training Courses

Page 161

THE BIG GREEN DEAL

Big Green Book UK Ltd
Old Station Building
Oswald Road, Oswestry
Shropshire, SY11 1RE

Biggreenbook

Solutions to environmental problems exist, but where do you find them?

This is a question that occurred to ecologist, Stephen Lings in 2003, when he was looking to solve some problems for a local company.

So Steve started putting together a database of companies that can help solve all kinds of problems in our environment. Nine years on, that database has grown into one of the UK's largest business membership organisations.

Now when a company wants help to become sustainable they only have to look to one place www.biggreenbook.com.

But if you don't really know what to look for, then the unique **GET A QUOTE** feature of their website allows you to email an expert about your issues and get suitable suppliers contacting you.

It is an incredible free service, and is one that has helped companies, large and small, throughout the UK.

Over 45,000 organisations have used the Big Green Book website in the last year alone and with over 750,000 hits a month it is a highly visited site.

Big Green Book also runs a face-to-face clinic service, travelling around the country and visiting major trade shows and events. Directors from Big Green Book, supported by experts from within the membership, are on hand to answer question about business and the environment.

Currently Big Green Book is on a membership drive, with special deals for companies that sign up to promote their solutions to environmental and sustainability issues.

If you would like more information on how your company can join their team is very approachable and friendly. Just ask for Gary and you will see what we mean.

With over 6,000 companies in 400 categories and sectors, the Big Green Book online directory is the place to start.

Call 01691 661 565
or email sales@biggreenbook.com
www.biggreenbook.com

GREEN PAGES UK G
The Green Directory

Decision-making help for everyday choices at
Work *or* Home

Your contacts directory source for:

Energy Efficiency
Eco-Design
Eco-Products
Green Services
Renewable Energy
Sustainable Building
Waste & Recycling
& much, much more!

Green Pages UK : The No1 Green Directory - Promoting Environmentally Sustainable Working and Living.

Green Pages UK is the United Kingdom's *bone fide* printed resource for locating genuine environmentally preferable products and services.

All businesses listed in the resource directory have been selected for their "green" attributes or sustainable business practices.

Green Pages UK is also the United Kingdom's premier online green directory (*www.greenpagesuk.com*), providing links between a broad range of suppliers and buyers wanting to do business in an environmentally sustainable way. It is the most popular and most visited directory for sustainable products and services.

Green Pages UK also provides services beyond the directory listings. Their unique free referral service provides users with direct answers to questions regarding products or services in a specific area.

directory**contents**

REAL
RENEWABLE ENERGY ASSURANCE LISTED

m&e
sustainability

Chartered Institute of
Architectural Technologists

The Consulting **Arborist**
SOCIETY

iema
The premier membership body
for environmental professionals

BPA
BRITISH PARKING ASSOCIATION

Painting
Decorating
Association

nqa.

CERTIFIED
ARBORIST

ISA

MICRO
POWER

BPVA British
Photovoltaic
Association

TCIA
VOICE OF TREE CARE

UNEP WCMC

Learning through Landscapes

FMB
FEDERATION OF MASTER BUILDERS
The sign of building quality

adba
ANAEROBIC DIGESTION AND BIOGAS ASSOCIATION

UKITA
UK IT Association
more business.collaboration.quality

wrap

atac

NATIONAL ENERGY FOUNDATION

TRUST MARK

The National Federation of Roofing Contractors Ltd (NFRC) is the UK's largest roofing trade association representing over 70% of the roofing industry by value. By using an NFRC registered contractor, clients have the assurance of guaranteed protection and quality.

NFRC actively ensures that members offer high standards of workmanship and sound business practice through a strict code of practice and independent vetting procedure, including regular site inspections.

- Trained solar and green roof installers
- National Heritage Roofing Contractors' Register
- Recognised national awards for roofing
- Members have been offering Insurance Backed Guarantees (IBG) since 1983. Today the insurance range covers IBGs & Latent Defect from 10 to 20 years
- CompetentRoofer - Government approved Competent Person Scheme; allowing roofers to 'self-certify' for Building Regulations on refurbishment work in all roofing sectors.

WATERPROOFING RAINSCREEN
ROOFING METAL
SOLAR FLAT
HERITAGE
TECHNICAL
VETTED SERVICES
PRODUCTS
QUALITY CLADDING
COMPETENTROOFER SLATING
TILING CONTRACTORS
EXPERTISE STANDARDS

GREEN SHEETING CODE OF PRACTICE UK INDUSTRIAL EXPERIENCED

nFRC

THE NATIONAL FEDERATION OF
ROOFING CONTRACTORS LIMITED

For all your roofing needs, go to
www.nfrc.co.uk

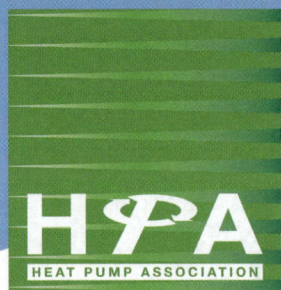

Reflex Type DD Flow Through Vessels – WRAS approved – anti - legionella

The Type DD integrated internal circulation anti - legionella expansion vessels have just been WRAS tested and approved suitable for drinking water applications to the UK standards.

The range of the DD vessels are from 8 ltr to 33 ltr 10 bar pressure rated with a Butyl bladder in accordance to KTW – C norms. All vessels have a pre charge pressure of 4 bar nitrogen from the factory and is manufactured EC norms. For pressure vessels 97/23/EC

The complete range of the flow through vessels are from 8 ltr to 3000ltr 10 bar and 16bar from 60 ltr to 3000ltr. The larger vessels are undergoing WRAS approval and would expect to have the complete range WRAS approved later 2012.

The DD vessels can be supplied with our special flowjet valves so the vessel can be isolated and / or media drained for replacement or modification. With all vessels supplied from 8 ltr to 33 ltr we include a ¾" T piece so can be installed with flowjet as a packaged unit.

The smaller DD WRAS approved range can be supplied with wall mounting straps where the 33 ltr has its own lugs for wall mounting.

The design of this unique expansion vessel is essential to the the prevention of legionella, as this is not a static media vessel, and there is circulation through the vessel as all times when installed in the system flow.

The UK market is now becoming more stringent on what type of vessels are installed, whether static or flow through, depending on the installation and system requirements, but definitely this specific "flow through" design will become a standard requirement for booster set installations. Reflex manufacture a large extensive range of Expansion Vessels static and flow through type for different application in Heating / Chilled Water / Drinking Water in 3 bar / 6 bar / 10 bar / 16 bar and 25 bar from 2 ltr to 5000ltr.

The quality of our vessels, as expected, are to a high standard but we also have to be market priced in order to retain our market share in the UK. Linked with similar system type products encompassing vacuum degassing, pressurisation pump and compressor systems (+/- 0.1 to 0.2 bar maintenance) etc. and our technical expertise in these fields, Reflex in the UK is quickly becoming a very useful partner to many installer and consultants for the heating and chilled water market.

If you are interested in this product range and need discussion on specific products please contact Reflex: **Mr Dan Testar**
Email: **dan.testar@reflexuk.co.uk**

Regional Section: SCOTLAND

01

Glasgow

Edinburgh

The Business Supporting The Scotland Section for the 2012/13 Local Sourcing Directory is:

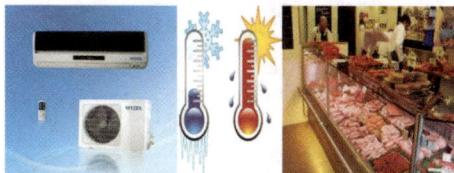

THE GREEN DIRECTORY

Accountancy

Bird Simpson & Co
Chartered Accountants
144 Nethergate , Dundee
DD1 4EB 01382 227841

Bell & Company
39 St John Street , Perth
PH1 5HQ 01738 632081

James Hair & Co
59 Bonnygate , Cupar
KY15 4BY 01334 654030

Hall Morrice LLP
Chartered Accountants
6 & 7 Queens Terrace , Aberdeen
AB10 1XL 01224 647394

Ian Macfarlane & Co
2 Melville Street , Falkirk
FK1 1HZ 01324 635991

ICW Accountancy Limited
9 Westport , Lanark
ML11 9HD 01555 665767

Gillespie Inverarity & Co
1 Torphichen Street ,
Edinburgh , EH3 8HX
0131 229 7088
gourlay.fairman@gillespiesca.co.uk
www.gillespiesca.co.uk

Blyth Smith Chartered Accountants
Axwel House , Broxburn
West Lothian , EH52 5AU
01506 862248
info@blythsmith.com
www.blythsmith.com

A & J Accountancy Services Ltd
57 Fairhaven Avenue , Airdrie
ML6 8EW 01236 767495

Fergusons Chartered Accountants
24 Woodside , Johnstone
PA6 7DD 01505 610412

Accreditation and Certification

ISO Assured Ltd
69-73 Crossgate , Cupar
KY15 5AS 08456 190860

Air Conditioning Systems

Greenergy Advice Ltd
Connemara , Johnstone
PA9 1AW 07908 264818

PDC Refrigeration Ltd
67 Whirlow Road , Glasgow
G69 6QE 07906 089405

Celsius Cooling Ltd
16 Colvilles Park , Glasgow
G75 0GZ 01355 242770

C & M Environmental Ltd
52 Strathmore Road , Glasgow
G22 7DW 01413 367774

Beaumont Services
18 Crowhill Road , Bishopbriggs
G64 1QY 01417 723999

Energy Efficient Cooling Ltd
Killearn Mill , Glasgow
G63 9LQ 01360 550303

D & K Refrigeration
7 Bishops Court , Moray
IV31 6TL 01343 814106

Lothian Refrigeration
31b High Street , Pencuik
EH26 8HS 07808 793993

Air Source Heat Pumps

Renew Green Energy Ltd
Langhaugh Industrial Estate , Galashiels
Scottish Borders , TD1 2AJ
01896 668055 or 07812 176129
info@renewgreenenergy.co.uk
www.renewgreenenergy.co.uk
(see half page advert for more information)

Barres Renewable Energy Systems
16 Carsegate Road South , Inverness
IV3 8LL 01463 713131

Anderson Floor Warming And Renewables
Atlas Express Industrial Estate , Glasgow
G73 1SX 01416 476716

Airport Transfers

Fortune Taxi Mini
2 Haddington Station , Haddington
EH41 5CP 01620 821000

Airport Transfers

Central Taxis
8 St Peter's Buildings , Edinburgh
EH3 9PG 01312 292468

Alternative and Renewable Energy

Gaelic Green Energy
Milliganton , Speddock
DG2 9UA 01387 820422

Ecoliving Ltd
60 High Craighall Road , Glasgow
G4 9UD 08453 013121

Adrian Laycock Ltd
The Marine Resource Centre , Oban
PA37 1SE 01631 720496

Architects

Planning & Building Design Ltd
24 West Nicolson Street , Edinburgh
EH8 9DA 01316 628430

Architects

Studio DuB
17a/2 West Crosscauseway , Edinburgh
EH8 9JW 01316 681536

Ash Architectural
6 Balgonie Drive , Paisley
Renfrewshire , PA2 6HH
0141 884 7272   or   07721 612 753
info@ash-architectural.com
www.ash-architectural.com

Vii Design in Architecture
294 Crow Road , Broomhill
G11 7LB 07951 992312

Air Source Heat Pumps

Renew Green Energy Ltd

Langhaugh Industrial Estate , Galashiels
Scottish Borders , TD1 2AJ

01896 668055

07812 176129

info@renewgreenenergy.co.uk

www.renewgreenenergy.co.uk

Architects

Building regulation compliance & testing services...

Stuart King Architecture & Design

www.stuartkingarchitecture.com

BM Plan & Design
144 Moraine Drive , Blairdardie
G15 6JD **01419 440594**

Cullinan Design
9 Phoenix Lane , Dunfermline
Fife , KY12 9EB
01383 739100
sales@cullinandesign.co.uk
www.cullinandesign.com

Douglas Stuart Chartered Architect
32 Church Street , Inverness
Highlands , IV1 1EH
01463 729 989
dhs@douglas-stuart.co.uk
www.douglas-stuart.co.uk

Giraffe Architecture Ltd
18 Weymouth Court , Glasgow
GL2 0ER **01413 399267**

Curve Architecture & Design
20 Links Gardens , Edinburgh
EH6 7JG **01312 082211**

Asbestos Handling and Removal

Asbestos Surveys & Advice
Cockenzie Business Centre , Cockenzie
East Lothian , EH32 0HL
01875 813999 or 07940 933045
info@asa-asbestos.uk.com
www.asa-asbestos.uk.com

Asbestos Survey and Assesment

Asbestos Surveys & Advice
Cockenzie Business Centre , Cockenzie
EH32 0HL **01875 813999**

Asbestos Training and Awareness

K S Safety Ltd
Polkemmet Business Park , Whitburn
EH47 0LH **01501 749500**

Biomass Energy and Biofuels

Scot Heating Company Ltd
East Gogar , Stirling
FK9 5QB **01259 727600**

Altyre Estate
Estate Office , Forres
IV36 2SH **01309 672265**

Renew Green Energy Ltd
Langhaugh Industrial Estate , Galashiels
TD1 2AJ **01896 668055**

Gaelic Green Energy
Milliganton , Speddock
DG2 9UA **01387 820422**

Barres Renewable Energy Systems
16 Carsegate Road South , Inverness
IV3 8LL **01463 713131**

Lauderdale Renewables Ltd
The Old Post Office , Earlston
Berwickshire , TD4 6BS
01896 849 829 or 07808 689 668
info@lauderdalerenewables.com
www.lauderdalerenewables.com

Bonnymans
Willowburn Road , Beith
KA15 1LN **08001 691131**

Speyside Plumbing Services Ltd
Tomneen Farm , Aberlour
AB38 9SB **01340 871360**

Branding & Marketing

Fraktul Marketing
Kinoull House , Perth
PH2 8DF **01738 237850**

Building and Construction

Robin Baker Architects
Tower Buildings , Dunkeld
Perthshire , PH8 0DS
01350 728 116 or 07789 725 556
info@robinbakerarchitects.com
www.robinbakerarchitects.com

Building and Construction

DRC Contracts
9 Main Street , Perth
PH1 3NJ **01738 583615**

**George W Simpson
Chartered Architect**
Tulloford Nil , Old Meldrun
AB51 0AQ **01651 873601**

Chris Jones
35-37 South Methven Street, Perth
PH1 5NU **07940 814370**

Accomplished Joinery & Building
35 Moira Terrace , Edinburgh
EH7 6TD **01316 030408**

Building Conservation and Preservation

Solway Solar Systems
The Old School , Dumfries
DG2 9RY **01387 720100**

Canopies, Carports & Covered Walkways

GRP Canopies plc
Edgcott House , Aylesbury
HP18 0QW **08007 833835**

Carpentry and Joinery

Mark D McCandlish Joinery
39 Beauly Court , Larbert
.............**01324 875455**

Southside Glazing and Joinery
84 East Crosscauseway ,
Edinburgh , EH8 9HQ
07910 045735 or 01316 679744
southsideglazingandjoinery@yahoo.co.uk

Derek Lawson Joinery Contractors
16 Russell Street , Perth
PH1 4NV **07740 588493**

Frank Walker Joinery
39 Kirktonhill Road , Aberdeen
Aberdeenshire , AB30 1UZ
01674 840138 or 07759 171557
wilmawalker_@hotmail.com

Carpentry and Joinery

Almond Building Company Ltd
107 Overton Crescent , East Calder
EH53 0RJ **07720 740670**

Harry E. Finlay.
Joiner & Contractor

89 Glasgow Road,
Perth
PH2 0PQ

07765 003 603

01738 504 895

highland382000@yahoo.co.uk

www.hefinlayjoinercontractorph2.co.uk

Jardine Joiners of Milngavie
4 Kersland Drive , Glasgow
G62 8DE **07832 328955**

Mach 3 Ltd Joinery and Interiors
43 Caledonia Crescent , Gourock
PA19 1UT **01475 630597**

Turner Joinery
26 Bourock Square , Glasgow
G78 2NQ **07545 226216**

Alasdair Watson Carpentry

**35 Burlington Avenue , Glasgow
Lanarkshire , G12 0LJ
07901 648 241**

alasdair@watsoncarpentry.co.uk
www.watson-carpentry.co.uk

THE **GREEN** DIRECTORY

LOCAL SECTION Scotland

THE GREEN DIRECTORY

Cleaning and Hygiene Services
A Touch of Class Cleaning Services
170 Blackness Road ,
DD1 5PQ **01382 646646**

Computer and Internet Training
Solutions Aberdeen Ltd
Bridge House , Aberdeen
AB11 6JN **01224 213033**

Computer Consultancy
Endrick IT
9a Bankers Brae , Glasgow
G63 0PY **08448 009188**

Computer Hardware
Endrick IT
9a Bankers Brae , Glasgow
Lanarkshire , G63 0PY
0844 8009188
biggreen@endrickit.com
www.endrickit.com

Computer Maintenance
IT Go
25 Duthie Street , Dundee
DD8 5DJ **01575 598128**

Computer Troubleshooters Edinburgh West
20 Parkwood Gardens , Broxburn
EH52 5RE **01506 205120**

Computer Services
Factotum Technical
1 Broughton Market , Edinburgh
EH3 6NU **08451 196006**

Computer Software
Solutions Aberdeen Ltd
1st Floor , Aberdeen
AB11 6JN **01224 213033**

Contaminated Land Management
Caledonia Environmental Ltd
29 Fir Grove , Livingston
EH54 5JP **01506 437967**

Counselling , Advice and Psychotherapy
Mairead Mackintosh
, Banchory Under Elgin Area
.............**07986 735197**

Act Counselling
135 Wellington Street , Glasgow
G2 2XD **07891 574099**

Development
Jumpstart (Scotland) Ltd
6 Atholl Crescent , Edinburgh
EH3 8HA **01312 402900**

Driving Schools
Stonehaven Trailer Training Services
35 Fetteresso Terrace , Stonehaven
Kincardinshire , AB39 2DS
01569 767905 or 07718 916007
gordon@stts-scotland.co.uk
www.stonehaventrailertrainingservices.co.uk

Ecology Surveys and Consultancy
Alpha Ecology Ltd
110 Main Street , Biggar
ML12 6XR **01659 74208**

Acorna Associates Ltd
50 Foxdale Drive , Aberdeen
FK4 2FE **07800 565809**

Ecotoxicology
NCIMB Limited
Ferguson Building , Bucksburn
AB21 9YA **01224 711100**

Electrical and Electricians
Michael Reekie Electrical Contracting
8 Anderson Drive , Perth
Ph1 1JZ **07867 780989**

PDMD Electrical Ltd
12 Craigiedar Close , Dunfermline
KY12 0XY **01383 625618**

Dunmar Electrical
40 Dronley Road , Dundee
DD2 5QD **07977 120175**

H Electrics
104 Bellevue Road , Edinburgh
EH7 4DE **07905 448166**

Electrical and Electricians

Neill Martin Electrical Contractors Ltd
56 Orchard Gate , Cupar
KY15 5AF 01334 653221

Clark Electrical
3 Froghall Terrace , Aberdeen
AB24 3JJ 07885 287783

Addison Electrical Ltd
Cairnton Road , Banff
AB45 2LR 01261 843870

PowerPlusElectrical.co.uk
21 Glenconner Road , Ayr
KA7 3HF 07912 447526

P&R Services (Glasgow) Ltd
31 Herschell Street , Glasgow
G13 1HT 01412 742065

A.C.M Electricians
83 Pirnifield Place , Edinburgh
EH6 7PZ 07854 441838

Electronic Component Recycling

The Easdale Group
Unit 6A Mid Road , Clumberland
North Lanarkshire , G67 2TT
01236 451 748
klausmoock@easdalegroup.com
www.easdalegroup.com

Energy Performance Certificates

Greenergy Advice Ltd
Connemara , Johnstone
PA9 1AW 07908 264818

Stuart King Architecture & Design
Rosyth Business Centre , Rosyth
KY11 2WX 01383 435996

Environmental Consultancy

Scottish Environment Protection Agency (SEPA).
Erskine Court , Stirling
Stirlingshire , FK9 4TR
01786 457700
info@sepa.org.uk
www.sepa.org.uk

Acorna Associates Ltd
50 Foxdale Drive , Aberdeen
FK4 2FE 07800 565809

Fair Trade Products

Rainbow Turtle
Greenlaw Industrial Estate , Paisley
PA3 4BT 01418 871881

Fireplaces & Wood Stoves

Blairquhan Castle
Maybole
KA19 7LZ 01655 770239

First Aid Training

Albacare
19 South Bridge Street , Bathgate
EH48 1TU 08003 899391

Moray Firth Training Group
32 Harbour Road , Inverness
IV1 1UF 01463 230036

Funding

Jumpstart (Scotland) Ltd
6 Atholl Crescent , Edinburgh
EH3 8HA 01312 402900

Gas and Central Heating (Domestic)

Haxtons of Dunkeld Ltd
Cally Industrial Estate , Dunkeld
PH8 0HU 07711 892700

Triple Point
4 Redhughes , Edinburgh
EH12 9DQ 08000 376525

Graphic Design

TBDA Scotland Ltd
112 John Player Building , Stirling
FK7 7RP 01786 446004

Wrights Graphic Design
4 Corberry Terrace , Dumfires
DG2 7SR 01387 419770

SSH Design
17 Sunart Gardens , Bishopbriggs
G64 1HW 07947 749754

Derek Collins Design
22 Walkerston Avenue , Largs
KA30 8ER 07780 811795

Adamson Design
60 Brook Street , Glasgow
G40 2AB 08451 305470

THE GREEN DIRECTORY

THE GREEN DIRECTORY

Ground Source Heat Pumps

Ecoliving Ltd
60 High Craighall Road , Glasgow
G4 9UD 08453 013121

Barres Renewable Energy Systems
16 Carsegate Road South , Inverness
IV3 8LL 01463 713131

Eco-Coil Heating Ltd
27 Newmiles Gardens , Glasgow
G72 0JA 07769 622311

Anderson Floor Warming And Renewables
Atlas Express Industrial Estate , Glasgow
G73 1SX 01416 476716

Speyside Plumbing Services Ltd
Tomneen Farm , Aberlour
AB38 9SB 01340 871360

Health and Safety

Hodgins Smith Consulting
151 West George Street , Glasgow
G2 2JJ 01292 678484

Heat Recovery and Ventilation Systems

Energy efficiency to Passive House performance

*Best indoor air quality
*No build-up of pollutants
*Reduced humidity
*Lower risk of mould, fungus & mites
*Surprisingly quiet

www.paulheatrecovery.co.uk
info@paulheatrecovery.co.uk
Tel: 0845 3885 123

PAUL
Heat Recovery Scotland

Renew Green Energy Ltd
Langhaugh Industrial Estate , Galashiels
TD1 2AJ 01896 668055

Anderson Floor Warming And Renewables
Atlas Express Industrial Estate , Glasgow
G73 1SX 01416 476716

Housing Adaptions

Jordan Shaw
Alloa Business Centre , Alloa
FK10 3SA 08450 550323

Hypnotherapy

Brecon Beds Hypnotherapy
Brecon Beds School House , Lockerbie
DG11 3NA 01461 500857

Act Counselling
135 Wellington Street , Glasgow
G2 2XD 07891 574099

Illustration, Art and Design

KOG Design
306 Oxgangs Road North , Edinburgh
EH13 9NE 01314 414791

Industrial Ecology

ECOIDEAM
22 Atholl Street , Dunkeld
Pertshire , PH8 0AR
01350 720902
john.ferguson@ecoideam.co.uk
www.ecoideam.co.uk
(see full page advert for more information)

Insulation

Blantyre Insulations
15 Forrest Street , Glasgow
G72 0JP 01698 327718

Fuelsave Insulation Ltd
20 Barrhill Lane , Glasgow
G65 9QD 08004 115151

Investment

Jumpstart (Scotland) Ltd
6 Atholl Crescent , Edinburgh
EH3 8HA 01312 402900

Land Reclamation, Site Clearance and Groundworks

Caledonia Environmental Ltd
29 Fir Grove , Livingston
EH54 5JP 01506 437967

Landscaping and Ground Maintenance

Careth Ltd
The Oaks , Glasgow
G65 0QN 01360 449042

ecoideaM

facilitating industrial ecology

EcoideaM Ltd is a Scottish based environmental facilitation and ideas company specializing in industrial ecology.

We work in a number of areas including environmental and clean technology development, eco innovation parks, recycling, residual waste treatment systems and residual waste fuels and renewable energy.

We are a new ideas business that develops new approaches to resolving material and resource efficiency, energy security, low carbon issues and closed loop soil nutrient cycles. We are system innovators and system linkers to define and develop new ways of creating integrated linked systems for a more resilient, sustainable and fairer world.

Our principles are simple. We aim to support the transition to sustainable economies at local, regional and national levels. We are an extensively networked company with a wide range of personal and associated expertise. Our primary business skill is the development of new ideas and the creation of new opportunities.

We work almost exclusively in the Scottish space but collaborate globally. If you need an entry to the Scottish clean technology; integrated resource management; small scale and decentralised renewable energy; clean energy from waste space and eco park development community we are the portal to use.

We work as development partners, rarely do consultancy but will provide opportunity analysis and network forming for new business.

John Ferguson, EcoideaM Ltd, 22 Atholl Street, Dunkeld, Perthshire, Scotland, PH2 9PX

Tel: 0044 (0)1350 720902
www.ecoideam.co.uk

Landscaping and Ground Maintenance

Neil Shaw Garden Maintenance Service
Criffel , Stranraer
DG9 8BT 01776 705338

Low Energy Building

Timber-Tec

**39 Girnigoe Street , Caithness
Caithness , KW1 4HP
07900 237482
01955 604983
timber-tec@toucansurf.com
www.timber-tec.net**

Craigs Eco Construction Ltd
19 Acredales , Linlithgow
West Lothian , EH49 6HY
01506 840157 or 07813 791933
michael@craigseco.co.uk
www.craigsecoconstruction.co.uk

Low Energy Lightbulbs, Lighting and L.E.D.

PowerPlusElectrical.co.uk
21 Glenconner Road , Ayr
KA7 3HF 07912 447526

Lampforce
Unit 10/2 , Loanhead
EH20 9QX 01314 482229

LPG & Catalytic Conversions

Seton Engineering
Seton Gardens , Edinburgh
EH32 0PG 01875 811651

Ace Tuning
Shore Street , Lossiemouth
IV 6PB 01343 814220

Motivational and Life Coaching

Life Bridging Coach
9 Macallan Road , Kintore
AB51 0QB 01467 632997

Networking and Cabling

DSIS
15 Edison Street , Glasgow
Renfrewshire , G52 4JW
0141 438 2030
miah@dsis.co.uk
www.dsis.co.uk

Solutions Aberdeen Ltd
56-58 Bridge Street , Aberdeen
AB11 6JN 01224 213033

Noise and Vibration Testing

Robin Mackenzie Partnership Ltd
42 Collington Road , Edinburgh
EH10 5BT 01315 573327

Office And Retail Furniture

Asplanned Ltd
20 Exchange Court , Dundee
DD1 3DE 01382 669174

Office Cleaning and Cleaning Services

Cleaning Services (Scotland) Ltd
6 Mill Place , Linlingtow
EH49 7TL 01506 843900

Painting and Decorating

Garty & Christie Decorators Ltd
66 Uist Place , Perth
PH1 3BY 07944 351735

LGS Contracts Ltd
Mayfield , Hurlford
KA1 5EX 07825 304570

Williamson & Sons Ltd
27 Deerhil , Broxburn
EH52 6LY 07521 540692

Decor8ing Solutions
41d Mains Loan , Dundee
DD4 7AF 07765 056827

Colin Campbell-Painters and Decorators
Quinaig , Golspie
Sutherland , KW10 6SL
01408 633 438 or 07788 873 556
campbell.quinag@btinternet.com

Payroll and Bookkeeping

Day2day Office Support
61 Woodburn Road , Falkirk
FK2 9BT **01324 281010**

McKenzie and Co
12a Chester Street , Edinburgh
EH3 7RA **01312 262299**

Infinity Partnership
37 Albert Street , Aberdeen
AB25 1XU **01224 618460**

Gillespie Inverarity & Co
1 Torphichen Street , Edinburgh
EH3 8HX **01312 297088**

Laing Bookkeeping Services
Braeview , Elgin
IV30 8RJ **01343 862933**

DCS Payroll
13 Beaumont Gate , Glasgow
G12 9ED **01413 331933**

Four Support Ltd
Stannergate House , Dundee
DD5 1NB **01382 480488**

**Hall Morrice LLP
Chartered Accountants**
6 & 7 Queens Terrace , Aberdeen
AB10 1XL **01224 647394**

Simply Balanced Business Services
Thainstone Business Centre , Inverurie
AB51 5TB **01467 624543**

Capital Payroll Services Ltd
Argyll House , Livingston
EH54 6 AX **08448 099346**

Pest Control

Graham Pest Control
Skimmie Park , Blairgowrie
PH10 6NP **08001 46544**

Burns Environmental
82B Talbot Terrace , Glasgow
G13 3RX **08002 343220**

R.E.D Pest Control
West Field , Bridge of Weir
PA11 3JJ **07769 802651**

Environmental Services Pest Control
Airlink Business Centre , Paisley
PA3 1RD **01418 480957**

Pest Control

**Precision Pest Management
Pest Solutions**
2 Front Lebanon , Cupar
KY15 4EA **01334 659250**

The Mole Man
5 Balmoral Crescent , Carstairs Junction
ML11 8RX **01555 840320**

Vermgon
4 North Isla Street , Dundee
DD3 7JQ **01382 523288**

Plumbing Services

Aqueous Plumbing Services
15 Craggenmore Place , Perth
PH1 3GJ **07941 307734**

Printing, Design and Mailing Services

GMP Print Solutions
Unit 17 , Loanhead
Midlothian , EH20 9LZ
0131 629 0071
roger.parry@gmpprint.co.uk
www.gmpprint.co.uk
(see full page advert for more information)

Pace Print
19 South Clerk Street , Edinburgh
EH8 9JD **01316 670737**

Minuteman Press
27 Coatbank Street , Coatbridge
ML5 3SP **01236 602527**

Tantallon Press
Mill Walk Business Park , North Berwick
EH39 5NB **01620 892767**

Rain Water Harvesting

GRP Canopies plc
Edgcott House , Aylesbury
HP18 0QW **08007 833835**

Recycled and Refilled Printer Cartridges

Printerwise
308 George Street , Aberdeen
AB25 1HL **01224 642222**

THE GREEN DIRECTORY

Printing, Design and Mailing Services

join us under the green umbrella

gmp
print solutions

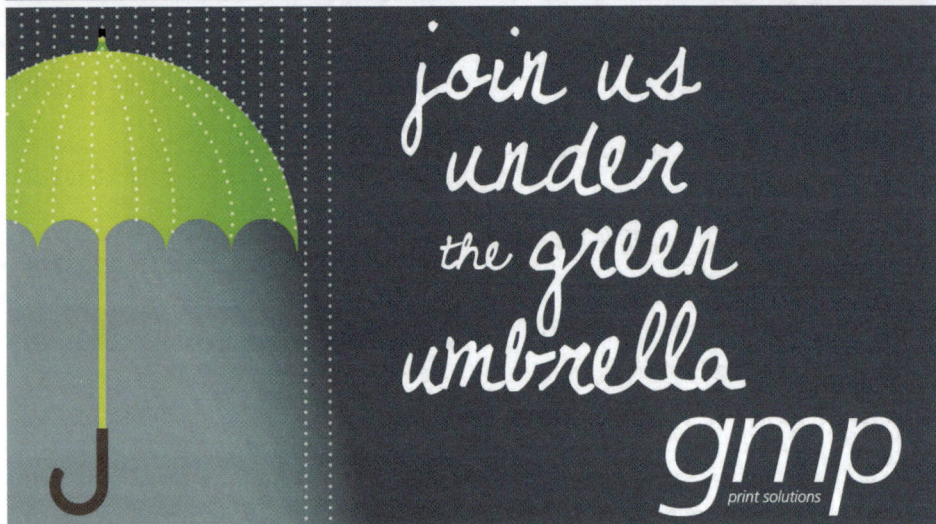

AT GMP WE LIKE TO KEEP THINGS SIMPLE.

WE HAVE 2 PASSIONS:

1: To provide our clients with the **BEST QUALITY** design & print at affordable prices. Quality is a necessity not a luxury in today's marketplace.

2: To offer this service in such a way that it has the **LEAST DETRIMENTAL IMPACT ON OUR ENVIRONMENT.**

HOW DO WE ACHIEVE THIS?

We carbon balance all our print projects by planting broadleaf trees in local community woodlands, enhancing the communities and their environs.

Contact **Roger Parry,** a 2009 Scottish Sustainable Development Forum Green List Champion:

07841 429 775

e: roger.parry@gmpprint.co.uk
www.gmpprint.co.uk
office: 0131 629 0071

OUR PRODUCT EXPERTISE INCLUDES

INDOOR & OUTDOOR
SIGNAGE
LARGE & SMALL FORMAT
POINT OF SALE
POSTERS
BANNERS
FLYERS
BROCHURES
EXHIBITION STANDS

Refrigeration

Energy Efficient Cooling Ltd
Killearn Mill , Glasgow
Scotland , G63 9LQ
01360 550303 or 07817 227088
enquiries@eecooling.co.uk
www.eecooling.co.uk

Research

Jumpstart (Scotland) Ltd
6 Atholl Crescent ,Edinbrugh
EH3 8HA 01312 402900

Roofing Services

Strathisla Roofing
Unit 3 Midfriarton , Perth
PH2 8DF 07736 030474

Safety and Protective Clothing

Seahawk Clothing Ltd
Unit 6 , Glenrothes
KY7 4PF 01592 630450

Corston Sinclair Ltd
36 Glenburn Road , Glasgow
G74 5BA 01355 238161

Safety Risk Assessment

Hodgins Smith Consulting
151 West George Street , Glasgow
G2 2JJ 01292 678484

Screen and T Shirt Printing

Digisin
12m Kinnoull House , Perth
PH2 8DF 07870 223243

Secretarial Service

Virtual Assistance@Virtual Angel
14 Polsons Crescent , Paisley
PA2 6AX 07981 333391

Fine Print Secretarial Services
6 Dick Street , Dunfermline
KY12 0AG 01383 741441

Septic Tanks

Symbiotic Trading Ltd
Farrenridge , Falkirk
FK1 2HN 01324 860050

Sewage and Effluent Products and Services

Symbiotic Trading Ltd
Farrenridge , Falkirk
FK1 2HN 01324 860050

Signs and Graphics

Mercury Signs and Designs Ltd
Inveralmond Industrial Estate, Perth
PH1 3WB 01735 451450

Skips and Skip Hire

Hamilton Waste and Recycling Ltd
Wally Ford Industrial Estate , Edinburgh
EH21 8QJ 01316 652173

Binn Skips
Binn Farm , Perth
PH2 9PX 01577 334569

Solar Energy

REAP Community Enterprises
177 Mid Street , Keith
AB55 5BL 01542 880200

Kellwood Electrical
Unit 9 Catherinefield Industrial Estate , Dumfries
DG1 3PQ 01387 255816

Solar Panels and Photovoltaics

PDMD Electrical Ltd
12 Craigiedar Close , Dunfermline
KY12 0XY 01383 625618

Renew Green Energy Ltd
Langhaugh Industrial Estate , Galashiels
TD1 2AJ 01896 668055

THE GREEN DIRECTORY

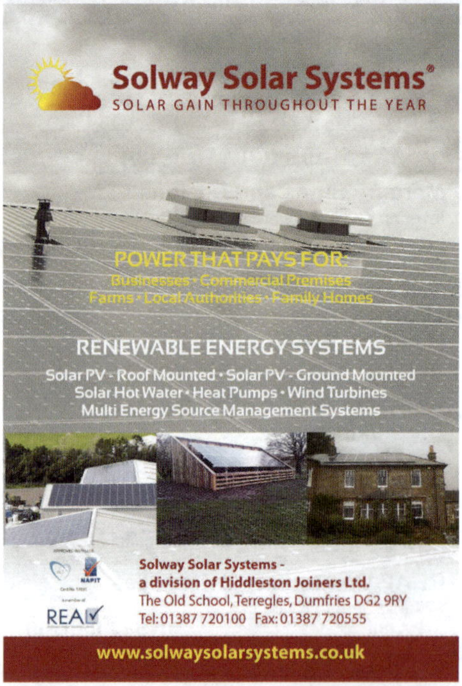

Solar Panels and Photovoltaics

THCL (Thomson Homes Construction Ltd) Construction & Renewable Energy
Office Unit , Kinross
KY13 0LB 08455 551015

Solar Energy Systems
4 Ross Street , Dunfirmline
KY12 0AN 01383 725499

Solas Renewable Energy
41 Bonhill Road , Dumbarton
Dumbartonshire , G82 2DL
0800 616203
karl@biggreenbook.com
www.solas.biz
(see half page advert for more information)

Richard Irvin Sustainable Energy Ltd
Irvin House , Aberdeen
Aberdeenshire , AB12 3LE
01224 367182
dave.mcgrath@richard-irvin.co.uk
www.richardirvinsustainableenergy.co.uk
(see full page advert for more information)

Solar Panels and Photovoltaics

ENERGY INDEPENDENCE - THE JOURNEY BEGINS

There's more to Sustainable Energy

Energy price hike, up 9% again

Renewable Energy Solutions

Domestic P.V.

- 4kW PV array, grid tied inverter
- Benefit typically £775
- Payback typically 9 years
- 25 year PV panel warranty
- Canadian Solar & Other leading brands
- Feed in Tarrif rate to drop from 1st November

P.V. for Agriculture

- Farm building up to £24/m²/year benefit
- Set aside/barron ground up to £25,000 per acre, beats barley!

Office & Industry P.V.

- Save up to 118kg CO_2/year/m²
- Payback 7-8 years
- Staff discount schemes available
- Car Park Solutions
- Roof Space worth up to £30/m² per annum benefit

1 SOLAR PV

Demand Reduction
- Voltage Optimisation
- LED Lighting
- Automatic Controls
- Thermal Insulation

2 SOLAR THERMAL

3 AIR SOURCE HEAT PUMPS

4 COMBINED HEAT & POWER

5 FLUE HEAT RECOVERY

6 BIOMASS

7 GROUND SOURCE HEAT PUMPS

8 HEAT RECOVERY

HR01

RICHARD IRVIN
A name trusted for generations
And for generations to come

INTEGRATED ENERGY SYSTEM

TIME TO CONSIDER WINTER SERVICING

THE GREEN DIRECTORY

Solar Panels and Photovoltaics

Solar Power Scotland
Unit 1 Bridge End , Montrose
DD10 8JA **01674 660000**

Speyside Plumbing Services Ltd
Tomneen Farm , Aberlour
AB38 9SB **01340 871360**

Alva Northern
New Albion Industrial Estate , Glasgow
G13 4DJ **08002 851260**

Solar Water Heating Systems

Renew Green Energy Ltd
Langhaugh Industrial Estate , Galashiels
TD1 2AJ **01896 668055**

Barres Renewable Energy Systems
16 Carsegate Road South , Inverness
IV3 8LL **01463 713131**

Speyside Plumbing Services Ltd
Tomneen Farm , Aberlour
AB38 9SB **01340 871360**

Anderson Floor Warming And Renewables
Atlas Express Industrial Estate , Glasgow
G73 1SX **01416 476716**

Spray on Coatings

Smart Refinishers
Dyce Drive , Dyce
AB21 0HP **01224 772999**

Stone Sculpture

Limburg Stonecraft
168e North High Street , Musselburgh
EH 21 6AR **07902 267119**

Taxi and Private Hire

Central Taxis
8 St Peter's Buildings , Edinburgh
EH3 9PG **01312 292468**

Telecommunications

Ross Telecom Consultancy
23 Foxes Grove , Glasgow
G66 5BN **01417 777183**

FES Ltd
Forth House , Stirling
FK7 8HW **01786 819600**

Timber Frame Buildings

Timber Design & Construction
Unit 2 Woodside Mid Road , Kirriemuir
Angus , DD8 4PJ
01575 575980
gaetangoub@hotmail.com
www.timberdesign.org.uk
(see full page advert for more information)

Moor Park Homes
The Sawmills , Lanark
ML11 7RX **01555 665087**

Tree Work and Surveys

John Meikle Contractors Ltd (Stump Masters)
Springhill House , Glasgow
South Lanarkshire , G78 2SE
0141 881 4269 or 07710 006 777
info@johnmeiklecontractorsltd.co.uk
www.johnmeiklecontractorsltd.co.uk

Yieldshields Tree Surgeons Ltd
Middle Hope Farm , Carluke
ML8 4QY **01555 771327**

Martin Plummers Tree Surgery Ltd
8 Preston Crescent , Fife
KY11 1DR **01383 428899**

A Robertson Tree Surgeon
68 Carseview , Alloa
FK10 2SS **01259 722746**

T.J.B. Landscapes
The Old Cannery , Blairgowrie
PH10 6NB **07999 031151**

Underfloor Heating

Renew Green Energy Ltd
Langhaugh Industrial Estate , Galashiels
TD1 2AJ **01896 668055**

Optimum Underfloor Heating
23 Lotland Streen , Inverness
IV1 1ST **01463 222800**

Barres Renewable Energy Systems
16 Carsegate Road South , Inverness
IV3 8LL **01463 713131**

Eco-Coil Heating Ltd
27 Newmiles Gardens , Glasgow
G72 0JA **07769 622311**

THE **GREEN** DIRECTORY

Underfloor Heating

**Anderson Floor Warming
And Renewables**
Atlas Express Industrial Estate , Glasgow
G73 1SX **01416 476716**

Vehicle Leasing and Rentals

Arnold Clark Car and Van Rental
Renault Complex , Stirling
FK7 7RU **08448 470649**

Green Motion Rental
Edinburgh Airport , Edinburgh
EH28 8AU **01312 240045**

Go Green Car and Van Rental
10-30 Nantwich Road , Crewe
CW2 6AD **08002 987957**

Waste Management and Disposal

Holden Environmental
Shore Road , Perth
Perthshire , PH2 8BH
01738 634747 or
donald@holdenenvironmental.co.uk
www.holdenenvironmental.com

Website and Internet Services

Steve Cardno
4/12 Bonnington Gate, Edinburgh
EH6 5NZ **07841 410762**

X Design 365
3 Coates Place , Edinburgh
EH3 7AA **01313 393838**

Impact Web Services
44 Harris Place , Dunfermline
KY11 3DE **07857 876262**

Think Extraordinary Design
Westercroft , Symington
KA2 9AT **07849 744536**

Organic Digital
5 Newton Place , Glasgow
G3 7PR **01413 534100**

Storr Media
9 Craigton Road , Glasgow
G62 7JH **07746 698682**

Netmedia Business Solutions
Old Drynie House , Kilmuire
IV1 3XG **01463 731000**

Website and Internet Services

Creative Designz
27 Whitehill Crescent , Carluke
ML8 5DU **01555 752258**

Simplistic Designs
5 Walnut Grove , Leven
KY8 5PP **01333 670067**

Digital Soul Design
8A Burnside , Fife
KY14 7AL **07429 476490**

Wind Energy

Gaelic Green Energy
Milliganton , Speddock
DG2 9UA **01387 820422**

GREENER TIMES
>SUSTAINABLE SOLUTIONS MAGAZINE

Old Station Building
Oswald Road, Oswestry
Shropshire, SY11 1RE

SUBSCRIBE TO THE UK'S BEST GREEN BUSINESS, LIFESTYLE AND SUSTAINABILITY MAGAZINE

If you enjoy reading the Greener Times magazine, why not take advantage of our special subscription rates and save yourself some money?   Each issue of Greener Times is enjoyable, informative reading that will also make you think!

As well as articles on environmental issues that can affect you at home as well as at work; there are interviews with celebrities like Gareth Southgate and successful businesses such as Stagecoach, quizzes that the whole family can get involved with and current affairs relating to local communities and businesses, all with an environmental and sustainable theme i.e. The Green Deal, The Renewable Heat Incentive (RHI) etc.

There is also a 'Whats On?' list of forthcoming shows and events that we will be attending where you can come along and meet us in person.

It costs just **£4.20 + P&P** Or if you want to save some money you can subscribe for a year for just **£42 + P&P** *(payable by monthly or annual direct debit)* Instruction to Greener Times Publishing Ltd

DON'T MISS AN ISSUE, SUBSCRIBE TODAY!

£42 + P&P

01691 661 565
info@greener-times.co.uk
www.greener-times.co.uk

01

02

03

05

04

06   **07**   **08**

09

10

11   **12**

02.

Newcastle

Middlesbrough

THE GREEN DIRECTORY

The Business Supporting The North East of England Section for the 2012/13 Local Sourcing Directory is:

Applied Heating Services

TRUST MARK

gas safe REGISTER

www.appliedheat.co.uk

Applied Heating Services Ltd provides heating and ventilation services to domestic and commercial clients throughout the North East of England. Supplying, installing and servicing boilers, heating systems and ventilation solutions, the Applied Heating team is proud of its excellent service, commitment to safety and outstanding reputation.

Never a company to stand still, the team is always seeking new ways to provide extra services to its customers.

With a belief in and passion for energy efficiency and conservation, the Applied Energy team is extremely knowledgeable about the best ways to save its customers money and conserve energy - a critical consideration in the current climate of rocketing fuel bills.

T: 0191 417 2428   F: 0191 417 1549   E: info@appliedheat.co.uk

Accountancy

Accounts and Business Management Limited
82 Low Lane , Middlesbrough
TS5 8EB **01642 592802**

A C Savage & Co
275 High Street , North Allerton
DL7 8DW **01609 773342**

Jacs Accountancy Ltd
The Rialto Exchange , Peterlee
SR8 3LA **01915 279288**

SDB Accountancy Services
110 Trewhitt Road , Newcastle upon Tyne
NE6 5LU **01912 766792**

Total Accounting Network
3 The Elms , Newcastle upon Tyne
NE3 4BD **01912 855339**

Wells Business Services
20 Rosedale Gardens , Stockton-on-Tees
TS23 3UB **01642 566170**

C Michael Hanby
8 Galgate , Barnard Castle
DL12 8BG **01833 638287**

Accountancy

C I Accountancy Ltd
Boatside Business Centre , Hexham
NE46 4SH **01434 601133**

Christopher Bailey Chartered Accountants
30 Yoden Way , Peterlee
SR8 1AL **01915 004421**

Air Conditioning Systems

Aircon Refrigeration Ltd
35e Dukesway , Stockton on Tees
TS17 9LE **01642 760565**

Home Air Ltd
Unit 1 City West Business Park , Meadowfield
DH7 8ER **01913 789385**

Air Source Heat Pumps

Applied Heating Services Ltd
9 Rosse Close , Washington
NE37 1EY **01914 172428**

Solarwall Ltd
Green Lane Trading Estate , York
YO30 5PY **08001 380079**

Airport Transfers

D & D Taxis
40 Meadow Dale , Chilton
DL17 0RW **07757 614920**

Alternative and Renewable Energy

Architects

Page 197

THE **GREEN** DIRECTORY

THE GREEN DIRECTORY

Architects

David Stovell and Millwater
5 Brentnall Centre , Middlesbrough
TS1 5AP **01642 232397**

William Gray Associates
Eggleston Hall , Barnard Castle
DL12 0AG **01833 650316**

Elder Lester McGregor
Reeds Mill , Yarm
Teeside , TS15 9AD
01642 782211 or 07710144806
ian@elderlester.co.uk
www.elderlester.co.uk

Derek Cansfield MCIAT, Chartered Architectural Technologist
6 Holywell Close , Whitley Bay
Northumberland , NE25 0LD
0191 237 4124 or 07960 457692
derek.cansfield@yahoo.com

BIM Architectural Services
53 Garnet Street , Saltburn
TS12 1EQ **01287 201398**

North East Architectural Plans
38 Grasmere Terrace , Hawkeys Lane ,
North Shields , NE29 0PW
0191 257 2020 or 07807 030574
mick@northeastplans.co.uk
www.northeastplans.co.uk

Design Lines Architects Ltd
19 John Street , North East England
NE30 4PJ **01912 510297**

Amamus Design
66 Claypath , Durham City
DH1 1QT **01913 843193**

Matthew TROTTER & MILLER Chartered Architects
82 Norton Road , Stockton on Tees
Tees Valley , TS18 2DE
01642 673 449
tony@trottermiller.co.uk
www.trottermiller.co.uk

Asbestos Training and Awareness

cnm training solutions ltd
14 Trent Place , Darlington
DL1 5TA **01325 353151**

Catering Services & Design

Restaurant Design Associates Limited
5 Apollo Court , Hebburn
NE31 2ES **07872 831131**

Counselling , Advice and Psychotherapy

Walton Counselling
Regus House , Sunderland
SR3 3XW **07988 119285**

Jean Coates Counselling & Psychologist
14 North Magdalene , Consett
DH8 6RG **07521 404924**

Design 2 Print

Kudos Print & Design Ltd
Durham Way, Newton Aycliffe
DL5 6HP **01325 307237**

Display and Exhibition Boards

Spot on Displays Ltd
42 Station Road , Stanley
DH9 0JL **01207 236909**

Drilling, Boring and Site Investigations

Dunelm Well Drilling Ltd
Foundation House , Durham
DH7 8TZ **01913 783151**

E-commerce and Search Engine Optimisation (SEO)

Longstone Solutions
15 East Field , Alnwick
NE66 3BZ **07513 334858**

NSM Web Design Ltd
8 Consett Innovation Centre , Consett
Durham , DH8 5XP
0845 643 2667
info@nsmwebdesign.com
www.nsmwebdesign.com

E-commerce and Search Engine Optimisation (SEO)

STCS Limited
Gear House , Gateshead
NE8 3AH 01914 903232

All Media Ltd
Media Exchange One , Newcastle upon Tyne
NE1 2QB 01912 212277

Stomp
20 Eskdale Terrace , Newcastle upon Tyne
NE2 4DN 07903 746868

Ecology Surveys and Consultancy

Total Ecology Ltd
3 St James Close , Riding Mill
NE44 6BS 01434 632285

Oak Bay Ecology
16 Waters Edge Fold, Manchester
OL1 4QJ 07775 186757

Electrical and Electricians

Solutions Electrical Services
105 Addington Drive , Wallsend
NE28 9UX 07974 704210

GLS Electrical Services
100 Basselton Lane , Stockton
TS17 0LD 01642 882859

DJH Maintenance Solutions
4 Dobson Close , Newcastle Upon Tyne
NE4 7EA 07500 019177

A & M Solutions UK Ltd
12 Bydales Drive , Redcar
TS11 7HJ 01642 287791

Daniel Hall Electrical Services
8 Tindale Avenue , Cramlington
NE23 2BS 07927 170640

Solec (North East) Ltd
14 Great North Road , Morpeth
NE61 6DQ 07900 555135

Electrolaze Electricians
447 Stanhope Road , South Shields
NE33 4QY 07824 862147

Embroidery

Yarm Logos
72a High Street , Stockton on Tees
TS15 9AH 01642 424553

Environmental Consultancy

Total Ecology Ltd
3 St James Close , Riding Mill
NE44 6BS 01434 632285

C J Molloy Grounds Maintenance
Unit 7 Bolam Business Park , Cramlington
Northumberland , NE23 8AL
01670 898619 or 07968 790128
john@cjmolloy.co.uk
www.cjmolloy.co.uk

Exhibition Stands

Spot on Displays Ltd
42 Station Road , Stanley
DH9 0JL 01207 236909

Exhibition Structural Systems

Spot on Displays Ltd
42 Station Road , Stanley
DH9 0JL 01207 236909

Fences, Fencing & Decking

Rennyco Ltd
West Tree Buildings , Darlington
DL3 0XE 08000 116144

Fire Risk Assessment and Training

G C Safety Services
11 Hedgefield Grove , Blyth
NE24 3XD 01670 362816

Funding

Class Fundraising Ltd
W9 Vienna Court , Redcar
TS10 5SH 01642 489000

Graphic Design

Spot on Displays Ltd
42 Station Road , Stanley
DH9 0JL 01207 236909

The Point Design
Hoults Yard , Newcastle-upon-Tyne
NE6 1AB 01912 244483

All Media Ltd
Media Exchange One , Newcastle upon Tyne
NE1 2QB 01912 212277

THE GREEN DIRECTORY

Graphic Design

Designs Unique
16 Rosedale Avenue , Shotley Bridge
DH8 0DZ **01207 502877**

November Design
7 Northumberland Gardens , Newcastle upon Tyn
NE2 1HA **07515 352298**

JPGraphics Creative Design Solutions
19 Melrose Crescent , Guisborough
TS14 7Az **07530 455926**

Gainford Design Associates
The Gymnasium , Stocksfield
NE43 7 RY **01661 844777**

Ground Source Heat Pumps

Applied Heating Services Ltd
9 Rosse Close , Washington
NE37 1EY **01914 172428**

Go Geothermal Ltd
Unit 3 Ridgeway , Newton Aycliffe
DL5 6SP **01388 720228**

Solarwall Ltd
Green Lane Trading Estate , York
YO30 5PY **08001 380079**

Health and Safety

Green Dragon Ltd
8 Bamburgh Drive , North Tyneside
NE28 6JX **01912 871399**

Dodds Associates
40 Queensway , Tynemouth
NE30 4NB **01912 583547**

The Way Forward North East
16 Chirton Avenue , South Shields
NE34 7BW **01914 271698**

Christian James Associates
112 Front Street , East Boldon
NE36 0SG **01915 373149**

Carmel Safety Training Service Ltd
9 Carmel Road South , Darlington
DL3 8DQ **01325 463500**

Heat Recovery and Ventilation Systems

Applied Heating Services Ltd
9 Rosse Close , Washington
NE37 1EY **01914 172428**

Heat Transfer Fluids

Kilfrost
32 Gallowgate , Newcastle upon Tyne
NE1 4SN **01434 323184**

Insulation

Solarwall Ltd
Green Lane Trading Estate , York
YO30 5PY **08001 380079**

Insurance

Coversure Middlesbrough
13 Kings Road , Middlesbrough
Clevland , TS3 6NG
0800 3081013
middlesbrough@coversure.co.uk
www.coversure.co.uk/branch/middlesbrough

Japanese Knotweed

C J Molloy Grounds Maintenance
Unit 7 Bolam Business Park , Cramlington
Northumberland , NE23 8AL
01670 898619 or 07968 790128
john@cjmolloy.co.uk
www.cjmolloy.co.uk

Landscaping and Ground Maintenance

C J Molloy Grounds Maintenance
Unit 7 Bolam Business Park , Cramlington
NE23 8AL **01670 898619**

Painting and Decorating

Into Painting and Decorating
31 Honeypot Road , Richmond
DL10 7HT **01748 906327**

Right Decorators
8 Etuel Avenue , Sunderland
SR2 0QG **07917 168436**

DJH Maintenance Solutions
4 Dobson Close , Newcastle Upon Tyne
NE4 7EA **07500 019177**

Dave Spencer Decorating
126 Sixth Avenue , Blyth
NE24 2SY **01670 364995**

Painting and Decorating Supplies

International Paint Ltd
Stoneygate Lane , Gateshead
NE10 0JY **01914 696111**

Payroll and Bookkeeping

Beaumont Accountancy Services
Unit 306 Vienna Court, Redcar
TS10 5SH **01642 489045**

Numiracle Ltd
28 Friars Wharf , Gateshead
Tyne & Wear , NE10 0QX
0191 447 9094 or   07514079090
susan@numiracle.co.uk
www.numiracle.co.uk

Unicorn Bookkeeping Service
2 Normont Gardens ,
Newcastle upon Tyne , NE4 8AP
0191 273 1593 or   07773 963349
shirleyafletcher@sky.com
www.unicorn-bookkeeping-service.co.uk

CC Payroll Service
54 Villette Road , Sunderland
Tyne & Wear , SR2 8RW
0191 5109400
jill@ccpayrollservices.co.uk
ccpayrollservices.co.uk

Peters Bookkeeping Services
Dean and Chapter Industrial Estate , Ferryhil
DL17 8LN **01740 664730**

Richardson Bookkeeping
47 Lime Street , Sunderland
SR4 6BQ **07723 650504**

The Three Little W s Limited
17 Sidney Street , Blyth
NE24 2RD **01670 362316**

NGJ Bookkeeping & Payroll Ltd
26 Bradwell Way ,
DH4 4XA **01915 121212**

SDB Accountancy Services
110 Trewhitt Road , Newcastle upon Tyne
NE6 5LU **01912 766792**

Nickalls and Co Ltd
4 Bridge Street , Amble
NE65 0DR **01665 710547**

Pest Control

Deadfast Pest Control
56 Grange Terrace , Chester Le Street
DH2 2PD **01913 887966**

Portable Appliance and Fixed Wire Testing

North East Electrical Test
41 Dene Gardens , Newcastle Upon Tyne
NE15 8RL **07811 855769**

Printing, Design and Mailing Services

Spot on Displays Ltd
42 Station Road , Stanley
DH9 0JL **01207 236909**

Graphic Print and Sign Co Ltd
Brynmill House , North Shields
NE29 7BN **01914 474013**

Printing.com (Middlesbrough)
Rede House , Middlesbrough
TS1 1LY **01642 226220**

Dave Dent Printers
56-60 Station Road , Newcastle upon Tyne
NE3 1QD **01912 848501**

Print Swift
212 High Street , Sunderland
Tyne & Wear , SR1 1UA
01915 676770
sales@printswift.co.uk
www.printswift.co.uk

Mags Laser Commercial Printers
Nelson Street Industrial Estate , South Bank
TS6 6BJ **01642 466091**

Penny Print
Unit 1 Dunston Industrial Estate , Gateshead
NE11 9JW **01914 611111**

MK Print Solutions
10 Woodlands , Durham
DH7 0NS **01207 529784**

Marford Lithographic
Windsor House , Darlington
DL1 5SF **01325 358456**

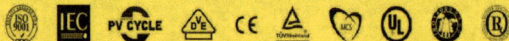

Solar Energy

LINUO
POWER UK

Leading global manufacturer & distributor of high quality high efficiency solar panels.

Established in 1994 Linuo Power is a leading global manufacturer and distributor of high quality high efficiency solar panels, offering power, performance, technology, excellence & partnership.

Linuo was one of the first 3 manufacturers to be TUV certified in Europe and it is part of the Linuo group which have 5 main industries (solarPV, glass, solar thermal, pharmaceutical, coating & sodium) With profit of 1.8 billion in 2011, it is one of the biggest private companies in the world.

Linuo Power currently has a 2000MW annual manufacturing capacity covering an area of 270 hectares (27,000000m2), consisting of two solar cell factories and 2 solar module production factories, a college and a university.

.All of Linuo's factories uses world class manufacturing equipment from Germany, Italy, USA etc.

Linuo also has the most highly educated work force in the solar industry, of its 13000 employees 70% have a university bachelor's degree or above and 30% are educated to HND standard or above.,

Linuo operate a fully automated manufacturing process with 100% EL testing before and after lamination.

Double 'A' rated silicon sourced from our own mine meaning globally bankable (investment grade) panels, suitable for financial institutions and other investors.

10 year warranty and 100% insured in Europe by CHUBB with a 25 year performance guarantee.

0191 206 4144
www.linuouk.com
facebook.com/linuouk
twitter.com/linuouk

Professional Office and Evening Wear

Ian Bone Business Tailor Ltd
89 Cheadle Avenue , Wallsend
NE28 9QP 01912 627254

Promotional Items and Incentives

Spot on Displays Ltd
42 Station Road , Stanley
DH9 0JL 01207 236909

Recycling

J & B Recycling Limited
Tomlinson Road , Hartlepool
TS25 1NS 01429 272810

Signs and Graphics

Spot on Displays Ltd
42 Station Road , Stanley
DH9 0JL 01207 236909

Ace Signs & Graphics
Unit 22G Damsone Way , Durham
DH1 2XL 01913 841136

Skips and Skip Hire

Hughes Waste Management
Old Stone Road , Cramlington
NE23 6XW 01670 734087

Solar Energy

Linuo Power UK
Rotterdam House , Newcastle upon Tyne
Tyne & Wear , NE1 3DY
0191 206 4144
sonia.sandhu@linuouk.com
www.linuouk.com
(see full page advert for more information)

T J Warr Electrical
34 Marlborough Road , Manchester
M41 5GQ 07793 046262

Solar Panels and Photovoltaics

A C Electrical
24 Errington Drive , Stanley
DH9 9PD 01207 235386

Northern Light Solar Systems Ltd
9 Heythrop Drive , Middlesbrough
TS5 8QA 08458 942230

Solar Panels and Photovoltaics

Genflux Renewables Ltd
1 Ferry Road , Hexham
NE46 4JW 01434 700770

Geo Light UK Ltd
Q16 Quarum Business Park , Newcastle
NE12 8BX 01915 114922

Solarwall Ltd
Green Lane Trading Estate , York
YO30 5PY 08001 380079

Helios Eco Solutions Ltd
26 Glenesk Road , Sunderland
SR2 9BN 01915 225827

Solec (North East) Ltd
14 Great North Road , Morpeth
NE61 6DQ 07900 555135

Linuo Power UK
Rotterdam House , Newcastle upon Tyne
Tyne & Wear , NE1 3DY
0191 206 4144
sonia.sandhu@linuouk.com
www.linuouk.com
(see full page advert for more information)

Solar Water Heating Systems

Genflux Renewables Ltd
1 Ferry Road , Hexham
NE46 4JW 01434 700770

Solarwall Ltd
Green Lane Trading Estate , York
YO30 5PY 08001 380079

Sustainable Materials

The Bongtree
Unit W8 , Hartlepool
Cleveland , TS25 5TG
07958491876 or 07917460330
info@thebongtree.co.uk
http://www.thebongtree.co.uk/

Tree Work and Surveys

Kevin Patton Tree Surgeon Ltd
Garden Cottage , Guisborough
Cleveland , TS14 8JT
07977 322702 or 07411 922881
kevin@99log.co.uk
www.99log.co.uk

C J Molloy Grounds Maintenance
Unit 7 Bolam Business Park , Cramlington
Northumberland , NE23 8AL
01670 898619 or 07968 790128
john@cjmolloy.co.uk
www.cjmolloy.co.uk

Oliver Tree Services
Langley Park Industrial Estate North , Witton Gilbert
DH7 6TX **01913 739771**

Underfloor Heating

Applied Heating Services Ltd
9 Rosse Close , Washington
Tyne & Wear , NE37 1EY
0191 417 2428
george@appliedheat.co.uk
www.appliedheat.co.uk

Website and Internet Services

Sean Hay Design & Development
2 Beechwood Avenue , Darlington
DL3 7HP **07538 798291**

Zine UK
174 Harton House Road , South Shields
NE34 6EA **07960 606676**

Website and Internet Services

Hiltonian Media
PO Box 612 , Durham
DH1 9HT **01913 038403**

Chocolate Grape
2 Clayport Street , Alnwick
NE66 1JU **07595 218004**

Alison Parker Web Design
Kirklevington, Yarm
. ...**01642 780962**

The Website-Lab
1 Pink Lane , Newcastle-upon-Tyne
NE1 5DW **01912 111975**

SDH Internet
8 Castleton Road , Middlesbrough
TS6 8AU **07920 301301**

tr10.com
26 The Grainger , Gateshead
NE8 2BG **01914 607331**

NSM Web Design Ltd
8 Consett Innovation Centre , Consett
Durham , DH8 5XP
0845 643 2667
info@nsmwebdesign.com
www.nsmwebdesign.com

Longstone Solutions
15 East Field , Alnwick
NE66 3BZ **07513 334858**

Wind Energy

Genflux Renewables Ltd
1 Ferry Road , Hexham
NE46 4JW **01434 700770**

01

02

05

04

03

06

07

08

09

10

11

12

03

York

Hull

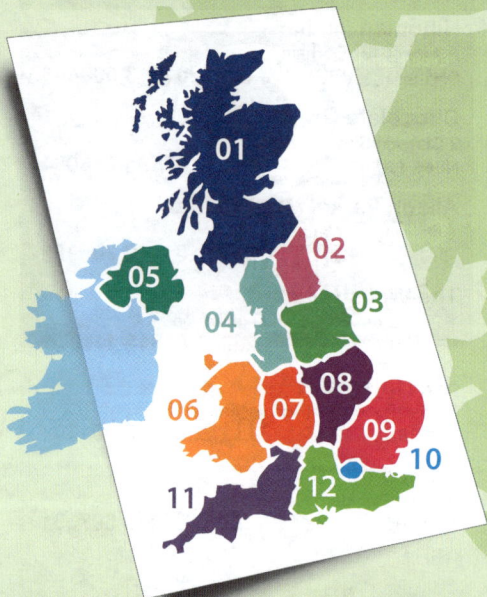

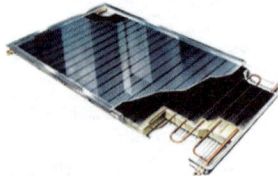

THE GREEN DIRECTORY

THE GREEN DIRECTORY

LOCAL SECTION

THE GREEN DIRECTORY

Accountancy

Liquid Consultants Limited
The Portergate , Sheffield
S11 8NX 01142 096283

Patten Accountancy
1 Cambridge Close , Doncaster
DN5 7JX 01709 880157

Brown Butler
Leigh House , Leeds
Yorkshire , LS1 2JT
0113 246 1234
info@brownbutler.com
www.brownbutler.com

Accounting Solutions
128 Saltergate , Chesterfield
S40 1NG 01246 202735

Meadowcroft & Co.
1 Castlegate , Thirsk
YO7 1HL 01845 523153

Abacus I55 Ltd
4 Spring Bank Meadow , Ripon
HG4 1HQ 08440 502257

MBS Payroll & Accountancy Services
Manor Farm , Scarborough
YO13 9LN 01723 863637

Seaman Herbert & Co Ltd
36-40 Doncaster Road , Barnsley
S70 1TL 01226 299962

Naylor Wintersgill
Carlton House , Bradford
BD1 4NS 01274 733184

ABS and Co Accountants Ltd
Nostell Estate , Wakefield
WF4 1AB 01924 866020

Air Conditioning Energy Assessments

Airmaster Air Conditioning Ltd
Wetherby House , Sheffield
S26 4UN 01142 889911

Air Conditioning Systems

Refrigeration Specialists (Huddersfield)
Unit 3D Spafields Industrial Estate , Huddersfield
HD7 5BB 01484 845124

Air Conditioning Systems

Al Cool Air Conditioning Ltd
3 Bells Road , Hull
Yorkshire , HU12 8QR
07966 131615 or 01482 899518
andy@alcool.co.uk
www.alcool.co.uk

Airmaster Air Conditioning Ltd
Wetherby House , Sheffield
Yorkshire , S26 4UN
0114 288 9911
team@airmaster.uk.com
www.airmaster.uk.com
(see full page advert for more information)

Advanced Building Maintenance Ltd
6 Cotswold Drive , Liversedge
West Yorkshire , WF15 8EG
0845 8386059 or 07713 693436
gavin@abm-limited.co.uk
www.abm-limited.co.uk

Air Con One (Halifax) Ltd
10 Highfield Avenue , Halifax
Yorkshire , HX4 8JD
01422 375366 or 07506 730525
enquiries@airconone.com
www.aircon-one.co.uk

Amazon Refrigeration Ltd
42 Shaw Drive , Grimsby
DN33 2JB 07821 577794

EBA Climate Ltd
Unit 4 Brockholes Business Park , Holmfirth
HD9 7BN 07854 938709

Pure Air Conditioning
Unit 4 New Brook Business Park , Mansfield
NG20 8GB 01623 741004

Air Source Heat Pumps

Matrix Energy Systems
23 Lathkill Close , Sheffield
S13 8DI 07931 801904

Yorkshire Renewable Energy Solutions
Evans Business Centre , Wakefield
WF2 7AS 08455 198854

Kingspan Environmental (was Kingspan Renewables)
Tadman Street , Wakefield
WF1 5QU 01924 376026

LOCAL SECTION

THE GREEN DIRECTORY

Air Source Heat Pumps

Solarwall Ltd
Green Lane Trading Estate , York
YO30 5PY 08001 380079

ECO Energy Smart Ltd
7 Kingsley Drive , Rotherham
S65 4GY 01709 702737

Pure Air Conditioning
Unit 4 New Brook Business Park , Mansfield
NG20 8GB 01623 741004

Airport Transfers

Flights, Ferries 'n' Fuddles
72 Hunt Lane , Doncaster
DN5 9SE 01302 783013

Benchmark Cars
52 Church Street , Leeds
LS23 6DN 07774 608860

Swift Travel
26 Timire Close , York
YO10 4NG 07921 841366

Alternative and Renewable Energy

Matrix Energy Systems
23 Lathkill Close , Sheffield
S13 8DI 07931 801904

Oak Apple Renewable Energy Ltd
Oak Apple Road , Leeds
LS12 6QA 01132 708052

Norcroft Electrical
Mustard Hill House , Sheffield
S36 7JA 01226 763127

Architects

Prospect Design
64 Newbiggin , Malton
YO17 7JF 01653 690272

Architects

AME Plans
38 Holderness Road , Hull
HU9 1EF 01482 215584

Time Architects
2 Hollins Drive , Sheffield
S6 5GP 01142 854554

Domestic Architecture
168 Leeds Road , Wakefield
WF1 2QA 01924 600250

C J A Architecture
47 Woodside Avenue , Leeds
LS4 2QX 01133 689911

Keir Architecture Limited
10A Abbey Road , Ulceby
DN39 6TJ 07813 006079

Richard Eves Architects
Alexandra Villa , Harrogate
HG1 1EQ 01423 504488

SIX Architecture + Design Ltd
Electric Works , Sheffield
S1 2BJ 01142 866263

Hansom Architects Ltd
Durham House , Northallerton
DL7 8PP 01609 772100

Asbestos Handling and Removal

D J Cleaning Ltd
43 White Gap Road , Cottingham
HU20 3XF 01430 827491

A1 Environmental Services Ltd
4 The Paddock , Catterick Village
DL10 7 RZ 01748 818683

Asbestos Survey and Assesment

Atmosphere Environmental Ltd
36 Rochdale Road , Tormorden
OL14 5HZ 01706 559743

A1 Environmental Services Ltd
4 The Paddock , Catterick Village
DL10 7 RZ 01748 818683

Coal Consultants Ltd
3 Phoenix Court , Brighouse
HD6 1PF 01133 971040

Asbestos Training and Awareness

Atmosphere Environmental Ltd
36 Rochdale Road , Tormorden
OL14 5hz 01706 559743

Asbestos Training and Awareness

Bridge Safety and Training Ltd
43 Southey Avenue , Sheffield
S5 7NN 01142 490312

Lighthouse Risk Services LLP
Airedale House , Leeds
LS20 8EH 08454 591724

Coal Consultants Ltd
3 Phoenix Court , Brighouse
HD6 1PF 01133 971040

Biomass Energy and Biofuels

NNFCC
Biocentre , York
YO10 5DG 01904 435182

DPR Services Ltd
Unit 6b Ashbrooke Park , Leeds
LS11 5SF 01132 743322

Matrix Energy Systems
23 Lathkill Close , Sheffield
S13 8DI 07931 801904

Yorkshire Solar
Lynwood , Leeds
West Yorkshire , LS20 8HY
01943 878 319 or 07989 356 923
amanda@yorkshiresolar.com
www.yorkshiresolar.com

Building & Roofing Products

Gradena Ltd
Beevor Street , Barnsley
South Yorkshire , S71 1HN
07799 635283
info@gradsol.com
www.gradsol.com
(see full page advert for more information)

Building Conservation and Preservation

Elden Minns & Co Ltd
453 Glossop Road , Sheffield
S10 2PT 01142 662458

C.A.D. and 3D Visualisation

Vector Design Concepts
4 St John's North , Wakefield
WF1 3QA 01924 332056

Carpentry and Joinery

JC Norton Joinery and Property Repairs
6 Wingfield Road , Barnsley
Yorkshire , S71 3PS
07973 489795 or 01226 321970
info@jcnortonjoinery.co.uk

Chauffeur Services

Benchmark Cars
52 Church Street , Leeds
LS23 6DN 07774 608860

Chemical Regulations (SDS, Reach, CSR)

Denehurst Chemical Safety Ltd
Denehurst , Burley in Wharfedale
LS29 7NS 01943 865448

Cleaning Products

Northern Environmental
Unit 427b Birch Park , Wetherby Leeds
LS23 7FG 01937 841070

Bonnetts Ltd
Corringham Industrial Estate , Gainsborough
DN21 1QB 01427 613240

Clinical Waste

SRCL
Indigo House , Leeds
LS10 2LF 08451 242020

Computer Consultancy

Atkins Solutions
128 Peckover Drive , Pudsey
LS28 8EG 07834 229487

Computer Maintenance

Clayton Computers
16 Gaythorne Terrace , Bradford
BD14 6LE 01274 883362

ETC
PO Box 519 , Doncaster
DN4 0GE 01302 337559

nd **chemical resistant**, insect, vermin pro
ot harmful to humans or animals, doesn'
rack or splinter, 3 x more fire resistant th
vood, nailable, screwable, cutable with ha
ower tools, **passed ASTM tests**, full UV
rotection, easy to clean and safe in use,
roduced in a range of colours and finishe
ompletely **recycleable**...

And if that's not enough,
we help you to meet your
sustainability build targets.

Contact Patric Kinstrey
E: info@gradena.co.uk T: 0845 155 2869

www.gradena.co.uk

GRADENA
REVOLUTIONARY BUILDING MATERIALS

Computer Maintenance

Atkins Solutions
128 Peckover Drive , Pudsey
West Yorkshire , LS28 8EG
07834 229487
dan.atkins@atkins-solutions.co.uk
www.atkins-solutions.co.uk

POW IT
30 Oakes Lane , Holmfirth
HD9 7AR 01484 660149

Computer Services

Yorks Computers Ltd
20 Thorpe Lane , Huddersfield
HD5 8TA 01484 768522

Atkins Solutions
128 Peckover Drive , Pudsey
LS28 8EG 07834 229487

Iveson Computer Services
15 Northfield Way , York
YO23 7EA 01904 744437

Haworth Computers
Oxen Hope Road , Hull
HU6 7BZ 01482 801550

Gritstone Computers
The Fleets , Skipton
BD23 6NA 01756 730030

Counselling , Advice and Psychotherapy

Anger Management Solutions.co.uk
Bradford , West Yorkshire
BD7 2PS 01274 419295

Jane Power
Toddington
.............08442 484718

Courier Services

NRT Freight
61 Field View , York
YO30 6EJ 07842 052181

PMF Transport Ltd
C/O 26 Wordsworth Drive , Rotherham
S65 2QQ 08002 983511

Design 2 Print

Printing.com @ Scunthorpe
105-107 Mary Street , Scunthorpe
DN15 6LA 01724 2852971

Maywell Trading as Whites Prints
Unit 2 Amberley Court , Sheffield
S9 2LQ 01142 562256

Loyalty Matters Ltd (printing.com)
104 Station Parade , Harrogate
HG1 1HQ 01423 857900

Document and Data Destruction

Secure Destruction of Electronic Media

Specialist data destruction facility for all types of electronic media. Materials shredded down to 2mm at our site or 6mm at your own site (IL6 MOD Standard) rendering all information stored completely unreadable. Software data erasure using CESG approved software. Asset tracking, witness destruction and degaussing options also available.

HARD DRIVE MEDIA
CD / DVD MEDIA
SOLID STATE STORAGE
PDA / MOBILE & PHONES

S2S Electronics Ltd
Unit B, Brookfield Park, Manvers Way
Wath Upon Dearne, Rotherham, S63 5DJ
Tel: 01709 878878   Fax: 01709 763878
www.s2s.uk.com

THE **GREEN** DIRECTORY

E-commerce and Search Engine Optimisation (SEO)

Loyalty Matters Ltd (printing.com)
104 Station Parade , Harrogate
HG1 1HQ **01423 857900**

Squashed Pixel Ltd
Fruition Building , Bradford
BD15 0DX **01535 958083**

Ecology Surveys and Consultancy

Naturally Wild Consultants Limited
Evans Business Centre , Middlesbrough
Cleveland , TS6 6UT
0845 260 1107 or 07817 634 504
graeme.skinner@naturallywild.co.uk
www.naturallywild.co.uk

Access Ecology Ltd
Sheaf Bank Business Park , Sheffield
S2 3EN **01142 587819**

Wildbanks Conservation
20 Holmdale Crescent , Holmirth
HD9 3HB **01484 681704**

Electrical and Electricians

May Electrical
11 Spring Grove , Sheffield
S20 1XE **01142 474313**

P K Electrical
41 Dewar Drive , Sheffield
S7 2GQ **01142 364313**

RH Electrical Contractor Ltd
57 Brookroyd Lane , Birstall
WF17 0BU **07817 390219**

Electrical and Electricians

JDP Electrical Solutions Ltd
1 Greenland , Bradford
Yorkshire , BD13 1HS
07866 051 555 or 01274 882023
jdp.ltd@tiscali.co.uk
www.electriciansinbradford.com

BMR Electrical Ltd
3 Back Lane , Castelford
WF10 2BN **08453 384880**

DPR Services Ltd
Unit 6b Ashbrooke Park , Leeds
LS11 5SF **01132 743322**

Paul Wilson Renewable Technologies
Orchard Cottage , Skipton
BD23 4SJ **07767 293886**

Corts Electrical Limited
27 Durkar Rise , Wakefield
West Yorkshire , WF4 3QB
07939 252611
pwcorts@live.co.uk

NC Electrical
25 Venetian Crescent , Barnsley
S73 9AZ **07870 972196**

Electrical Maintenance and Installation

B & P Electrical Contractors
16 Borrage Lane , Ripon
HG4 2PZ **01765 690896**

PAB Electrics
3 Wordsworth Avenue , Sheffield
S36 6EX **07850 407128**

Allan Davis Electrical Contractors
13a Farrar Lane , Leeds
Yorkshire , LS16 6AD
0800 611 855 or 07860 444758
allandavis@hotmail.co.uk
www.allandavis.co.uk
(see full page advert for more information)

BH Electrical
21 Moat House Way, Doncaster
DN12 3GE **07912 608792**

Electrical Maintenance and Installation

Celect Electrical Uk Ltd
416b Hessle Road Hull , Hull
HU3 3SE **07831 473043**

Hainsworth Electrical Ltd
2 Roe House , Balldon
BD17 5LF **07805 034071**

AJH Electrical Services
13 Milton Road , Doncaster
DN3 3NX **07793 750884**

Embroidery

Embroidery In-House
182 Highgate Road , Bradford
BD13 1DS **01274 889299**

Kmbroidery
Priestroyd , Huddersfield
HD1 3BD **07879 655832**

Vega Corporate Embroidery
Central Buildings , Hull
HU2 0HG **01482 606622**

Butler Embroidery
Unit 4B Spence Mill , Leeds
LS13 3HE **01132 557860**

Laughing Whale Print & Embroidery
Ridgewood , Whitby
YO21 3SU **01947 893392**

Eagle Expressions
Unit 1 Saddle Bridge , Dewsbury
WF12 9AF **01924 464664**

Energy Assessors & Consultants

DPR Services Ltd
Unit 6b Ashbrooke Park , Leeds
LS11 5SF **01132 743322**

Energy Performance Certificates

Bonham Energy
4 Fairview Gardens , Richmond
DL10 4NP **01748 826057**

Energy Saving Heating

DPR Services Ltd
Unit 6b Ashbrooke Park , Leeds
LS11 5SF **01132 743322**

Environmental Consultancy

D J Cleaning Ltd
43 White Gap Road , Cottingham
HU20 3XF **01430 827491**

Environmental Strategies Limited
81 Harland Way , Hull
East Yorkshire , HU16 5PT
01482 841164 or 07789 936398
info@esltd.co.uk
www.esltd.co.uk

Greensafe Consulting LLP
Unit 8 Meersbrook Works , Sheffield
S8 9FT **07877 698214**

A S Associates
10 Briar Close , Leeds
LS28 5TW **07740 409797**

Wildbanks Conservation
20 Holmdale Crescent , Holmirth
HD9 3HB **01484 681704**

Exhibition Display Banners

SDD Exhibitions
Unit 1 Parkway Business Park , Sheffield
S9 4WN **01142 317810**

Exhibition Stands

GPA Concepts Ltd
Unit 1 Aylesham Industrial Estate, Bradford
BD12 0NQ **01274 606633**

SDD Exhibitions
Unit 1 Parkway Business Park , Sheffield
S9 4WN **01142 317810**

Financial Auditing

Fire Risk Assessment and Training

Kingstown Training Services Ltd
16 Green Road , Hull
HU12 8EQ 01482 890909

Fire Safety Specialists Ltd
10 Martin Rise , Sheffield
S21 4HH 01246 434314

Craven Safety Services
P.O Box 36 , Skipton
BD23 0AE 01756 730632

Forensec (UK) Ltd
7A Kings Road , Leeds
LS16 9JW 01132 676954

Cedar GB Ltd
Equinox House , York
YO30 5PA 07709 879948

Miles Safety Ltd
502 Fullwood Road , Sheffield
South Yorkshire , S10 3 QD
0114 230 2200 or   07711 049829
info@dcmfire.co.uk
www.dcmfire.co.uk

Fire Safety Protection and Equipment

Hydro Fire Limited
9 Kings Close , Wakefield
WF5 8QU 01924 264074

First Aid Medical Services
80-88 Eyre Lane , Sheffield
S1 4RB 07729 010034

Fireplaces & Woodstoves

DPR Services Ltd
Unit 6b Ashbrooke Park , Leeds
LS11 5SF 01132 743322

First Aid Training

Kingstown Training Services Ltd
16 Green Road , Hull
HU12 8EQ 01482 890909

Craven Safety Services
P.O Box 36 , Skipton
BD23 0AE 01756 730632

First Aid Medical Services
80-88 Eyre Lane , Sheffield
S1 4RB 07729 010034

Food Hygiene

A S Associates
10 Briar Close , Leeds
LS28 5TW 07740 409797

Geothermal Energy

Earthtest Energy
Bridge Mills , Holmfirth
HD93TW 01484 681314

Graphic Design

K Design Branding & Marketing
Hunsworth
BD19 4DX
01274 877092 or   07711 511848
info@kdesignwork.com
www.kdesignwork.com

Kinetic Marketing & Design
50 Park Drive , Grimsby
DN32 0EQ 01472 269016

The Big Ideas Collective
20 Fountayne Street , York
YO31 8HL 08456 431656

Pink Custard Design
Danish Buildings , Hull
HU1 1PS 01482 337780

Micron Graphics
9 Pyramid Court , York
YO26 5NB 01904 792059

Rubber Band
156A Haxby Road , York
YO31 8JN 01904 633800

Slater Clark Associates Ltd
New Street , Doncaster
DN1 3QU 01302 325306

Graphic Design

Tractor Creative Ltd
Bullace Farm , Harrogate
HG3 4AZ **01943 880296**

Solo and Jones Design
56 Warneford Road , Huddersfield
HD4 5TP **01484 644295**

Green Roofing

Ground Source Heat Pumps

Earthtest Energy
Bridge Mills , Holmfirth
HD93TW **01484 681314**

Matrix Energy Systems
23 Lathkill Close , Sheffield
S13 8DI **07931 801904**

Yorkshire Renewable Energy Solutions
Evans Business Centre , Wakefield
WF2 7AS **08455 198854**

DPR Services Ltd
Unit 6b Ashbrooke Park , Leeds
LS11 5SF **01132 743322**

Ground Source Heat Pumps

Solarwall Ltd
Green Lane Trading Estate , York
YO30 5PY **08001 380079**

Health and Beauty Products

Forever Young Yorkshire. Group
Moore Farm , York
YO60 7QZ **01904 468088**

Health and Safety

Cedar GB Ltd
Equinox House , York
YO30 5PA **07709 879948**

Denehurst Chemical Safety Ltd
Denehurst , Burley in Wharfdale
LS29 7NS **01943 865448**

S.D.L Health and Safety Services
P.O Box 109 , Ripon
HG4 1WT **07768 505170**

A S Associates
10 Briar Close , Leeds
LS28 5TW **07740 409797**

At Risk ? Health & Safety Consultancy
Brookbank House , Rotherham
S66 9JX **01709 739961**

HSE Group
PO Boz 109 , Ripon
HG4 1WT **07768 505170**

Ralph N Bennett Health & Safety Management
27 Tardrew Close , Beverley
HU17 7QH **07508 028841**

Health and Safety

B K Safety
20 Pembroke Rise , Doncaster
DN5 8PP 01302 785063

Hemp Crete

K J Voase
and son

**Growers of Industrial Hemp and Supplier
of Hemp Shiv for insulated Hempcrete
buildings. For more information
Tel: 01964 542477
E-mail: info@kjvoaseandson.co.uk**

Human Resources and Training

Cedar GB Ltd
Equinox House , York
YO30 5PA 07709 879948

Hypnotherapy

The Caring Clinic
35 Barkers Road , Sheffield
S7 1SD 01142 551345

Karen April Mills Dip.Hyp, Dip.Couns.
28 Sycamore Avenue , Sheffield
S26 5QU 01909 515585

Insulation

Foamspray Technology
67 Ash Hill Drive , Leeds
LS17 8JR 01132 930068

Solarwall Ltd
Green Lane Trading Estate , York
YO30 5PY 08001 380079

Insurance

Senior Wright Ltd
Jason House , Leeds
LS18 4JR 01132 588155

Japanese Knotweed

Nimrod Environmental Ltd
Glendene , Barnsley
South Yorkshire , S75 4BZ
01924 830961 or 07843 680483
enquiries@nimrodenvironmental.co.uk
www.nimrodenvironmental.co.uk

Low Energy Lightbulbs, Lighting and L.E.D.

DPR Services Ltd
Unit 6b Ashbrooke Park , Leeds
LS11 5SF 01132 743322

JDP Electrical Solutions Ltd
1 Greenland , Bradford
BD13 1HS 07866 051555

Modular Buildings

Cabin Locator
Oak Tree Cottage , York
YO42 4PP 08708 030755

Motivational and Life Coaching

UME Coaching
3 Rombalds Way , Skipton
BD23 2SG 01138 151558

New Habits
Cherry Tree , Sheffield
S11 9EF 01142 214876

Networking and Cabling

DTX Telecommunications Ltd
2C Harewood Yard , Leeds
LS17 9LF 08448 870700

Atkins Solutions
128 Peckover Drive , Pudsey
LS28 8EG 07834 229487

Office And Retail Furniture

Lab Systems Furniture Ltd
Rotary House , Hull
HU5 4HF 01482 444650

Office/Shop Fitters

Line and Level Interiors
Leeds West Industrial Estate, Leeds
LS13 4EN 01132 559998

Organic Recycling and Green Waste

Land Network (Hull) Ltd
Inncarr Farm , Driffield
YO25 8LZ **01964 542477**

Outdoor/Street Furniture

Sustainable Options
Unit 11 Riverside Place, Leeds
LS9 0RQ **01132 492222**

Painting and Decorating

Ian Stokes Decorating
15 Wheatfield Close , Epworth
North Lincolnshire , DN9 1SY
01427 873372 or 07930 371969
stokessustainabledecor@live.co.uk
www.stokesdecorating.co.uk

Stewart Morley Decorators
3 Carr Lane , Malton
YO17 8RP **01944 728318**

T Bailey Decorating
21 Compass Road , Hull
HU6 7AU **07710 028217**

T J Roberts Painter & Decorator
9 Charlton Avenue , Harrogate
North Yorkshire , HG5 0DN
07843 767263 or
info@tjrobertsdecorating.co.uk
tjrobertsdecorating.co.uk

Mark Galley Decorators Ltd
1 Nunwood House , Bradford
BD10 0PB **07973 310275**

D W Decorators
27 Neville Road , Scunthorpe
DN16 1TN **07788 447891**

Paul Crosby Painter & Decorator
26 Broome Way , York
YO32 9RL **01904 331782**

Mky Property Services
4 Hazel Court , Wakefield
WF2 0UD **07825 616082**

DKS Decorating
21 Berks Road , Huddersfield
HD3 4TD **01484 657097**

Payroll and Bookkeeping

MBS Payroll & Accountancy Services
Manor Farm , Scarborough
YO13 9LN **01723 863637**

BME Book-Keeping
17 North Road , Driffield
YO25 9TN **01377 217273**

Acorn Business Services
146 Westminster Crescent , Sheffield
S10 4EZ **01142 306670**

Double M Bookkeeping
34 Ormesby Road , Scunthorpe
DN17 2JG **07903 866812**

And Counting Ltd
The Catalyst , York
YO10 5GA **01904 409749**

John S Danson & Co
35 Salisbury Road , Dronfield
S18 1UG **01246 290261**

Painless Payroll
Green Trees , Gilberdyke
HU15 2XH **01430 473389**

Westside Payroll Services
24 Mona Avenue , Sheffield
S10 1NE **01142 684427**

Carol Rayner Book Keeping Service
Onward B , Ackworth
WF7 7BE **01977 618161**

Payroll People
37 Ellesmere Road , Chiswick
W4 3DU **02087 479575**

Pest Control

Sykes Pest Control
271 Cliffe Lane , Gomersal
BD19 4SB **07796 615260**

HUNTCATCHKILL PEST CONTROL SOLUTIONS
33 Barley Rise , York
.............**01904 492535**

Pest Control
14 Regent Street , Harrogate
HG1 4BD **01423 541040**

Discreet Pest Control Services
Titan House , Leeds
LS18 5PA **01132 818237**

MJ Backhouse Pest Control
Cambridge Court , Leeds
LS27 8LH **08005 426359**

Pest Control

Pest-Kill Direct
Grove Dene , Goole
DN14 9AH 01405 785439

Photography and Photographers

ICS Photography Ltd
The Studio , Doncaster
DN5 7JP 01709 910599

Rowland Fawcett Photography
20 Westminster Drive , Harrogate
HG3 1LW 08452 300596

Plumbing Services

W.E. Hargrave Ltd
Hargrave House , York
YO26 5RX 01904 792105

R.P.H Plumbing
46 Cleveland Way , York
YO32 9PH 01904 762093

Portable Appliance and Fixed Wire Testing

Electech 7671
Doncaster
DN2 5NG 07714 291993

A M Electrical and Consultancy Ltd
26 Springfield Avenue , Brough
HU15 1BU 01482 662790

Tech Services Corporate Ltd
28 Woodmoor Rise , Wakefield
WF4 3NT 01924 255574

Naldera Electrical Services
Naldera Leeds Road , Halifax
HX3 7AG 01422 202752

TSL Electrical & Data Services Ltd
Unit 2 Yorvale Business Park , York
YO10 3DR 01904 413798

Johnsons Electrical Contractors
13 Mayfield Grove , Harrogate
HG1 5HD 07852 721829

BCM Electrics
25 Ryshworth Crescent , Bingley
BD16 2EJ 01535 211306

Dave Mason Electrical
262 Kiveton Lane , Sheffield
S26 6NL 01909 772040

Portable Appliance and Fixed Wire Testing

Prolec Hull
319 James Rickett Avenue , Hull
HU8 8LQ 01482 796933

PAT Safety Ltd
28 New Park Street , Leeds
LS27 0PS 01132 525441

Printer Cartridges

Direct Printer Supplies Ltd
134 Archer Road , Sheffield
S8 0JZ 08453 888081

Printing, Design and Mailing Services

Evolution Print Ltd
9 Atlas Way , Sheffield
South Yorkshire , S4 7QQ
0114 249 3000
julie@evolutionprint.co.uk
www.evolutionprint.co.uk

Printing.com@Leeds
40 Great George Street , Leeds
LS1 3DL 01132 467374

Westwood Printers Ltd
Willowbridge Way , Castleford
WF10 5NP 01977 604647

Fuzz Digital
Unit 8 Bullroyd Industrial Estate , Bradford
BD8 0LH 08452 419921

Community Communication Ltd
1a Emgate , Bedale
North Yorkshire , DL8 1AH
01677 426 487
theteam@bcsofficepoint.co.uk
www.communitycommunication.co.uk

AKS Design and Print
Sandall Stones Road , Doncaster
DN3 1QR 01302 880200

Tiger Print, the business printer
The Vivars Industrial Centre , Selby
YO8 8BE 01757 706821

FMP Print & Projects
101 Waterloo Road , Huddersfield
HD5 0AB 01484 300790

THE GREEN DIRECTORY

Printing, Design and Mailing Services

Print 4 Sheffield
30 Scotland Street , Sheffield
S3 7AA **01142 701582**

Hull Print Zone
78-16th Avenue , Hull
HU6 9JS **01482 852163**

Promotional Items and Incentives

Gdock Promotions / Gwenagen Ltd
30-38 Dock Street , Leeds
West Yorkshire , LS10 1JF
0113 318 28 27
info@gdock.co.uk
www.gdock.co.uk

Chillbuddy
Birklands Avenue , Hull
East Yorkshire , HU8 0LJ
01482 240020 or 07834 929000
mail@chillbuddy.com
www.chillbuddy.com

Property Maintenance

JC Norton Joinery and Property Repairs
6 Wingfield Road , Barnsley
Yorkshire , S71 3PS
07973 489795 or 01226 321970
info@jcnortonjoinery.co.uk

Cottingham Home Solutions Ltd
396 Bricknell Avenue , Hull
HU5 4QD **01482 843653**

Allan Davis Electrical Contractors
13a Farrar Lane , Leeds
LS16 6AD **08006 11855**

Recycled and Refilled Printer Cartridges

The Little Ink Shop
80a Easy Road , Leeds
LS9 0AB **01132 496555**

Refrigeration

Econo Freeze Ltd
Unit 4 Enterprise Park ,
Leeds , LS11 8HA
0113 276 0722
barrie@econofreeze.co.uk
www.econofreeze.co.uk

Refrigeration Specialists (Huddersfield)
Spafields Industrial Estate , Huddersfield
HD7 5BB **01484 845124**

Safety and Convenience Products

Heatshot Limited
Unit 1 Sovereign Business Park , Leeds
LS10 1AW **07814 503566**

Signs and Graphics

Bizarre Signs
Unit 5 Safeguard House , Wakefield
WF4 5EB **01924 724526**

Signarama (York)
34/36 Auster Road , York
YO30 4XA **01904 692588**

Signarama (Harrogate)
100-A Knaresborough Road , Harrogate
HG2 7NN **01423 883700**

Insignia Signs & Graphics Ltd
87 Owston Road , Doncaster
DN6 8DR **01302 723003**

Artsign Ltd
76A Tickhill Road , Doncaster
DN4 8QG **01302 850271**

Magenta Signs
25 Folder Lane , Doncaster
DN5 7PD **07738 261247**

S&S Signs and Graphics
Unit 4 Kendray Business Park , Barnsley
S70 3NA **01226 748761**

Simply Signs of Penistone
Unit 2A , Penistone
Sheffield , S36 6HH
01226 379400
studio@simplysigns-penistone.co.uk
www.simplysigns-penistone.co.uk

Uniq Renewable Energy Solutions Ltd

URES Ltd is a mission led company, dedicated to reducing emmissions of climate changing gases such as carbon dioxide

The Earth's resources are becoming increasingly exhausted and we are putting a strain on our environment. Energy is now becoming an expensive commodity and we are seeing prices increase year on year.

We can offer a wide range of high quality microgeneration solutions. We are focused on helping you choose the best products suited to your requirements and will guide you through the whole process, from initial enquiry, to installation, to aftercare.

URES Ltd is a mission led company, dedicated to reducing emissions of climate changing gases such as carbon dioxide. The inconvenient truth is that we are exploiting the Earth's energy and other resources at a rate of about 3 times of that which is sustainable. Continuing down this path will have terrible global consequences in human and economic terms.

Our aim is therefore to help achieve sustainability in the UK so that we live within the resources of the planet we call home.

Contact
Tel: 01777 816379 - Mob: 07713575249
Web: www.ures.co.uk   - Email: ures@live.co.uk

THE GREEN DIRECTORY

Signs and Graphics

Awesome Signs and Printing
172 Plantation Hill , Worksop
S81 0DT **01909 509964**

Social Media and Internet Marketing

Squashed Pixel Ltd
Fruition Building , Bradford
BD15 0DX **01535 958083**

Solar Energy

Eco Solar Smiths Ltd
25 Appleton Drive , Glossop
SK13 8RX **07970 744221**

Energy and Environmental Consultants Ltd
28 Signhills Avenue , Cleethorpes
DN35 0BT **03331 234987**

Yorkshires Green With Energy Ltd
51 Darfield Road , Barnsley
S72 8HF **01226 718789**

Trust Renewable
Bradley Mill , Halifax
HX4 8BH **01422 382822**

Uniq Renewable Energy Solutions Ltd
The Barn , Gringley-On-The-Hill
South Yorkshire , DN10 4RA
01777 816379
ures@live.co.uk
www.ures.co.uk
(see full page advert for more information)

RP Dowsland Ltd
20A Blackwall , Halifax
HX1 2BE **01422 366336**

DPR Services Ltd
Unit 6b Ashbrooke Park , Leeds
LS11 5SF **01132 743322**

AWE Energy Ltd
212 Middlewood Road , Sheffield
S6 1TE **08452 256001**

Yorkshire Solar
Lynwood , Leeds
LS20 8HY **01943 878319**

Matrix Energy Systems
23 Lathkill Close , Sheffield
S13 8DI **07931 801904**

Solar Panels and Photovoltaics

Eco Solar Smiths Ltd
25 Appleton Drive , Glossop
SK13 8RX **07970 744221**

Solar Panels 4 U
Unit 6B Claypit Lane, Boroughbridge
YO51 9LS **01423 322915**

Solar Northern Ltd
6 Ryefield Gardens , Sheffield
S11 9UD **07971 415787**

Advanced Electro-Mechanical Services Ltd
192 Sandringham Road , Doncaster
DN2 5JE **01302 246538**

Solarwall Ltd
Green Lane Trading Estate , York
YO30 5PY **08001 380079**

Arc Solar Renewables Ltd
35 East Bawtry Road , Rotherham
S60 4BX **01709 542717**

Paul Wilson Renewable Technologies
Orchard Cottage , Skipton
BD23 4SJ **07767 293886**

ECO Energy Smart Ltd
7 Kingsley Drive , Rotherham
S65 4GY **01709 702737**

Yorkshire Solar
Lynwood , Leeds
LS20 8HY **01943 878319**

Strategic Energy Ltd
Strategic Business Centre , Castleford
WF10 4UA **01977 555550**

Solar Water Heating Systems

Matrix Energy Systems
23 Lathkill Close , Sheffield
S13 8DI **07931 801904**

Kingspan Environmental (was Kingspan Renewables)
Tadman Street , Wakefield
WF1 5QU **01924 376026**

ECO Energy Smart Ltd
7 Kingsley Drive , Rotherham
S65 4GY **01709 702737**

Solarwall Ltd
Green Lane Trading Estate , York
YO30 5PY **08001 380079**

Stress Management

The Caring Clinic
35 Barkers Road , Sheffield
S7 1SD 01142 551345

Surveyors

Bradley-Mason LLP
Evans Business Centre , Harrogate
HG3 2XA 01423 534604

Parker Beevers Ltd
Brockville , Spofforth
HG3 1AT 01937 590794

Taxi and Private Hire

Blue Line Taxis Ltd
43 York Avenue , Scunthorpe
DN16 3SB 01724 844222

Top Line Private Hire
84 Raymond Street , Bradford
BD5 8DY 01274 371222

Havacab
2 Doublegates Avenue , Ripon
HG4 2TP 01765 601888

Telecommunications

DTX Telecommunications Ltd
2C Harewood Yard , Leeds
LS17 9LF 08448 870700

Timber Frame Buildings

Mexframes Limited
Unit 5 Globe Court , Doncaster
South Yorkshire , DN12 4LH
01709 252588 or 07710 785 346
info@mexframes.co.uk
www.mexframes.co.uk
(see half page advert for more information)

Stonewood Timber Frames Limited
Kaileys Barn , Todmorden
OL14 7JF 01706 810101

Turner Timber Frames
5C Wyke Street , Hull
HU9 1PA 01482 218945

THE GREEN DIRECTORY

Tree Work and Surveys

Crown Consultants Ltd
Crown House , Halifax
HX6 3PS 08000 141330

Expert Tree Care
68 Kensington Street , York
YO23 1JA 01904 651378

Chevin Tree Surgeons
2 Silverdale Close , Guiseley
LS20 8BQ O1943 879016

Ross Hanley Tree Specialists
Hill Top Farm , Harrogate
HG3 5EU 01423 3711282

Valeside Tree Care
9 Warren Vale , Rotherham
S62 7SS 01709 710164

Underfloor Heating

DPR Services Ltd
Unit 6b Ashbrooke Park , Leeds
LS11 5SF 01132 743322

Waste Management and Disposal

Augean Plc
4 Rudgate Court , Leeds
LS23 7BF 01543 468832

Website and Internet Services

Radian IT Ltd
Louis Pearlman Centre, Hull
HU3 4DL 01482 221882

Pixel Builders Ltd
The Tannery , Leeds
LS3 1HS 01132 473895

Blue Mantis Ltd
23 Langley Crescent , Leeds
LS13 1AY 01132 883240

Jumble Design
Tapton Park Innovation Centre , Chesterfield
S41 0TZ 01246 541909

Waindigo Limited
The Catalyst , York
North Yorkshire , YO10 5GA
01904 409 748
hello@waindigo.com
waindigo.com

Website and Internet Services

Web Design Solution
143 St Johns Road , Huddersfield
HD1 5EY 07588 563615

Squashed Pixel Ltd
Fruition Building , Bradford
BD15 0DX 01535 958083

Rusola LLP
49 Windmill Crescent , Halifax
HX3 7DG 07413 037696

Mindbullet
16 Blundell Avenue , Cleethorpes
DN35 7PT 07733 047401

Wind Energy

AWE Energy Ltd
212 Middlewood Road , Sheffield
S6 1TE 08452 256001

Window Film

Solarshade Window Films Ltd
Springfield Place , Huddersfield
HD3 4AE 01484 515933

GREENER TIMES

> SUSTAINABLE SOLUTIONS MAGAZINE

Old Station Building
Oswald Road, Oswestry
Shropshire, SY11 1RE

SUBSCRIBE TO THE UK'S BEST GREEN BUSINESS, LIFESTYLE AND SUSTAINABILITY MAGAZINE

If you enjoy reading the Greener Times magazine, why not take advantage of our special subscription rates and save yourself some money? Each issue of Greener Times is enjoyable, informative reading that will also make you think!

As well as articles on environmental issues that can affect you at home as well as at work; there are interviews with celebrities like Gareth Southgate and successful businesses such as Stagecoach, quizzes that the whole family can get involved with and current affairs relating to local communities and businesses, all with an environmental and sustainable theme i.e. The Green Deal, The Renewable Heat Incentive (RHI) etc.

There is also a 'Whats On?' list of forthcoming shows and events that we will be attending where you can come along and meet us in person.

It costs just **£4.20 + P&P** Or if you want to save some money you can subscribe for a year for just **£42 + P&P** *(payable by monthly or annual direct debit)* Instruction to Greener Times Publishing Ltd

DON'T MISS AN ISSUE, SUBSCRIBE TODAY!

£42 + P&P

01691 661 565
info@greener-times.co.uk
www.greener-times.co.uk

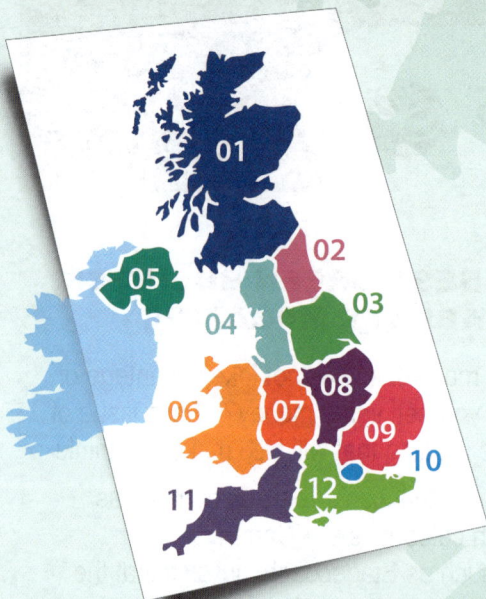

01
02
03
04
05
06
07
08
09
10
11
12

04

Manchester
Liverpool

The Business Supporting The North West of England Section for the 2012/13 Local Sourcing Directory is:

Accountancy

Morgan & Co
The Shakespeare Centre , Southport
PR8 5AB **01704 539636**

Accounting 4
8 Cobbler Hall , Wakefield
WF4 4LJ **07899 964895**

Alexander Bursk
Parkgates , Prestwich
M25 0JW **01617 737737**

Christopher D Jones
Strawberry Cottage , Chester
CH1 6LL **01244 851893**

P R Moss
12 Hankshaw Bank Road , Blackburn
BB1 8JS **01254 670756**

Kenwright and Co.
Unit A15 Champion Business Park , Wirral
CH49 0AB **01516 043904**

ABL Accountancy Services Ltd
6 Goose Butts Lane , Clitheroe
BB7 1JT **01200 438186**

ALX Chartered Certified Accountants
Charter House , Burnley
BB12 6LY **01282 437421**

Supreme Accountancy Services
Fieldview Garage & Stables , Barnston Village
CH61 1BW **08009 704386**

ADC Accountants
15 Market Street , Wigan
WN6 0HW **01257 423114**

Accreditation and Certification

Successful Safety Solutions
Wirral
CH49 6QL **08458 901427**

Acoustic Products

Hush (UK) Limited
44 Canal Street , South Sefton
L20 8QU **01519 332026**

Air Conditioning Energy Assessments

Rourke Environmental Services Ltd
Crown Point South Industrial Park , Manchester
M34 6PF **01613 367554**

Air Conditioning Systems

P & M Coppack Air Conditioning Ltd
Unit 5 Pippin Bank , Bacup
OL13 0BU **01706 879336**

Gear Services
35 Eden Street , Wigton
CA7 4Ad **07588 419456**

Andrews Air Conditioning & Refridgeration Ltd
Claverton Road , Wythenshaw
M23 9FT **0800 7318833**

Icecap Cooling Ltd
Cheethams Mill Industrial Park , Stalybridge
SK15 2BT **01613 433919**

Pro Temp Airconditioning Ltd
Unit 17 Farriers Way , Bootle
L30 4XL **01515 233086**

AirFrost Ltd
Harkers Farm , Ormskirk
L39 7JY **07710 556137**

Rourke Environmental Services Ltd
Crown Point South Industrial Park , Manchester
M34 6PF **01613 367554**

Air Source Heat Pumps

Jacob ECO Energy Ltd
8 Exchange Quay , Manchester
M5 3EJ **01617 938536**

Gatehouse Renewables
Lancaster Environment Centre , Lancaster
LA1 4YQ **01524 510469**

Ground Therm Ltd
129 Mill Lane , Denton
M34 7RS **07796 811072**

GDI
AIR CONDITIONING

Our Company specialises in Air Conditioning solutions to the commercial, industrial & domestic sectors throughout the U K. We offer a comprehensive package including: Site Surveys, Specification Advise and an Estimating Service ensuring an accurate and quick quotation.

GDI Air Conditioning Limited offers total support before, during and after the project to ensure piece of mind to you, our client, and our highly qualified engineers will be on hand to offer technical advice during the project ensuring a smooth operation from start to finish.

GDI Air Conditioning Ltd is one of the latest of successful companies to join a leading edge scheme, designed to help industry improve its safety record.
Our Manchester based firm recently received accreditation from SAFE contractor, & B&ES *(formerly HVCA)* all Companies that recognise very high standards of health and safety practice amongst UK Contractors. The Company's application for B&ES & SAFE contractor accreditation was driven by the need for a uniform standard across the business.

DAIKIN   **FUJITSU**   **MITSUBISHI ELECTRIC** PRESENTATION PRODUCTS   **HITACHI** Inspire the Next   **LG** Life's Good

B&ES BUILDING & ENGINEERING SERVICES ASSOCIATION   **SAMSUNG**   **TOSHIBA** Leading Innovation >>>   **MITSUBISHI HEAVY INDUSTRIES, LTD.**   SAFEcontractor APPROVED

Tel/Mob: 0161 790 0001 or 07738 177555
Web: www.gdi-airsolutions.com
Email: sales@gdiairsolutions.com

THE GREEN DIRECTORY

Airport Transfers

Cumbria Cabs Carlisle
26 Crindledyke , Carlisle
CA6 4BZ **01228 899599**

Autozone Travel
Cablehouse , Liverpool
L2 28X **07528 860074**

Affordable FS
16 Stone Croft , Preston
PR1 9EX **07894 72889**

Pegasus Fairways Travel
156 Lindale Gardens , Blackpool
FY4 3PL **01253 346609**

Airport Specials
76 Blackburn Road , Accrington
BB5 1LE **01254 393969**

Greenmount Cars
209 Holcombe Road , Bury
BL8 4BQ **01204 322505**

Architects

Flanagan Design Associates Ltd
Spring House , Oswaldtwistle
BB5 3EG **01254 385095**

Colin Hayes Associates
78 Hill Lane , Manchester
M96 PF **01617 407220**

Constructive Thinking Studio Limited
Liverpool Science Park Innovation Centre
L3 5TT **01517 053433**

sR arcitecture & design
78 Holm Lane , Oxton
CH43 2HS **07738 975242**

Johnston and Wright Architects
15 Castle Street , Carlisle
CA3 8TD **01228 525161**

Ralph Hilton & Co
The Family Life Centre , Southport
PR8 6JH **01704 513377**

CTA Architects
54 Hamilton Square , Birkenhead
CH41 5AS **01516 662990**

RJG Architectural Design Services
18 Russet Close , St. Helens
WA10 2NE **01744 28453**

Green Design Group
Sutton House , Cockermouth
CA13 0PW **01900 822945**

Architects

Martin Rigby Architects
Wilbank House , Nantwich
CW5 8JG **01270 524577**

Asbestos Handling and Removal

Northern Insulation Contractors LLP
Caroline House , Stalybridge
SK15 1SE **08450 760055**

D R Environmental Consultants Ltd
35 Barton Road , Manchester
M32 9FA **08007 569906**

Asbestos Survey and Assesment

D R Environmental Consultants Ltd
35 Barton Road , Manchester
M32 9FA **08007 569906**

REC Asbestos Ltd
Unit 19 Kenfig Industrial Estate , Port Talbot
SA13 2PE **01656 749823**

Asbestos Training and Awareness

Lighthouse Risk Services LLP
Airedale House , Leeds
LS20 8EH **08454 591724**

One Stop Asbestos Consultants and Services Ltd
Brendan House ,
Widnes , WA8 6AD
0845 833 8156 or 0151 257 2719
admin@onestopasbestos.com
www.onestopasbestos.com

QHS Solutions Ltd
Queens Park Lodge , Burnley
Lancashire , BB11 3QW
01282 839103
a.stansfield@qhs-solutions.com
www.qhs-solutions.com

Biomass Energy and Biofuels

Jacob ECO Energy Ltd
8 Exchange Quay , Manchester
M5 3EJ **01617 938536**

Branding & Marketing

Wash Design Ltd
The Watermark Studios , Preston
PR1 5EZ 01772 880000

Primo Website Design
Manchester (Central) , Manchester
M13 9AB 01612 744513

Builders Merchants

Benchmark Building Supplies Ltd
200 Guide Lane , Audenshaw
M34 5EE 01613 378555

Building Integrated Photovoltaics(BIPV)

Gatehouse Renewables
Lancaster Environment Centre , Lancaster
LA1 4YQ 01524 510469

Business Management, Coaching and Consultancy

Absolute HR
1 Meadow Walk , Bolton
BL4 0AF 07809 498949

True Progress
Suite 7 Fulshaw Hall, Wilmslow
SK9 1RL 01625 525100

Chauffeur Services

Chameleon Luxury Chauffeur Services
Desside Enterprise , Shotton
CH5 1PP 01244 810355

Cleaning and Hygiene Services

Eco Extreme Clean
57 Mount Pleasant , Dalton-In-Furness
LA15 8BQ 01229 465366

Westgrove Group
940 Lakeside Drive , Warrington
WA1 1QX 01925 414190

Cleaning Products

The Green House Keeper Cafe
16 Yewdale Road , Coniston
LA21 8DU 01539 441925

Computer & IT Recycling

Computer Recycling Technologies Ltd.
11A Trident Industrial Estate , Warrington
WA3 6AX 01925 813030

Computer Recycling Centre
Coalshaw Green Road , Oldham
OL9 8JW 01612 900762

Computer Maintenance

Leigh Computers
Unit L2 The Market Hall, Leigh
WN7 4PG 01942 677777

RSG IT Plus LTD
Coronation Drive , Leigh
Greater Manchester , WN7 2YZ
07929 251134 or 0844 096 1819
lee@rsgitplus.com
www.rsgitplus.com
(see full page advert for more information)

IT247NW
32 Coniston Drive , Preston
PR5 4RP 01772 369247

BH Computers
Glendale Avenue , Preston
PR5 5XY 01772 330994

PC PAL Support Group
Adamson House , Manchester
M20 2YY 07751 771661

Computer Services

Computer Recycling Centre
Coalshaw Green Road , Oldham
OL9 8JW 01612 900762

Hit F1
47 Knutshaw Crescent , Bolton
BL3 4SB 01204 400347

S & N Computer Services
45 Abbey Road , Warrington
WA3 1EP 01942 730854

Counselling , Advice and Psychotherapy

4 Therapy UK
229 Bury New Road , Whitefield
M45 8GW 01617 989443

Counselling , Advice and Psychotherapy

Elizabeth Hammond
Manchester
.............07960 610942

Adam Prince Counselling, Psychotherapy & Hypnotherapy
37 Granby House , Manchester
M1 7AR 01612 355187

Aspects by Christine
14 St Andrews Avenue , Thornton-Cleveleys
FY5 3NJ 01253 864419

Kevin Rodgers
Wirral Sports Medicine & Physiotherapy Clinic
CH63 4JG 07866 657316

Debra Maxwell
79 Pategill Road , Penrith
LA11 8LH 07887 968059

Dove Tail
2 Pine Close , Stockport
SK6 7QU 01614 845012

Your Lifes Puzzles
25 Taylors Lane , Wigan
WN3 4TZ 07944 120532

Maurcia Mitchell
Paragon House , Old Trafford
M16 0LN 07908 522523

John Monk-Steel Associates
43 Stoneygate Road , Leicester
LE2 2BP 01162 700290

Courier Services

Patriot Express Deliveries
Patriot House , Wirral
CH62 8EG 01515 135198

Document and Data Destruction

IBEX Information Management
IBEX House , Preston
PR1 1QE 01772 563146

Document Management

IBEX Information Management
IBEX House , Preston
PR1 1QE 01772 563146

Drains, Drainage and Pipes

Driver, CPC, Periodic Training

Handson Safety Services Ltd
The Training Centre , Crewe
Cheshire , CW2 7RP
01270 252009
enquiries@handson-safety-services.co.uk
www.handson-safety-services.co.uk

E-commerce and Search Engine Optimisation (SEO)

Cyberfrog Design
1 Valencia Road , Liverpool
L15 8LL 07595 596877

Primo Website Design
Manchester (Central) , Manchester
M13 9AB 01612 744513

Simply Creative Software
332 Whalley Range , Blackburn
BB1 6NN 01254 664282

Zine UK (Cheshire)
2 Abbey House , Northwich
CW8 1LY 08458 384698

E-commerce and Search Engine Optimisation (SEO)

Singleframe Design
78 Princes Reach , Preston
PR2 2GB **01772 721144**

Ecology Surveys and Consultancy

Oak Bay Ecology
16 Waters Edge Fold, Manchester
Lancashire , OL1 4QJ
07775 186757
cp.ecology@yahoo.co.uk
www.cp-ecology.co.uk

Ecological Land Management Ltd
Prospect Industrial Estate , Llay
Wrexham , LL12 0PB
07970 570777
mail@elm.uk.net
www.elm.uk.net
(see half page advert for more information)

Ecology Surveys and Consultancy

Angela Graham Bat Consultancy Service Ltd
47 Bury Business Centre , Bury
Lancashire , BL9 6BU
0161 763 6171 or 07710 184142
bat.consultancy@talktalk.net
www.batconsultant.co.uk

Electrical and Electricians

R H Electrics Ltd
62 Rutherford , Bolton
BL5 1DL **07973 140627**

Paul Robertson Electrical
224 Sale Road , Manchester
M23 0FR **07810 806611**

PP Electrical Ltd
11 Hopefold Drive , Manchester
M28 3PN **07768 368051**

K.F.Electrical
4 Dye House Cottages , Macclesfield
SK11 0NN **07710 054826**

Electrical and Electricians

BB Electrical Ltd
57 Adrian Road , Bolton
BL1 3LQ **07771 697136**

ARM Electrical Contractors Ltd
20 Trent Close , St. Helens
WA9 4TS **01744 609229**

Watsons Electrical
23 Meyrick Road , Norris Green
L11 5BL **07883 383303**

P.I. Electrical Services
37 Wilton Avenue , Cheadle
SK8 3LY **07921 787517**

Standish Electrical
19 Church Street , Wigan
WN6 0JT **01257 427100**

Ian Fisher Electrical
warwick Mill Business Village , Carlisle
CA4 8RR **07860 684270**

Electrical Maintenance and Installation

C J Electrical
28 Cranbourne Avenue , Meols
CH47 7BW **01516 320699**

W H Services
18 Claymore Street , Abbeyhay
M18 8SP **07540 698258**

I.C Electrical Ltd
121 Elm Drive , Crewe
CW1 4EL **07546 245807**

J D Mounsey Electrics
Sowarth Industrial Estate , Settle
BD24 5AF **01729 825677**

Embroidery

Opal Embroidery
9 Clarence Street , Burnley
BB11 3HG **07974 817570**

Carlisle Embroidery Ltd
8b Port Road Business Park , Carlisle
CA2 7AF **01228 597649**

Lucky Seven Embroidery
Unit 9 Albion Mill , Havannah
CW12 2AQ **01260 299777**

Barbaton Ltd
14 Rydal Road , Poulton-le-Fylde
FY6 9BN **01253 701171**

Embroidery

A&K Embroidery & Print
8 Rydal Mount , Crewe
CW1 4PR **01270 257653**

Acorn Embroidery
12 Almond Drive , Warrington
WA5 4QE **01925 224351**

Energy Assessors & Consultants

Envantage Ltd
8 Grange Lane , Manchester
M20 6RW **01614 487722**

Energy Saving Heating

Ecopod Heating Systems Limited + Belfry Group Limited
Unit 12 Cameron Court , Warrington
WA2 8RE **01925 633311**

Energy Saving Products and Services

Ecopod Heating Systems Limited + Belfry Group Limited
Unit 12 Cameron Court , Warrington
WA2 8RE **01925 633311**

Gatehouse Renewables
Lancaster Environment Centre , Lancaster
LA1 4YQ **01524 510469**

Environmental Consultancy

Kate Mansfield ECO
6 Nelson Close , Milton Keynes
MK8 0DL **01908 566068**

GeoCon Site Investigations Ltd
15 Belmont Drive , Stockport
SK8 5EA **0844 5043901**

S.I.S (GB) Ltd
Hanover House , Liverpool
L1 3DZ **01512 853884**

Rintoul Integrated Solutions
106 Prenton Hall Road , Prenton
CH43 0RA **01516 080023**

Environmental Training and Awareness

Liverpool Environmental Training
41-51 Greenland Street , Liverpool
L1 0BS **01517 083563**

Event Organisers

Discovery Events Limited
5 Dunham Court , Northwich
CW8 2EX **01606 884162**

Exhibition Stands

Fred and Ginger Productions Limited
94 Wilderspool Causeway , Warrington
WA4 6PU **01925 636634**

Unique Exhibitions Limited
Whitebirk Industrial Estate , Blackburn
BB1 5UA **08450 704456**

Discovery Events Limited
5 Dunham Court , Northwich
CW8 2EX **01606 884162**

Financial Services

Calculus Accountants
38 Wardley Hall Avenue , Worsley
M28 2RL **01617 905909**

Fire and Smoke Detection

FirePro
48 Whalley Road , Accrington
BB5 5EF **01254 600002**

Fire Risk Assessment and Training

TLC Learning Academy Limited
1-3 The Courtyard , Bolton
BL1 8PB **01204 404140**

Fire Risk Management Solutions Ltd
27-29 Wellhouse Road , Barnoldswick
Lancashire , BB18 6DB
01282 876336 or 07958 102838
brianstrickland2@gmail.com
www.frms-ltd.co.uk

Fire Risk Assessment Solutions Ltd
20 Beacon View , Marple/Stockport
SK6 6PX **07739 263886**

Apollo Training & Consultancy Ltd
111 Brackenwood Road , Bebington
CH63 2LU **01516 082405**

Applecore Consultancy
634A Liverpool Road , Southport
PR8 3BH **01704 260486**

First Aid Training

TLC Learning Academy Limited
1-3 The Courtyard , Bolton
Greater Manchester , BL1 8PB
01204 404 140 or 07737 239 278
sharon@tlclearningacademy.com
www.tlclearningacademy.com

S.I.S (GB) Ltd
Hanover House , Liverpool
L1 3DZ **01512 853884**

BDS Group
Charles Court Business Centre , Urmston
M41 9EH **01617 476310**

Centaur Training Services
Centurion Industrial Estate , Leyland
PR25 4GU **01772 433080**

Apollo Training & Consultancy Ltd
111 Brackenwood Road , Bebington
CH63 2LU **01516 082405**

First Aid Academy
2 Railway Road , Urmston
M41 0XL **08443 571426**

Food Hygiene

TLC Learning Academy Limited
1-3 The Courtyard , Bolton
BL1 8PB **01204 404140**

S.I.S (GB) Ltd
Hanover House , Liverpool
L1 3DZ **01512 853884**

BDS Group
Charles Court Business Centre , Urmston
M41 9EH **01617 476310**

Fraud Investigation

Applecore Consultancy
634A Liverpool Road , Southport
PR8 3BH **01704 260486**

Fuel Saving Products

Greenfoot Global
117 Greenwood , Preston
PR5 8JY **07595 643797**

Gas and Central Heating (Domestic)

Green Deal Solutions
150c Holland Street , Denton
Greater Manchester , M34 3GG
0844 477 0995
info@greendealsolutions.net
www.greendealsolutions.net

Gear Services
35 Eden Street , Wigton
CA7 4Ad 07588 419456

Graphic Design

Gill Tatlock Graphic Design
10 Runshaw Lane , Chorley
PR7 6AU 01257 412888

Beepea
Swarbrick Close , Blackpool
FY1 3RZ 01253 301803

Meme Media
Tonge Bridge Industrial Estate , Bolton
BL2 6BD 01204 381283

Wash Design Ltd
The Watermark Studios , Preston
PR1 5EZ 01772 880000

Brotherhood Design Studio
6a Kew Road , Southport
PR8 4HH 01704 566446

Campbell Graphics
14 Cavendish Road , Stockport
SK4 3DN 01614 420865

Reform Creative
31 Dale Street , Manchester
M1 1EY 01612 360054

Cooper Design
12 Seat Hill , Penrith
Cumbria , CA10 1BD
01768 870979 or 07775 791747
mike@cooperman.uk.com

Design & Print @ RAS Ltd
11 Mollington Graqnge , Chester
CH1 6NP 01244 346120

Inspire Graphic Design
12 Rowan Lane , Skelmersdale
WN8 6UL 01695 722137

Green Roofing

The Better Roofing Company
35 Coverdale road , Lancaster
LA1 5PY 07972 815797

Ground Source Heat Pumps

Gatehouse Renewables
Lancaster Environment Centre , Lancaster
LA1 4YQ 01524 510469

Ground Therm Ltd
129 Mill Lane , Denton
M34 7RS 07796 811072

Habitat Management.

Ecological Land Management Ltd
Prospect Industrial Estate , Llay
Wrexham , LL12 0PB
07970 570777
mail@elm.uk.net
www.elm.uk.net
(see half page advert for more information)

Health and Safety

TLC Learning Academy Limited
1-3 The Courtyard , Bolton
BL1 8PB 01204 404140

Rintoul Integrated Solutions
106 Prenton Hall Road , Prenton
CH43 0RA 01516 080023

Applecore Consultancy
634A Liverpool Road , Southport
PR8 3BH 01704 260486

Successful Safety Solutions
CH49 6QL 08458 901427

Handson Safety Services Ltd
The Training Centre , Crewe
CW2 7RP 01270 252009

BDS Group
Charles Court Business Centre , Urmston
M41 9EH 01617 476310

SafetyForce Safety Services
161 Mottram Road , Hyde
SK14 2NX 07853 288080

International Safety Service
Enterprise House , Penwortham (Preston)
PR4 4BA 08445 625109

Health and Safety

Comply at Work Ltd Health & Safety Consultancy & Training
5 Vale Coppice , Bolton
BL6 5RP **01204 690851**

TL Safety Ltd
4 Wenlock Close , Bolton
BL6 7PE **07749 838367**

Health and Social Care

TLC Learning Academy Limited
1-3 The Courtyard , Bolton
BL1 8PB **01204 404140**

Hypnotherapy

Phoenix Clinic
26 Knutsford Avenue , Stockport
SK4 5LQ **01614 323022**

Aspects by Christine
14 St Andrews Avenue , Thornton-Cleveleys
FY5 3NJ **01253 864419**

Hypnotherapy

The Mobile Massage Man & Advanced Hypnotherapist
Radcliffe
M26 1BG **01617 231771**

Insulation

Warm Front Ltd
Shepley Industrial Estate North , Audenshaw
M34 5DR **08000 834333**

Sprayseal Contracts Ltd
Bollin House , Mobberley
WA16 7LX **01565 872303**

Global Heatsave
Unit G2A Newton Business Park, Hyde
SK14 4UQ **01613 688300**

Insulation

Kelsey Insulation
70 Falbarn Cresent , Rossendale
NN4 6BD **01706 240007**

Modern Plan Insulation
Church Street , Bolton
BL5 3QW **01942 811839**

Insurance

M G P Group
Easter House , Manchester
M16 0ND **07747 621055**

Landscaping and Ground Maintenance

B S Bardsley
8 Caroton Avenue , Stockport
SK6 4EG **07900 298009**

Lawyers

Farleys Solicitors
1-2 Richmond Terrace , Blackburn
BB1 7AT **01254 606060**

Low Energy Lightbulbs, Lighting and L.E.D.

LED Switchover Ltd
Unit D3C Edgefold Industrial Estate , Bolton
BL4 0JW **01618 500906**

Motivational and Life Coaching

Brian McMinn
1A Anderton Road , Liverpool
L36 4HS **01514 803108**

Networking and Cabling

CIS Northwest
45 Hillside Close , Wigan
WN5 7PJ **01744 416450**

Q2Q IT
Bridge Mill , Cowan Bridge
LA6 2HS **01524 274000**

High Blade Cables
The Shire Hall , Appleby
CA16 6XN **01768 352560**

Noise and Vibration Testing

Robin Mackenzie Partnership Ltd
42 Collington Road , Edinburgh
EH10 5BT **01315 573327**

Red Acoustics Ltd
Cottam Lane Business Centre , Preston
PR2 1JR **01772 722182**

Office Cleaning and Cleaning Services

AbleArrow Cleaning Services
PO Box 2301 , Wrexham
LL11 0FN **01829 271720**

Painting and Decorating

Chris Thwaites Painter and Decorator
21 Heads Road , Keswick
CA12 5Ex **01768 771035**

B S Bardsley
8 Caroton Avenue , Stockport
SK6 4EG **07900 298009**

A M Robinson Decorators
68 Belmont Road , Cheadle
SK8 4AQ **07857 177074**

Dave Rainford Decorator
24 Whinfell Drive , Lancaster
LA1 4PB **07702 882837**

Steve's
20 Laburnum Drive , Skelmersdale
WN8 8HA **01695 729525**

JDS Decorating Services
18 Tilstock Crescent , Prenton
CH43 0ST **01512 001368**

Keith Olive Decorating
11 Aire Drive , Bolton
BL2 3FS **07885 251364**

D P Mattinson Ltd
2 Wharfe Court , Morecombe
LA3 3SD **01524 388138**

Louise Robinson
13 Willow Street , Accrington
BB5 5SX **07922 883817**

Decor8 4 You
228 Leyland Lane , Leyland
PR25 1XJ **07731 439431**

PESTOCLEAR
your local pest control experts

Pest Control Services Provided by Pestoclear

Welcome to the full range of pest control services from **PESTOCLEAR**. We are delighted to have established a first class reputation for providing a professional and comprehensive pest control service tailor made to your exact needs.

Fumigation - Commodities & Bulk Grain
Pest Control • Heat Treaments
Bird Control & Proofing • Barn Spraying

OUR PROMISE TO YOU
- ✔ Free Survey & Quote
- ✔ No Callout Charges
- ✔ Fast Response 24/7
- ✔ Competitive Rates
- ✔ Yearly Service Plans

Tel: 0151 513 1996   Mob: 07806 498 186

BPCA MEMBER
BRITISH · PEST · CONTROL · ASSOCIATION

Pests dealt with include:-
- • Wasps • Ants • Fleas • Rats
- • Mice • Moles • Bed Bugs

Partitioning Services

MF Ceilings Ltd
144 Brownlow Road , Bolton
Lancashire , BL6 7EH
07968 979081 or 01204 698334
mfceilings@talktalk.net
http://mfceilings.wix.com/mfceilingsltd

Payroll and Bookkeeping

Many Happy Returns Ltd
Oxford Road , Macclesfield
SK11 8HS **01625 507401**

John Greenall & CO
20 Crewe Road , Sandbach
CW11 4NE **01270 762547**

D C Computer Accounting
4 Oxford Road , Wigan
WN5 8PQ **01942 222310**

Key Business Solutions Ltd
335 Bury Old Road , Manchester
M25 1PY **07794 286958**

BCS Partnership
Merlin House , Rochdale
OL11 5NL **01706 646664**

Phil Clayton Accountancy
460 Blackpool Road , Preston
PR2 1HX **01772 464822**

Alexander Bursk
Parkgates , Prestwich
M25 0JW **01617 737737**

Minsters Bookkeeping Services
2 Kingsley Court , Sandbach
CW11 3GJ **01270 766751**

Alpha Bookkeeping Limited
15 Lynton Drive , Southport
Merseyside , PR8 4QP
07432 598237
enquiries@alpha-bookkeeping.co.uk
www.alpha-bookkeeping.co.uk

Justines Payroll Services
18 Hinchley Road , Manchester
M9 7FG **01616 830642**

Pest Control

Pestoclear Chester and Wirral Ltd
99 Heygarth Road , Wirral
Merseyside , CH62 8AJ
0151 513 1996 or 07806 498186
steveharwood.pestoclear@virginmedia.com
www.pestoclear.co.uk
(see full page advert for more information)

Alpha Pest Control
The White House , Stoke on Trent
Staffordshire , ST4 3AR
0800 0925999
info@alphapest.co.uk
www.alphapest.co.uk
(see full page advert for more information)

DPD Services
13A Belmont Road , Bolton
BL1 7AF **08007 817984**

Guardian Pest Management
25 Canaan , Warrington
WA3 1EG **01942 677967**

Photography and Photographers

Soulchild Photography
Brentwood Street , Manchester
M16 7LE **07533 341104**

Damien Haywards Photography
Failsworth
M35 9PL **07815 969361**

Plumbing Services

Standish Electrical
19 Church Street , Wigan
WN6 0JT **01257 427100**

Portable Appliance and Fixed Wire Testing

Safety-PAT
56 Berkshire Drive , Congleton
CW12 1SB **08006 128807**

MAC Electrical (UK) Ltd
130 Mossway , Middleton
M24 1NT **07814 836359**

BPD Building Services Ltd
The Kingwood , Ashton-Under-Lyme
OL6 6TN **01618 705576**

Portable Appliance and Fixed Wire Testing

EST-NW
9 Lime Grove , St Helens
WA11 8DS **01744 889602**

BB Electrical Ltd
57 Adrian Road , Bolton
BL1 3LQ **07771 697136**

Calbarrie Cumbria Ltd
67 Scotland Road , Carlisle
CA3 9HT **01228 512237**

Print Management

Print 4 Less
10 Yorkshire Street , Burnley
BB11 2DY **01282 421000**

Printing, Design and Mailing Services

Rubell Print Ltd
College Lane , Tarporley
CW6 9PQ **01829 260420**

AFP Design and Print
15 Hunt Street , Manchester
M46 9JF **01942 873574**

The Print Quarter.Com
Cottam Street , Chorley
PR7 2DT **01257 269707**

PWD Creative
122a Station Road , Preston
PR5 6LA **01772 312554**

Candyprint @ printing.com
 103 Castlerigg , Carlisle
CA2 6PG **07736 930043**

Kaleido Print
14 Briarfield Road , Cheadle
SK8 5PA **01614 854902**

Minuteman Press (Blackburn)
8 Walker Street , Blackburn
BB1 1BG **01254 677655**

The Printroom UK
Unit C2 Kingfisher Business Park , Liverpool
L20 6PF **01519 228516**

BAYTYPE - Digital Artwork & Print
Manderley House , Heysham
LA3 1LN **01524 850056**

Design & Print @ RAS Ltd
11 Mollington Graqnge , Chester
CH1 6NP **01244 346120**

Quality Management (ISO Accreditation)

Rintoul Integrated Solutions
106 Prenton Hall Road , Prenton
CH43 0RA **01516 080023**

Recycling

Eden Community Recycling
Mardale Road , Penrith
Cumbria , CA11 9JH
01768 840259 or 077156 07327
info@ecreden.com
www.ecreden.com

Refrigeration

AirFrost Ltd
Harkers Farm , Ormskirk
L39 7JY **07710 556137**

Rourke Environmental Services Ltd
Unit 14 Crownpoint South Industrial Park, Manchester
M34 6PF **01613 367554**

Renewable Energy Training.

Easy MCS Ltd
Viscount House , Chester
CH4 8RH **08444 146041**

Roofing Services

Crescent Roofing Ltd
20 West Crescent , Manchester
M24 4DA **01616 533152**

Safety Risk Assessment

Applecore Consultancy
634A Liverpool Road , Southport
PR8 3BH **01704 260486**

SafetyForce Safety Services
161 Mottram Road , Hyde
SK14 2NX **07853 288080**

Signs and Graphics

Signarama
128 London Road , Stockport
SK7 4DJ **01614 562003**

Signarama (Preston)
Sheraton House , Preston
PR1 2QD **01772 258494**

Signs and Graphics

R J Signs & Graphics
39 Birches Lane , Northwich
CW9 7SN 01606 41374

PC Signs
18 Harewood Avenue , Nr Burnley
BB12 7JB 01282 774713

Creative Design and Workwear Ltd
Unit 5 Cowling Business Park , Chorley
PR6 0QL 01257 231414

S J Signs & Graphics
St Johns Industrial Estate , Oldham
OL4 3DZ 01617 858616

Solar Energy

Eco Solar Smiths Ltd
25 Appleton Drive , Glossop
SK13 8RX 07970 744221

T J Warr Electrical
34 Marlborough Road , Manchester
M41 5GQ 07793 046262

D.R Energy Solutions
54 Gloucester Road , Wirral
CH45 3JT 01516 473599

Solar Panels and Photovoltaics

The Better Roofing Company
35 Coverdale Road , Lancaster
LA1 5PY 07972 815797

Eco Solar Smiths Ltd
25 Appleton Drive , Glossop
SK13 8RX 07970 744221

Green Deal Solutions
150c Holland Street , Denton
Greater Manchester , M34 3GG
0844 477 0995
info@greendealsolutions.net
www.greendealsolutions.net

Global Roofsave
Unit G2A Newton Business Park , Hyde
SK14 4UQ 01613 688300

Brill Energy Ltd
11 Warrington Road , Northwich
CW8 2LH 08456 009029

Jacob ECO Energy Ltd
8 Exchange Quay , Manchester
M5 3EJ 01617 938536

Solar Panels and Photovoltaics

Gatehouse Renewables
Lancaster Environment Centre , Lancaster
LA1 4YQ 01524 510469

Macclesfield Renewables
2 The Whitfields , Macclesfield
SK10 3PX 07590 893877

Standish Electrical
19 Church Street , Wigan
WN6 0JT 01257 427100

The Greener Group
48 Wharton Court , Chester
CH2 3DH 01244 405285

Solar Water Heating Systems

The Better Roofing Company
35 Coverdale Road , Lancaster
LA1 5PY 07972 815797

Jacob ECO Energy Ltd
8 Exchange Quay , Manchester
M5 3EJ 01617 938536

Gatehouse Renewables
Lancaster Environment Centre , Lancaster
LA1 4YQ 01524 510469

Stress Management

TLC Learning Academy Limited
1-3 The Courtyard , Bolton
BL1 8PB 01204 404140

**Jo Mathieson Counselling/
NLP Coaching Services**
Stockport
SK3 8AB 07746 156144

Suspended Ceilings - Installation and Manufacture

MF Ceilings Ltd
144 Brownlow Road , Bolton
BL6 7EH 07968 979081

Tax Advice and Taxation

Calculus Accountants
38 Wardley Hall Avenue , Worsley
M28 2RL 01617 905909

Taxi and Private Hire

Cumbria Cabs Carlisle
26 Crindledyke , Carlisle
CA6 4BZ **01228 899599**

KVN Travel
22 Ellen Grove , Salford
BL4 8RQ **07791 630617**

Telecommunications

BlueBox Communications Ltd
Network House , Bolton
BL1 6AH **01204 494950**

Wirral Telecom
8 Prenton Lane , Wirral
CH42 9NX **01516 093400**

The Complete Solutions Group Ltd
Alexander House , Manchester
M32 0AZ **08443 443443**

Thermal Insulation

Knauf Insulation Ltd
PO Box 10 , St Helens
WA10 3NS **08700 668660**

Timber Frame Buildings

Stonewood Timber Frames Limited
Kaileys Barn , Todmorden
OL14 7JF **01706 810101**

Lakeland Timber Frame Ltd
Unit 38c Holme Mills Industrial Estate , Carnforth
LA6 1RD **01524 782596**

CHESHIRE OAK STRUCTURES

TEL: 01829 250919 ■ WWW.CHESHIREOAKSTRUCTURES.CO.UK

Travel Insurance

Consumer Alliance in Travel (CAT)
Easter Road , Manchester
M16 0ND **07747 621055**

Tree Work and Surveys

Bowland Tree Services
6 Ashford Close , Lancaster
LA1 4QH **01524 33373**

Arundel Tree Surgeons
Lees Hall Quarry , Glossop
SK13 6JT **01619 298939**

Frankland Tree Services Ltd
Hillside , Altrincham
WA15 0RD **01619 415410**

Treework Arboricultural Services
HaresteadsFarm , Stockport
.............**01625 850320**

Bergen Tree Services
Lindeth , Holme
Cumbria , LA6 1QP
01524 782898 or 07771 931193
info@bergentreeservices.co.uk
www.bergentreeservices.co.uk
(see full page advert for more information)

A Binns & Co
Knarrs Hill Cottage , Colne
BB8 7ES **01282 862770**

Chartley Tree Services
3 Chartley Grove , Middlewich
CW10 9GG **01606 738622**

Astra Tree Services Ltd
2 Ebenezer Cottages , Sandbach
CW11 4SD **01270 753072**

Davenham Tree Tech
358 London Road , Northwich
CW9 8EE **01606 40681**

Underfloor Heating

UK Underfloor Heating Systems
Unit 14 Riverside Business Park , Wilmslow
SK9 1BJ **01625 460221**

Redheat Limited
26 Princes Park Mansions , Liverpool
L8 3SA **07702 705033**

Vehicle Accident Management and Recovery

FARG - Green
PCLE House , Swinton
M27 9HF **07825 506250**

Tree Work and Surveys

Bergen Tree Services

professional tree care

'excellence should be the standard rather than the exception'

Bergen have been providing professional tree care and vegetation management solutions to customers across the North West since 1990.

From planting a single tree to maintaining an entire woodland or estate, we are qualified and equipped to advise and assist and all our work is carried out in accordance with current legislation and arboricultural industry best practice.

Bergen - competent, professional and impartial advice

- Specialist training provider
- Qualified surveyors
- Weed control specialists
- Green waste processing
- Stump removal
- Winter maintenance service

Andrew C Hancock RFS Cert Arb.

Tel: 01524 782898 Mob: 07771 931193
www.bergentreeservices.co.uk
Email: info@bergentreeservices.co.uk
Lindeth, City o Pinch, Holme, Cumbria. LA6 1QP

Vehicle Washing Equipment
Sales & Service

Tammer T.UK

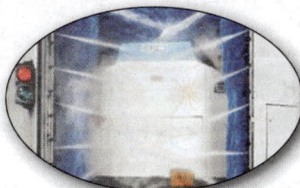

- Truck Washing
- Vehicle Cleaning Chemicals
- Car Wash
- Tanker Cleaning
- Jet Wash Equipment & Mobile Pressure Washers
- Water Recycle & Rainwater Harvesting Systems
- Coach & Bus Wash

TAMMERMATIC group
CLEAN BY NATURE

Please contact us to discuss your vehicle cleaning needs.

Call: 01695 727 994

Tammer UK Ltd
Greenhey Place, Gillibrands, Skelmersdale, Lancashire WN8 9SA
Fax: 01695 724456 Email: sales@tammer.co.uk
www.tammeruk.co.uk

Van Wash   Tractor Wash
Wheel Washers
Vehicle Washing Equipment supplied by Tammer UK

Vehicle Cleaning and Car Washes

Tammer UK Ltd
34 Greenhey Place , Skelmersdale
WN8 9SA **01695 727994**

Vehicle Cleaning Equipment

Tammer UK
34 Greenhey Place , Skelmersdale
Lancashire , WN8 9SA
01695 7281191
john@tammer.co.uk
www.tammeruk.co.uk
(see full page advert for more information)

Vehicle Leasing and Rentals

Go Green Car and Van Rental
10-30 Nantwich Road , Crewe
CW2 6AD **08002 987957**

UK Carline Limited
Sunnybank House , Preston
PR3 0RN **01995 641111**

Website and Internet Services

Marketise
703B Cameron House , Lancaster
LA1 4XF **08444 480444**

**Patrick M Higgins Photography /
Primary Web Design**
Liverpool
L15 7LW **01517 226239**

JG1 Ltd
Unit 5 Penfield Road , Leigh
WN7 3PG **01942 375704**

Wolf Web Solutions
Advantage Business Centre , Manchester
M4 6DE **07825 959074**

SuBBlime WeBB Design
The Granary , Tarvin
CH3 8BE **07812 207571**

Geni-i Creations Ltd
Studio 14 , Bootle
Merseyside , L20 4AP
07704 157872
helen@geni-i.co.uk
www.geni-i.co.uk

Website and Internet Services

Viral Web Consultancy
19 Mathers Street , Bolton
BL4 8AT **07970 880687**

Tsw - Systems Solutions Ltd
3 Padstow Bramhall , Stockport
SK7 2HU **01614 409055**

JSayerWeb Design
17 Hastings Road , Nantwich
CW5 6GL **07912 761729**

Jellis Design
225 Ravenhead Road , St. Helens
WA10 3LR **01744 21246**

Wildlife Protection and Conservation

Ecological Land Management Ltd
Prospect Industrial Estate , Llay
LL12 0PB **07960 570777**

Wind Energy

Gatehouse Renewables
Lancaster Environment Centre , Lancaster
LA1 4YQ **01524 510469**

Window Film

Nu Window Films
2 Hansom Drive , Manchester
M46 0SE **01942 701810**

Reflecta
5 Melbecks , Keswick
CA12 5TL **01768 800193**

Big Green Book UK Ltd
Old Station Building
Oswald Road, Oswestry
Shropshire, SY11 1RE

Biggreen**book**

Solutions to environmental problems exist, but where do you find them?

This is a question that occurred to ecologist, Stephen Lings in 2003, when he was looking to solve some problems for a local company.

So Steve started putting together a database of companies that can help solve all kinds of problems in our environment. Nine years on, that database has grown into one of the UK's largest business membership organisations.

Now when a company wants help to become sustainable they only have to look to one place www.biggreenbook.com.

But if you don't really know what to look for, then the unique **GET A QUOTE** feature of their website allows you to email an expert about your issues and get suitable suppliers contacting you.

It is an incredible free service, and is one that has helped companies, large and small, throughout the UK.

Over 45,000 organisations have used the Big Green Book website in the last year alone and with over 750,000 hits a month it is a highly visited site.

Big Green Book also runs a face-to-face clinic service, travelling around the country and visiting major trade shows and events. Directors from Big Green Book, supported by experts from within the membership, are on hand to answer question about business and the environment.

Currently Big Green Book is on a membership drive, with special deals for companies that sign up to promote their solutions to environmental and sustainability issues.

If you would like more information on how your company can join their team is very approachable and friendly. Just ask for Gary and you will see what we mean.

With over 6,000 companies in 400 categories and sectors, the Big Green Book online directory is the place to start.

Call 01691 661 565
or email sales@biggreenbook.com
www.biggreenbook.com

05

Belfast

THE **GREEN** DIRECTORY

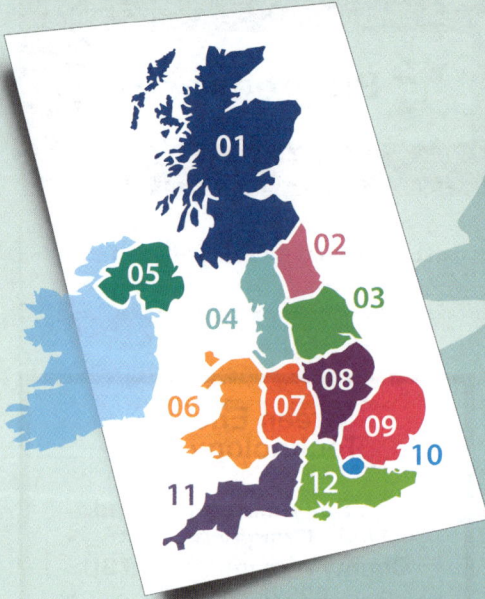

The Business Supporting The Northern Irish Section for the 2012/13 Local Sourcing Directory is:

LOCAL SECTION

THE **GREEN** DIRECTORY

Air Conditioning Systems

AM Air Conditioning
6 Rowallane Dale , Ballynahinch
County Down , BT24 7LE
02897 511574 or 07808 828812
david.porter@btinternet.com

East Coast Cooling
2 Watercrest Road , Newcastle
BT33 0NL **07515 486944**

Air Source Heat Pumps

Daly Renewables Ltd
Rosevale Industrial Estate , Lisburn
BT28 1RW **02892 667745**

Architects

Ctwo Design
Wilson House , Carrickfergus
BT38 8AD **02893 369542**

David Young Architectural Consultant
11 Lettercarn Road , Castlederg
BT81 7QY **02881 679657**

O'Neill Architecture
11 Bellfield , Castlewellan
BT31 9RG **07815 679947**

Chris Spratt Design
5 Grange Avenue . Londonderry
BT47 5YN
07792 757935
info@chrissprattdesign.com
www.chrissprattdesign.com

9yards architecture
Victoria House , Carrickfergus
BT38 8AE **02893 365999**

Modus Architectural
62 Trench Road , Newtownabbey
BT36 4TY **02890 849086**

Dickson Architectural Services
17 Main Street , Newtownards
BT22 2PG **02842 758097**

Dunmurry Design
47 Glenhead Avenue , Dunmurry
BT17 9AX **02890 279810**

Maine Designs
51a Killyless Road , Cullybackey
BT42 1HD **02825 881514**

Catering Equipment and Supplies

Environmental Products & Services Ltd
5 Shepherd's Drive , Newry
BT35 6JQ **02830 833081**

Computer Hardware

Garts Computer Services
7 Glenluce Drive , Belfast
BT4 2QN **07731 492780**

Computer Maintenance

Garts Computer Services
7 Glenluce Drive , Belfast
BT4 2QN **07731 492780**

Computer Services

Stem Systems
37a Mallusk Enterprise Park , Belfast
BT36 4GN **02890 998080**

Asylia Ltd (Lisburn)
64 Hillsborough Road , Lisburn
BT28 1JJ **08008 402039**

Asylia Ltd (Londonderry)
Coleraine , Londonderry
BT **08008 402039**

Erne Computer
65 Riverside Cornagrade , Enniskillen
BT74 6BR **02866 329835**

Computer Sales Direct
39 Ballynahatty Road , Omagh
BT78 1PW **02882 251596**

Garts Computer Services
7 Glenluce Drive , Belfast
BT4 2QN **07731 492780**

Ground Source Heat Pumps

Daly Renewables Ltd
Rosevale Industrial Estate , Lisburn
BT28 1RW **02892 667745**

Insulation

FMN Contracts
115 Coolkill Road , Tynan
BT60 4TA **02837 569777**

Legionella

BWT(NI) Anerobic Digestion Consultancy
23 Shore Street , Donaghdee
BT21 0DS **07989 421512**

Plumbing Services

Environmental Products & Services Ltd
5 Shepherd's Drive , Newry
BT35 6JQ **02830 833081**

Printing, Design and Mailing Services

B.E. Print
29a Charlemont Street , Moy-Dungannon
BT71 7SL **02887 784822**

Promotional Items and Incentives

JWA Promotional Products Ltd
12 Spittal Hill , Coleraine
BT52 2BY **02870 342420**

Solar Panels and Photovoltaics

Twim Ltd t/a Solec Renewables
57 Meadowlands , Newtonabbey
BT37 0UR **07894 473953**

Green Energy Technology Ltd
30a Ballynabragget Road , Craigavon
BT66 7SH **02838 881228**

Altec Solar
88 Dowland Road , Limavady
BT49 0HR **02877 778177**

Solar Water Heating Systems

Daly Renewables Ltd
Rosevale Industrial Estate , Lisburn
BT28 1RW **02892 667745**

Telecommunications

Telecom Systems
The King Building , Belfast
BT5 4GS **02890 998989**

JMC Mobile Ltd
75 Belfast Road , Newry
BT34 1QH **02830 256444**

Timber Frame Buildings

MBC Timber Frame Ltd
Cahir Business Park , Cahir
............**07909 667241**

Town Planning

Chris Spratt Design
5 Grange Avenue , Londonderry
BT47 5YN
07792 757935
info@chrissprattdesign.com
www.chrissprattdesign.com

Waste Water Heat Recovery

shower save

Don't throw £ down the drain
• Save money and Co2
• Pays for itself in 3 years
• No maintenance

T: 028 9334 4488
www.showersave.net

Website and Internet Services

SMK Creations
10 Vionille Way , Belfast
BT5 7SQ **02890 486844**

JMCIT
15 Dunnesmullan Road , Markethill
BT60 1TJ **07921 834936**

Goat Web Design
Bury House , Enniskillen
BT93 1BP **02868 631317**

Omega Digital Ltd
68-72 Newtownards Road , Belfast
BT4 1GW **07843 566114**

Blackthorn Design
43A Knockmoyle Road , Omagh
BT79 7TB **02882 258347**

David Henderson Design
10 Nicholson Road , Kilkeel
BT34 4JN **07742 898311**

Belfast SEO
64 North Parade , Belfast
BT7 2GJ **07708 534364**

THE **GREEN** DIRECTORY

01
02
03
05
04
06 07 08 09 10
11 12

06

Swansea
Cardiff

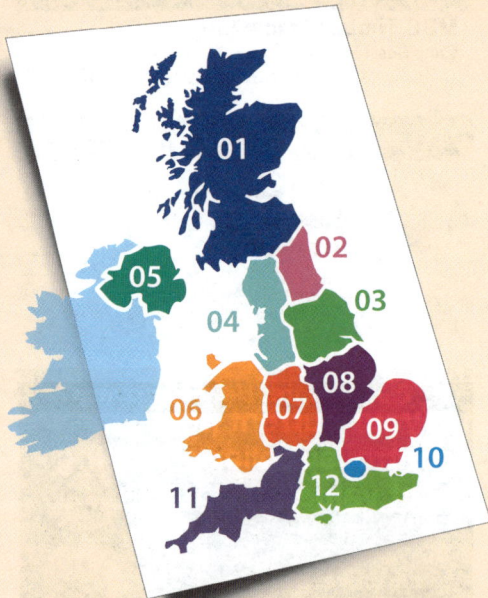

The Business Supporting The Welsh Section for the
2012/13 Local Sourcing Directory is:

Renewable Energy Association
Installer of the Year 2012

Quality installations that earn you maximum returns on your renewable energy system

- ✓ **High performing solutions**
- ✓ **Great financial returns**
- ✓ **Quality certified installations**

Contact us today for a free quote

dulas
inspiring renewable energy
ynni adnewyddadwy ysbrydoledig

3 dulas
YEARS

three decades
of excellence in
renewable energy
engineering

☼ solar ◎ biomass
◊ hydro ❈ wind

01654 705000   info@dulas.org.uk   www.dulas.org.uk   Ref: A70

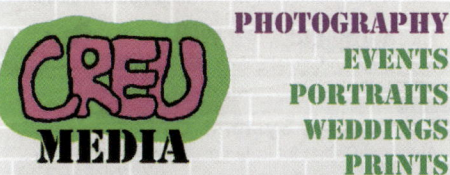

THE GREEN DIRECTORY

Accountancy

N S Accounting Services Ltd
7 Banc-Yr-Afon , Cardiff
CF15 9TU 02920 810668

Brooke-Rankin & Co

**104 High Street , Mold
Clwyd , CH7 1BH**

01352 744963

admin@brooke-rankin.co.uk
www.brooke-rankin.co.uk

**Hart Parry ACCA, Accountants &
Business Advisors**
2 Llys y Fedwen , Bangor
LL57 4BL 01248 360067

Anne Rattue & Co
41 Gladstone Street , Newport
NP11 7PL 01495 270316

Fingertips Business Services
Sun Alliance House ,
Swansea , SA1 4DQ
01792 587353 or 07723 074065
fingertips2@ntlworld.com

Andrew Turford & Co Ltd
33 Stow Park Avenue , Newport
NP20 4FN 01633 214658

Michael A Colley F.C.A
Leicester House , Pembroke
SA71 4DE 01646 682582

Francis Gray
Ty Madog , Aberstwyth
SY23 2HN 01970 625754

Criterion Accounting
37 Oxford Street , Bridgend
CF32 8DD 01656 871195

Davies & John (Powys) Accountants
Commeroe Chambers , Llandrindod Wells
LD1 5DB 01597 824848

Administration and Payroll Software

Cambrian Software (UK) Ltd
43 High Street , Pwllheli
LL53 5RT 08458 620149

Advertising and Promotional Material

Martin Hopkins Partnership Ltd
The Maltings   , Cardiff
CF24 5EA 02920 461233

Air Conditioning Systems

Air-Tech UK Ltd
16 Hop Gardens , Tenby
SA70 8SF 01646 651327

Watts Air Conditioning Ltd
7 Cilgant Y Meillion , Barry
CF62 3LH 07967 806072

F & T Refrigeration Ltd
D C Griffiths Way , Port Talbot
SA11 1BT 01639 634171

M4 Cooling Ltd
6 Tramway Close , Cwmbran
NP44 6US 01633 862442

West Coast Cooling
12 Gilfach Road , Neath
SA10 8EH 01792 793355

Coldpoint Ltd
Cilowen , Pontargothi
SA32 7NE 01267 290382

Blue Mountain Air Conditioning Ltd
Unit 17 Pontnewydd Industrial Estate, Pontypool
NP4 6AD 01495 769922

Air Source Heat Pumps

F & T Refrigeration Ltd
D C Griffiths Way , Port Talbot
SA11 1Bt 01639 634171

Exenergy Ltd
38 Rassau Industrial Estate , Ebbw Vale
NP23 5SD 08005 26107

Cool Energy Systems Uk Ltd
Abernant Centre for Enterprise , Swansea
SA8 4TY 07774 532270

Solar Installations Wales Ltd
The Barn , Port Talbot
SA10 8HD 07855 960752

Air Source Heat Pumps

J W Jones & Son
3-5 Bay View Road , Colwyn Bay
LL29 8DW **01492 531414**

Pearce Elite Plumbing & Heating Ltd
74 St Johns Street , Bridgend
CF32 7BB **01658 863328**

Airport Transfers

Arrow Travel
36 Griffin Drive , Hengoed
CF82 6AH **07806 730041**

Vale Cabs
2 Place , Caeathro
LL55 1SG **01286 676161**

Prestige Cars
56 Fairhill Walk , Torfaen
NP44 4QZ **01633 480480**

Alternative and Renewable Energy

Gemini Solar
Ty'n Y Weirglodd , Caernarfon
Gwynedd , LL55 4AX
01286 650701 or 07876 302484
info@geminisolar.co.uk
www.geminisolar.co.uk

Dulas Ltd
Unit 1 Dyfi Eco Park , Machynlleth
SY20 8AX **01654 705000**

Architects

Llwyd Edwards Architects
The Old Stable , Cardigan
Ceredigion , SA43 1HA
01239 614 365
llwyd.edwards@btconnect.com

(see full page advert for more information)

AGW Architecture
18 Dulais Drive , Neath
West Glamorgan , SA10 8HB
01639 645 179
info@agwarchitects.co.uk
www.agwarchitects.co.uk

Architects

Boccan Ltd
School Lane , Oswestry
Shropshire , SY10 0ET
01691 860435
info@boccan.co.uk
www.boccan.co.uk
(see full page advert for more information)

**Convergence Consultancy
(Cymru) Ltd**
86A Albany Road , Cardiff
CF24 3RS **02920 494772**

WRAY architects
Tan-y-coed , Boduan
LL53 8YE **01758 720635**

Air Architecture
1 Brynmill Terrace , Brynmill
Swansea , SA2 0BA
01792 465584 or
robin.campbell@airarchitecture.co.uk
www.airarchitecture.co.uk

**GERAINT EFANS PENSAER
ARCHITECTS**
Yr Hen Ysgol , Caernarfon
Gwynedd , LL55 3NR
01286 685483
swyddfa@geraintefans.com

Building Design & Surveying Services
15 Beach Road , Porthcawl
CF36 5NH **01656 788606**

FTAA Limited
Torfaen Business Centre , Blaenavon
NP4 9RL **01495 792732**

Ab Iestyn Architect Pensaer RIBA
3 Kingsland Road , Canton
CF5 1HU **02920 318855**

Asbestos Handling and Removal

Pars Ltd
43 Heol Hendre , Rhyl
LL18 5PG **01745 590424**

LLWYD EDWARDS
Chartered Architects
The Old Stables
St Mary Street
Cardigan
Ceredigion
SA43 1HA

Tel: 01239 614 365
Email: llwyd.edwards@btconnect.com

It is imperative that the best use is made of technology to mitigate the worst consequences of Global Warming. Sustainability through built in design will be the most effective method given the short time available.

We have experience through the use of a variety of methods such as 'Heat Recovery' Ground Source, Air Source, Wind and Heat store to reduce the carbon footprint of new development.

As an established business of over 35 years with experience in domestic, commercial, leisure and agricultural developments, we pride our selves in providing a quality service.

sustainability
low ENERGY low CARBON

Llwyd Edwards Architect

THE **GREEN** DIRECTORY

Asbestos Survey and Assesment

ASM Environmental
12 Devon Place , Newport
NP20 4NN **01633 224422**

REC Asbestos Ltd
Unit 19 Kenfig Industrial Estate , Port Talbot
SA13 2PE **01656 749823**

Asbestos Training and Awareness

West Environmental Services Ltd
Unit 5 Park Road Industrial Estate , Newport
NP11 6PU **01633 613882**

ActOn Group
Miskin Manor Estate , Pontyclun
CF72 8ND **08456 436201**

Towner Asbestos Consultancy & Training
65A New Road , Llanelli
Carmarthenshire , SA15 3DS
07875 448162 or 01554 753800
gareth.towner@talktalk.net

Audio Visual

Trytom Ltd
Unit 2 Lon Parcwr Business Park , Ruthin
LL15 1NJ **01824 705003**

Biomass Energy and Biofuels

Dulas Ltd
Unit 1 Dyfi Eco Park , Machynlleth
SY20 8AX **01654 705000**

Castle Heating and Gas Services
9 Bro Gorwel , Newcastle Emlyn
SA38 9PJ **01239 711313**

Branding & Marketing

Martin Hopkins Partnership Ltd
The Maltings , Cardiff
CF24 5EA **02920 461233**

Carpentry and Joinery

**Nick Parkes & Son,
Carpentry & Joinery Services**
Tai-ucha , Conwy
LL32 8UW **01492 650015**

CCTV and Surveillance

3-E Electrical
Gorder Garn , Pwllheli
LL53 5UE **07974 931823**

Cleaning and Hygiene Services

Quality Assured Facility Services Ltd
2 Heol Y Delyn , Cardiff
CF14 0SQ **02920 709670**

Andrew's Cleaning Services
Cherry Tree House , Swansea
SA1 1HE **01792 446368**

Anglesey Contract Cleaning
Old Police House , Bodedern
LL65 3UD **01407 742622**

Computer Maintenance

Cybercure IT Support
17 Powell Close , Pembroke
SA71 4QQ **07765 201292**

Computabilda Ltd
Retail Outlet , Carmarthen
SA31 1QY **01267 233651**

Computer Services

Triple 'E' Recycling Limited
Unit 2 Baglan Energy Park, Neath
SA11 2HZ **01639 822855**

Counselling , Advice and Psychotherapy

Nicola Dunkley Counselling
3 Powell Street , Aberystwyth
.............**01970 832001**

Annie Davis Allen
10 Pantllyn Terrace , Swansea
SA18 3JT **01269 853902**

Ty Eillian
Chirk
.............**01691 778906**

Diana Wellens Counselling

LL11 5UA **07880 510270**

Courier Services

2ulogistics Ltd
HTM Business Park , Rhuddlan
LL18 5UZ **08704 214388**

Display and Exhibition Boards

Jaspa Digital Print
13 The Dell , Bridgend
CF32 0HR **01656 769050**

E-commerce and Search Engine Optimisation (SEO)

New Wave Design Ltd
9 Nevill Street , Abergavenny
NP7 5AA **01873 851225**

Visualcode Ltd
Medley Park , Craven Arms
SY7 9LL **01584 861597**

MJ Software Solutions Ltd
2 Narbeth Close , Newport
NP10 8EE **01633 810543**

Silverfen Web Design
P.O Box 316 ,
Denbighshire , LL18 9GL
01745 583012 or   07729 622374
mail@silverfen-web.com
www.silverfen-web.com

Net Marketing
6 Longhouse Grove , Torfaen
NP44 6HQ **08456 440963**

Daydream Designs
Newlands , Holywell
CH8 8SZ **01352 710054**

Trimast Systems Ltd
7 Oaktree View , Llandrindod Wells
LD1 6HN **01597 851036**

Mandala Designs
Hazeldene , Boncath
SA37 0JW **01239 841381**

Design Four
32 Church Road , Cardiff
CF14 2EA **02920 520205**

Snowdonia IT Services
17 Lon Y Bedw , Bangor
LL57 4TN **07545 808144**

Ecology Surveys and Consultancy

Ecological Land Management
Prospect Industrial Estate , Wrexham
Wales , LL12 0PB
07960 570777
mail@elm.uk.net
www.elm.uk.net
(see half page advert for more information)

Electric & Plug In Vehicle Charging Systems

Charging Solutions Ltd
Border Chase , Nr Alberbury
Powys , SY5 9AN
0843 289 0125 or   07950 750511
info@charging-solutions.com
http://www.charging-solutions.com

Electrical and Electricians

A Lloyd Electrical and Solar
39 Pastoral Way , Swansea
SA2 9LY **01792 205679**

DLR Electrical Contractor
Maesteg Star , Gaerwen
LL60 6AW **01248 712249**

MB-lec Electrical Solutions
6 St. Briavels Mews , Newport
NP10 8SX **08432 892059**

Ivor Rees and Sons Ltd
The Mill , Haverfordwest
SA66 7JY **01437 532326**

NGEC Ltd
Holly Cottage , Frodsham
WA6 6NR **07714 155163**

Peter Sheppard Electrical Services
Oakview , Welshpool
SY21 8NB **01938 580144**

Anthony Pease Electrical
52 Stone Street , Llandovery
SA20 0JW **01550 721971**

3-E Electrical
Gorder Garn , Pwllheli
LL53 5UE **07974 931823**

GKM Electrical Services
23 Wrenwood , Neath
SA10 7PU **01639 501585**

Electrical and Electricians

IGR Electrical
29 Bryn Tirion , Bangor
LL57 3NG 07887 931152

Electrical Maintenance and Installation

Irfon Electrics
Bryn Ifron , Builth Wells
LD2 3HN 01982 552676

Gwendraeth Valley Electrical Services
16 Troed Y Bryn , Llaneli
SA14 6BP 07854 266243

NG Electrical Services Ltd
231 Christchurch Road , Newport
NP19 8BE 01633 278762

EPS Electrical
Y fedw Peppercorn Lane , Brecon
LD3 9EG 01874 625689

JG Electrical
4 Queensway , Haverfordwest
SA61 2PB 07979 535708

Electrical Maintenance and Installation

Richard Kavanagh Electrical Services
Blynderi , Camarthen
SA33 5NN 01994 232978

Gee Cee Electrical and Building Maintenance
37 Southminster Road , Cardiff
CF23 5AT 07721 468701

Serica Electrical
43 Appledore Road , Cardiff
CF14 ....07982 193720

A and B Electrics Ltd
Cae Fedw , Swansea
SA7 9NN 07976 746584

Western Electrical Installations Ltd
53 Glyn Eiddew , Caerphilly
CF83 3PH 07812 997791

Embroidery

Cardiff Embroidery Ltd
34 Bessemer Road , Cardiff
CF11 8BA 02920 224880

Embroidery

Pride of Place (Embroidery) Ltd
Unit 11 Dyffryn Business Park, Ystrad Mynach
CF82 7RY **01443 812726**

Images Design, Print & Embroidery Ltd
1 Sheppard Street , Pontypridd
CF37 1HT **01443 402030**

J's Embroidery
4 Trelawney Square , Flint
Flintshire , CH6 5NN
01352 734636 or 07764 475359
blythinm@gmail.com

Mid Wales Embroidery
Ael Y Bryn , Welshpool
Powys , SY21 0AX
01938 811883
midwales.emb@btinternet.com
www.midwalesembroidery.com

UK Leisure
Kingsbridge Business Park , Gorseinon
SA4 4HJ **01792 897853**

Energy Control

Sustainable Energy & Building Ltd
Glynhelig Villa , Machynlleth
Powys , SY20 8JP
01970 832736 or 07813 107303
info@rsbl.co.uk
www.susbe-ltd.co.uk

Energy Performance Certificates

South Wales Home Inspectors
3 Pen-Y-Wain Place , Cardiff
CF24 4GA **07796 350383**

Cedar Professional Services (UK) Ltd
Crocadwr , Monmouth
NP25 5RY **01989 770400**

Kimberley Gulf
Unit A6 Peblig Industrial Park , Caernarfon
LL55 2SE **01286 672430**

William Morris Energy Assessments
Arvon House , Dolwyddelan
LL24 0NZ **01690 750288**

Environmental Consultancy

Smith Grant LLP
Station House , Ruabon
LL14 6DL **01978 822367**

Occhnet Ltd
Elm Grove , Carmarthen
SA33 5PB **01994 232977**

Estate and Letting Agents

The Letting Company
35 Oxford Street , Bridgend
CF32 8DD **03309 991010**

Exhibition Display Banners

Jaspa Digital Print
13 The Dell , Bridgend
CF32 0HR **01656 769050**

Exhibition Stands

Semaphore (Cardiff) LImited
28 Bessemer Road , Cardiff
CF11 8BA **02920 224111**

Facilities Management

Quality Assured Facility Services Ltd
2 Heol Y Delyn , Cardiff
CF14 0SQ **02920 709670**

Fences, Fencing & Decking

Ark Fencing and Landscaping Supplies Ltd
Phoenix Way , Gorseinon
SA4 9WF **01792 896540**

Fireplaces & Wood Stoves

Sandersons Eco Fuel
Unit 2 The Village Workshops , Four Crosses
SY22 6ST **01691 830075**

Fire Risk Assessment and Training

Atrium
Redwither Tower , Wrexham
LL13 9XT **01978 660000**

EPS Fire Safety Training
34 Chester Road , Deeside
CH5 3LZ **01244 550253**

THE **GREEN** DIRECTORY

Fire Risk Assessment and Training

H & S Compliance Ltd
10 Kingfisher Road , Bridgend
CF33 4NZ **07813 857432**

CS Fire Risk Management
Fernleigh , Ebbw Vale
NP23 6EJ **01495 301975**

Springboard Safety Services
18 Turnberry Avenue , Wrexham
LL13 9GG **07805 112019**

Fire Safety Protection and Equipment

Border Fire Protection
1 Bryn Ucha , Wrexham
LL11 4PL **01978 361384**

Springboard Safety Services
18 Turnberry Avenue , Wrexham
LL13 9GG **07805 112019**

Premier Fire And Safety Services Ltd
7 Maddocks Place , Bridgend
CF1 3BS **01656 649805**

First Aid Training

Atrium
Redwither Tower , Wrexham
LL13 9XT **01978 660000**

Bigfoot Services Limited (ISO9001)
The Shambles , Brecon
LD3 7RH **01874 625077**

Springboard Safety Services
18 Turnberry Avenue , Wrexham
LL13 9GG **07805 112019**

Flooring and Carpets

W S Flooring
Pine Cottage , Knighton
LD7 1SA **01547 529061**

B Smith Carpets
1 Elm Grove , Rhyl
LL18 3PD **01745 336108**

Food Hygiene

Michelle Symes, Health and Safety Consultants
2 Tan Y Foel , Machynlleth
SY20 8SY **07984 501479**

Food Hygiene

Atrium
Redwither Tower , Wrexham
LL13 9XT **01978 660000**

Gas and Central Heating (Domestic)

Pritchard Services 2011 Ltd
Hill Street Industrial Estate , Cwmbran
NP44 7PG **01633 740741**

Graphic Design

Sugar Salt Media
17 Gwynt Mews , Cardiff
CF11 9LZ **07972 610393**

Plum Design & Advertising Ltd
The Old Green Store , Swansea
SA5 7JD **01792 701937**

Suburbia Design & Communications
The Malt House , Regent Street
LL20 8HS **01978 860307**

Bigger Boat Marketing Communications Ltd
Dolargae Barn , Welshpool
SY21 8BQ **01686 640784**

Annakristen Ltd
Belmont Villas , Denbigh
LL1 63SN ....**08448 843044(**

Green Roofing

AAC Waterproofing Ltd
Industrial Estate , Angelsey
LL60 6HR **01248 421955**

Ground Source Heat Pumps

Solar Installations Wales Ltd
The Barn , Port Talbot
SA10 8HD **07855 960752**

Habitat Management.

Ecological Land Management Ltd
Prospect Industrial Estate , Llay
Wrexham , LL12 0PB
07970 570777
mail@elm.uk.net
www.elm.uk.net
(see half page advert for more information)

Habitat Management.

Ecological Land Management
Conservation & Wildlife Protection
www.elm.uk.net

Rheoli Tir Ecolegol
Cadwraeth a Gwarchod Bywyd Gwyllt
www.elm.uk.net

Woodland felling

Meadow Management

Newt Fencing

Badger Fencing

Wetland Management

· Providing nature reserve and protected species management from our base in North East Wales

· A deep understanding of countryside management, ecology & wildlife law

· An established close working relationship with government licensing agencies

· An ability to understand & implement our clients expectations on time & on budget

Pond Creation

Platforms

G.C.N. Surveys

For more information, contact
Phil Pearce on: 01978 800 193
Or Email: mail@elm.uk.net

THE GREEN DIRECTORY

Health and Safety

Springboard Safety Services
18 Turnberry Avenue , Wrexham
Clwyd , LL13 9GG
07805 112019 or   0771 889 8510
mail@springboardsafetyservices.com
www.springboardsafetyservices.com

Atrium
Redwither Tower , Wrexham
LL13 9XT 01978 660000

CDM Consulting Ltd
Ashdene , Alltami
Flintshire , CH7 6SB
01244 550169 or   07747 800811
mail@cdmconsultingltd.co.uk
cdmconsultingltd.co.uk

JCT
12 Water Street , Pembroke
SA72 6DN 01646 685376

EPS Fire Safety Training
34 Chester Road , Deeside
CH5 3LZ 01244 550253

Health and Safety

H and S Compliance Ltd
10 Kingfisher Road , Bridgend
Glamorgan , CF33 4NZ
07813 857432
allan.charles@hotmail.co.uk
www.handscomplianceltd.co.uk
(see full page advert for more information)

Michelle Symes, Health and Safety Consultants
2 Tan Y Foel , Machynlleth
SY20 8SY 07984 501479

Occhnet Ltd
Elm Grove , Carmarthen
SA33 5PB 01994 232977

LOCAL SECTION **Wales**

THE **GREEN** DIRECTORY

Heat Recovery and Ventilation Systems

Sustainable Energy & Building Ltd
Glynhelig Villa , Machynlleth
Powys , SY20 8JP
01970 832736 or 07813 107303
info@rsbl.co.uk
www.susbe-ltd.co.uk

Insulation

Exenergy Ltd
38 Rassau Industrial Estate , Ebbw Vale
NP23 5SD 08005 26107

Sustainable Energy & Building Ltd
Glynhelig Villa , Machynlleth
Powys , SY20 8JP
01970 832736 or 07813 107303
info@rsbl.co.uk
www.susbe-ltd.co.uk

Excel Industries Ltd
Maerdy Industrial Estate , Rhymney
NP22 5PY 01685 845200

Landscaping and Ground Maintenance

My Tidy Garden
1 Plassey Close , Wrexham
LL13 9Gt 07931 158398

Ark Fencing and Landscaping Supplies Ltd
Phoenix Way , Gorseinon
SA4 9WF 01792 896540

Low Energy Building

Ty Afal Design Ltd
Bryn Afal , Welshpool
SY22 6HT 01938 500899

Low Energy Lightbulbs, Lighting and L.E.D.

Sustainable Energy & Building Ltd
Glynhelig Villa , Machynlleth
Powys , SY20 8JP
01970 832736 or 07813 107303
info@rsbl.co.uk
www.susbe-ltd.co.uk

Modular Buildings

Ty Afal Design Ltd
Bryn Afal , Welshpool
SY22 6HT 01938 500899

Noise and Vibration Testing

Robin Mackenzie Partnership Ltd
42 Collington Road , Edinburgh
EH10 5BT 01315 573327

Office And Retail Furniture

Sandersons Fine Furniture & Joinery Ltd
1,5 &6 The Village Workshops , Four Cross
SY22 6ST 01691 830075

Office Cleaning and Cleaning Services

Quality Assured Facility Services Ltd
2 Heol Y Delyn , Cardiff
CF14 0SQ 02920 709670

Office Supplies

Swallow Office Supplies
58 Pendre , Cardigan
SA43 1JR 01239 621500

Office/Shop Fitters

Clansmen Joiners and Shopfitters Ltd
25 Maes Becca , Llanelli
SA14 6AX 07736 104486

Painting and Decorating

Haydn Adams. Painter & Decorator
10 Queen Street , Llandovery
SA20 0BU 01550 721754

J T Painter & Decorator
10 Cwm Yfstrad Parc , Carmarthen
SA31 3NZ 07891 832316

LDC Painters
21 The Twinings , Cwmbran
NP44 4ST 07895 944879

Ian Richards Decorating and BuildingMaintenance
54 Daphne Road , Neath
SA10 8DU 07970 409402

K & J Decorators
18A West Hook Road , Haverfordwest
SA62 4LS 07967 408432

Painting and Decorating

Longshanks
83 Shakespear Avenue , Milford Haven
SA73 2JJ 01646 692281

Nathan's Decorating Service
20 Crescent Road , Ammanford
SA18 1HL 01269 492053

Viv Morris
154 Llanrumney Avenue , Cardiff
CF3 4EA 07786 592080

Berwyn Painters
1Ceibiog Cottage , Corwen
LL21 0PH 07856 360330

Neil Jones Decorating Specialist
3 Oakridge Drive , Llandrindod Wells
LD1 5EW 01597 829202

Partitioning Services

Ombler Williams Ltd
Builders Street , Llandudno
LL30 1DR 01492 860603

Payroll and Bookkeeping

Inforstat
20 Hoel Ger-Y-Felin , Llanwit Major
CF61 2XA 01446 794600

Business Beacon
33 Cae Rhos , Caerphilly
CF83 3JG 07837 807646

Nick Price Bookkeeping Services
35 Holbrook Road , Haverfordwest
SA62 3HZ 01437 781064

Dorrell Oliver Ltd
Linden House , Abergavenny
NP7 5NF 01873 852113

Oxley Accountants Ltd
Greyhound Building , Chepstow
NP16 5DB 01291 627613

Karen Rogers Chartered Accountants
16 Llantarnam Drive , Cardiff
CF15 8GA 02920 024630

Groves Davey Chartered Accountants
34 Wellfield Road , Cardiff
CF24 3PB 02920 482622

Francis Gray
Ty Madog , Aberstwyth
SY23 2HN 01970 625754

Payroll and Bookkeeping

Andrew Turford & Co Ltd
33 Stow Park Avenue , Newport
NP20 4FN 01633 214658

YDH Ltd
71 Pen Y Bryn Road , Colwyn Bay
LL29 6NN 01492 532222

Pest Control

Rid-It Pest Control
Trebeoth Fach , Fishguard
SA65 9QT 01348 431556

MITIE Pest Control
3 Oaktree Court , Cardiff
CF23 8RS 08450 171069

Pest Force (Pembrokeshire)
26 Milton Close , Haverfordwest
SA61 1SW 01437 765732

Pest Force North Wales
20 Tegid Drive , New Broughton
LL11 6QA 07766 318119

General Pest Control
27 Traston Road , Newport
NP19 4RQ 01633 275996

G A Howell and Sons
Baiden Farm , Bridgend
CF32 0BS 01656 740379

B Firm Pest Control
30 Coopers , Ammanford
SA18 3SN 01269 594761

Dragon Pest Control
Canol Y Stryd , Treorchy
CF42 6UU 07852 527531

P Morris Pest & Vermin Control
Ty Derwen Bach , Dyffryn
LL15 2EP 01824 704067

Aderyn Pest Control
61 Trealaw Road , Tonypandy
CF40 2NR 0845 5192486

Physiotherapy

Andrew Seary Chartered Physiotherapy
The Coach House , Whitchurch
CF14 1AA **07802 454589**

Portable Appliance and Fixed Wire Testing

Touchscreen
3 Dovedale Close , Cardiff
CF23 5LS **02920 481543**

PAT 4U
54 Commercial Street , Swansea
SA9 1JH **07976 714443**

D.J Electrical Consultants Ltd
2 Chatsworth Drive , Wrexham
LL11 4XD **01978 661011**

NWPT
Lyons Winkups Holiday Park , Conwy
LL22 9EL **01745 222045**

Earth Connection
Argraig , Amlwch
LL68 9RU **01407 831473**

Print Management

AA Media. Print & Media Management
The Coach House , Penarth
CF64 2LA **02920 003846**

Printing, Design and Mailing Services

Pembrokeshire and Canine Press
6 High Street , Fishguard
SA6 9AR **01348 218027**

Creative Images
Brackig , Bridgend
CF31 2JF **01656 645110**

Stephens & George Print Group
Goat Mill Road , Merthyr Tydfill
CF48 3TD **01685 388888**

C S M Printing Services
Unit 36 Bowen Industrial Estate , Caerphilly
CF81 9EP **01443 875086**

Rhymney Print Services
Unit 5/6 The Lawn Industrial Estate , Tredegar
NP22 5PW **01685 841321**

K C Graphics Printers
The Croft , Wrexham
LL11 5HG **01978 752197**

Printing, Design and Mailing Services

Cynlluniau Dysynni Designs
Godrer Graig , Tywyn
LL36 9LP **01654 710930**

Gwasg Teifi Press
32 Feidrfair , Cardigan
SA43 1EB **01239 614051**

Dalton Printers
Dalton House , Cardiff
CF24 4BN **02920 236832**

Promotional Items and Incentives

MR Products
94a Greenfield Business Centre , Holywell
CH8 7GR **01352 717917**

Property Maintenance

Quality Assured Facility Services Ltd
2 Heol Y Delyn , Cardiff
CF14 0SQ **02920 709670**

NP Construction and Landscaping
6 Clos Llywellyn , Cardiff
CF15 7AT **02920 813205**

Recycling

Dyfed Recycling Services
Dafen Industrial Estate , Llanelli
SA149RQ **01554 772478**

Refrigeration

Watts Air Conditioning Ltd
7 Cilgant Y Meillion , Barry
CF62 3LH **07967 806072**

F & T Refrigeration Ltd
D C Griffiths Way , Port Talbot
SA11 1BT **01639 634171**

West Coast Cooling
12 Gilfach Road , Neath
SA10 8EH **01792 793355**

Safety Risk Assessment

H & S Compliance Ltd
10 Kingfisher Road , Bridgend
CF33 4NZ 07813 857432

Screen and T Shirt Printing

Carian
The Caban , Blaenau Ffestiniog
LL41 3UN 01766 830838

Secretarial Service

Hi-Tech Secretarial Services Limited
13 Camddwr Rise , Llandrindod Wells
LD1 5BF 01597 823375

Signs and Graphics

Jaspa Digital Print
13 The Dell , Bridgend
CF32 0HR 01656 769050

Atlantic Hardware
Unit B Entrec Site , Wrexham
LL13 9RD 01978 660729

d3Signs
85 Woodstock Gardens , Bridgend
CF35 6ST 07702 422490

Complete Signs & Graphics
Unit 10 The Quarry , Welshpool
SY21 7NA 01938 556695

Eagle Signs of St Clears
Unit 3 & 4 Parc Tiron , Carmarthen
SA33 4BN 01994 231749

A B Sign Writing
4 Maes yr Eglwys , Caersws
SY17 5LA 07813 105119

Andrew Bromley Sign Writing
4 Maes Yr Eglwys , Caersws
Powys , SY17 5LA
07813 105119 or 01686 688112
absignwriting@tiscali.co.uk
www.absignwriting.co.uk

Stik-It
New Road , Hengoed
CF82 8AU 01443 821917

Skips and Skip Hire

Dyfed Recycling Services
Dafen Industrial Estate , Llanelli
SA149RQ 01554 772478

Skips and Skip Hire

A Lewis Skip Hire Ltd
Milfraen View , Nantyglo
NP23 4PQ 01495 310438

Solar Energy

3-E Electrical
Gorder Garn , Pwllheli
LL53 5UE 07974 931823

Paul O'Brien Solar Installations
Unit 6 Brookgate , Bristol
BS3 2UN 01179 533234

Gemini Solar
Ty'n Y Weirglodd , Caernarfon
Gwynedd , LL55 4AX
01286 650701 or 07876 302484
info@geminisolar.co.uk
www.geminisolar.co.uk

Solar Panels and Photovoltaics

Dulas Ltd
Unit 1 Dyfi Eco Park , Machynlleth
SY20 8AX 01654 705000

DLR Electrical Contractor
Maesteg Star , Gaerwen
LL60 6AW 01248 712249

Dick Manteuffel & Son Ltd
Dugoed , Boncath
SA37 0LW 01239 698286

AP Electrical & Renewable Energy Ltd
Unit 4 Seawall Court, Cardiff
CF24 5TH 02920 495791

Solar Installations Wales Ltd
The Barn , Port Talbot
SA10 8HD 07855 960752

Cool Energy Systems UK Ltd
Abernant Centre for Enterprise , Pontardawe
SA8 4TY 07774 532270

A Lloyd Electrical and Solar
39 Pastoral Way , Swansea
SA2 9LY 01792 205679

**Renewable Energy Installations Ltd
t/a Solar Harvester**
Mor Olwg , Amlwch
LL68 9ND 01407 831377

Gwres Glas-Green Heat
Brynawelon , Llanfair Caereinion
SY21 0BL 01938 552020

Solar Panels and Photovoltaics

Pearce Elite Plumbing & Heating Ltd
74 St Johns Street , Bridgend
CF32 7BB **01658 863328**

Solar Water Heating Systems

Gemini Solar
Ty' N Y Weirglodd , Caernarfon
Wales , LL55 4AX
01286 650701
dave@geminisolar.co.uk
www. geminisolar.co.uk
(see half page advert for more information)

Paul O'Brien Solar Installations
Unit 6 Brookgate , Bristol
BS3 2UN **01179 533234**

Cosywarm Heating & Plumbing
112C The Philog , Cardiff
CF14 1ED **02920 615111**

Cool Energy Systems UK Ltd
Abernant Centre for Enterprise , Pontardawe
SA8 4TY **07774 532270**

Solar Water Heating Systems

Solar Installations Wales Ltd
The Barn , Port Talbot
SA10 8HD **07855 960752**

Exenergy Ltd
38 Rassau Industrial Estate , Ebbw Vale
NP23 5SD **08005 26107**

Sustainable Energy & Building Ltd
Glynhelig Villa , Machynlleth
Powys , SY20 8JP
01970 832736 or   07813 107303
info@rsbl.co.uk
www.susbe-ltd.co.uk

Staff and Work Wear

Cardiff Embroidery Ltd
34 Bessemer Road , Cardiff
CF11 8BA **02920 224880**

U Design Ltd
129 Bute Street , Treorchy
CF42 6BB **01443 776661**

Solar Water Heating Systems

THE **GREEN** DIRECTORY

Suspended Ceilings - Installation and Manufacture

Ombler Williams Ltd
Builders Street , Llandudno
LL30 1DR **01492 860603**

Taxi and Private Hire

Abacus Taxis (Wales)
99 Foryd Road , Rhyl
LL18 5LU **01745 360054**

Georges Taxis
Nyddfa Yard , Blackwood
NP12 3UZ **01443 832874**

Eco Taxi
Fenton Home Farm , Haverfordwest
SA62 4PY **07857 275217**

Johns Taxis
39 Heol Dinas , Aberystwyth
SY23 3SB **01970 627139**

Stanways Taxis Pwllheli
Arley House , Pwllheli
LL53 5PN **07788 788044**

Telecommunications

Pace Telecom Ltd
Unit 2 Zenith House , Wrexham
LL12 8LX **01978 858585**

Marina Telecom
Cherry Tree House , Swansea
SA1 1HE **01437 760200**

Faces UK Ltd T/A Beta Telecoms
16 Bulwark Avenue , Chepstow
NP16 5QG **01291 620189**

Timber Frame Buildings

ADEPT Consulting (UK) Ltd
Riverside Court , Chepstow
NP16 5UH **01291 635522**

Benfield Advanced Timberframe Technology
1 Symondscliffe Way , Caldicot
Monmouthshire , NP26 5PW
01291 437 050
prof.b@benfieldattgroup.co.uk
www.simplyselfbuild.co.uk
(see full page advert for more information)

Timber Frame Buildings

Castle Gates
Castle Ring Wood , Presteigne
LD8 2PB **01547 560231**

Crossframes
31 Brook Estate , Monmouth
NP25 5AN **01600 711675**

Town Planning

Llwyd Edwards Architects
The Old Stable , Cardigan
Ceredigion , SA43 1HA
01239 614 365
llwyd.edwards@btconnect.com

(see full page advert for more information)

Tree Work and Surveys

Mighty Oaks Tree Solutions
34 Nantgarw Road , Caerphilly
CF 83 3FB **02920 863635**

Cambrian Woodland Services
20 Parc Alafowlia , Denbigh
LL16 CH2 ....**07753 662938**

Anderson Tree Specialists Ltd
Penysgynfa Cottage , Dolgellau
LL40 2LU **01341 421415**

Lampeter Tree Services
Gwel-Y-Coed , Lampeter
SA48 8EL **01570 422819**

Tops Services
The Old Police Station , Lloc
CH8 8RD **01352 715996**

Clive Francis Tree Care

8 Western Road , Abergavenny Monmouthshire , NP7 7AA

01873 859273

clive4trees@gmail.com

LLWYD EDWARDS
Chartered Architects
The Old Stables
St Mary Street
Cardigan
Ceredigion
SA43 1HA

Tel: 01239 614 365
Email: llwyd.edwards@btconnect.com

It is imperative that the best use is made of technology to mitigate the worst consequences of Global Warming. Sustainability through built in design will be the most effective method given the short time available.

We have experience through the use of a variety of methods such as 'Heat Recovery' Ground Source, Air Source, Wind and Heat store to reduce the carbon footprint of new development.

As an established business of over 35 years with experience in domestic, commercial, leisure and agricultural developments, we pride our selves in providing a quality service.

Page 277

sustainability
low ENERGY low CARBON

Llwyd Edwards Architect

THE **GREEN** DIRECTORY

Underfloor Heating

GES Underfloor Heating Systems Ltd
Pentre Meurig Road , Carmarthen
SA33 6AA **01267 237920**

Pearce Elite Plumbing & Heating Ltd
74 St Johns Street , Bridgend
CF32 7BB **01658 863328**

Universal Construction Products

Dragonboard
Grosvenor House , Mold
CH7 1EJ **01352 700088**

Ventilation and Filtration

F & T Refrigeration Ltd
D C Griffiths Way , Port Talbot
SA11 1Bt **01639 634171**

Waste Management and Disposal

Dyfed Recycling Services
Dafen Industrial Estate , Llanelli
SA149RQ **01554 772478**

Website and Internet Services

Net Marketing
6 Longhouse Grove ,
Torfaen , NP44 6HQ
0845 644 0963
enquiries@nmuk.com
www.nmuk.com

Jerboa Design
Grofield , Abergavenny
NP7 5BB **08000 432190**

Selina Taylor Web Design
The Gables , Swansea
SA3 1PH **01792 390339**

Visualcode Ltd
Medley Park , Craven Arms
SY7 9LL **01584 861597**

DASO Interactive Development
LLwyn Leloc , Rhayader
LD6 5LT **01597 810248**

Tasty Code Website Creation
20 Llys Gwyrdd , Cwmbran
NP44 7LS **01633 875752**

Bay View Systems Ltd
215 Technium Digital , Swansea
SA2 8PP **01792 602566**

Website and Internet Services

Distinct Graphics
51 St. Kingsmark Avenue , Chepstow
NP16 5LY **08007 101502**

IB Computing
IB Computing , Llanarth
SA47 0NN **01545 558158**

MJ Software Solutions Ltd
2 Narbeth Close , Newport
NP10 8EE **01633 810543**

Wildlife Protection and Conservation

Ecological Land Management Ltd
Prospect Industrial Estate , Llay
LL12 0PB **07960 570777**

Wind Energy

Dulas Ltd
Unit 1 Dyfi Eco Park , Machynlleth
SY20 8AX **01654 705000**

Sustainergy
Fronhaul , Newport
SA42 0QG **01239 821120**

Enegis
10 Banbury Road , Stratford Upon Avon
CV37 7HZ **08456 861846**

Window Film

Stik-it Window Films
New Road , Hengoed
CF8 2AU **01443 821917**

Madol Ltd
Unit 4 Quay Point , Cardiff
CF24 5HF **02920 467100**

Wood Recycling and Waste

Sandersons Eco Fuel
Unit 2 The Village Workshops , Four Crosses
SY22 6ST **01691 830075**

Reseiclo Community Wood Recycling
Unit 2 Harlequin Trading Estate, Newport
NP20 5NH **01633 856622**

Big Green Book UK Ltd
Old Station Building
Oswald Road, Oswestry
Shropshire, SY11 1RE

Solutions to environmental problems exist, but where do you find them?

This is a question that occurred to ecologist, Stephen Lings in 2003, when he was looking to solve some problems for a local company.

So Steve started putting together a database of companies that can help solve all kinds of problems in our environment. Nine years on, that database has grown into one of the UK's largest business membership organisations.

Now when a company wants help to become sustainable they only have to look to one place www.biggreenbook.com.

But if you don't really know what to look for, then the unique GET A QUOTE feature of their website allows you to email an expert about your issues and get suitable suppliers contacting you.

It is an incredible free service, and is one that has helped companies, large and small, throughout the UK.

Over 45,000 organisations have used the Big Green Book website in the last year alone and with over 750,000 hits a month it is a highly visited site.

Big Green Book also runs a face-to-face clinic service, travelling around the country and visiting major trade shows and events. Directors from Big Green Book, supported by experts from within the membership, are on hand to answer question about business and the environment.

Currently Big Green Book is on a membership drive, with special deals for companies that sign up to promote their solutions to environmental and sustainability issues.

If you would like more information on how your company can join their team is very approachable and friendly. Just ask for Gary and you will see what we mean.

With over 6,000 companies in 400 categories and sectors, the Big Green Book online directory is the place to start.

Call 01691 661 565
or email sales@biggreenbook.com
www.biggreenbook.com

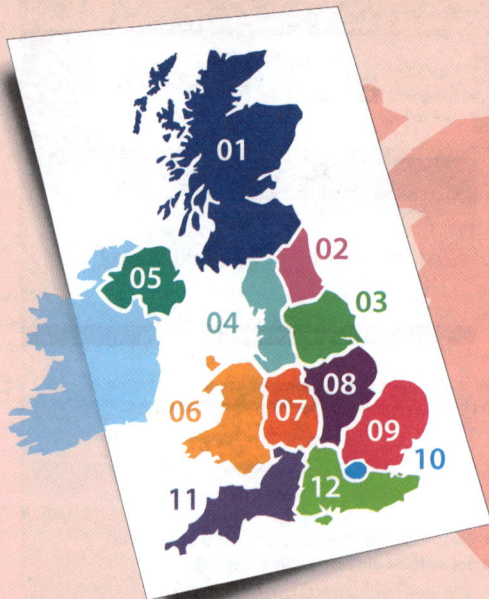

Shrewsbury

Birmingham

07

Accountancy

Robert Powell. Chartered Accountant
A4 Spinnaker House , Gloucester
GL2 5FD **01452 527700**

Hampton & Co
Canalside Office Complex , Worcester
WR1 2RS **01905 25464**

Suretax Accounting
279 Leamington Road , Coventry
West Midlands , CV3 6NB
02476 697300 or 07850 898178
msparrow@suretax.co.uk
www.suretax.co.uk

C M Watson & Co Ltd
Cromwell House , Cannock
Staffordshire , WS11 0DP
01543 577 377
clive.watson3@yahoo.co.uk
www.accountantsincannock.co.uk

Regency Chartered Management Accoutants
8 Richmond Terrace , Stoke-on-Trent
ST1 4ND **01782 286334**

Ramar & Co
2 Whitridge Way , Oswestry
SY10 9FB **01691 655678**

Thorpe Thompson
2 Tettenhall Road, Wolverhampton
NV1 4SA **01902 713477**

Joe Martin Business Services
11 Green Meadows , Cheltenham
GL51 6SN **01452 859057**

Julia Walters Chartered Accountants
The Dairy Bookwell Lane , Rugby
CV25 0BJ **01788 569005**

Hayward Accounting Services
6 Terry Ruck Close , Cheltenham
Gloucestershire , GL51 0XR
01242 698661
anna@haywardaccountingservices.co.uk
www.haywardaccountingservices.co.uk

MM Accountancy Services
205 Kings Road, Birmingham
B11 2AP **01217 070711**

Accreditation and Certification

The Quensh Consultancy
435 Holyhead Road , Coventry
CV5 8HS **02476 599503**

Air Conditioning Systems

Green Man Environmental Services Ltd
Mill House , Dymock
GL18 2BL **01531 890685**

Airtech UK Ltd
Unit 3A Pole Position , Sutton Coldfield
B75 5SA **01213 081447**

AGS Technical Solutions
Brywood House , Solihull
B91 2JU **01217 052000**

Temp Air Solutions Ltd
7 Bottrill Court , Nuneaton
Warwickshire , CV11 5JS
02476421380 or 02476352300
info@tempairsolutions.co.uk
www.tempairsolutions.co.uk

Jones Air Conditioning
Rivermead , Gloucester
Gloucestershire , GL2 9AB
01452 561179
tim@jonesairconditioning.co.uk

(see full page advert for more information)

RMV Cooling Services
The Relm, Alderton , Shrewsbury
SY4 1AP **01743 4741236**

CPL Response Ltd
11 Paper Mill , Birmingham
West Midlands , B44 8NH
0800 118 2503
markpritchard@cpl-group.co.uk
www.cpl-group.co.uk
(see full page advert for more information)

PJ Refrigeration
5 Castle Close , Tenbury Wells
WR15 8AY **01584 819881**

MG Cooling Services Ltd
19 Norman Road , Birmingham
B31 2ES **07771 966839**

WELCOME TO JONES AIR CONDITIONING

At Jones Air Conditioning all of our engineers are qualified to City&Guilds Level 3 and are 2079 Refrigerant Handling Certified.
We also offer a wide range of air-conditioning services and below are some of the main services we are able to support and offer.

- Service and repairs to all air conditioning systems
- Air conditioning maintenance
- Air conditioning installation
- Technical Support

SERVICE AND MAINTENANCE

Jones Air Conditioning offer Service & Maintenance contracts designed to keep your equipment running smoothly and efficiently throughout the year. Our service support is available 365 days a year, 24 hours a day. We have fully equipped vehicles enabling us to attend breakdowns within a 4 hours response.

Some of the benefits of a regular maintenance are:

- Increases system life span
- Increases energy efficiency
- Cleaner, more aesthetically pleasing equipment
- Effectiveness of system enhanced
- Help reduce your monthly electricity bill

OUR MISSION

At Jones Air Conditioning our mission is to keep your air conditioning system running safely and efficiently throughout the year and to provide you with our technical support 24/365.

CONTACT US

Office:	01452 561179 **Mobile:** 07904 976933
Fax:	01452 546501
Email:	info@jonesairconditioning.co.uk
Address:	Jones Air Conditioning Ltd
	Rivermead
	Sandhurst Lane
	Gloucester
	GL2 9AB

Air Conditioning Systems

Pure Air Conditioning
Unit 4 New Brook Business Park , Mansfield
NG20 8GB **01623 741004**

Air Source Heat Pumps

Nu-Heat UK Ltd
Heathpark House , Honiton
EX14 1SD **01404 549770**

Robert R Mcgowan Ltd
4 Campbell Road , Hereford
HR1 1JE **01432 356984**

EZ Solar
Ditton Mill House , Cleobury Mortimer
Shropshire , DY14 0DH
01299 270011
sales@ezsolar.co.uk
www.ezsolar.co.uk

Viessmann Limited
Hortonwood 30 , Telford
Shropshire , TF1 7YP
01952 675000
info-uk@viessmann.com
www.viessmann.co.uk

Pure Air Conditioning
Unit 4 New Brook Business Park , Mansfield
NG20 8GB **01623 741004**

Alternative and Renewable Energy

CD Electrical Design & Installation Ltd
Unit 11 Ptarmigan Place , Nuneaton
CV11 6RX **08008 498110**

Green Whale Energy Ltd
212-222 Hagley Road West , Birmingham
B68 0NP **01212 225120**

Worcester Bosch Group
Cotswold Way , Wardon
WR4 9SN **08448 929900**

Architects

Edge Design Workshop Ltd
Royal Mews , Cheltenham
Gloucestershire , GL50 3PQ
01242 528 111 or 07595 218 104
jdp@edgedesignworkshop.com
www.edgedesignworkshop.com

Architects

Macona Architects Ltd
53 Warwick Street , Coventry
Warwickshire , CV5 6ET
07969 831 211 or 07411 132 947
clive@cdrarchitects.co.uk
www.maconaarchitects.co.uk

**JBD Architects RIBA,
Chartered Practice**
Lea House , Worcester
WR3 8JE **01905 611667**

Tesha Ltd
4 Hazeley , Birmingham
B17 8AY **01214 294056**

Synergy Architects Ltd
8 Euston Place , Leamington Spa
CV32 4LN **01926 450391**

**David Yarnall, MCIAT
Architectural Services**
Heather Bank , Upper Longdon
WS15 1QE **01543 491205**

Masefields Architects and Surveyors
Studley Point , Studley
B80 7AS **01216 282332**

**CSB Architects -
CSB Architectural Designs**
47 Priest Meadow , Redditch
B96 6HT **01527 893940**

YAPP Design Limited
126 Station Road , Birmingham
B30 1DB **01214 582886**

David Rudge Associates
Green Farm Cottage , Rugely
Staffordshire , WS15 3QG
01889 223388
davidrudgeassociates@hotmail.co.uk
www.davidrudgeassociates.com
(see full page advert for more information)

Asbestos Handling and Removal

Maylarch Recycling Ltd
Andoversford Industrial Estate , Cheltenham
GL54 4LB **01242 821450**

THE **GREEN** DIRECTORY

THE **GREEN** DIRECTORY

Asbestos Training and Awareness

Asbestos Surveying Limited
Vernon Place , Birmingham
B16 9SQ **01212 462526**

Audio Visual

Agnito
Miller's Barn , Lechlade
GL7 3NP **01865 524524**

Integrated Audio Visual
Unit 8 Amherst Business Centre , Warwick
CV34 5XH **01926 499800**

Backing Gates

Fabdec Limited
Grange Road , Ellesmere
SY12 9DG **01691 627210**

Biomass Energy and Biofuels

EZ Solar
Ditton Mill House , Cleobury Mortimer
Shropshire , DY14 0DH
01299 270011
sales@ezsolar.co.uk
www.ezsolar.co.uk

Viessmann Limited
Hortonwood 30 , Telford
Shropshire , TF1 7YP
01952 675000
info-uk@viessmann.com
www.viessmann.co.uk

Ecovision Systems Ltd
Barley Court , Tetbury
GL8 8TQ **01666 501580**

Worcester Bosch Group
Cotswold Way , Wardon
WR4 9SN **08448 929900**

Boilers and Water Heaters

Fabdec Limited
Grange Road , Ellesmere
SY12 9DG **01691 627210**

Broadband

Utility Bill Money Saver.com
332 Marsh Lane , Birmingham
West Midlands , B23 6HP
0121 377 6600 or 07961 746 519
andrewdakin@utilitywarehouse.org.uk
www.utilitybillmoneysaver.com

Builders Merchants

E H Smith
Westhaven House , Solihull
West Midlands , B90 4NH
0121 713 7100
mark.mallinder@ehsmith.co.uk
www.sustainablebuildingmaterials.co.uk
(see full page advert for more information)

Jewson Ltd
Merchant House , Coventry
CV3 2TT **08005 39766**

Building Integrated Photovoltaics(BIPV)

Worcester Bosch Group
Cotswold Way , Wardon
WR4 9SN **08448 929900**

Business Management, Coaching and Consultancy

First Success Partnership
6 Sugarloaf Close , Malvern
WR14 1FQ **08006 226033**

Forever
Acacia House , Cirencester
Gloucestershire , GL7 6AZ
01285 898 093
info@mandie-cran.info
www.mandiecran.flppro.biz

Positive Management Services
17 Whitbourne Hall , Worcester
WR6 5SE **01886 822222**

IPT Business Development
The Cedars , Lechlade
GL7 3DL **01367 253780**

Canals and Waterways

The Planning Company
51 Battenhall Rise , Worcester
WR5 2DE **01905 360277**

Carpentry and Joinery

Doors to Floors
Telford
TF4 3RE **01952 591575**

RPM
18 Baker Street , Walsall
WS7 4QD **07977 149653**

Heritage Oak Builders
The Old Mill , Shrewsbury
SY5 9HQ **01743 891638**

Craig Hancock Joinery
106 Riceymon Road , Newcastle Under Lyme
ST5 8LH **07786 437162**

Mark Massey Carpentry
340 Blenheim Road , Kingswinford
DY6 8SL **01384 76967**

Chauffeur Services

PRL Executives
East Road , Wolverhampton
WV10 7NP **01902 798766**

Cleaning and Hygiene Services

J B Cleaning Services
7 Battisson Crescent , Stoke on Trent
Staffordshire , ST3 4DS
0800 4346282 or 01782 311333
john@jb-cleaningservices.com
www.jb-cleaningservices.com

Ultra Clean Oswestry Ltd
Glovers Meadow , Oswestry
SY10 8NH **01691 880827**

Regent Office Care Ltd
Unit 2 Oak Court , Coventry
CV6 4QH **02476 339890**

Cleaning Products

GreenBuying.co.uk
Festival House , Cheltenham
GL50 3SH **08452 178995**

Clothing for Schools

Bristows Club & School
157 Victoria Road , Bridgnorth
WV16 4LL **01746 761701**

Computer Maintenance

MNComputer Services
980 Tyburn Road , Erdington
B24 0TL **01213 825302**

Croft IT Services Ltd
Electric House , Tamworth
B77 5DE **01827 216544**

Computer Services

Agnito
Miller's Barn , Lechlade
GL7 3NP **01865 524524**

Professional Computer Services
2 Clive Close , Birmingham
B75 6NE **07791 837684**

CC Miller Ltd
21 Kelvin Drive , Cannock
WS11 6ED **01543 502013**

Firebird IT Solutions Ltd
The Techno Centre , Coventry
CV1 2TT **08458 387039**

DMC Systems
6 Leaper Street , Derby
DE1 3ND **01332 363404**

Datasyche
140a Longden Coleham , Shrewsbury
SY3 7DN **01743 236000**

Design IT
6 Oak Drive , Seisdon
WV5 7ET **07774 895373**

I.T. Systems & Solutions Ltd
The Old Vicarage , Stoke-on-Trent
ST12 9HD **01782 372000**

MJC Group Ltd
MJC House , Stourport-on Severn
DY13 9EF **08452 718000**

Cosnet Computing Ltd
Arden Forest Industrial Estate , Alcester
CV37 0ES **01789 762202**

Conference & Event Management

TVP-Accounts
Maxima Forum , Cheltenham
GL50 2JA **01242 227520**

THE GREEN DIRECTORY

Cooling Products

Fabdec Limited
Grange Road , Ellesmere
SY12 9DG 01691 627210

Counselling , Advice and Psychotherapy

Geoff T Cox
47 Castle Road , Kidderminster
DY10 3TE 01562 852145

Patience O'Neill
16a Russell Terrace , Leamington
CV31 1EZ 01926 330128

Maggie Peet
Meadow View , Stoke on Trent
ST10 4AZ 01538 702502

Duncan Stoddart Counselling, Psychotherapy & Consultancy
Phoenix Psychological Services , Kenilworth
CV8 1LQ 07900 307903

Courier Services

Jogle Couriers Ltd
6 Rainbow Street , Wolverhampton
WV14 8SX 07743 604500

Davis Sameday Courier
105 The Medway , Birmingham
B97 5AE 01527 401810

Avon Express and Main Taxis
43 Woodlands Road , Stratford upon Avon
CV37 0DH 01789 414514

ACS Couriers
61 Kings , Leominster
HR6 9UY 07989 431913

HCS Courier Service Ltd
1 Old Railway Inn , Parkend
GL15 4UN 01594 560101

Blue Box Logistics Ltd
Eastleigh , Oswestry
SY10 9QJ 01691 830889

PA Couriers
Hanbury Court , Stourbridge
DY8 1BQ 01562 882780

SGoS
160 Barrs Road , Sandwell
B64 7EX 07990 523972

Design 2 Print

Printworks
Purbrook Road , Wolverhampton
WV1 2EJ 01902 458800

A.L.K Printed Limited
4 Suffolk Close , Wednesfield
WV11 1LB 01902 865330

Wildfire Creative
140a Longden Coleham , Shrewsbury
SY3 7DN 01743 236000

Document and Data Destruction

WN Security Shredding
Shifnal Trading Estate , Shifnal
TF11 8OD 01952 463379

Double/Triple Glazing

Extraglaze
Telford
TF4 3RE 01952 591575

Drilling, Boring and Site Investigations

Hughes Geothermal Ltd
Leebotwood , Church Stretton
Shropshire , SY6 6LU
01694 751251   or   07881 555978
office@hughesdrilling.co.uk
www.hughesdrilling.co.uk
(see half page advert for more information)

ADP Group Ltd
Firing Close Farm , Wotton-Under-Edge
GL12 8PE 01454 227115

M and J Drilling Services
Unit 44 Coneygree Industrial Estate , Tipton
West Midlands , DY4 8XP
01902 885241
enquiry@mandjdrilling.com
www. mandjdrilling.com
(see full page advert for more information)

E-commerce and Search Engine Optimisation (SEO)

Social Presence
1 Worcester Road , Great Malvern
WR14 4QY 01684 577247

E-commerce and Search Engine Optimisation (SEO)

Websyche
140a Longden Coleham , Shrewsbury
SY3 7DN **01743 236000**

Ecology Surveys and Consultancy

WWT Consulting
Wildfowl & Wetlands Trust , Slimbridge
GL2 7BT **01453 891222**

Stuart Thomas Ecological Associates
Marine & Terrestrial Ecology , Oswestry
SY10 8LN **01691 680036**

Electric Cycles

Pedego Europe
Walnut Tree House , Stonehouse
GL10 3PW **02032 394722**

Electrical and Electricians

MOR Electrical
27 Cardinals Close , Telford
TF2 7HW **01952 670533**

Electrical and Electricians

T A Raza
25 Cookson Avenue , Stoke-on-Trent
ST3 4NR **07543 151146**

RJW Electrical and Solar Ltd
44 Garden Village , Oswestry
SY11 3AX **01691 770958**

Baker Electrical Services
Unit 6 Leys Business Park , Cheltenham
GL52 9QH **07973 772751**

Live Wires Electrical and Property Maintenance
9 Dunley Road , Stourport-on-Severn
DY13 0AY **07515 729719**

Electrical and Electricians

P. Hudson & Son Ltd
Stratford House , Hereford
HR4 8AZ **01432 830106**

Tandy Cunningham Electrical Contractors Ltd
42 Wilton Road , Gloucester
GL1 5NJ **07739 429892**

Streetly Electrical
46 Lowlands Avenue , Sutton Coldfield
B74 3QW **01213 537932**

Pure Electrics/Pure Energy
Unit 6 Maesbury Road , Oswestry
SY10 8NH **01691 681051**

Electrical Maintenance and Installation

Arden Electrical Services UK Ltd
24 Hurst Green Road , Solihull
West Midlands , B93 8AF
01564 778515 or   07986 837024
info@ardenes.co.uk
www.ardenes.co.uk
(see half page advert for more information)

Electrical Maintenance and Installation

Elec SP
P.O Box 5333 , Nuneaton
Warwickshire , CV11 9GX
07595 326853
sparky@elecsp.co.uk

(see full page advert for more information)

Just Power Plus Ltd
10 Royville Place , Stoke
ST6 1RP **07980 000398**

Gary Hanlon Electrician
Fairview Industrial Estate , Sutton Coldfield
B76 9EE **07771 677699**

Alan Tarling Electrical Ltd
28 Bonnington Drive , Hereford
HR4 0RU **07976 407129**

Activate Energy
Parbrook Close , Coventry
CV4 9XY **08456 011833**

SJD Electrical Services Ltd
134 Deansway Friars Croft , Bromsgrove
B61 7PN **01527 559568**

Electrical Maintenance and Installation

Arden Electrical Services UK Ltd

Mobile: 07986 837024
Tel: 01564 778515
Email: info@ardenes.co.uk
Web: www.ardenes.co.uk

Page 293

Arden Electrical Services offer an efficient and reliable service, with fully qualified electricians to Domestic, Commercial and Industrial customers throughout the UK. We have the knowledge and experience to provide a comprehensive electrical service to suit all needs.

Our customers include: hotels, leisure facilities, retail outlets, motorway service stations, industrial premises, schools and residential properties including landlord's certification.

We are Part P certified to the latest 17th edition of IEE Wiring Regulations (BS7671) and members of NAPIT and ECS. Qualified to City & Guilds level we are also members of the Trust Mark scheme which promotes local, trustworthy and reliable tradesmen.

Our services include Inspection & Testing, Fire Alarms & Emergency Lighting, Security Alarms, CCTV Systems , Energy Management, Portable Appliance Testing, Communication systems, Fuse Board upgrades, Installations & Re-wiring and minor works.

THE **GREEN** DIRECTORY

Page 295

Electrical Maintenance and Installation

ET Electrical Partners
11 Waddington Way , Gloucester
GL2 2DQ **07544 389742**

Prospark Electrical Contractors Ltd
304 Penn Road , Wolverhampton
West Midlands , WV4 4AQ
01902 829992 or 0800 955 2526
info@prospark.co.uk

(see full page advert for more information)

TSM Electrical Services
59 Henry Street , Kenilworth
CV8 2HL **07966 366516**

Embroidery

Jaslyn Embroidery & Print Ltd
Unit D2 Innsworth Technology Park , Gloucester
GL3 1DL **01452 731336**

Go-Go Designs Ltd
12 St Edwards Street , Leek
ST13 8DS **01538 381781**

Image Maker
Park Lane Industrial Estate, Wolverhampton
WV10 9QA **07970 022134**

Employee Share Schemes

David Craddock Consultancy Services
10 Smokies Way , Biddulph
ST8 6TZ **01782 519925**

Energy Assessors & Consultants

The Home Buyers Friend Ltd
4 Arthur Street , Oswestry
SY11 1JP **01691 658197**

Energy Issues Ltd
10 Mossbank Way , Shrewsbury
SY3 8XW **07970 609350**

Energy Performance Certificates

The Home Buyers Friend Ltd
4 Arthur Street , Oswestry
SY11 1JP **01691 658197**

Assessahome Property Services
8 Willowdale Gardens , Shrewsbury
SY1 3SS **07939 678907**

Energy Saving Heating

L W Cooling
48 Sykes Moor , Tamworth
B77 4LE **07518 582173**

Energy Saving Products and Services

Schneider Electrics Ltd
Stafford Park 5 , Telford
TF3 3BL **08706 088608**

Worcester Bosch Group
Cotswold Way , Wardon
WR4 9SN **08448 929900**

Environmental Consultancy

The Planning Company
51 Battenhall Rise , Worcester
Worcestershire , WR5 2DE
01905 360277 or   07747 533170
info@theplanningcompany.co.uk
www.theplanningcompany.co.uk

Safe Environment Ltd
4 Bridle Road , Stafford
ST17 0QD **01785 662967**

Exhibition Display Banners

Replicolour
Arosfa , Oswestry
SY10 0AN **01691 860409**

Signs4you (UK Limited)
The Station , Lydney
GL15 5HE **01594 888120**

Exhibition Stands

Revolution X
Unit 4 , Coleshill
Birmingham , B46 1HT
01675 463353 or   07545 392131
info@revolutionx.co.uk
www.revolutionx.co.uk

Abbey Lighting Ltd
27 Tything Road West , Alcester
B49 6EP **01789 400705**

Raphael Design Limited
Raphael Court , Lichfield
WS14 9DX **01543 261220**

Exhibition Stands

Smart XS Limited
35 Chesterton Close , Redditch
B97 7CG **01527 457784**

External Wall Insulation

Green Whale Energy Ltd
212-222 Hagley Road West , Birmingham
B68 0NP **01212 225120**

Fences, Fencing & Decking

Sil Landscapes
153 Quinton Lane , Quinton, Birmingham
B32 2TY **01214 215078**

Longford Fencing and Landscaping
Unit 1A Northbrook Road, Gloucester
GL4 3DP **01452 500478**

Pontesbury Fencing
Park Peadow , Shrewsbury
SY5 0HL **07720 844888**

Financial Auditing

C M Watson & Co Ltd
Cromwell House , Cannock
WS11 0DP **01543 577377**

Financial Services

Thompson & Co.
Shiretown House , Hereford
HR4 9AR **01432 273353**

Morris Cook
6 Salop Road , Oswestry
SY11 2NU **01691 654545**

ABCS
4 Pike Villas , Bibury Nr Cirencester
GL7 5WB **01285 740796**

Fire Risk Assessment and Training

JPB Pinney Ltd
4 Warneford Place , Moreton in Marsh
GL56 0LR **01608 650606**

Fire Safe International Ltd
48 Atcham Business PArk , Shrewsbury
SY4 4HG **01743 761000**

Safe Environment Ltd
4 Bridle Road , Stafford
ST17 0QD **01785 662967**

Fire Safety Protection and Equipment

Fire Safe International Ltd
48 Atcham Business Park , Shrewsbury
SY4 4HG **01743 761000**

First Aid Training

PGL Associates Ltd
Hobbits Hall , Derbyshire
DE12 6JP **01283 762999**

Flooring and Carpets

MWB Flooring
2 Oak Drive , Oswestry
SY11 3EU **01691 778032**

Food Hygiene

First Class Safety Ltd, Consultancy & Training
24 Warwick Street , Rugby
CV21 3DW **01788 569774**

Food Waste Processing

Jack Moody Ltd Landscaping and Civil Engineering Contractors
Hollybush Farm , Shareshill
WV10 7LX **01922 417648**

Fuel Saving Products

Motrak Fleet Monitoring
Minton Hollins Building , Stoke On Trent
ST4 7RY **01782 221100**

Garage Services

Elite Vehicle Services
Unit 12 Progress Drive, Cannock
WS11 0JE **01543 502440**

Gas and Central Heating (Domestic)

J.A.G. Plumbing & Heating
4 Queensway , Hereford
HR1 1HF **01432 350715**

Geothermal Energy

Hughes Geothermal Ltd
Leebotwood , Church Stretton
SY6 6LU **01694 751251**

THE GREEN DIRECTORY

Geothermal Energy

Worcester Bosch Group
Cotswold Way , Wardon
WR4 9SN 08448 929900

Graphic Design

Wildfire Creative
140a Longden Coleham , Shrewsbury
Shropshire , SY3 7DN
01743 236 000
mark@websyche.com
www.websyche.com

Humphrey John Stanley
Blaisdon , Ross-On-Wye
HR9 6AT 01989 770760

Bright Light Design
Connaught House , Leamington Spa
CV32 5SZ 01926 678570

Artful Limited
15 Ullenwood Court , Cheltenham
GL53 9QS 01242 221556

Stratford Marketing
Bay Tree House , Lichfield
WS13 6RF 01543 263942

Swoon Marketing Ltd
Liverage Hill , Henley in Arden
B95 5QS 01564 972098

VS Design
88 Moseley Road , Wolverhampton
WV14 6JE 07539 828874

RMA (Design) Ltd
The Cemetary Lodge , Birmingham
B18 6NN 07725 044960

Chris Wheeler Graphic Design
14 Rothen Street , Stratford upon Avon
CV37 6LU 01789 413936

Graphic Dragon Limited
36 Elmdene Road , Kenilworth
CV8 2BX 01926 779140

Green Roofing

SkyGarden GREEN SOLUTIONS

Greenroofs are part of our sustainable future.

The leading independent UK supplier of green roofs have the expertise to provide environmental solutions within the urban landscape.

**01242 620905
www.sky-garden.co.uk
enquiries@sky-garden.co.uk**

ACSAP A.C. Smith (Applications) Ltd
133 Weddington Road , Nuneaton
CV10 0AN 02476 340308

Ground Source Heat Pumps

REHAU Ltd
Hill Court , Ross-on-Wye
HR9 5QN 01989 762600

Nu-Heat UK Ltd
Heathpark House , Honiton
EX14 1SD 01404 549770

Robert R Mcgowan Ltd
4 Campbell Road , Hereford
HR1 1JE 01432 356984

EZ Solar
Ditton Mill House , Cleobury Mortimer
Shropshire , DY14 0DH
01299 270011
sales@ezsolar.co.uk
www.ezsolar.co.uk

Ground Source Heat Pumps

Viessmann Limited
Hortonwood 30 , Telford
Shropshire , TF1 7YP
01952 675000 or
info-uk@viessmann.com
www.viessmann.co.uk

Health and Beauty Products

Forever
Acacia House , Cirencester
GL7 6AZ **01285 898093**

Health and Safety

Three Spires Safety Ltd
6 Palmerston road , Coventry
CV5 6FH **02476 712244**

Callsafe Services Ltd
Yardley House , Rugeley
WS15 2EJ **01889 577701**

The Quensh Consultancy
435 Holyhead Road , Coventry
CV5 8HS **02476 599503**

First Class Safety Ltd, Consultancy & Training
24 Warwick Street , Rugby
CV21 3DW **01788 569774**

Northleigh Safety Ltd
7 Sandbeds Road , Willenhall
WV12 4HH **07970 628223**

The Worksafe Partnership Ltd
8 Lancelot Court , Slimbridge
GL2 7BU **01453 890031**

AMPA Associates Ltd
4 Manor Road , Solihull
B93 8DX **01564 230294**

Height & Safety Ltd
Orchard Business Centre , Cheltenham
GL52 7RZ **01242 701250**

Positive Management Services
17 Whitbourne Hall , Worcester
WR6 5SE **01886 822222**

The Health and Safety Service Ltd
E-Innovation Centre , Telford
TF2 9FT **08451 634444**

Heat Detection

Fabdec Limited
Grange Road , Ellesmere
SY12 9DG **01691 627210**

Heat Recovery and Ventilation Systems

Internal Climate Systems Ltd
1 Wyecliffe Terrace , Hereford
HR1 2HG **01432 272118**

Fabdec Limited
Grange Road , Ellesmere
SY12 9DG **01691 627210**

Human Resources and Training

The Quensh Consultancy
435 Holyhead Road , Coventry
CV5 8HS **02476 599503**

Hypnotherapy

Lavendergate
20 Hornyold Road , Malvern
WR14 1QQ **01684 568502**

Insulation

Alba Insulation Limited
Central City Industrial Estate , Coventry
West Midlands , CV6 5RY
0800 731 9477 or 07723474946
info@albainsulation.co.uk
www.albainsulation.co.uk

Seal Insulation
Smethwick Energy Action Ltd , Birmingham
B66 4PH **08001 073847**

Total Homefix Solutions
Unit 15 Ollerton Business Park , Childs Ercall
TF9 2DB **08006 121170**

Rockwarm Energy Saving Solutions
4 Trident Business Park , Nuneaton
CV11 4PN **02476 345554**

Insurance

Jelf Group
Chequers Close , Malvern
WR14 1BF **01684 571835**

Insurance

Berkeley Applegate & Webb Company (Midlands) Ltd
Lowcroft , Wolverhampton
WV5 9EZ **01902 324194**

Mercer Jones and Co Ltd
48 Broad Street , Stoke-on-Trent
ST1 4EU **01782 202007**

Key and Asset Management Systems

Keytracker Limited
Keyper House , Rowley Regis
B65 0JY **01215 599000**

Lake & Pond Construction

DE Spencer & Sons (UK) Ltd
Nupend , Stonehouse
GL10 3SS **01453 822764**

Landscaping and Ground Maintenance

GBD (Evesham) Ltd
Murcot Turn Business Park , Broadway
WR12 7LT **01386 834090**

D S Landscapes
34 Viscount Avenue , Telford
TF4 3SW **07968 271046**

Greenfields Garden Services Ltd
Kites Nest Yard , Gloucester
GL2 8BL **01452 790190**

Bricks and Roses
28 Pulton Close , Birmingham
B13 9SD **07816 620841**

Classic Landscape
44 Moor Lane , Tamworth
B77 3LJ **01827 54764**

First Pave Ltd
17b Kenilworth Road , Balsall Common
CV7 7EW **01676 532826**

D J Davies
Stonehouse , Oswestry
Shropshire , SY10 8BE
07967 022231 or 01691 682743
davedaviesmorton@tiscali.co.uk

(see full page advert for more information)

Landscaping and Ground Maintenance

Vision Landscape
66 Trostrey Road , Birmingham
B30 3NG **07773 137167**

Lighting

Abbey Lighting Ltd
27 Tything Road West , Alcester
B49 6EP **01789 400705**

Low Energy Lightbulbs, Lighting and L.E.D.

Lustre & Lighting Electrical Ltd
Cuckoo's Corner , Ross on Wye
Herefordshire , HR9 5SQ
01989 567 961 or 07745 791 027
rob.powell@btconnect.com

(see full page advert for more information)

Pass Electrical Ltd
2 King Charles Court . Worcester
WR5 3HF **08006 566693**

OCIP Energy Ltd
Montpellier House , Cheltenham
Gloucestershire , GL50 1TY
01242 250633
aiden.brown@ocip.co.uk
www.ocip.co.uk
(see full page advert for more information)

Abbey Lighting Ltd
27 Tything Road West , Alcester
B49 6EP **01789 400705**

Eco Lightstore Ltd
137 Western Road , Hockley
Birmingham , B18 7QD
0870 766 9606
admin@ecolightstore.com
www.ecolightstore.com

Magazine Publishers

Energy Now
County House , Worcester
WR1 1HB **01905 616665**

Lustre and Lights Electrical Ltd.

Electrical instillation, testing & lighting engineering

With over 30 years' experience offering electrical,

Mechanical and lighting refurbishment to the private

Sector, museums, galleries and period property owners.

Based in the west Midlands covering the UK and

Further afield as required.

- **Chandelier and Period Lighting restoration**
- **Low energy/LED conversions for majority of fittings**
- **Refurbishment and refinishing to the highest standards**
- **Installation, in-service testing and maintenance**
- **Own fully equipped studio workshops**
- **On-site mobile workshop facilities**
- **Specialist advice**

Electrical Safety Register

ELECSA ✚ ECA

N EIC DOMESTIC INSTALLER

UKAS

Cuckoos Corner, Deep Dean, Ross-on-Wye, HR9 5SQ

Phone - 01989 567961   Mobile - 07745791027
E.mail – rob.powell@btconnect.com

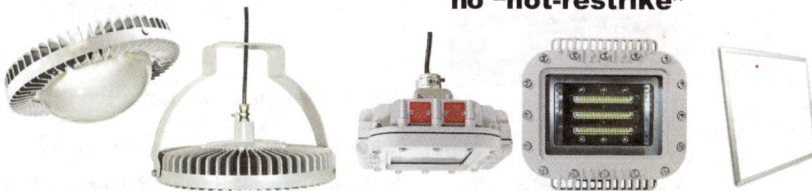

ocipenergy

- **REDUCES Energy Costs**
- **LOWERS Maintenance**
- **ENHANCES CCTV images**
- **IMPROVES Security**
- **FAST return on investment**
- **WIDE RANGE of indoor & outdoor products**

- **British Manufactured LEDs (plus EU & US)**
- **100% TAX DEDUCTABLEYr 1**
- **REDUCE Carbon Footprint**
- **LONG LIFE L70 at 100,000hrs**
- **BETTER quality light**
- **INSTANT LIGHT no "hot-restrike"**

REDUCE operating & maintenance costs

FAST return on investment

REDUCE carbon footprint and costs of carbon tax

IMPROVE light quality

Tel: +44 (0) 1 242 250633
web: www.ocip.co.uk email: info@ocip.co.uk
OCIP ENERGY LTD, MONTPELLIER HOUSE, MONTPELLIER DRIVE, CHELTENHAM, GL50 1TY

THE **GREEN** DIRECTORY

THE **GREEN** DIRECTORY

Milking Equipment

Fabdec Limited
Grange Road , Ellesmere
SY12 9DG **01691 627210**

Mobile Phone and Blackberry Service and Supplies

Complete ICT
Twyford House , Stoke on Trent
ST5 9QH **01782 200030**

Mobile Phones

Utility Bill Money Saver.com
332 Marsh Lane , Birmingham
B23 6HP **01213 776600**

Mobi Techno Ltd
23 Chapel Ash , Wolverhampton
WV3 0TZ **01902 313666**

Motivational and Life Coaching

David Craddock Consultancy Services
10 Smokies Way , Biddulph
ST8 6TZ **01782 519925**

Inner Kalm
Unit 16 Llanfyllin Work House , Llanfyllin
SY22 5LD **01691 870398**

Networking and Cabling

Data Craft Installations Services Ltd
31 Mount Road , Wolverhampton
WV5 9EP **07973 241669**

PC Cables Ltd
The Seasons , Penkridge
ST19 5HE **01785 715588**

Office Cleaning and Cleaning Services

Green Mop Commercial and Domestic Cleaning
The Nursery Bungalow , Rushwick
WR2 5SN **07947 248494**

Office Stationery

GreenBuying.co.uk
Festival House , Cheltenham
GL50 3SH **08452 178995**

Office/Shop Fitters

Mike Newey Interiors
Unit 4 New Road industrial Estate , Burntwood
WS7 0AZ **01543 685577**

Organic Recycling and Green Waste

Jack Moody Ltd Landscaping and Civil Engineering Contractors
Hollybush Farm , Shareshill
WV10 7LX **01922 417648**

Painting and Decorating

Restyle Painting & Decorating
27 Lyndhurst Road , Cannock
WS12 3HD **07967 472902**

Solver Painters
39 Edinburgh Place , Cheltenham
GL51 7RH **07561 520255**

Watkins
Ashe House , Hereford
HR1 3QR **01432 820631**

P Brandon
1 Cladswell Close , Alcester
B47 5JX **07977 575742**

Aces Decorators
63 Cleeve Road , Birmingham
B14 4EE **01215 373107**

A Hopkins General Maintenace
31 The Hobbins , Bridgnorth
WV15 5HH **07837 736314**

Steven Francis
15 Alfred Green Close , Rugby
CV22 6DN **07904 263316**

Beacon Painting and Decorating
53 Richborough Drive , Dudley
DY1 3PZ **07801 709607**

Acacia Property Maintenance Ltd
73 Elmdene Road , Kenilworth
CV8 2BW **07709 907883**

Dan Williams. Painting & Decorating
68 Dodington , Whitchurch
SY13 1EU **01948 663890**

Paving and Driveways

Holley Contractors
Mount Pleasant , Broseley
TF12 5AN **01952 882671**

Payroll and Bookkeeping

BR Accounts
8 Derby Drive , Birmingham
B37 5QR 01216 807903

Suretax Accounting
279 Leamington Road , Coventry
CV3 6NB 02476 697300

Jem Accountancy Service
Tamworth Lane , Solihull
West Midlands , B90 4DD
0121 744 8813 or   0121 604 6356
jem2012@btinternet.com

C M Watson & Co Ltd
Cromwell House , Cannock
WS11 0DP 01543 577377

Clifford & Co
11 Manor Farm Drive , Market Drayton
Shropshire , TF9 2SN
01952 551166
info@cliffordandco.co.uk
www.cliffordandco.co.uk

L.A.D. Bookkeeping
32 Country Meadows , Market Drayton
TF9 3LR 01630 657126

J J & N Associates Ltd
Planetary Business Park , Wolverhampton
WV13 3SW 01902 866405

MAS Accountancy & Bookkeeping
23 Allman Road , Erdington
B24 9DY 07940 534714

Expressway Business Services
Business Development Centre , Birmingham
B23 6HP 01213 776600

Bruton Young Bookkeeping
127 Woodvale , Gloucester
GL2 2BU 01452 725458

Pest Control

Express Pest Control
No 3 Victoria Parade , Oswestry
Shropshire , SY11 2ES
01691 662978 or   07916 322280
alexbrindle@hotmail.co.uk

Cedar Pest Management
Cedar View , Lower Tean
ST10 4LW 07837 049387

Tracey Farnan Local Lady Pest Controller
 Tracey Farnan Pest Control , Bromsgrove
B61 ....07596 465710

Alpha Pest Control
The White House , Stoke on Trent
Staffordshire , ST4 3AR
0800 092 5999
info@alphapest.co.uk

(see full page advert for more information)

Severn Pest Control
12 Rowton Road , Shrewsbury
Shropshire , SY2 6JG
01743 617247 or   07773 355334
glenn.langford@btinternet.com
www.severnpestcontrol.co.uk

The Pest Man
112 Caernarvon Road , Cheltenham
Gloucestershire , GL51 3JR
01242 706099
info@thepestman.co.uk

(see full page advert for more information)

Photography and Photographers

Paul Tristram Photography
19 Ormes Lane , Wolverhampton
West Midlands , WV6 8LL
07576 888631
info@paultristram.com

7 Star Media Care Ltd
11 Louise Court , Birmingham
B20 3QG 07505 652071

THE GREEN DIRECTORY

Photography and Photographers

John Quinn Photography
18 English Walls , Oswestry
SY11 2PA **01691 657555**

Plumbing Services

Doug Baker Plumbing & Heating
19 Armscote Road , Shipston-on-Stour
CV36 4NP **01608 664349**

A Top Services
32 Arvon Way , Birmingham
B38 8XH **07970 495102**

Portable Appliance and Fixed Wire Testing

C.R Electrical
10 St Johns Close , Shipston-On-Stour
CV36 5HR **01608 685978**

Daybury Electrical Services Ltd
Sandy Lane Industrial Estate , Stourport-On-Severn
DY13 9QB **01299 822070**

Elecexcel Electrical Contractors
18 Pates Avenue , Cheltenham
GL51 8EQ **01242 279583**

Portable Appliance and Fixed Wire Testing

Adam Kirkham Electrical
4 Belfield Avenue , Newcastle Under Lyme
ST5 9NH **01782 612617**

RMP Guarding (UK) Ltd
Security House , Telford
TF3 3BJ **08708 883100**

Leam Electrical
12 High View Road, Leamington Spa
CV32 7JB **07825 428264**

PR and Media Management

Gravitas Public Relations
7 Lansdown Place , Cheltenham
GL50 2HU **01242 211000**

Print Management

Signature Communications Ltd
6 Mead Close , Cheltenham
Gloucestershire , GL53 7DX
01242 256022 or 07792023578
paresh@scl.gb.com
www.signature-comms.co.uk

Printing, Design and Mailing Services

GREEN PRINTING
in full colour

One of the UK's most progressive and innovative print companies, printing.com offer high end litho print which is kind to the environment and extremely cost effective.

Our state of the art production hub produces **full colour print** that comes with a **guaranteed turnaround time**, which means you don't have to worry about missing your deadlines. All of our prices are **fixed** and we're up to **76% cheaper than other printers**. This is because we use as few resources as we can. Fewer resources equal less waste. We simply couldn't afford to offer you such low prices if we were wasteful or inefficient.

Our Environmental Management System has been assessed by BSI and we're certified for **ISO 14001**, the **Environmental Standard**. We're also certified under FSC's Chain-of-Custody programme which means that **FSC certified** wood is tracked all the way through production until it ends up as your finished printing. Over the past few years we've **planted 60,000** trees with our partners, **Tree Appeal**.

Leaflets, stationery, business cards, booklets, folders, stickers, flyers... CONTACT US NOW for a free buying guide and sample pack, quoting "BGB"

Page 309

[printing.com® @ røgue design print

74b Warwick Road | Kenilworth | CV8 1HL
t: **01926 851234**
e: **info@kenilworth-printing.com**
www.kenilworth-printing.com

Printing, Design and Mailing Services

BPM-UK (Print Bromsgrove)
26 Stratford Road , Bromsgrove
B60 1AP **01527 872436**

Restart Print Ltd
Unit 6 Amington industrial Estate , Tamworth
B77 4DR **01827 302554**

Mallard Independent Printing and Publishing
T3 Training and Enterprise Centre , Cradley Heath
B64 6EW **07729 328851**

Russell Printers Ltd
2 Ringway Business Park , Birmingham
B7 4AA **01213 590783**

Ben Baker Printers
Brantley Barn , Wolverhampton
WVV5 7AY **01384 221400**

Printing.com @centrepoint Print & Design Ltd
73 Gravelly Lane , Birmingham
B23 6LR **01213 548001**

Phatt Printing
239A London Road , Stoke on Trent
Staffordshire , ST4 5AA
01782 411211
ssales@phattprinting.com

(see half page advert for more information)

Printing.com@ Rogue Design
74b Warwick Road , Kenilworth
Warwickshire , CV8 1HL
01926 851234
adam@kenilworth-printing.com

(see full page advert for more information)

Severnprint
Units 8-11 Ashville Industrial Estate , Gloucester
GL2 5EU **01452 416391**

Gr8 Digi Prints
10 Birmingham Road , Oldbury
B69 4ED **01215 447588**

Professional Office and Evening Wear

Effective Use of Information
PO Box 4545 , Stourport-on-Severn
DY13 3AG **07796 974607**

Property Maintenance

GFC Property Maintenance Ltd
23 Miserden Road , Cheltenham
GL51 6BP **01242 511584**

Publishing, Packaging and Corporate ID

Mallard Independent Printing and Publishing
T3 Training and Enterprise Centre , Cradley Heath
B64 6EW **07729 328851**

Quality Management (ISO Accreditation)

QSI Advisory Services Ltd
1 Mawley Bank , Ludlow
SY8 3QH **01584 890942**

Rain Water Harvesting

Nu-Heat UK Ltd
Heathpark House , Honiton
EX14 1SD **01404 549770**

Recruitment and Employment Services

A & D Recruitment
Shop 1 Traitors Gate , Shrewsbury
SY1 2BX **01743 247774**

Positive Management Services
17 Whitbourne Hall , Worcester
WR6 5SE **01886 822222**

Recycled and Refilled Printer Cartridges

Cartridge World Lichfield
2 Dam Street , Lichfield
WS13 6AA **01543 410072**

GenetINKS Ltd
11 West Road , Bromsgrove
B60 2NG **01386 570425**

Cartridge World (Solihull)
Robin Hood Island , Birmingham
B28 9FT **01217 332707**

Recycling

Maylarch Recycling Ltd
Andoversford Industrial Estate , Cheltenham
GL54 4LB **01242 821450**

Pete Wall Refuse Removal and Recycling
1 Lingfield Road , Bewdley
DY12 1JZ **07956 172825**

Refrigeration

RMV Cooling Services
The Relm, Alderton , Shrewsbury
SY4 1AP **01743 4741236**

PJ Refrigeration
5 Castle Close , Tenbury Wells
WR15 8AY **01584 819881**

Removal Services

Heal Enterprises
1 Blowers Green Place , Dudley
DY2 8XG **07818 243144**

Gary Mulkin
46 Goring Road , Coventry
CV2 4LW **07830 897279**

Whites Removals Ltd
270 Great Lister Street , Birmingham
B7 4DB **01213 593571**

SGoS
160 Barrs Road , Sandwell
B64 7EX **07990 523972**

Reuse and Reduction

GreenBuying.co.uk
Festival House , Cheltenham
GL50 3SH **08452 178995**

Safety Risk Assessment

PGL Associates Ltd
Hobbits Hall , Derbyshire
DE12 6JP **01283 762999**

Callsafe Services Ltd
Yardley House , Rugeley
WS15 2EJ **01889 577701**

John Smith Associates Ltd
167 Birmingham Road , Water Orton
B46 1TE **01217 301474**

Scanners

PLUSTEK (UK)
33 Mayfair Grove , Telford
TF2 9GJ **01952 210280**

Screen and T Shirt Printing

ATELIER SCREEN PRINT LTD.
130 Pershore Street , Birmingham
B5 6ND **01216 226301**

Secretarial Service

The Typing Co.
Walterscott Road , Bedworth
BV12 9HD **02476 312869**

Caroline Daniels - Virtual Secretarial Services.
65 Robert Burns Avenue , Cheltenham
GL51 6NU **01242 521414**

VA Extra
11 Croft Road , Birmingham
B26 1SG **01217 848627**

Eagle Express Secretarial Services
3 George Street , Evesham
WR11 4LD **01386 571026**

Signs and Graphics

Apple Signs
Unit 12 New Enterprise Centre, Wolverhampton
WV1 2TZ **07717 398811**

Signarama (Oxford)
3 Bessel Sleigh Road , Wootton
OX13 6DN **01865 730046**

Signarama (Birmingham South)
328-330 Hobsmoat Road , Solihull
B92 8JT **01217 425888**

IDEOSYNC Creative Marketing Solutions
123 Thoresby Avenue , Gloucester
GL4 0TF **07865 086180**

Blizzard Graphics
Unit 6b Runway Farm , Kenilworth
CV8 1NQ **01676 533000**

De-Sign UK
108-110 Woodland , Erdington
B24 9QL **07970 869322**

Abbey Signs Ltd
1629 Bristol Road South , Birmingham
B45 9UA **01214 536604**

LOCAL SECTION

THE GREEN DIRECTORY

Signs and Graphics

Mark Latchford Screen and Digital Print Ltd
Unit 10E Alstone Trading Estate, Cheltenham
GL51 8HF 01242 584588

Sign Webb Ltd
23 Fairford Road , Birmingham
B44 8DJ 07921 569186

Spa Display Ltd
Design House , Droitwich Spa
WR9 8JB 01905 775428

Social Media and Internet Marketing

Social Presence
1 Worcester Road , Great Malvern
WR14 4QY 01684 577247

Solar Energy

Eco Solar Smiths Ltd
25 Appleton Drive , Glossop
SK13 8RX 07970 744221

WIN A FREE Solar PV Installation by entering our free Prize Draw conditions apply please email info@dynamicenergies.co.uk

OR CALL NOW ON 0845 880 3665
www.dynamicenergies.co.uk

Windscout Ltd
Lyde Arundel , Hereford
Herefordshire , HR4 7SN
0117 230 2789
lloydscott@windscout.co.uk

(see full page advert for more information)

Nu-Heat UK Ltd
Heathpark House , Honiton
EX14 1SD 01404 549770

Solar Time UK
3 School Lane , St Martins
SY11 3BX 01691 662445

Solar Energy

Kempowell Electrical Services Ltd
Unit 3a Foley Trading Estate , Hereford
HR1 2SF 01432 379300

Be Green Energy Ltd
1 Nimrod Drive , Hereford
HR1 1UG 01432 358261

UK Solar Direct Ltd
Nuneaton Railway Station , Nuneaton
CV11 4BU 08450 178847

ECO Energy UK Ltd
18 Abbotts Drive , Stoke on Trent
ST1 6HU 01782 534708

Worcester Bosch Group
Cotswold Way , Wardon
WR4 9SN 08448 929900

Solar Panels and Photovoltaics

Excess Solar Limited
26 Kingfisher Drive , Stafford
ST18 0FH 08008 488007

MOR Electrical
27 Cardinals Close , Telford
TF2 7HW 01952 670533

GreenTech
Holly Farm Business Park, Kenilworth
CV8 1NP 08455 194277

Greensphere Renewable Energy Ltd
Greensphere House , Oswestry
SY10 8NN 01691 688527

Viessmann Limited
Hortonwood 30 , Telford
Shropshire , TF1 7YP
01952 675000
info-uk@viessmann.com
www.viessmann.co.uk

EOS Energy
Senator House , Southam
CV47 0NA 08456 080680

J T Vobe Electrical Contracting
9 Bell Lane , Tenbury Wells
WR15 8QX 07966 238936

Eco Solar Smiths Ltd
25 Appleton Drive , Glossop
SK13 8RX 07970 744221

SureSpark Solar
Communications House , Stafford
ST18 0FS 01785 413105

Solar Panels and Photovoltaics

Pure Electrics/Pure Energy
Unit 6 Maesbury Road , Oswestry
SY10 8NH **01691 681051**

Solar Water Heating Systems

EZ Solar
Ditton Mill House , Cleobury Mortimer
Shropshire , DY14 0DH
01299 270011
sales@ezsolar.co.uk
www.ezsolar.co.uk

Solar Time UK
3 School Lane , St Martins
SY11 3BX **01691 662445**

Viessmann Limited
Hortonwood 30 , Telford
Shropshire , TF1 7YP
01952 675000
info-uk@viessmann.com
www.viessmann.co.uk

Greenshop Solar Ltd
Cheltenham Road , Stroud
GL6 7BX **01452 772030**

Renewable Heat Installers (UK) Limited
55 Beamhill Road , Burton-on-Trent
DE13 0AE **01283 515846**

Stress Management

Angryfish Training
33 Bickley Grove , Sheldon
B26 3DJ **07811 217648**

Surveyors

ADP Group Ltd
Firing Close Farm , Wotton-Under-Edge
GL12 8PE **01454 227115**

Gooch & Burley
4 High Street , Newent
GL18 1AN **08453 007677**

**Nigel Bullimore MRICS Chartered
Building Surveyor**
1 Charles Road , Solihull
B91 1TR **01217 042423**

Tanks and Cylinders

Fabdec Limited
Grange Road , Ellesmere
SY12 9DG **01691 627210**

Tax Advice and Taxation

Davies & John (Powys) Accountants
Commeroe Chambers , Llandrindod Wells
LD1 5DB **01597 824848**

Bickerstaff and Co
Emerald House , Walsall
WS9 8PH **01922 744117**

C M Watson & Co Ltd
Cromwell House , Cannock
WS11 0DP **01543 577377**

Gorman Evans Ltd
Emstrey House (South) , Shrewsbury
SY2 6LG **01743 248456**

Michael Stephens Accountancy
3 Fells Avenue , Worcester
Worcestershire , WR4 0LN
01905 22880 or 07702 205919
michstep@supanet.com
www.michael-stephens.co.uk
(see full page advert for more information)

C B Accountancy
29 Birkdale Crescent , Coventry
CV6 4PJ **07961 891275**

Robert Powell. Chartered Accountant
A4 Spinnaker House , Gloucester
GL2 5FD **01452 527700**

Taxi and Private Hire

A to B Taxis
Enterprise Unit 28 , Oswestry
SY10 8NN **01691 679911**

Ultimate Taxis Limited
70 High Street , Newport
TF10 7BA **01952 813636**

Comet Cars Ltd
27 Castle Foregate , Shrewsbury
SY1 2EE **01743 344444**

COMCAB (BIRMINGHAM) LTD
118-122 Charles Henry Street , Birmingham
B12 0SJ **01215 669000**

Michael Stephens Accountancy

Chartered Management Accountants

- **Tax Advice to Sole Traders,**
- **Partnerships and Limited Companies**
- **Payroll (including RTI)**
- **VAT Preparation of Tax Returns**
- **Free Initial Consultation**
- **Advice &support in setting up your business Preparation of Monthly Accounts to help in the running of the business**

We cover the whole of the Midlands Contact Ian Barnett CMA 07702 205919

Quality service at a reasonable price we look after the finances so that you can look after your business

3 Fels Avenue Harley Warren Worcester WR4 0LN
Telephone 01905 22880
Email michstep@supanet.com
www.michael-stephens.co.uk

Telecommunications

Business Telephone Network Solutions Ltd
Heavens Field , Nailsworth
GL6 0DH **08448 710100**

Acuity Networks Ltd
Sheldon Chambers , Birmingham
West Midlands , B26 3NW
0800 130 3020
sales@acuitynetworks.co.uk
www.acuitynetworks.co.uk

Midland Communications Co Ltd
Orchard Works , Worcester
WR8 0JH **08447 881000**

Complete ICT
Twyford House , Stoke on Trent
Staffordshire , ST5 9QH
01782 200 030
tim@complete-ict.net
www.complete-ict.net

Total Telecom Ltd
Stafford Park 4, Telford
TF3 3BA **01952 616601**

Agnito
Miller's Barn , Lechlade
GL7 3NP **01865 524524**

Telecoms Providers

Utility Bill Money Saver.com
332 Marsh Lane , Birmingham
B23 6HP **01213 776600**

Thermal Insulation

Total Homefix Solutions
Unit 15 Ollerton Business Park , Childs Ercall
TF9 2DB **08006 121170**

Timber Frame Buildings

Go Eco Homes Ltd
Cradley Heath Factory Centre,
Birmingham , B64 7AB
01384 560055
simon@goecohomes.co.uk
www.goecohomes.co.uk

Timber Frame Buildings

R G Stones (Buildings) Ltd
The Saw Mills , Oswestry
Shropshire , SY10 7TG
01691 773391   or   01691 774316
rgstones@btconnect.com
www.rgstonesbuildingsltd.co.uk

Timber Kit Solutions
Long Lane , Telford
Shropshire , TF6 6HA
01952 770990
simon@timberkitsolutions.co.uk

(see full page advert for more information)

Glosford Timber Solutions Ltd
Mortimer House , Hereford
HR4 9TA **01432 842999**

Town Planning

The Planning Company
51 Battenhall Rise , Worcester
WR5 2DE **01905 360277**

Tracking Systems

Motrak Fleet Monitoring
Minton Hollins Building , Stoke On Trent
ST4 7RY **01782 221100**

Complete ICT
Twyford House , Stoke on Trent
ST5 9QH **01782 200030**

Tree Work and Surveys

David Alviti Tree Services
Burnt House Farm , Ludlow
Shropshire , SY8 4LD
07976 901536   or   01584 711544
d.alviti@hotmail.com

Bartlett Tree Experts (Gloucestershire)
Fosse Cross Industrial Estate , Cheltenham
GL54 4NE **01285 690890**

Antony Charles Treescapes
The Bungalow , Walsall
WS4 1LG **01922 630942**

THE GREEN DIRECTORY

Tree Work and Surveys

Green Tree Care Ltd
120 Bromley , Dudley
West Midlands , DY5 4PH
07779 800717
james.green.tree.care@gmail.com

Broadleaf
34 Wyche Road , Malvern
Worcestershire , WR14 4EG
01684 568091
broadleaftreecare@hotmail.co.uk

(see full page advert for more information)

Wood Matters
27 Brook Road , Shrewsbury
Shropshire , SY5 0QZ
01743 791818
woodmatters@btinternet.com

(see full page advert for more information)

Shropshire Tree Services
Unit 1 Brogyntyn Estate , Oswestry
SY10 7DA **01691 680018**

Cedarwood Tree Care
3 Howton Grove Barns , Wormbridge
Herefordshire , HR2 9DY
01981 570426 or 07888838360
m.chester28@hotmail.co.uk
www.cedarwoodtreecare.co.uk

Broadacre Tree Service
5 Beech Close , Wellington
TF1 3NQ **01952 247088**

Wharton Aboricultural Ltd
1C Atherstone Hill , Stratford upon Avon
CV37 8NF **01789 459458**

Trees, Plants & Seeds

Garden Plant Supply
34 Grace Road , Coventry
CV5 9AT **01676 522122**

Trophies and Engraving

HNS Signs
Unit 5 Sandpits Industrial Estate , Birmingham
B1 2PD **01212 123977**

Underfloor Heating

Ecovision Systems Ltd
Barley Court , Tetbury
GL8 8TQ **01666 501580**

Vehicle Leasing and Rentals

Motiva Group
Minton Hollins Building , Stoke on Trent
ST4 7RY **01782 211442**

Waste Machinery

Orwak Environmental Services
Unit 6 Alpha Industrial Park , Smethwick
B66 1BZ **01215 657436**

Waste Management and Disposal

Maylarch Recycling Ltd
Andoversford Industrial Estate , Cheltenham
GL54 4LB **01242 821450**

Waste Transportation

A1 Ltd Recycling Consultancy
Stanleys Barn , Nuneaton
CV13 6BL **07970 783299**

Water Wells & Bore Holes

ADP Group Ltd
Firing Close Farm , Wotton-Under-Edge
GL12 8PE **01454 227115**

Website and Internet Services

AMI Creative Ltd
Cinderhill Industrial Estate , Stoke-on-Trent
ST3 5LB **01782 593073**

HD Pixel Design - Small business web site design
Telford , Shropshire
.............**07502 417997**

Websyche
140a Longden Coleham , Shrewsbury
SY3 7DN **01743 236000**

Wood Matters

Sustainable Solutions to the Management of Trees, Hedges & Woodlands

Professional Tree Care

FULLY QUALIFIED with £5 million Public & Employee Liability Insurance

All Aspects of Tree Work
Tree Planting & Management
Hedge Management
Orchard Tree Work
Hedgelaying
Woodland Management

MEMBER
INTERNATIONAL SOCIETY OF ARBORICULTURE
ISA

Shrewsbury, Shropshire

Tel: 01743 791818   Mobile: 07974 300328
E-mail: woodmatters@btinternet.com

www.wood-matters.co.uk

THE **GREEN** DIRECTORY

Website and Internet Services

Reflection Creative Media Ltd
Snuff Mill Warehouse , Bewdley
DY12 2EL **01299 400932**

Brand 29
21 St. Mary's Court , Worcester
WR1 1NU **08712 379350**

Web Function Limited
118 Boldmere Road , Sutton Coldfield
B73 5UB **01213 554474**

Real Point Design Ltd
Patrick Farm Barns , Solihull
B92 0LT **01676 521444**

Nicholas Evans Web Solutions
2c Woodthorne Road , Wolverhampton
WV6 8TP **01902 652403**

Zang Web
12 Binton Croft , Birmingham
B13 9RS **07786 115610**

Formation Media Ltd
7 Smith Street , Warwick
CV34 4JA **01926 298777**

Wind Energy

Ecotricity Group Ltd
Unicorn House , Stroud
GL5 3AX **08452 306102**

FuturEnergy
Ettington Park Business Centre , Stratford Up
Warwickshire , CV37 8BT
01789 450280
sandra@futurenergy.co.uk
www.futurenergy.co.uk
(see full page advert for more information)

GreenTech
Unit F3 Holly Farm Business Park, Kenilworth
Warwickshire , CV8 1NP
0845 5194277   or   07733 366701
enquiries@greentech-uk.com
www.greentech-uk.com

Enegis
10 Banbury Road , Stratford Upon Avon
CV37 7HZ **08456 861846**

Worcester Bosch Group
Cotswold Way , Wardon
WR4 9SN **08448 929900**

Window Cleaning

J K Cleaning Services
11 Royal Crescent , Coventry
CV3 3DY **02476 304956**

Wood Recycling and Waste

Jericho Wood Recycling
Unit 8 Metro Triangle, Birmingham
B7 5QT **01213 285082**

Big Green Book UK Ltd
Old Station Building
Oswald Road, Oswestry
Shropshire, SY11 1RE

Biggreenbook ®

Solutions to environmental problems exist, but where do you find them?

This is a question that occurred to ecologist, Stephen Lings in 2003, when he was looking to solve some problems for a local company.

So Steve started putting together a database of companies that can help solve all kinds of problems in our environment. Nine years on, that database has grown into one of the UK's largest business membership organisations.

Now when a company wants help to become sustainable they only have to look to one place www.biggreenbook.com.

But if you don't really know what to look for, then the unique **GET A QUOTE** feature of their website allows you to email an expert about your issues and get suitable suppliers contacting you.

It is an incredible free service, and is one that has helped companies, large and small, throughout the UK.

Over 45,000 organisations have used the Big Green Book website in the last year alone and with over 750,000 hits a month it is a highly visited site.

Big Green Book also runs a face-to-face clinic service, travelling around the country and visiting major trade shows and events. Directors from Big Green Book, supported by experts from within the membership, are on hand to answer question about business and the environment.

Currently Big Green Book is on a membership drive, with special deals for companies that sign up to promote their solutions to environmental and sustainability issues.

If you would like more information on how your company can join their team is very approachable and friendly. Just ask for Gary and you will see what we mean.

Page 323

With over 6,000 companies in 400 categories and sectors, the Big Green Book online directory is the place to start.

Call 01691 661 565
or email sales@biggreenbook.com
www.biggreenbook.com

Lincoln

Nottingham

08

01
02
03
05
04
08
06 07
09
10
11 12

The Business Supporting The East Midlands Section for the 2012/13 Local Sourcing Directory is:

THE **GREEN** DIRECTORY

Access Control and Entry Systems

Atmos Heating Systems
TBS Depot , Daventry
NN11 4ES **01327 871990**

Accountancy

AA Accountancy
38 Skegby Road , Sutton-in-Ashfield
NG17 4EZ **01623 430022**

Dronfield Accounting Services
5 Ingleby Close , Dronfield
S18 8RB **01246 411227**

Huw Williams Chartered Accountants
217 Musters Road , Nottingham
Nottinghamshire , NG2 7DT
0115 914 6846
info@huwwilliams.co.uk
www.huwwilliams.co.uk

Accounting Solutions
128 Saltergate , Chesterfield
Derbyshire , S40 1NG
01246 202735
info@accounting-solutions.biz
www.accounting-solutions.biz

Suretax Accounting
279 Leamington Road , Coventry
West Midlands , CV3 6NB
02476 697300 or   07850 898178
msparrow@suretax.co.uk
www.suretax.co.uk

Paul Jennings & Associates Ltd IFA
Bramley House , Grantham
Lincolnshire , NG32 2HF
01949 843535 or 07710 290184
paul.jennings@aol.co.uk

(see full page advert for more information)

Alison Revill trading as Pyramid Management Accounts
The Stables , Bakewell
DE45 1GB **01629 812126**

Michael Stack
Unit 4 Stoke Lyne Road , Bicester
OX27 9AU **01869 277973**

Accountancy

Ask Accountancy
154 Rothley Road , Mountsorrel
LE12 7JX **01162 352244**

Sadika-Vale Ltd
276 Banbury Road , Oxford
OX2 7ED **01865 511898**

Accreditation and Certification

The Quensh Consultancy
435 Holyhead Road , Coventry
CV5 8HS **02476 599503**

Acoustic Products

Silvaperl
Albion Works , Gainsborough
DN21 2QB **01427 675094**

Acoustic Wall Panels And Tiles

Green Footprint Solutions
14 Inham Fields Close , Gunthorpe
NG14 7FH **01159 665546**

Air Conditioning Systems

Coolbox Air Conditioning Solutions Ltd
29 St Mary's Road , Bingham
NG13 8DX **08003 345048**

Pure Air Conditioning
Unit 4 New Brook Business Park , Mansfield
NG20 8GB **01623 741004**

Cooling Techniques Ltd
5 Park View , Northampton
NN3 7TP **01604 670676**

ASVC Air Conditioning Services
38 Lodge Way , Wellingborough
NN9 5YJ **08009 551281**

HD Engineering Ltd
55 High Street , Kettering
Northamptonshire , NN14 3Df
07528 270888
miles@hdeng.co.uk
www.hdeng.co.uk

PJA

Accountancy

PJA Means Business

Incorporated Financial Accountants

Services to: Individuals & Small to Medium Sized Businesses of all types Including:

- **VAT & Payroll (RTI)**
- **Accounts Preparation**
- **Taxation Services**
- **Business & Financial Management Training**
- **Monthly Fee Option**

Paul has over 30 years experience in preparation of accounts and dealing with taxation matters for individuals and small businesses of all types.

Paul also spent a number of years as a partner/director with day to day involvement in 2 retail businesses and gained valuable "hands on" experience at the sharp end of small business operations.

Currently, in addition to heading his accountancy practice, Paul is now currently FD of a successful SME in the IT industry and therefore very much in touch with managing SME commercial organisations at senior level.

If you are looking for a professional accountant with wide business experience and a pro active approach then please take the opportunity of an initial free consultation with Paul Jennings.

Page 327

ifa
Est. 1916

FOR ALL YOUR ACCOUNTING NEEDS...

ICPA

Please contact Paul for an initial free consultation and advice

Tel: 01949 843535 **Email:** paul.jennings@aol.co.uk
Mobile: 07710 290184

LOCAL SECTION **East Midlands**

THE GREEN DIRECTORY

Air Conditioning Systems

WM Air Conditioning
Unit 26 , Stanton Harcourt
Oxfordshire , OX29 5UX
01865 884333 or
jason@wmaircon.co.uk
www.wmaircon.co.uk

ORAC, Oxford Refrigeration and Air Conditioning
79/81 Magdalen Road , Oxford
OX4 1RF **01865 424424**

J B Refrigeration Ltd
22 Main Street , Oakham
LE15 9EP **07813 838402**

VA Refrigeration & Air Con
18 Meadow View , Towcester
NN12 7PH **05600 940481**

Air Source Heat Pumps

Ice Energy
Unit 2 Oakfield House, Eynsham
OX29 4TH **01865 882202**

Valley Heating Services Ltd
Unit 12B Vincent Works , Hope Valley
S33 9HG **01433 620220**

Atmos Heating Systems
TBS Depot , Daventry
NN11 4ES **01327 871990**

SmartGen
14 Craddock Street , Loughborough
LE11 1AH **01509 611500**

Radiant Heating Solutions Ltd
Hougham , Grantham
NG32 2HZ **01400 250572**

Underfloor Warehouse Ltd
The Eco Hub , Blaby
Leicestershire , LE8 4GZ
0116 258 1410
enquiries@ufw.co.uk
www.ufw.co.uk

Airport Transfers

Emerald Executive Cars
Harlow-Stansted
.............**01279 310562**

Architects

Architect John Woodward
High House , Lincoln
LN4 3PA **01526 320298**

ADJ Architectural Services
156 Westfield Road , Wellingborough
NN8 3HX **07976 799139**

Luke Williamson Architect
26 Field Street , Bicester
OX26 2NP **01869 240382**

Kay Smith Architect Ltd
Studio 2 Waterside Court, Burton-on-Trent
DE14 2WQ **01283 564041**

I-Plan Architectural
22 Cambridge Road , Stamford
PE9 1BN **01780 767088**

Studio G Architects
Business Centre , Newark
NG23 7NB **01636 894913**

PP Building Design Ltd
The Old Court House , Bingham
NG13 8AL **01949 838026**

Dickinson Building Design Ltd
24 Rectory Lane , Breadsall
DE21 5LL **01332 831429**

Gil Schalom Design
9 Patrick Road , West Bridgeford
Nottinghamshire , NG2 7JY
07981 501322
email@gilschalom.com

(see full page advert for more information)

Asbestos Handling and Removal

Midlands Asbestos Solutions Ltd
Nexsis House , Ilkeston
DE7 5DA **01159 326521**

Asbestos Survey and Assesment

Midlands Asbestos Solutions Ltd
Nexsis House , Ilkeston
DE7 5DA **01159 326521**

Asbestos Survey And Management Ltd
New Media Centre , Long Eaton
NG10 2DL **07870 585934**

GIL SCHALOM DESIGN
Advanced low energy and eco design for life

Page 329

Engaging an architect isn't something you do everyday - but you live and work with the results forever so it is vital that your building – whether new build, eco retrofit or extension meets your needs for beauty, function and low energy performance.

Gil Schalom's friendly open approach to client's ideas and attention to detail make the design process a pleasure and when you couple his nationally respected ecological design flair into the mix – you can be sure you are in safe hands.

Gil offers advanced low energy and ecological design services including PassivHaus methodology from small domestic projects to larger clients across a range of sectors.

Contact Gil today on 07981 501322
Email email@gilschalom.com
www.gilschalom.com

Asbestos Training and Awareness

XL HAZMAT LTD
16 Rosemary Drive , Derby
Derbyshire , DE24 0TA
0115 888 2797 or   07546 171160
enquiries@xlhazmat.co.uk
www.xlhazmat.co.uk

Monitor Environmental Ltd
Unit 7 Ascot Park Estate , Nottingham
NG10 5DL **01159 394535**

Bainbridge Asbestos Services Ltd
62 Rillwood Court , Northampton
NN3 8JS **07772 557635**

Biomass Energy and Biofuels

Dragon Heat Ltd
Loves Lane , Boston
Lincolnshire , PE20 2EU
01205 461594 or   07811147803
sales@dragonheat.co.uk
www.dragonheat.co.uk

Boilers and Water Heaters

Atmos Heating Systems
TBS Depot , Daventry
NN11 4ES **01327 871990**

Valley Heating Services Ltd
Unit 12B Vincent Works , Hope Valley
S33 9HG **01433 620220**

Heatwell
Croft Avenue , Hucknell
NG15 7JD [...........**01159 681273**]

Radiant Heating Solutions Ltd
Hougham , Grantham
NG32 2HZ **01400 250572**

Builders Merchants

Travis Perkins Plc
Lodge Way House , Northampton
NN5 7UG **01604 752424**

Buildbase
Gemini One , Cowley
OX4 2LL **01865 871700**

Building and Construction

Green Footprint Solutions
14 Inham Fields Close , Gunthorpe
Nottingham , NG14 7FH
0115 966 5546 or   07876 791499
info@greenfs.co.uk
www.greenfs.co.uk

SRS Limited
4 Elizabeth Way , Northampton
NN9 5LE **07973 418354**

A.J.S Property Services
Cherrytree Cottage , Lincoln
LN1 2LX **01522 703799**

Building Integrated Photovoltaics(BIPV)

Radiant Heating Solutions Ltd
Hougham , Grantham
NG32 2HZ **01400 250572**

Carpentry and Joinery

Leigh Hudson
16 Almond Crescent , Lincoln
LN5 9BT **01522 721200**

Carpet and Floor Care

John Beresford Cleaning Services
4 Derwent Crescent , Nottingham
NG5 6TA **07767 607855**

Chauffeur Services

Emerald Executive Cars
Harlow-Stansted
............**01279 310562**

Cleaning Products

Eco EZEE
West Hill Manor Barn , Welford
NN6 6HF **01858 575454**

Compost

Welland Waste Management Ltd
Pebble Hall , Lutterworth
LE17 2NJ **07889 821844**

Computer & IT Recycling

DTC International
Park End Works , Brackley
NN13 5LX 01869 810600

PCB - Plus Computers
City Road Business Centre , Derby
DE1 3RQ 01332 366352

Computer Consultancy

Binary Royale
2 Chevin Vale , Duffield
DE56 4DT 01332 890460

Computer Maintenance

Daftech (UK) Ltd
33 Lynmouth Drive , Wigston
LE18 1BP 07730 598318

Octopus Computers
Octopus Business Centre , North Luffenham
LE15 8LF 08451 662318

Computer Services

PCB - Plus Computers
City Road Business Centre , Derby
DE1 3RQ 01332 366352

ACC Computers Ltd
69 West Gate , Mansfield
NG18 1RU 01623 646694

Iasotech Ltd
The Manor , Leicester
LE8 0PJ 08458 623697

Peakweb Ltd
Icon Business centre , Nottingham
NG15 0DT 08006 527871

DMC Systems
6 Leaper Street , Derby
DE1 3ND 01332 363404

Counselling , Advice and Psychotherapy

Katherine Akroyd Talking Support - Counselling & Coaching
3 Vernon Street , Derby
DE1 1FR 07808 584203

Family Therapy
17 Brookhouse Avenue , Leicester
LE2 0JE 07550 012923

Counselling , Advice and Psychotherapy

Anna Walker Counselling
3 Stud Farm Bungalows , Mansfield
NG18 4HX 01623 472902

John Monk-Steel Associates
43 Stoneygate Road , Leicester
LE2 2BP 01162 700290

David Woodall
31 Marigold Drive , Burbage
LE10 2SJ 01455 636787

Monica Hanaway Psyc and Meditation Services
79 Fairacres Road , Oxford
OX4 1TQ 01865 436538

Courier Services

Cabserve Ltd
55 Chieftan Way , Lincoln
LN6 7RY 01522 542732

Design 2 Print

Eight Days A Week Print Solutions
3 Church View , Sandiacre
NG10 5EA 01159 399797

Printing.Com (Nottingham)
94 Lower Palment Street , Nottingham
NG1 6DQ 01159 484626

Drilling, Boring and Site Investigations

Fugro Engineering Services
Fugro House , Wallingford
OX10 9RB 01491 820423

E-commerce and Search Engine Optimisation (SEO)

Momentum Web Solutions Ltd
14 Hanborough Business Park , Oxfordshire
OX29 8LH 07814 043651

MBS Wizzywebs
15 Bishops Close , Louth
LN11 8BT 03330 442674

Graphics & Web Design Ltd
The Mayfair Walk , Nottingham
NG10 1JR 08001 123011

Ecology Surveys and Consultancy

Herpetosure
Piper Hole Farm , Melton Mowbray
LE14 4SS **01664 444660**

Scarborough Nixon Associates
Brookfield House , Tattershall Thorpe
LN4 4PG **01526 344726**

Oak Bay Ecology
16 Waters Edge Fold, Manchester
OL1 4QJ **07775 186757**

Electrical and Electricians

Blackman Electrical
27 Masefield Crescent , Newark
Nottinghamshire , NG24 3QG
07920 776630 or 01636 659326
blackmanelectrical1@gmail.com
www.blackmanelectrical.co.uk

Michael Tobin Electrical Contractors
27 Lambley Lane , Nottingham
NG14 5BG **07542 052208**

Reset Renewables Ltd
Unit 18 Packway Court , Nottingham
NG8 4GN **01158 378322**

Atkinson Electrical Services
16 Pond Lane , Chesterfield
S42 6TW **07890 171515**

TRJ Electric and PV Solar
Sheaf Cottage , Skegness
PE24 5DH **01754 811331**

Ben Langridge Electrical
3 Strubby Cottages , Market Raisen
LN8 5Qa **07799 763351**

H J C Services Ltd
The Rise Office , Bicester
OX25 4SA **01869 349090**

Pegasus Property Maintenance Ltd
27 Calder Close , Derby
DE65 5HP **07809 228614**

Energy Electrical Contracting Ltd
8c Mobbs Miller House , Northampton
NN1 5LL **01604 788895**

A.J.S Property Services
Cherrytree Cottage , Lincoln
LN1 2LX **01522 703799**

Electrical Maintenance and Installation

Finch Electrical
28A Clare Street , Northampton
NN1 3JF **07885 298611**

Electro-Care Electrical Services
Unit 8 Howit Building, Nottingham
NG7 2BG **07989 115521**

Xy Electrical
6 Culpins Close , Spalding
PE11 2JL **07843 232700**

CSP Electrical Services
147 Harwill Crescent , Nottingham
NG8 5LE **07540 587119**

Embroidery

Embroidery 4 U
13 Moira Road , Ashby - De - La Zouch
LE65 2GB **07810 287185**

Quality Embroidery Design Ltd
650 Woodborough Road , Nottingham
NG3 5FS **08455 200007**

Energy Performance Certificates

Energy Measures 4u
344 Heanor Road , Ilkeston
DE7 8TJ **07709 285770**

Energy Performance Certificates Direct
15 Raven Drive , Kettering
Northamptonshire , NN15 6SD
07976 969 808
enquiries@energyperformancecertificatesdirect.com
www.energyperformancecertificatesdirect.com

Associated Corporation Ltd
Rosemary Centre , Mansfield
NG18 1RW **01623 654300**

Energy Saving Heating

Solar Sunpower UK Ltd
Jubilee Business Park, Appleby Magna
DE12 7AJ **08005 876527**

Intercity Marketing Ltd
Unit 5 Sketchley Road , Hinckley
LE10 3EN **07826 844698**

Energy Saving Products and Services

SmartGen
14 Craddock Street , Loughborough
LE11 1AH 01509 611500

Radiant Heating Solutions Ltd
Hougham , Grantham
NG32 2HZ 01400 250572

Exhibition Stands

Premier Display Ltd
Mill Lane Industrial Estate, Leicester
Leicestershire , LE3 8DX
0116 231 3335
paul@premierdisplay.co.uk
www.premierdisplay.co.uk

Bizgraphics
22 Annies Wharf , Loughborough
LE11 1LD 01509 214880

Off the Wall Imaging Ltd
Mill House Studio , Nether Broughton
LE14 3XB 01664 822000

Fences, Fencing & Decking

Beddow Tree Specialists
Thorney Fields Farm , Leicester
LE9 2BE 08002 888733

Fire Risk Assessment and Training

LRB Consulting Ltd
19 The Office Village , Loughborough
LE11 1QJ 01509 550023

Fire Safety Protection and Equipment

Silvaperl
Albion Works , Gainsborough
DN21 2QB 01427 675094

Cannon Safety Ltd
16 Quarrydale Avenue , Sutton in Ashfield
NG17 4DS 01623 465503

First Aid Training

Medrock Training Ltd
2 Carr Gate , Billinghay
LN4 4HD 08000 433822

First Aid Training

PGL Associates Ltd
Hobbits Hall , Derbyshire
DE12 6JP 01283 762999

Flashings for Solar Systems

Radiant Heating Solutions Ltd
Hougham , Grantham
NG32 2HZ 01400 250572

Food Hygiene

LRB Consulting Ltd
19 The Office Village , Loughborough
LE11 1QJ 01509 550023

Active Hygiene & Safety Training
35 Ilkeston Road , Trowell
NG9 3PY 07971 076645

Key Consultancy Services Ltd
15 Bulwer Road , Leicester
LE2 3BW 07849 414285

Fuel Saving Products

Clean Drive Systems uk Ltd
98 Uplands , Leicester
LE2 4ND 07812 743232

Garage Services

Truck Loaders
Unit 5 Drake House Court , Sutton in Ashfield
NG17 5LD 01623 558222

Garden Sculptures

Sculptures by Karen Williams
15 East Street , Nottingham
NG10 2DH 01158 492977

Gas and Central Heating (Domestic)

Valley Heating Services Ltd
Unit 12B Vincent Works , Hope Valley
S33 9HG 01433 620220

Graphic Design

One Hat Design
73a High Street , Witney
OX28 6JA 01993 702075

Graphic Design

Gem Graphic Design
Lincoln
.............**01522 689285**

Russfussuk Design
17 Costal Row , Newark
NG23 5DY **07952 285920**

Trident Design & Print
The Silk Warehouse , Hinckley
LE10 1QH **01455 557766**

Shinebright
13 University Road , Leicester
LE1 7RA **01162 553400**

Mark-Making Ltd
Harraden Court , Chiiping Norton
OX7 5AD **01608 649601**

BigStuff Media
Dunston Hole Farm , Chesterfield
S41 9RL **01246 261617**

Admen Partnership
Blakemoore House , Burton-on-Trent
DE14 3BY **01283 510369**

Liane J Robinson - Design Services
3 Vantage Meadow , Northampton
NN3 5EJ **07730 876916**

Connect Design and Print Ltd
Dabell Avenue , Nottingham
NG6 8WA **01159 755900**

Green Roofing

Green Footprint Solutions
14 Inham Fields Close , Gunthorpe
Nottingham , NG14 7FH
0115 966 5546 or 07876 791499
info@greenfs.co.uk
www.greenfs.co.uk
(see full page advert for more information)

Silvaperl
Albion Works , Gainsborough
DN21 2QB **01427 675094**

Green Roof Systems
Unit 5 Churchfield Court , Nottingham
NG5 9JL **07702 882234**

Ground Source Heat Pumps

Ice Energy
Unit 2 Oakfield House, Eynsham
OX29 4TH **01865 882202**

Ground Source Heat Pumps

SmartGen
14 Craddock Street , Loughborough
LE11 1AH **01509 611500**

Radiant Heating Solutions Ltd
Hougham , Grantham
NG32 2HZ **01400 250572**

Fusion G Source Ltd
Smeckley Wood Close , Chesterfield
S41 9PZ **01246 262721**

Health and Safety

Barnett's Safety Equipment Services Ltd (BSES)
363 Curie Avenue , Didcot
Oxfordshire , OX11 0QQ
01235 821593 or 07721 671301
barnett.pa@hotmail.com

Riskblitz Ltd
10 Cowbeck Close , Wootton
NN4 6JF **01604 709008**

The Quensh Consultancy
435 Holyhead Road , Coventry
CV5 8HS **02476 599503**

SLM PPE Technical Services
1 Adit View , Irthlingborough
NN9 5PH **01933 652284**

Singleton Associates
The Limes Training Centre , Lincoln
LN2 4JB **01522 531112**

ARC CONSULTANTS 2000 Ltd
Denby Yard , Derby
DE22 3BA **01159 220669**

Safety Fitz
Ashbourne
DE6 2DT **01335 330910**

Longland Safety Management Ltd
Gilmorton Road , Lutterworth
LE17 4BA **01455 559903**

Heatherwood Risk Management
Brook House , Wellingborough
NN8 2QY **01933 276871**

Safety Lincs
Garridan , Waddington
LN5 9RU **07514 550883**

Page 335

Human Resources and Training

The Quensh Consultancy
435 Holyhead Road , Coventry
CV5 8HS **02476 599503**

Insulation

Green Footprint Solutions
14 Inham Fields Close , Gunthorpe
Nottingham , NG14 7FH
0115 966 5546 or 07876 791499
info@greenfs.co.uk
www.greenfs.co.uk

Kingspan Tarec Industrial Insulation Ltd
Glossop Brook Road , Glossop
Derbyshire , SK13 8GP
0870 733 0021
info.uk@kingspantarec.co.uk
www.kingspantarec.com

Silvaperl
Albion Works , Gainsborough
DN21 2QB **01427 675094**

Seal Insulation
Smethwick Energy Action Ltd , Birmingham
B66 4PH **08001 073847**

BASF Polyurethanes U.K. Ltd
Wimsey Way , Alfreton
DE55 4NL **07557 012683**

Rockwarm Energy Saving Solutions
4 Trident Business Park , Nuneaton
CV11 4PN **02476 345554**

Insurance

Independent Warranty
20 Billing Road , Northampton
NN1 5AW **01604 604511**

Spink Insurance Consultants Ltd
Kirtlington Business Centre , Kidlington
OX5 3JA **01869 352711**

J C Steels (Insurance Consultants)
38 Glumangate , Chesterfield
S40 1TX **01246 540404**

Japanese Knotweed

Herpetosure
Piper Hole Farm , Melton Mowbray
LE14 4SS **01664 444660**

Landscaping and Ground Maintenance

Carrier Landscapes Ltd
Station Road , Melton Mowbray
LE14 3BQ **01664 822722**

Westwood Ground Maintenance
11 Rutland Road , Westwood
NG16 5JQ **07971 792531**

Low Energy Lightbulbs, Lighting and L.E.D.

Sunshine Energy Solutions
64 Hedgerley , Oxon
OX39 4TJ **07838 417528**

SmartGen
14 Craddock Street , Loughborough
LE11 1AH **01509 611500**

Solar Sunpower UK Ltd
Jubilee Business Park, Appleby Magna
DE12 7AJ **08005 876527**

Mobile Device Apps

Flexyweb Ltd
4 Stoney Street , Nottingham
NG1 1LG **08704 020108**

Networking and Cabling

Infront Communications Ltd
Hillcroft House , Lincoln
LN6 3QJ **08450 710670**

Cableguys Ltd
W24 Lenton Business Centre , Nottingham
NG7 2BY **01159 783896**

Off Grid Power

Office And Retail Furniture

Office Furniture Midlands, Restored & Recycled Furniture
Concept House , Melbourne
DE73 1DY 01332 864806

Office Stationery

Atlas Office Ltd
Business Exchange , Kettering
NN16 8DA 01536 417414

Painting and Decorating

Newport Decorators
8 Beech Avenue , Nottingham
NG17 8BP 01623 722252

Painting and Decorating

James Leddie Decorating And Maintenance
Lodge Cottage , Lincoln
Lincolnshire , LN1 2RB
07927 657959
j.leddie@hotmail.co.uk

(see full page advert for more information)

Bob Hooker & Son
10 Becketts Close , Daventry
NN11 6XS 01327 260845

F and CD Wells Ltd
Rowlands Way , Leicester
LE2 9HS 01162 771771

K Clarke Painting and Decorating
67 Grantham Road , Leicester
LE5 1HP 07753 219510

Decorating Solutions
31 Queen Street , Swadlincote
DE11 9LZ 01283 216556

Paul Frost Painter & Decorator
22 Boston Road , Grantham
NG34 7ET 07940 309700

Pinehirst Decorating Contractors Ltd
30 Meadow Lane , Loughborough
LE11 1JY 01509 217199

Gary Byrne & Son Decorators
24 Brostock Way , Abingdon
OX14 4BY 07759 341525

A.J.S Property Services
Cherrytree Cottage , Lincoln
LN1 2LX 01522 703799

Painting and Decorating Supplies

Eco EZEE
West Hill Manor Barn , Welford
NN6 6HF 01858 575454

Paving and Driveways

LMR Blockpaving
25 Hawkins Grove , Grimsby
DN32 8JB 01472 601263

Payroll and Bookkeeping

B B A Payroll
64 High Street , Belper
DE56 1GF 01773 826071

THE GREEN DIRECTORY

LOCAL SECTION   East Midlands

THE **GREEN** DIRECTORY

James Leddie
Decorating and
Maintenance

**Painting and
Decorating
Joinery, Tiling,
Plastering**

Call now:
07927 657959

Lodge Cottage, Middle Street, Burton, Lincoln, LIncolnshire, LN1 2RB, UK

LOCAL SECTION

THE **GREEN** DIRECTORY

Payroll and Bookkeeping

Value Added Accountancy Ltd
23 Saint Mary Street , Ilkeston
DE7 8AB **01159 320878**

H J C Services Ltd
The Rise Office , Bicester
OX25 4SA **01869 349090**

Adkins & Morris (Rugby) Ltd
23a High Street , Welford
NN6 6HT **01858 571197**

Brian James F.C.A
Chartered Accountant
45 Wide Bargate , Boston
PE21 6SH **01205 362900**

Moore Book-keeping Services
25 Howitt Street , Heanor
DE75 7AU **01773 767992**

Suretax Accounting
279 Leamington Road , Coventry
CV3 6NB **02476 697300**

Kate Jarvis Secretarial Services
The Granary , Inglby
D73 7HW **01332 862101**

Tye's Bookkeeping
74 Coton Park , Swadlincote
DE12 6RF **07579 006932**

Sadika-Vale Ltd
276 Banbury Road , Oxford
OX2 7ED **01865 511898**

Pest Control

Nottingham Pest Control Ltd
Kestrel Business Centre , Nottingham
NG9 2JR **01159 872968**

SP Pest Control
3 Dervale Villas , Matlock
Derbyshire , DE4 5HN
01629 826951   07907 954142
spmoleman@aol.co.uk
www.spmoleman-derbyshire.co.uk
(see full page advert for more information)

Pestwise
34 Hayway , Northamptonshire
NN9 5QP **01933 388177**

Acclaim Environmental
25 Granville Street , Market Harborough
LE16 9EU **01858 432797**

Pest Control

We Kill Any Pests
Markfield Lodge , Leicester
Leicestershire , LE9 9FH
01455 828967
davidrhysmorris@aol.com

(see full page advert for more information)

Rid-It-Pest Control
Brackley
NN13 5LZ **01869 810643**

Photography and Photographers

Ian Pickering Photography
27 Leicester Road , Hinckley
LE10 3PP **01455 271371**

Plastering and Tiling

A.J.S Property Services
Cherrytree Cottage , Lincoln
LN1 2LX **01522 703799**

Plumbers Merchants

Travis Perkins Plc
Lodge Way House , Northampton
NN5 7UG **01604 752424**

Buildbase
Gemini One , Cowley
OX4 2LL **01865 871700**

Plumbing Services

Valley Heating Services Ltd
Unit 12B Vincent Works , Hope Valley
S33 9HG **01433 620220**

A.J.S Property Services
Cherrytree Cottage , Lincoln
LN1 2LX **01522 703799**

Portable Appliance and Fixed Wire Testing

Oxfordshire PAT Testing Services
15 Poplar Close , Oxford
OX44 9BP **01865 599212**

Electrical Testers Ltd
Hawthorn Park , Northampton
NN6 8LD **01604 820220**

THE GREEN DIRECTORY

THE GREEN DIRECTORY

Print can contribute to the bottom line and be environmentally friendly

Discarded printed paper waste is a major component of landfill sites!

Good understanding of the print requirements marrying with the right processes reduces wastage. This requires experience and understanding of the processes available.

The team of six at Evolution Print have *over 30+ years* each of print experience. They ensure that your printed products are the right quality, on time, competitive and printed using the right processes - all contributing to the bottom line and importantly to the environment.

Contact Girish Naker for more details:

EVOLUTION
PRINT AND DESIGN LIMITED

Unit 12, Lewisher Road, Leicester LE4 9LR.
Tel: 0116 274 7700 | Fax: 0116 274 2691
Email: sales@evolutiondc.co.uk | Website: www.evolutiondc.co.uk

Portable Appliance and Fixed Wire Testing

Initial PAT Testing
122 Lubbesthorpe Road , Leicester
LE3 2XE **08000 831639**

RJ PAT Testing Services
10 Shields Crescent , Derby
DE74 2JS **07757 034879**

Electrosafe Electrical Services
75 Aspley Park Drive , Aspley
NG8 3EG **07968 536345**

Printing, Design and Mailing Services

Ruddocks
56 Great Northern Terrace , Lincoln
LN5 8HL **01522 529591**

Tbag Productions Limited
Unit 4 Network House, Nuns Street,
Derby , DE1 3LP
01332 372020 or 0773 0527652
info@tbagproductions.com
www.tbagproductions.com
(see full page advert for more information)

Kall Kwik Business & Print
85 Abington Street , Northampton
Northamptonshire , NN1 2BH
01604 635177
robert@kallkwiknorthampton.co.uk
www.kallkwik.co.uk/northampton

Evolution Print & Design Limited
37 Lewisher Road , Leicester
Leicestershire , LE4 9LR
0116 274 7700
sales@evolutiondc.co.uk

(see full page advert for more information)

Connect Design and Print Ltd
Dabell Avenue , Nottingham
NG6 8WA **01159 755900**

Blue Star Print Solutions
21 Patenall Way , Northants
NN10 8PL **08442 729109**

Colorgrafix (Louth) Ltd
114 Eastgate , Louth
LN11 9AA **01507 600541**

Printing, Design and Mailing Services

Quick Print UK Ltd
Unit 23 Prince William Road , Loughborough
LE11 5GU **01509 236987**

Poppy Print
Satra Innovation Park , Kettering
NN16 9JH **01536 533275**

Easy Green Print.com
Horspath Road industrial Estate, Oxford
OX 4 2SE **01865 395252**

Promotional Clothing

Maverick Promotions
4 Paddock Close , Grantham
NG32 3RP **01400 230180**

Promotional Items and Incentives

Perfect Promotional Products Limited
36 Coniston Close , Rushden
NN10 8NL **01933 420624**

Micromarketing Ltd
The Barrel House , Witney
OX28 4AW **01993 773350**

Publishing, Packaging and Corporate ID

Bizgraphics
22 Annies Wharf , Loughborough
LE11 1LD **01509 214880**

Recycling

Ellgia Recycling Limited
Westville , Boston
PE22 7RH **01205 750910**

Acclaim Environmental
25 Granville Street , Market Harborough
LE16 9EU **01858 432797**

National Paper Recycling Ltd
Pilot Road , Corby
NN17 5YH **07779 003591**

Roofing Services

Green Roof Systems
Unit 5 Churchfield Court , Nottingham
NG5 9JL **07702 882234**

PGL ASSOCIATES

**Health and Safety
Training and Consultancy**

"Talk to us for effective commonsense
Safety Advice or Training"

PRODUCTS AND SERVICE SECTORS

- City and Guild Assesment
- Health and Safety Training
- IOSH Courses

MARKETS SERVED

- Commercial
- Industrial
- Government

Page 345

PRODUCTS AND SERVICES OFFERED

- Safety Equipment Hire
- Safety Equipment Servicing
- Health and Safety Consultancy

**PGL Associates Ltd, Hobbits Hall, Green Lane, Overseal
Derbyshire, DE12 6JP, UK
www.pglassociates.com
Tel: 01283 762999**

THE GREEN DIRECTORY

Safety and Convenience Products

Kaizen Distribution Services Ltd
98 Uplands Road , Leicester
LE2 4NQ **07812 743232**

Safety Risk Assessment

PGL Associates
Hobbits Hall , Overseal
Derbyshire , DE12 6JP
10283 762999
enquiries@pglassociates.com

(see full page advert for more information)

Michael W White Associates Ltd
94 Manor Road , Borrowash
DE72 3LN **01332 671730**

Riskblitz Ltd
10 Cowbeck Close , Wootton
NN4 6JF **01604 709008**

SLM PPE Technical Services
1 Adit View , Irthlingborough
NN9 5PH **01933 652284**

Heatherwood Risk Management
Brook House , Wellingborough
NN8 2QY **01933 276871**

Secretarial Service

Dragon Virtual Assistants
NFU Offices , Spalding
PE12 6ET **01775 302101**

Signs and Graphics

Direct Signs (UK) Ltd
Venture Court , Hinckley
LE10 3BT **01455 230122**

Signarama (Oxford)
3 Bessel Sleigh Road , Wootton
OX13 6DN **01865 730046**

DNA Signs
Wood Burcote Business Farm , Towcester
NN12 8TA **01327 350106**

Apollo Signs & Engraving
5 Tannery Road , Nottingham
NG16 2WP **01159 384200**

Graphics To Go
Greenfield Business Park , Hinkley
LE10 1BB **01455 239760**

Signs and Graphics

Bizgraphics
22 Annies Wharf , Loughborough
LE11 1LD **01509 214880**

Solar Accessories

Klober Limited
East Midlands Distibution Centre , Castle Donnington
DE74 2HA **08007 833216**

Solar Energy

Eco Solar Smiths Ltd
25 Appleton Drive , Glossop
SK13 8RX **07970 744221**

Sunshine Energy Solutions
64 Hedgerley , Oxon
OX39 4TJ **07838 417528**

JHS Solar Solutions
Cherwell Business Village , Banbury
OX16 2SP **08453 024779**

Radiant Heating Solutions Ltd
Hougham , Grantham
NG32 2HZ **01400 250572**

Rockwarm Energy Saving Solutions
4 Trident Business Park , Nuneaton
CV11 4PN **02476 345554**

Solar Panels and Photovoltaics

1 Melton Electrical Services
25 Palmerston Road , Melton Mowbray
Leicestershire , LE13 0SS
01664 564223
shaun.nolan@btinternet.com

(see full page advert for more information)

Eco Solar Smiths Ltd
25 Appleton Drive , Glossop
SK13 8RX **07970 744221**

Ice Energy
Unit 2 Oakfield House, Eynsham
OX29 4TH **01865 882202**

Beco Energy Ltd
Beco Energy Centre , Nottingham
NG10 1GA **01159 461392**

Carrino Eco Ltd
4 Gorse Hill , Nottingham
NG15 9AF **08452 000836**

Solar Panels and Photovoltaics

An East Midlands based company dedicated to the business of delivering free electricity from the sun

Non-polluting, safe, reliable, silent, long-lasting and with zero running cost

PRODUCE YOUR OWN RENEWABLE ENERGY

On April 1st 2010, feed in tariffs(FITS) were introduced allowing individuals and communities who produce their own renewable energy through microgeneration and low carbon sources to sell any excess electricity back to the grid. Domestic and commercial solar panels can provide you with excellent returns, we are leading solar panel suppliers. The scheme guarantees a minimum payment incentive for all energy produced by the system as well as a payment for the energy sold back for general usage

WHY CHOOSE SOLAR

Traditional sources of electricity generation emit large amounts of carbon dioxide and various other noxious gases into the atmosphere. Solar electricity is a completely environmentally friendly alternative as it harnesses energy directly from the sun which can produce a constant source of power without damaging the environment. Having domestic solar panels is a completely clean energy source. Save money on your energy bills.

Solar PV provides a FREE source of electricity which can cover up to 50% of your energy needs each year. With the governments newly introduced Feed In Tarrifs(FITS), you also have the option to sell electricity back to the national grid which will provide additional income as well as enrgy.

Tel: 01664 564 223
shaun.nolan6@btinternet.com
http://www.meltonelectricalservices.co.uk/
Melton Electrical Services ltd, 25 Palmerston Road, Melton Mobray, Leicestershire, LE13 0SS

Solar Panels and Photovoltaics

Electricmover Ltd
Hillcrest , Alfreton
DE55 6JR **08456 432155**

Solar Sunpower UK Ltd
Jubilee Business Park, Appleby Magna
DE12 7AJ **08005 876527**

SmartGen
14 Craddock Street , Loughborough
LE11 1AH **01509 611500**

Reset Renewables Ltd
Unit 18 Packway Court , Nottingham
NG8 4GN **01158 378322**

Underfloor Warehouse Ltd
The Eco Hub , Blaby
Leicestershire , LE8 4GZ
0116 258 1410
enquiries@ufw.co.uk
www.ufw.co.uk

Solar Water Heating Systems

Valley Heating Services Ltd
Unit 12B Vincent Works , Hope Valley
S33 9HG **01433 620220**

Atmos Heating Systems
TBS Depot , Daventry
NN11 4ES **01327 871990**

SmartGen
14 Craddock Street , Loughborough
LE11 1AH **01509 611500**

NSA Solar Thermal Ltd
Unit 3 Coal Cart Road , Leicester
LE4 3BY **01162 675835**

Radiant Heating Solutions Ltd
Hougham , Grantham
NG32 2HZ **01400 250572**

Underfloor Warehouse Ltd
The Eco Hub , Blaby
Leicestershire , LE8 4GZ
0116 258 1410
enquiries@ufw.co.uk
www.ufw.co.uk

Spray Foam Insulation.

BASF Polyurethanes U.K. Ltd
Wimsey Way , Alfreton
DE55 4NL **07557 012683**

Staff and Work Wear

Graphics To Go
Greenfield Business Park , Hinkley
LE10 1BB **01455 239760**

Maverick Promotions
4 Paddock Close , Grantham
NG32 3RP **01400 230180**

Sustainable Bathroom Equipment.

Ecotoilets
The Canal Shop , Crick Road , Rugby
Warwickshire , CV21 4PW
01327 844442
richard@ecotoilet.org.uk
www.ecotoilet.org.uk
(see full page advert for more information)

Telecommunications

Infront Communications Ltd
Hillcroft House , Lincoln
LN6 3QJ **08450 710670**

RFH Communications Ltd
6 Sycamore Close , Swadlincote
DE12 6PS **07980 449803**

Torkard Telecom Ltd
150 Common Lane , Nottingham
NG15 6TG **08448 111299**

Sempervox
Consort House , Leicester
LE1 7GZ **08442 510521**

DTC International
Park End Works , Brackley
NN13 5LX **01869 810600**

Town Planning

Planning & Development

Archaeology

Historic Buildings

CgMs
CONSULTING

Practical solutions for landowners and developers

Contact: Richard Atkinson, CgMs Consulting, Newark Beacon, Cafferata Way, Newark, Nottinghamshire NG24 2TN.
Email: richard.atkinson@cgms.co.uk Tel: 01636 653 060

THE GREEN DIRECTORY

Transport Equipment Installations

Truck Loaders
Drake House Court , Sutton in Ashfield
NG17 5LD **01623 558222**

Tree Work and Surveys

Beddow Tree Specialists
Thorney Fields Farm , Leicester
LE9 2BE **08002 888733**

Northants Tree Services
105 Bush Hill , Northampton
NN3 2PF **01604 787222**

Midland Tree Management Ltd
Woodside Farm , Turnditch
DE56 2LU **01335 370491**

TREES : AN INTEGRAL PART OF
A SUSTAINABLE LANDSCAPE
• TREE CONDITION SURVEYS
  AND RISK ASSESSMENTS
• SURVEYS FOR PLANNING &
  DEVELOPMENT
• DESIGN & MANAGEMENT

RGS
Aboricultural
Consultants

CONTACT: ROBERT YATES
(Principal) Tel. 01604 581044
e. info@rgs-treeservices.co.uk
www.rgs-treeservices.co.uk

P.M Tree Services Ltd
12 Candlery Lane , Nottingham
NG12 3JG **07970 449929**

Trophies and Engraving

Joblot Trophies
467 Westdale Lane , Nottingham
NG3 6DH **01159 245577**

Underfloor Heating

Atmos Heating Systems
TBS Depot , Daventry
NN11 4ES **01327 871990**

Ice Energy
Unit 2 Oakfield House, Eynsham
OX29 4TH **01865 882202**

SmartGen
14 Craddock Street , Loughborough
LE11 1AH **01509 611500**

Underfloor Heating

UFW Limited - The Renewable Energy Centre
The Eco Hub , Blaby
LE8 4GZ **01162 581410**

Water Coolers

Jack In the Box Vending
11 Cara Close , Leicester
LE2 3UD **08002 343777**

Water Saving Products and Services

Ecotoilets
The Canal Shop , Rugby
CV21 4PW **01327 844442**

Water Treatment and Purification Systems

B & V Water Treatment
A division of Global Chemical Technologies Lt
NN11 8YH **08443 727344**

Website and Internet Services

RouteToWeb
4 Russell Close , Peterborough
PE6 0SW **01733 270872**

Flaminga Design
8 Hillfield Gardens , Nottingham
NG5 5BA **07707 995969**

Push Dot Play Ltd
Sparkhouse Studio , Lincoln
LN6 7DQ **01522 837258**

In 1 Design
62 Swallowfield , Peterborough
PE4 5BN **07952 067685**

Purpose Media
Unit 14, The Village , South Normanton
DE55 2DS **01773 864500**

Website and Internet Services

Matthew Stuart Design
Yew Tree Close , Banbury
OX18 2SU **01295 713813**

Xtremis Web Design
48 Marlborough Road , Northampton
NN5 5DS **01604 758730**

Defining Design
2-14 The Crescent , Leicester
LE1 6RX **07969 559087**

1point3
14 Proclamation Avenue , Rothwell
NN14 6GY **01536 711263**

Wind Energy

SmartGen
14 Craddock Street , Loughborough
LE11 1AH **01509 611500**

Evance Wind Turbines Ltd
Unit 6 Weldon Road , Loughborough
LE11 5RN **01509 215669**

Window Cleaning

Gerald McKeever
2a Devonshire Drive , Nottingham
NG9 8GU **01158 565219**

JM Window Cleaning
3 Bull Furlong Lane , Hinckley
LE10 2HQ **07974 550515**

Ivory Towers
39 Orchard Street , Ibstock
LE67 6LL **07963 561834**

Window Film

Solar Control Films Ltd
Unit 18 The Weavers , Newark
Nottinghamshire , NG24 4RY
01636 613222 or   07799 664442
sales@solarcontrolfilms.co.uk

GREENER TIMES
>SUSTAINABLE SOLUTIONS MAGAZINE

Old Station Building
Oswald Road, Oswestry
Shropshire, SY11 1RE

SUBSCRIBE TO THE UK'S BEST GREEN BUSINESS, LIFESTYLE AND SUSTAINABILITY MAGAZINE

If you enjoy reading the Greener Times magazine, why not take advantage of our special subscription rates and save yourself some money?   Each issue of Greener Times is enjoyable, informative reading that will also make you think!

As well as articles on environmental issues that can affect you at home as well as at work; there are interviews with celebrities like Gareth Southgate and successful businesses such as Stagecoach, quizzes that the whole family can get involved with and current affairs relating to local communities and businesses, all with an environmental and sustainable theme i.e. The Green Deal, The Renewable Heat Incentive (RHI) etc.

There is also a 'Whats On?' list of forthcoming shows and events that we will be attending where you can come along and meet us in person.

It costs just **£4.20 + P&P** Or if you want to save some money you can subscribe for a year for just **£42 + P&P** *(payable by monthly or annual direct debit)* Instruction to Greener Times Publishing Ltd

Page 353

DON'T MISS AN ISSUE, SUBSCRIBE TODAY!

£42 + P&P

01691 661 565
info@greener-times.co.uk
www.greener-times.co.uk

Norwich

09

Cambridge

01
02
03
04
05
06
07
08
09
10
11
12

The Business Supporting The East of England Section for the 2012/13 Local Sourcing Directory is:

Page 355

_gh_
George Hay
Chartered Accountants

Local advice equals
a low carbon footprint

At George Hay, we don't think you should have to go
a long way to find the best advice for your business and
personal finances. With offices in Biggleswade, Huntingdon
and Letchworth, it's easy to access our high quality accountancy,
business development and tax services. We also offer expert
advice in more specialist areas, including:

- Payscheme, our outsourced payroll service
- charities
- academy schools
- business start-ups
- business strategy
- inheritance tax planning
- research and development tax credits.

So it's good to know that whatever
advice you need, it isn't far away
with **George Hay.**

www.georgehay.co.uk

Biggleswade office
T: 01767 315010

biggleswade@georgehay.co.uk

Huntingdon office
T: 01480 426500

huntingdon@georgehay.co.uk

Letchworth office
T: 01462 708810

letchworth@georgehay.co.uk

George Hay is registered to carry on audit work and regulated for a range of investment business activities by the Institute of Chartered Accountants in England and Wales.

Access Control and Entry Systems

Oakpark Alarms Security Services Ltd
34 High Street , Winslow
MK18 3HB **01296 713010**

Accountancy

Trueman Brown
7 Foxglove Road , South Ockenden
RM15 6EU **01708 854943**

Abacus 161 Ltd
408 Linnet Drive , Chelmsford
Essex , CM2 8AL
08440 502265
enquiries@abacusaccounts-chelmsford.co.uk
www.abacusaccounts-chelmsford.co.uk

George Hay Chartered Accountants
St. Georges House , Huntingdon
Cambridgeshire , PE29 3GH
01480 426500
toni.hunter@georgehay.co.uk
www.georgehay.co.uk
(see full page advert for more information)

Julian Ellis
15a Bull Plain , Hertford
Hertfordshire , SG14 1OX
01992 550424
ellis-julian@btconnect.com
www.julianellis.co.uk

Lescott Courts (Wickford)
10 Station Court , Wickford
SS11 7AT **01268 560060**

Astons
19-21 Manor Road , Nr. Luton
LU1 4EE **01582 459500**

James Johnson and Co (Accountancy) Limited
7 Peddars Drive , Hunstanton
Norfolk , PE36 6HF
01485 534948 or 07876 523861
james@jamesjohnsonltd.co.uk
www.jamesjohnsonltd.co.uk

Accountancy

Clouders
Charter House , Leigh-on-Sea
Essex , SS9 1JL
01702 470033 or
david@clouders.co.uk
www.clouders.co.uk

D & E Accountancy Ltd
2 Walsworth Road , Hitchin
Hertfordshire , SG4 9SP
01462 437 562 or
david@d-and-e.co.uk
www.d-and-e.co.uk

Accreditation and Certification

SCILP Ltd
144 Beccles Road , Great Yarmouth
Norfolk , NR31 3AE
01493 304493 or 07840 523028
ian.thynne@scilp.co.uk
www.scilp.co.uk

Acupuncture

The Lotus and The Serpent
134 Girton Road , Girton
CB3 0LW **01223 277177**

Bluebell Practice
2 Woodview Road , Norwich
NR9 5EU **01603 880214**

Administration and Payroll Software

BusinessPlus (Letchworth) Ltd
39 Parker Close , Letchworth
SG6 3RT **01462 486877**

Air Conditioning Systems

Climate Building Services Ltd
Bella Vista , High Wycombe
Buckinghamshire , HP14 4DW
07976 256 641
simon@climatebuildingservices.com

Interactive Components

Flexibility Moves

With the addition of the new type 300 series to the current Type 200 series of actuators, **GRUNER** *Schalten und Bewegen* is now able to offer actuators from 2 to 40 Nm for use in air movement systems and for use with ball and butterfly valves.

Offering rotary actuators with or with out the spring return function for HVAC applications, a quick running range from 1 – 35 seconds, a dedicated range for use in fire and smoke protection applications and a range of OEM types. With linear types, which include spindle drive variants that offer performance from 150 to 600 N and with a dedicated range of products for use in air volume, pressure and temperature control with the quickest set up time of any current manufacturer , **GRUNER** *Schalten und Bewegen* is truly your flexible partner

For more information on the actuator range and actuated ball valves, including a range for use in drinking water applications, visit the **GRUNER** *Schalten und Bewegen* website at :- **www.gruner.de** and click on to the actuators section, or contact us for samples and pricing information.

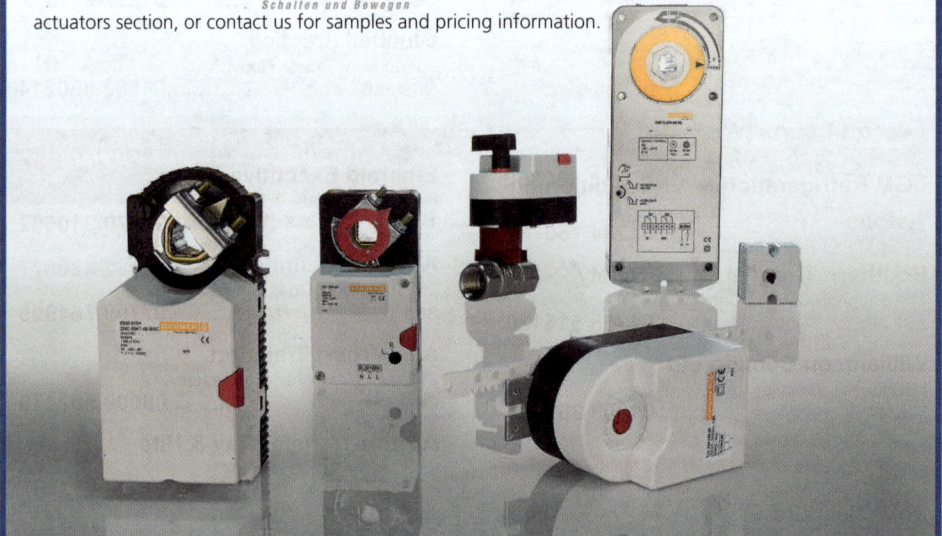

Air Conditioning Systems

ETS Ltd
22 St Marys Road , Stowmarket
Suffolk , IP14 1LP
07989 383823
sj.barrett@btconnect.com

Techni-Cool Ltd
1 Redbury Farm Cottages , Colchester
CO7 7PQ **07760 350717**

Airelec Services Ltd
12 The Cotes , Ely
CB7 5EP **01353 721122**

C Taylor Electrical & Mechanical Services
74 Dukes Avenue , Epping
CM16 7HF **07973 179324**

Interactive Components
2A Patrick Way , Aylesbury
Buckinghamshire , HP21 9XH
01296 425 656 or 07836 694 463
interactive@bucksnet.co.uk

(see full page advert for more information)

ARC Ltd
Silver Springs , Wisbech
Cambridgeshire , PE13 5LG
07971 595726 or 01945 871081
info@perfectenvironment.co.uk
www.perfectenvironment.co.uk

LGM Refrigeration & Air Conditioning
31 Gloucester Road , Bury St Edmonds
IP32 6DL **01284 750780**

Southern Thermal Fire & Safety
The Shannon Centre , CanveyIsland
SS8 0PE **01268 515130**

Williamson Cooling Ltd
Mill House , Bletchley
MK2 2UZ **01908 366605**

Air Source Heat Pumps

SolarTech Ltd
Unit 2 Sterling Business Park , Buckingham
MK18 1TH **08458 382477**

Air Source Heat Pumps

Miller Installations Ltd
8 Paston Road , Norwich
NR12 0JA **01692 531082**

Climate Building Services Ltd
Bella Vista , High Wycombe
HP14 4DW **07976 256641**

AngliaEcoheat Ltd
Elco Building , Newmarket
CB8 0AT **01638 662955**

Affordable Renewables
Unit 1 Chamberlayne Road , Bury St. Edmunds
Suffolk , IP32 7EY
0800 032 0944 or 07770 765 328
richard@affordablerenewables.org.uk
www.affordablerenewables.org.uk

Airport Transfers

1st Goldstar Taxis
6 Drayton Industrial Estate , Norwich
NR8 6RL **01603 700700**

Envirocab MK Ltd
168 Newton Road , Milton Keynes
MK3 5DE **01908 645300**

Airport Express
4 Hazel Close , Colchester
Essex , CO7 8HJ
0330 555 1122 or 01206 251 122
ed@et-taxi.co.uk

Emerald Executive Cars
Harlow-Stansted
..............**01279 310562**

ATC Taxis Limited
295 Eastwood Road North , Leigh
SS9 4LT **07799 764905**

A B Airport Transfers
25 Steed Crescent , Colchester
CO2 7SJ **08009 552470**

Airport Transfer Day & Nite
65 High Street , Kelvedon
CO5 9AE **07903 818813**

THE GREEN DIRECTORY

Airport Transfers

Home Counties Chauffeur Co.
14 Warren Close , Aylesbury
Buckinghamshire , HP17 8YL
01296 748701 or 07973 635396
stuart@homecountieschauffeur.com
www.homecountieschauffeur.com

Thurrock Airport Cars
78 Bradleigh Avenue , Grays
RM17 5RJ **01375 399300**

Airport Direct
4 Moulsham Drive , Chelmsford
CM2 9PX **01245 347070**

Alternative and Renewable Energy

Bidwells
Bidwell House , Cambridge
CB2 9LD **01223 559406**

Alternative and Renewable Energy

Natural Sparx
313-333 Rainham Road , Dagenham
Essex , RM10 8SX
0845 218 6938
marketing@naturalsparx.co.uk
www.naturalsparx.co.uk
(see half page advert for more information)

SolarTech Ltd
Unit 2 Sterling Business Park , Buckingham
MK18 1TH **08458 382477**

Ambulance Services

Aero Medical Ambulance Service
71 The Crescent , Abbotts Langley
Hertfordshire , WD5 0DR
07717 478648
info@aeromedicalambulance.com

(see full page advert for more information)

We Listen to you,
We have Time for you,
We treat you with Care.

Aero Medical Ambulance Service is based in the South East of England, located close to the main road routes to access areas quickly.

Aero Medical Ambulance Service is an independent provider of quality private ambulance services. We have a well known reputation for specialising in medical repatriations within the UK and Europe since 1974. Aero Medical Ambulance Service offer a friendly and professional service to meet your requirements. All our ambulances are kitted to deal with all needs of the patient. Patients receive a high level of care, from the moment of first contact to ensure all their needs are met.

24/7 365 Days   Tel: 07717 478 648   www.aeromedicalambulance.com

We offer:
- Ambulance Transfers
- Hospital Appointments/Visits
- Emergency Ambulance Response
- Air Ambulances
- Medical Cover for events
- First Aid and Medical Training

LOCAL SECTION East of England

Page 361

THE GREEN DIRECTORY

THE GREEN DIRECTORY

Architects

Manns Property Services
4 Chestnut Close , Mildenhall
Suffolk , IP28 7NL
01638 716 432 or 07777 800 413
david@mannspropertyservices.co.uk
www.mannspropertyservices.co.uk
(see half page advert for more information)

Design & Development Consultancy
Herringbone , Frinton-on-Sea
Essex , CO11 1BP
01255 675376 or 07801 546 398
info@design-development.co.uk
www.design-development.co.uk

Water Lane Architects
Water Lane Cottage , Colchester
CO6 4DG 07827 414847

Richard Pike Associates
4 Netherconesford , Norwich
NR1 1PW 01603 611323

Calvert Brain & Fraulo Architectural Ltd
3 Portland Street , King's Lynn
PE30 1PB 01553 766220

Architects

Ely Design Group
3 Short Road , Stretham
CB6 3LS 01353 649649

E & P Building Design
The Gables , Mildenhall
IP28 7AH 01638 563086

Graham Blyth Building Design & Planning
Acanthus House , North Walsham
NR28 9BN 01692 402385

Hibbs and Walsh Associates
53 High Street , Saffron Walden
CB10 1AR 01799 523660

Graham Page Designs
11 Northgate Street , Ipswich
IP1 3BX 01473 231876

Whitworth Co-Partnership Ltd (Suffolk)
18 Hatter Street , Bury St Edmunds
IP33 1NE 01284 760421

Architects

Asbestos Handling and Removal

Four Seasons Environmental
Swinbourne Road , Southend on Sea
SS13 1EP **01268 729747**

Asbestos Survey and Assesment

Pinpoint Asbestos Ltd
11 High Street , St Neots
PE19 5YE **01480 477292**

Asbestos Training and Awareness

Bainbridge Asbestos Services Ltd
62 Rillwood Court , Northampton
NN3 8JS **07772 557635**

1-2 Call Worksafe Ltd
1 Empire Avenue , Kings Lynn
Norfolk , PE30 3AU
07794 505 712 or 01553 672449
info@1-2callworksafe.co.uk
www.1-2callworksafe.co.uk

Audio Visual

Hyde AV
17 Puckleside , Basildon
SS16 5XD **07540 615125**

Biomass Energy and Biofuels

Affordable Renewables
Unit 1 Chamberlayne Road , Bury St. Edmunds
Suffolk , IP32 7EY
0800 032 0944 or 01284 763969
richard@affordablerenewables.org.uk
www.affordablerenewables.org.uk

(see full page advert for more information)

Branding & Marketing

Mike Spike
12 Millington Gate , Milton Keynes
MK15 9HT **01908 677994**

Builders Merchants

MKM Building Supplies (Chelmsford)
7 Montrose Road , Chelmsford
CM2 6TE **01245 399711**

Builders Merchants

MKM Building Supplies
Vulcan Road North , Norwich
NR6 6AQ **01603 795377**

Building and Construction

Building Conservation and Preservation

Whitworth Co-Partnership Ltd (Norfolk)
1 The Close , Norwich
NR1 4DH **01603 626782**

Business Management, Coaching and Consultancy

Langdale Consulting
Windsor House , Holmer Green (Bucks)
Buckinghamshire , HP15 6SG
07973 766747
ptodd@langdaleconsulting.co.uk
www.langdaleconsulting.co.uk

Coach4resultS Ltd
Russell Drive , Willington
MK44 3QX **01234 831282**

Carpentry and Joinery

Julie Chamberlain
58 Hatfield Road , Ipswitch
Suffolk , IP3 9AF
07940 310316
jcchippy@hotmail.com

(see half page advert for more information)

Handmade Kitchen Co
18A Woodfield Terrace , Epping
CM16 6LL **01992 577998**

Page 364

THE GREEN DIRECTORY

Carpentry and Joinery

JULIE CHAMBERLAIN
Carpentry & Joinery

Julie Chamberlain
58 Hatfield Road, Ipswich, Suffolk
IP3 9AF, UK
Tel: 07940 310 316
jcchippy@hotmail.com

Page 365

CCTV and Surveillance

Sygma Security Systems
Blois Meadow Business Park , Steeple Bumstead
CB9 7BN 01440 731912

Concept Security Solutions
117 Watford Road , St. Albans
AL2 3JY 07884 000682

Chauffeur Services

Emerald Executive Cars
Harlow-Stansted
.............01279 310562

Home Counties Chauffeur Co.
14 Warren Close , Aylesbury
HP17 8YL 01296 748701

Cleaning and Hygiene Services

Spalls Ltd
29 Mitchell Way , Chelmsford
CM35 5PJ 01245 429178

The Tudor Cleaning Company
155 Waterloo Road , Norwich
NR3 3HY 01603 889034

Cleaning and Hygiene Services

Klean Well Bedford Ltd
154 Honey Hill Road , Bedford
MK40 4PD 01234 218014

County View Commercial Cleaning Services Ltd
Wrest Park Enterprise Centre , Silso
MK45 4HS 01582 968605

B & M Cleaners Ltd
11 Overbury Road , Norwich
NR6 5LB 01603 424202

Clothing for Schools

Pauls Discount Clothing
38/40 Southchurch Road , Southend
SS1 2ND 01702 466431

Computer Maintenance

Arrow Ltd
17 Middlefield Drive , Stowmarket
IP14 3AH 01449 674102

Computer Maintenance

ARK IT Services & Supplies Ltd
Unit 16 Cockridden Farm , Brentwood
CM13 3LH **01277 811188**

Herts IT and Telecom Services
77 Elderbek Close , Cheshunt
EN7 8HT **01992 878584**

Andrews Computer Services Ltd
Nash House , Hemel Hempstead
Hertfordshire , HP3 9SR
01442 241 200
sales@andrews-computers.com
www.andrews-computers.com

Octopus Computers
Octopus Business Centre , North Luffenham
LE15 8LF **08451 662318**

Computer Services

Softlink Solutions Ltd
Foundry Place , Maldon
CM9 8JT **08450 940010**

Softcraft Computer Services Ltd
Norwich House , Norwich
NR28 9AL **01692 535355**

Sunrise Technologies
25 Seax Court , Basildon
SS15 6SL **01268 543995**

Andrews Computer Services Ltd
Nash House , Hemel Hempstead
Hertfordshire , HP3 9SR
01442 241 200
sales@andrews-computers.com

Bridon IT Support Limited
77 High Street , Benfleet
SS7 1RS **01702 389432**

You Services Ltd
6B Belgic Square , Peterborough
PE1 5XF **01733 563900**

C.J. Computer Solutions
3 Kingshill , Earl Soham
IP13 7RY **01728 746122**

ITS 4 BIZ
Unit 1 Sackville Place, Norwich
NR3 1JU **01603 766716**

Abacus Data Entry Ltd
Abacus House , Luton
LU2 0NS **01582 702704**

Computer Services

SD Colour Services
155 Abercromby Avenue , High Wycombe
HP12 3BN **01494 474928**

Counselling , Advice and Psychotherapy

Margaret Kelly MBA, MBACP
Counselling and Psychotherapy

Tel: 05602 684991
www.margaretkelly.org.uk
margaret @ margaretkelly.org.uk

22 Great Brickhill Lane
Little Brickhill
Milton Keynes MK17 9NW

Mary Neave Counselling (Princes Risborough)
19 Gardiner Street , Oxford
OX3 7AW **07722 840563**

Ian Farmer
35 Bowland Drive , Milton Keynes
MK4 2DN **07913 911704**

Rachel King
6 St Johns Road , Clacton on Sea
.............**07507 884825**

Jean Carrington
19 Glenrose Avenue , Bedford
MK44 2SB **01234 306784**

Sandra Banks Psychotherapy & Counselling Services
Rushden
NN10 0SX **07790 368586**

Mandi Jacksons Counselling & Psychotherapy
11 Pottergate , Norwich
NR1 2DS **07990 932832**

Jasmine Heaps
11 Burns Green , Nr Stevenage
SG2 7DA **01438 869808**

Brenda Bulmer (M.A) Counselling
62 Kings Hedges , Hitchin
SG5 2QE **01462 623164**

Dawn Kemp Therapuetic Counselling
Braemar , Felixstowe
IP11 2EX **01394 272645**

Courier Services

Rapid Dispatch
The Brewery Warehouse , Ipswich
IP3 0BE **01473 259999**

Mid Anglia Executive Services
Huntsman Site , Cambridge
CB22 4QB **01223 836000**

Design 2 Print

Grafixbiz
8 Venus Way , Cambridgeshire
PE2 8GF **01733 308198**

Printing Limelight Design
40 Eastgate Street , Bury St Edmunds
IP33 7YW **01284 719342**

Drilling, Boring and Site Investigations

Borehole Solution Site Investigation Ltd
13 Great North Road , St Neots
PE19 5XJ **07969 715655**

E-commerce and Search Engine Optimisation (SEO)

Websiteaday.co.uk
6a Jessop Close , Dereham
NR19 2PZ **08432 896972**

The Calico Tree
54A Waverley Road , St Albans
AL3 5PE **01727 769718**

SME-Web
1 Dukes Orchard , Bishops Stortford
CM22 7HJ **01279 718912**

Wholething
5 Jupiter House , Reading
RG7 8NN **01255 815555**

Ecology Surveys and Consultancy

Skilled Ecology Consultancy Ltd
The Cherries , Clare
CO10 8LG **07747 477307**

Hone Ecology Ltd
12 High Street , Headcorn
TN27 9NE **07967 013972**

Tim Moya Associates
8 Feitimore Park , Harlow
CM17 0PF **08450 943268**

Electrical and Electricians

CN Electrics
53 Church Road , Boston
PE21 0LW **07962 171262**

JHD Electrical
96 Lemsford Road , Hatfield
AL10 0EA **07951 673653**

Barton Electrical Ipswich Ltd
64 Dales View Road , Ipswich
IP1 4HL **07976 685746**

Manpreet Singh
57 Limbury Street , Luton
LU3 2PJ **01582 260010**

DSG Electrical
90 Beechwood Drive , Norwich
NR7 0LP **07758 331816**

Interactive Components
2A Patrick way , Aylesbury
HP21 9XH **01296 425656**

Townsend Electrical
Broadway Drive , Halesworth
IP19 8QR **01986 875397**

J H Electrical
24 Priory Avenue , Essex
CM17 0HJ **01279 441060**

Holgate & French (Shelford) Ltd
71a Newham Street , Ely
CB7 4PQ **01353 668811**

Electrical Maintenance and Installation

DB Electrical
3 Glenhurst Avenue , Ipswich
IP4 4RA **07701 016915**

THE GREEN DIRECTORY

Embroidery

Native Promotions
110 Coast Road , Colchester
CO5 8NA 08452 581000

Embroidery Hut
65 Beachampstead Road , St Neots
PE19 5DX 01480 861406

Ipstitch Embroidery
10 Penshurst Road , Ipswich
IP3 8QZ 01473 430001

TL Productions Ltd
6 Wellcreer Road , Wisbech
Cambridgeshire , PE14 8SD
01945 772490
info@badges.tv
www.badges.tv

Energy Performance Certificates

Chiltern PSC Energy Assessors
35 Jackson Court , High Wycombe
HP15 7TZ 01494 860011

AJR Energy
1 Ward Place , Amersham
HP7 0EU 01494 725490

Equinox Energy Performance Certificates
PO Box 2171 , Rayleigh
SS6 0AY 08458 063352

Rodgers Energy Assessments
31 Hydean Way , Stevenage
SG2 9XJ 07882 370403

Keith Garnett Energy Assessor
21 Reeve Gardens , Ipswich
IP5 2FG 01473 636935

Hopton EPCs
58 Old Church , Great Yarmouth
NR31 9BZ 01502 735724

Energy Saving Products and Services

Energenie
Unit 5 Harolds Close , Harlow
CM19 5TH 01279 422022

MS Electronics
Unit 5 Harvey Close , Basildon
SS13 1EY 03336 661176

Energy Saving Products and Services

Big Green Smile Ltd
First Floor , Amersham
Buckinghamshire , HP6 5BX
01494 727 575
nbuhler@biggreensmile.com
www.biggreensmile.com

Environmental Consultancy

SHE Solutions Ltd
18 Saint Johns Road , Kings Lynn
PE34 4QL 01945 881345

SCILP Ltd
144 Beccles Road , Great Yarmouth
Norfolk , NR31 3AE
01493 304493 or 07840 523028
ian.thynne@scilp.co.uk
www.scilp.co.uk

Kate Mansfield ECO
6 Nelson Close , Milton Keynes
Buckinghamshire , MK8 0DL
01908 566068 or 07875 325700
kate@katemansfieldeco.co.uk
www.katemansfieldeco.co.uk

Environmental Water Treatment

Exhibition Stands

The Exhibition Hub.Com
42 High Street , Tilbrook
PE28 0JP 01480 861777

Stylize Display Graphics
3 Hollands Road , Haverhill
CB9 8PU 01440 712713

Exhibition Stands

John Davey Exhibitions Ltd
Lewis Farm Business Park , Stowmarket
IP14 6AU 01473 892591

Fences, Fencing & Decking

Robert Fencing
Estuary Farm , Kings Lynn
PE30 2HY 01553 828190

S.M. Fencing and Paving Services
15 Kennedy Avenue , Halesworth
IP19 8EF 01986 874021

AMR Services
Sunnyside , Norwich
NR12 0LS 07917 645859

Fire and Smoke Detection

Oakpark Alarms Security Services Ltd
34 High Street , Winslow
MK18 3HB 01296 713010

Fire Risk Assessment and Training

Akeva Safety Solutions Ltd
181 Wisbech Road , Littleport
CB6 1RA 08458 902511

Fenland Fire Appliance LLP
Unit 4 Grassgate Lane, Wisbech
PE14 7AN 01945 582358

DBA Safety Consultancy & Training Services
The Old Bake House , Warboys
PE28 2TU 01487 824624

P and K Training Services
Saint Anne's House , Kings Lynn
PE20 1LT 01553 692045

Fire Safety Protection and Equipment

Three Counties Fire Protection
100 Cambridge Road , Cambridge
Cambridgeshire , CB23 7AR
01223 265550 or 0800 052 2727
james.allen2@btconnect.com
www.threecountiesfire.co.uk

Eastern Fire Extinguishers
113 Ongar Road , Chelmsford
CM1 3ND 01245 422862

Fireplaces & Woodstoves

Fireplace Products
Lower Barn Farm , Rayleigh
SS6 9ET 01268 200139

First Aid Training

Aero Medical Ambulance Service
71 The Crescent , Abbots Langley
WD5 0DR 07717 478648

P and K Training Services
Saint Anne's House , Kings Lynn
PE20 1LT 01553 692045

B & D M Johnson
7 Riverdown , March
PE15 8RA 07980 884218

First Aid Tech
29 Lindlings , Hemel Hempstead
Hertfordshire , HP1 2HB
01442 506342 or 07950 033742
andy@firstaidtech.co.uk
www.firstaidtech.co.uk

Focus Training Anglia Ltd
Hockleys Business Centre , Clacton-On-Sea
CO15 4AE 01255 476589

Food Hygiene

Focus Training Anglia Ltd
Hockleys Business Centre , Clacton-On-Sea
CO15 4AE 01255 476589

Gas and Central Heating (Domestic)

Save Your Energy
172 Bushey Mill Lane , Watford
WD24 7PB 01923 338285

Jim Patten Gas
523 Ashingdon Road , Rochford
SS4 3HE 01702 530624

Empire Plumbing and Heating
19 Kelly- Pain Court , Lowestoft
NR32 4TX 01502 564297

MG Plumbing & Heating
65 Cubb Field , Aylesbury
HP19 7SJ 01296 509609

Simon Kerr Plumbing and Gas
86 Bill Rickaby Drive , Newmarket
CB8 0HQ 01638 663992

Gas and Central Heating (Domestic)

Gas Monster Ltd
2 Wilkin Walk , Cambridge
CB24 8TS **07734 356741**

Simon Worrell Plumbing and Heating
21 Nairn Road , Stamford
PE9 2YR **07739 755565**

CJ Walsh Plumbing and Heating Ltd
2 Brookhill , Stevenage
SG2 8RR **01438 353928**

Gastec Installations Limited
9 New Pier Street , Walton on the Naze
Essex , CO14 8EB
01255 319138 or 07889 912088
gastecinstall@yahoo.co.uk

Graphic Design

Double S Design
67 Severn Road , Ipswich
Suffolk , IP3 0PU
07879 636 038
soo@doublesdesign.com
www.doublesdesign.com

Jet the Dog
8 The Hawthorns , Henlow
SG16 6BW **01462 816216**

rhiannon williams

Independent designer providing solutions
for your communication needs.

Specialising in:
· Brand development
· Document creation
· Marketing campaigns
· Event & exhibition design

01702 551531
design@rhiannonwilliams.com
rhiannonwilliams.com

Inception Design
11 St Johns Close ,
Rutland , PE9 4HS
01780 728 003
contact@inceptiondesign.co.uk
www.inceptiondesign.co.uk

Graphic Design

Mike Spike
12 Millington Gate , Milton Keynes
, MK15 9HT
01908 677994 or 07973 444401
mail@mikespike.co.uk
http://www.mikespike.co.uk/
(see half page advert for more information)

Thomson Design Associates Ltd
The Cottage School Lane , Ongar
CM5 0PH **01277 899268**

Cream Ink Ltd
88 High Street , Cambridge
CB2 14JT **01223 892892**

Sharon Davidson Graphic Designer
6 Springfields , Welwyn Garden City
AL8 6XP **07712 210436**

Vinspirational Designs
67A Wimblington Road , March
PE15 9QW **07872 996981**

Green Roofing

COVEREDINGREEN
56 Hall Farm Cottage , Nr Bungay
NR35 2AP **07917 113466**

Ground Source Heat Pumps

Miller Installations Ltd
8 Paston Road , Norwich
NR12 0JA **01692 531082**

AngliaEcoheat Ltd
Elco Building , Newmarket
CB8 0AT **01638 662955**

Affordable Renewables
Unit 1 Chamberlayne Road , Bury St. Edmunds
Suffolk , IP32 7EY
0800 032 0944 or 01284 763969
richard@affordablerenewables.org.uk
www.affordablerenewables.org.uk
(see full page advert for more information)

Health and Safety

Akeva Safety Solutions Ltd
181 Wisbech Road , Littleport
CB6 1RA **08458 902511**

THE GREEN DIRECTORY

THE GREEN DIRECTORY

Health and Safety

Birchtree Consultants Ltd
Birchtree House , Peterborough
PE7 2HW **01733 841199**

PRF Health, Safety & Environmental Services Ltd
60 Rivermead , Lincoln
LN6 8FE **01522 883824**

PMR Solutions Ltd
37 Wayside Avenue , Hornchurch
RM12 4LL **01708 452000**

Health and Safety

Securing A Family Environment (S.A.F.E.) Limited
399-401 High Street , London
E154QZ **07557 432582**

DBA Safety Consultancy & Training Services
The Old Bake House , Warboys
PE28 2TU **01487 824624**

Graphic Design

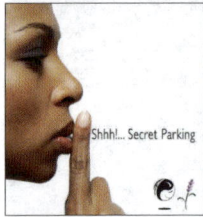

Health and Safety

Anglia Safety Advisors
65 Juniper Road , Bury St Edmunds
IP28 8TX **01638 551292**

Health and Social Care

**Leading Health & Safety
Consultants Ltd**
26 Chaplin Walk , Sudbury
CO10 0YT **01787 377265**

Heat Recovery and Ventilation Systems

Affordable Renewables
Unit 1 Chamberlayne Road , Bury St. Edmunds
Suffolk , IP32 7EY
0800 032 0944 or 01284 763969
richard@affordablerenewables.org.uk
www.affordablerenewables.org.uk

Hypnotherapy

Terry Westwood Hypnotherapy
1 Linden Grove , Milton Keynes
MK14 5HF **01908 674062**

**Vernon Harris Hypnotherapy,
Aim 4 Total Health**
Queens Road Clinic ,
SS1 1NL **01702 305781**

Illustration, Art and Design

Andrew Roberts Graphic Design
16 Shelford Park Avenue , Cambridge
CB22 5LU **01223 571538**

Insulation

Devana Insulation Ltd
34 Mill Road , Cambridge
CB24 5PY **01954 201834**

Insight Insulation
282A High Road , Loughton
IG10 1RB **02081 447836**

ARAN Services Limited
Units 1-6 The Old Station , Bury St Edmunds
IP28 6NE **01284 812577**

Insulation

Zero Environment Ltd
PO Box 1659 , Warwick
CV35 8ZD
01926 624966
enquieies@zeroenvironment.co.uk
www.zeroenvironment.co.uk

Maven Services Ltd
Unit 1 Waterloo Farm Courtyard , Arlesley
Bedfordshire , SG15 6XP
0800 466 1006 or
info@mavenservices.co.uk
www.mavenservices.co.uk

AOK Insulation
36 Grainger Road , Southend On Sea
Essex , SS2 5DD
0845 838 1508
sales@aokinsulation.com

(see full page advert for more information)

Insurance

HIA International Ltd
45-47 Mill Street , Bedford
MK40 3EU **01234 346495**

NW Brown Insurance Brokers Ltd
Richmond House , Cambridge
CB2 1DB **01223 720211**

Landscape Design and Architecture

Haskett
Rowan Cottage Cannons Lane , Ongar
CM5 0TG **01277 899325**

Landscaping and Ground Maintenance

CR Swift Landscaping Ltd
8 Over Road , Longstanton
Cambridgeshire , CB24 3GP
01954 288870
info@swiftlandscaping.co.uk
www.swiftlandscaping.co.uk
(see full page advert for more information)

AOK Insulation ltd

We would like to introduce you to AOK Insulation Ltd; we are a leading online supplier of insulation and construction products in the UK.

AOK Insulation and its associate leading national distributors are able to provide a fully comprehensive range of thermal, acoustic and fire protection insulation products to all sectors of the construction industry, from major contractors and house builders to DIY and Domestic Clients.

We offer an efficient and reliable service to all our clients, to meet exacting standards of modern construction methodology.

Our Products are from all major manufacturers of thermal and acoustic insulation; our stocks also include all relevant accessories

free delivery on orders over £200 to UK main land.

Find us at **www.aokinsulation.com**

If you cannot find what you are looking for please call **0845 838 1508**

Or Email us on **sales@aokinsulation.com**

East of England

LOCAL SECTION

Page 375

THE GREEN DIRECTORY

THE GREEN DIRECTORY

Landscaping and Ground Maintenance

Pro-Scape Ltd
Burnside , Bury St Edmunds
IP29 4SZ **01284 735779**

Hislop & Co Horticulture Ltd
12 West Lane , Hitchin
Hertfordshire , SG5 3AL
01462 768587 or 07790 772150
info@hislophorticulture.co.uk
www.hislophorticulture.co.uk

Business Gardens - Office Landscaping
32 + 34 The Row , High Wycombe
Buckinghamshire , HP14 3JS
01494 882433
businessgardens@onetel.com

(see full page advert for more information)

ECOPRO
Unit 1 Hill House Farm , Earl Stonham
IP14 5DP **01449 710066**

S.M. Fencing and Paving Services
15 Kennedy Avenue , Halesworth
IP19 8EF **01986 874021**

D W Woods Landscaping Ltd
Burbank House , Spalding
PE12 8JG **07958 229726**

Low Energy Lightbulbs, Lighting and L.E.D.

Ledi Solutions Limited
Kingsway Industrial Estate , Luton
Bedfordshire , LU1 1LP
01582 488 800 or 07540 872 545
paul@ledisolutions.co.uk
www.ledisolutions.co.uk

Sunshine Energy Solutions
64 Hedgerley , Oxon
OX39 4TJ **07838 417528**

Martial Arts

Strike-Zone Ltd
45-48 Croft St , Lincoln
LN2 5AZ **01522 531112**

Medical Checkups and Health Monitoring

Aero Medical Ambulance Service
71 The Crescent , Abbots Langley
WD5 0DR **07717 478648**

Motivational and Life Coaching

RKCounsellingservices
20 Cherry Orton Road , Peterborough
PE2 5EF **07717 171043**

Christine Des Dayes
CM21 9LF **01279 722022**

Jamili Coaching
12 Caister Close , Hemel Hempstead
HP2 4UQ **07703 069547**

Networking and Cabling

DJS Communications
12 Long Lane , Thetford
IP26 4BJ **01842 828518**

Bluepoint Technologies Ltd
Hawkins Road , Colchester
CO2 8JX **08443 350618**

Softcraft Computer Services Ltd
Norwich House , Norwich
NR28 9AL **01692 535355**

Andrews Computer Services Ltd
Nash House , Hemel Hempstead
Hertfordshire , HP3 9SR
01442 241 200
sales@andrews-computers.com
www.andrews-computers.com

Business Gardens

01494 882 433

www.businessgardens.co.uk

Gardening Services for Business and Industrial Parks around Oxford and the Thames Valley Corridor

David Clilverd
Business Gardens
32/34 The Row
Lane End
High Wycombe
Bucks. HP14 3JS
01494-882433
07775-683931
businessgardens@onetel.com
www.businessgardens@co.uk and .com

Dear Sirs,

We are a small *"Grounds Maintenance"* team of friends who provide a quality service facility to look after the landscaped grounds and car parks on Business Parks and offices in the M40/M4/Western M25/ Thames Valley corridor.

We are accredited as a *"Safe Contractor"* team by Connaught PlC/ Contractor Plus / Human Focus.

Customers include managing agents such as *Cushman Wakefield, Workman Partners, Lambert Smith Hampton, Sorbon Estates ltd, Mattel Toys, Persimmon Homes, Clinimed ltd, Jones Lang LaSalle.*

Our services include :- *Grass Cutting/Pruning/ Hand Weeding/Hoeing/ Stimming/Hedge Cutting/light small tree pruning/ Weed control with Roundup spray/ Car Park cleaning/ Spot litter collection.*

We provide regular maintenance visits to look after office grounds and can provide winter and summer bedding if required.

Business Gardens is keen to find new business opportunities with private clients, and can provide excellent references if required.

We can visit on a weekly, fortnightly, or monthly basis.

Do please contact us on **www.businessgardens.co.uk** and .com or on **01494-882433.**

Thank you for your interest and we wish you all every success and prosperity!

Page 377

Email: **businessgardens@onetel.com**
Web: **www.businessgardens.co.uk & www.businessgardens.com**
Tel: **01494 882 433**

Office And Retail Furniture

Diamond Office Furniture Limited
No 4 East Wing , Harlow
CM19 5TJ **01279 406756**

Office Cleaning and Cleaning Services

Spalls Ltd
29 Mitchell Way , Chelmsford
CM35 5PJ **01245 429178**

Office Stationery

Essex Stationery Ltd
10 Briarfields , Frinton-On-Sea
CO13 0HE **01255 671125**

STP Office Supplies
1 Rookwood Way , Haverhill
CB9 8PB **01440 703303**

Office/Shop Fitters

PLW Interiors Ltd
Leighton Lodge , Leighton Buzzard
LU7 0GF **07966 292323**

D K F Interiors
Eco Innovation Centre , Peterborough
PE1 1SA **03306 600275**

A E Howlett Ltd
The Old Stables , Ongar
CM5 0GN **01277 364187**

Painting and Decorating

J M Chapman
44 Central Avenue , Stanford Le Hope
SS17 7NG **01375 640688**

Graham Halfpenny
7 Buchan Street , Cambridge
CB4 2XF **01223 522562**

Pointers Painters
217 Cotlandswick , St Albans
AL2 1EG **01727 821799**

Alastair Simmons Painting & Decorating
12 Ellis Gardens , Norwich
NR4 6RX **07583 351358**

Godstone Decorators Ltd
Unit E The Dixon Centre , Norwich
NR6 5PA **01603 414130**

Painting and Decorating

Mason Decorators Ltd
10 East View Crescent , Derham
NR20 5TD **01328 700318**

Fawden Decor
61 Springfield Road , Bury St Edmunds
IP33 3AS **07557 506723**

J B Decor
340 Sutton Road , Southend on Sea
SS2 5EX **07850 811315**

Steve Marley Decorating
51 Lower Ickinield Way , Tring
HP23 4LW **01296 660750**

RPM Painting & Decorating Services
2 The Priory , St Neots
PE19 2PZ **01480 211049**

Paving and Driveways

Supreme Surfacing Ltd
Meadow View , Kings Lynn
PE34 4DN **01553 771342**

P.Jays Ltd
7 Cemetary Road , East Anglia
IP27 9DY **01842 861766**

Payroll and Bookkeeping

Seago and Stopps Payroll Solutions
61 Station Road , Sudbury
Suffolk , CO10 2SP
01787 880080
info@sandspayroll.co.uk
www.sandspayroll.co.uk

Cook the Books Ltd
1 St Johns Barn , Toddington
LU5 6BT **01525 875949**

S.A Bell Accountancy Services
30 Cumberland Close , Braintree
CM7 9NQ **01376 346850**

Wispay Payroll Ltd
107 Norwich Road , Wisbech
PE13 2BB **01945 464146**

James Johnson & Co (Accountancy) Limited
7 Peddars Drive, Hunstanton
PE36 6HF **01485 534948**

Lescott Courts (Wickford)
10 Station Court , Wickford
SS11 7AT **01268 560060**

Payroll and Bookkeeping

CME Personnel Consultancy Ltd
CME House , Leigh on Sea
SS9 2HA 01702 713848

J & M Payroll Services Ltd
12 West Avenue , Hullbridge
SS5 6JU 01702 233290

Jet Bookkeeping Services
44d Lynn Road , Downham Market
PE38 9NN 07806 792211

Lynn Business Services
13 Old Rectory Close , Kings Lynn
PE30 3RG 01553 631745

Pest Control

DRE Pest Control
19 Wallmans Lane , Swavesey
CB24 4QY 01954 230708

Rodent Service (EA) Ltd
24 Cooke Road , South Lowestoft
NR33 7NA 01502 517292

Pest Control

MIBC Services
Wheelstay , Wymondham
Norfolk , NR18 9DH
01953 850923
mibcservices@talk21.com
www.mibcservices.co.uk
(see full page advert for more information)

Pest Defence Ltd
44 Waterhouse Business Centre , Chelmsford
CM1 2QE 01245 392555

Rentakeeper
Lincoln Grounds , Castlethorpe
Milton Keynes , MK19 7HJ
01908 510189
rent@rentakeeper.co.uk
www.rentakeeper.co.uk
(see half page advert for more information)

ECOPRO
Unit 1 Hill House Farm, Earl Stonham
IP14 5DP 01449 710066

Pest Control

LOCAL SECTION

Page 380

THE **GREEN** DIRECTORY

MIBC SERVICES

Pest Control

Established in the UK since 1999
Your *local* pest control company
Offering a comprehensive service at reasonable prices
Servicing the whole of Norfolk

For an efficient, discrete and friendly service
For the control of
Wasps, rats, mice, flies, fleas, ants, cockroaches, moles etc
Call
MIBC SERVICES

MIBC Services
Wheelstay, The Green, Deopham,
Wymondham, Norfolk
Telephone: 01953 850923
Mobile:07801351478
Email: mibcservices@talk21.com

Pest Control

Pro-Pest Services
12 Northumberland Road , Stanford-Le Hope
SS17 0PT 01375 670777

Black Dog Wildlife Services
Folly Sneath Road , Norwich
NR15 4DS 01379 677876

Pest Force (Essex)
8 Wype Road , Peterborough
PE7 2AX 01245 701041

Bugs Pest Control
11 High Street , St Neots
PE19 5YE 01480 477292

Photography and Photographers

Blackblue Ltd
6 Little Burrows , Welwyn Garden City
AL7 4SW 01707 351828

Plastic and UPVC Recycling

Jigsaw Recycling Ltd
19 Shuttleworth Road , Bedford
MK41 0EP 01234 349898

Pollution & Fire Water Containment Equipment

Environmental Innovations Ltd
The Innovation Farm , Nr Bishop Stortford
CM22 7QU 01279 600440

Portable Appliance and Fixed Wire Testing

CN Electrics
53 Church Road , Boston
PE21 0LW 07962 171262

S E Electrical Services
20 Magnus Drive , Colchester
CO4 9WQ 0845 4732863

CK Compliance
23 Haselmere Close , Bury St Edmunds
IP32 7JQ 01284 723045

M-PAT
7 School Lane , Bishop Stortford
CM22 6BP 07899 658363

CMC Electrical Testing
6A Venetia Road , Luton
LU2 7XD 07813 141085

Portable Appliance and Fixed Wire Testing

Electrix Celutions Ltd
34 High Street , Lincoln
LN4 4AD 07887 762645

Chong Electrical Limited
22 Halford Close , Attleborough
NR17 2HY 07916 888484

Powerlec Electrical & Testing
124 Ronald Park Avenue , Westcliff-On-Sea
SS0 9QW 01702 952951

C.K. Electrical
9 Ashurst Drive , Chelmsford
CH1 6TN 01245 465850

Sparks PAT Testing
Lampits Hill , Stanford - Le - Hope
SS17 9AG 01375 642067

Print Management

Grafixbiz
8 Venus Way , Cambridgeshire
PE2 8GF 01733 308198

Trade Search UK Ltd
Unit 16 Globe Industrial Estate , Grays
RM17 6ST 01375 768515

Printing, Design and Mailing Services

Eco Colour Print
155 Waterloo Road , Norwich
Norfolk , NR3 3HY
01603 633804
info@ecocolourprint.co.uk
www.ecocolourprint.co.uk
(see half page advert for more information)

354
Enterprise House , Basildon
SS14 3JB 01268 293794

Diverze
13 The Enigma Centre , Milton Keynes
MK1 1HW 08444 148061

PDS. The print & design specialists.
2 Repton Court , Basildon
SS13 1LN 08000 964874

LOCAL SECTION East of England

THE GREEN DIRECTORY

Promotional Items and Incentives

741 Awards Ltd
Syderstone Business Park , Syderstone
PE31 8RX 08455 000741

Property Maintenance

Brian Painting & Decorating
6 Elephant Castle , Cambridge
PE2A 5YN 07502 106844

Quality Management (ISO Accreditation)

Des Bennett Consultants Ltd
66a The Wroe , Peterborough
PE14 8AN 01945 587205

Rain Water Harvesting

Miller Installations Ltd
8 Paston Road , Norwich
NR12 0JA 01692 531082

Recycled and Refilled Printer Cartridges

Cartridge World Chelmsford
243 Broomfield Road , Chelmsford
CM1 4DP 01245 284992

Recycling

Recycling

PMK Recycling Ltd
Outgang Road , Baston
PE6 9PT 01778 561144

Refrigeration

ARC Ltd
Silver Springs , Wisbech
PE13 5LG 07971 595726

LGM Refrigeration & Air Conditioning
31 Gloucester Road , Bury St Edmonds
IP32 6DL 01284 750780

Roofing Services

Scofield and Lait Roofing Ltd
The Coach House ,
CO7 6LZ ....,.........08456 777035

Safety and Protective Clothing

Shelving, Storage and Shopfitting Supplies

Base-Line
Unit 3 The Square, Braintree
CM77 7WW 01376 551030

Signs and Graphics

Frame Art Display
4 Old Forge Close , Tingewick
MK18 4RH 01280 847444

SK Signs & Labels
Unit 16 Brookside Centre , Southend On Sea
SS2 5RR 01702 462401

Arrow Screen Print
Unit 3 Fletcher Way , Norwich
NR3 3ST 01603 485942

Signs and Graphics

Innovar Sign and Design
6 Wall Court , Braintree
CM7 1YN 01376 332121

Fordesigns
Hook Farm Workshops , Maldon
CM9 6PN 01621 744115

Skips and Skip Hire

1st Choice Asbestos Ltd
21c Hellesdon Park Road , Norwich
NR6 5DR 01603 426217

Solar Energy

Sunshine Energy Solutions
64 Hedgerley , Oxon
OX39 4TJ 07838 417528

Solar Energy

Natural Sparx
313-333 Rainham Road , Dagenham
Essex , RM10 8SX
0845 218 6938
marketing@naturalsparx.co.uk
www.naturalsparx.co.uk

Solar Green Ltd
7 East Hanningfield Industrial Estate , Chel
CM3 8AB 01245 400550

Ardenham Energy Ltd
Cane End Lane , Aylesbury
HP22 5BH 08003 698980

Aspiration Energy
Unit 6 Diss Business Centre , Diss
IP21 4HD 01379 658959

Solar Panels and Photovoltaics

Affordable Renewables
Unit 1 Chamberlayne Road , Bury St. Edmunds
Suffolk , IP32 7EY
0800 032 0944 or 01284 763969
richard@affordablerenewables.org.uk
www.affordablerenewables.org.uk
(see half page advert for more information)

Manor Solar
Unit 30 King Street Industrial Estate , Peter
PE6 9NF **01778 338337**

Solar Domestic Energy
Cassiobury , Buntingford
SG9 9DJ **01763 282237**

AVB Solar
103 Hookfield , Harlow
CM18 6QJ **01279 639154**

Panel Energy
13 a Penn Road , High Wycombe
HP15 7LN **01494 711471**

AngliaEcoheat Ltd
Elco Building , Newmarket
CB8 0AT **01638 662955**

Wildwood Renewable Energy Systems Ltd
The Croft , Billericay
CM12 9SN **01277 656750**

Axios Energy Ltd
60 Hillgrove Business Park , Nazeing
EN9 2HB **01992 447344**

Simon Waite Electrical
Mill House , North Walsham
NR28 9PJ **07787 269693**

Solar Water Heating Systems

Solar Domestic Energy
Cassiobury , Buntingford
SG9 9DJ **01763 282237**

AngliaEcoheat Ltd
Elco Building , Newmarket
CB8 0AT **01638 662955**

Wildwood Renewable Energy Systems Ltd
The Croft , Billericay
CM12 9SN **01277 656750**

Affordable Renewables
Unit 1 Chamberlayne Road , Bury St. Edmunds
IP32 7EY **08000 320944**

Solar Water Heating Systems

Solar Green Ltd
7 East Hanningfield Industrial Estate , Chelmsfordl
CM3 8AB **01245 400550**

Miller Installations Ltd
8 Paston Road , Norwich
NR12 0JA **01692 531082**

Staff and Work Wear

Maverick Promotions
4 Paddock Close , Grantham
NG32 3RP **01400 230180**

Surveyors

Manns Property Services
4 Chestnut Close , Mildenhal
Suffolk , IP28 7NL
01638 716432
david@mannspropertyservices.co.uk

Whitworth Co-Partnership Ltd (Norfolk)
1 The Close , Norwich
NR1 4DH **01603 626782**

Suspended Ceilings - Installation and Manufacture

PLW Interiors Ltd
Leighton Lodge , Leighton Buzzard
LU7 0GF **07966 292323**

Tax Advice and Taxation

Kerry Butcher Accountancy Service
Exchange House Centre , Attleborough
NR17 2AB **01953 457173**

James Johnson and Co (Accountancy) Limited
7 Pedders Drive , Hunstanton
PE36 6HF **01485 534948**

Taxi and Private Hire

1st Goldstar Taxis
6 Drayton Industrial Estate , Norwich
NR8 6RL **01603 700700**

A B Airport Transfers
25 Steed Crescent , Colchester
CO2 7SJ **08009 552470**

Taxi and Private Hire

Mid Anglia Executive Services
Huntsman Site , Cambridge
CB22 4QB 01223 836000

Team Building

RK Counselling Services
20 Cherry Orton Road , Peterborough
PE2 5EF 07717 171043

Telecommunications

RPM Solutions
Unit 8 Beech Avenue , Norwich
NR8 6HW 03336 006999

Pandala
Unit 79 Centaur Court , Ipswich
IP6 0NL 08448 117966

Services First Ltd
P.O. Box 791 , Cambridge
CB24 5WW 08454 023686

Fusion Four Telecoms Ltd
Unit 7 Saffron Court , Basildon
SS15 6SS 01268 417500

E S P Systems Ltd
3 Chapman Lane , Buckinghamshire
SL8 5 PB 01628 531531

Timber Frame Buildings

Chris Holmes Carpentry
Greenfields Bungalow , Thetford
IP25 6RE 07789 222427

Tree Work and Surveys

J O'Callaghan
76 Barnshaw House , Aylesbury
HP21 8FH 01296 392059

Lawrence Tree Services
4 Fairstead Cottages , Halesworth
IP19 0RF 01986 875036

Aborcare
Shangri-la , Stevenage
SG1 2JE 01438 726425

Tree Work and Surveys

Deben Forestry
18 Acer Road , Woodbridge
Suffolk , IP12 2EA
01394 331687
debenforestry@gmail.com

(see full page advert for more information)

Plantscape Tree Services Ltd
Church Nursery , Norwich
NR14 8HT 01508 570777

East of England Tree Surgeons
26 Pollard Road , Norwich
Norfolk , NR10 3BE
01603 279520
tc@eastofenglandtreesurgeons.co.uk
www.eastofenglandtreesurgeons.co.uk

Arboricultural Solutions LLP
3 Walnut Close , Whittlesey
PE7 1LL 01733 208661

AM and MJ Green Tree Work
41 Vanessa Drive , Colchester
CO7 9PB ....

Hallwood Associates
34 Victoria Road , Maldon
CM9 5HF 01621 874694

Tim Moya Associates
8 Feitimore Park , Harlow
CM17 0PF 08450 943268

Trees, Plants & Seeds

Q Lawns
Corkway Drove , Thetford
IP26 4JR 01842 880010

Trophies and Engraving

Sportsform
Fenlake Road Industrial Estate , Bedford
MK42 0HB 01234 210005

Turf and Top Soil.

Q Lawns
Corkway Drove , Thetford
Norfolk , IP26 4JR
01842 880010 or 01842 828266
sales@qlawns.co.uk
www.enviromat.co.uk

East of England

LOCAL SECTION

Page 387

THE GREEN DIRECTORY

Underfloor Heating

Miller Installations Ltd
8 Paston Road , Norwich
NR12 0JA 01692 531082

Affordable Renewables
Unit 1 Chamberlayne Road , Bury St. Edmunds
IP32 7EY 08000 320944

Thermotec
10 Menzies Road , Hastings
TN38 9BB 01424 205544

Vehicle Leasing and Rentals

Green Motion Stansted
London Stansted Airport , Stansted
CM24 1SF 01279 799060

Video Conferencing Services

Applied Inbound
15 Bindon Abbey , Bedford
MK41 0AZ 07760 757186

Website and Internet Services

SME-Web
1 Dukes Orchard , Bishops Stortford
CM22 7HJ 01279 718912

BYTE Internet
Dereham Road , Norwich
NR5 8UA 01603 458677

4DSites
6 Philips Road , Braintree
CM77 6DA 01376 350001

Design Quest Internet Marketing
Pegtile House , Hitchin
Hertfordshire , SG5 3QB
01462 712578 or 07973 623 611
sales@designquest.co.uk
www.designquestwebdesign.co.uk

Just Website Designs Ltd
64 Squirrel Lane , High Wycombe
HP12 4RS 01494 524141

Chelmer Web Design
15 Hayes Close , Chelmsford
CM2 0RN 01245 262082

Website and Internet Services

Applied Inbound
15 Bindon Abbey , Bedford
Bedfordshire , MK41 0AZ
07760 757 186
info@appliedinbound.com
www.appliedinbound.com

Viron Media
22 Catherine Close , Peterborough
PE2 7FD 07917 624611

Websmart Design
7 Oldmeadow Road , Kings Lynn
PE30 4JJ 01553 766760

Website Facility
2 Linford Forum , Milton Keynes
MK14 6LY 01908 711409

Wildlife Protection and Conservation

Black Dog Wildlife Services
Folly Sneath Road , Norwich
NR15 4DS 01379 677876

Wind Energy

Drakes Renewables
118 Lower Luton Road , Harpenden
AL5 5AN 07866 494952

Window Cleaning

Diamond Shine
81 Langham Crescent , Billericay
CM12 9RF 07743 415141

Window Film

The Window Film Centre
K Line House West Road, Ipswich
IP3 9SX 01473 272600

Chameleon-Co
Unit 97 Caxton Court , Milton Keynes
MK8 8DD 01908 562939

Flowline 2000 Ltd
1 West Avenue , Hockley
SS5 6JU 08009 247323

Wood Recycling and Waste

Q Lawns
Corkway Drove , Thetford
IP26 4JR 01842 880010

Big Green Book UK Ltd
Old Station Building
Oswald Road, Oswestry
Shropshire, SY11 1RE

Biggreen**book** ©

Solutions to environmental problems exist, but where do you find them?

This is a question that occurred to ecologist, Stephen Lings in 2003, when he was looking to solve some problems for a local company.

So Steve started putting together a database of companies that can help solve all kinds of problems in our environment. Nine years on, that database has grown into one of the UK's largest business membership organisations.

Now when a company wants help to become sustainable they only have to look to one place www.biggreenbook.com.

But if you don't really know what to look for, then the unique **GET A QUOTE** feature of their website allows you to email an expert about your issues and get suitable suppliers contacting you.

It is an incredible free service, and is one that has helped companies, large and small, throughout the UK.

Over 45,000 organisations have used the Big Green Book website in the last year alone and with over 750,000 hits a month it is a highly visited site.

Big Green Book also runs a face-to-face clinic service, travelling around the country and visiting major trade shows and events. Directors from Big Green Book, supported by experts from within the membership, are on hand to answer question about business and the environment.

Currently Big Green Book is on a membership drive, with special deals for companies that sign up to promote their solutions to environmental and sustainability issues.

If you would like more information on how your company can join their team is very approachable and friendly. Just ask for Gary and you will see what we mean.

With over 6,000 companies in 400 categories and sectors, the Big Green Book online directory is the place to start.

Page 389

Call 01691 661 565
or email sales@biggreenbook.com
www.biggreenbook.com

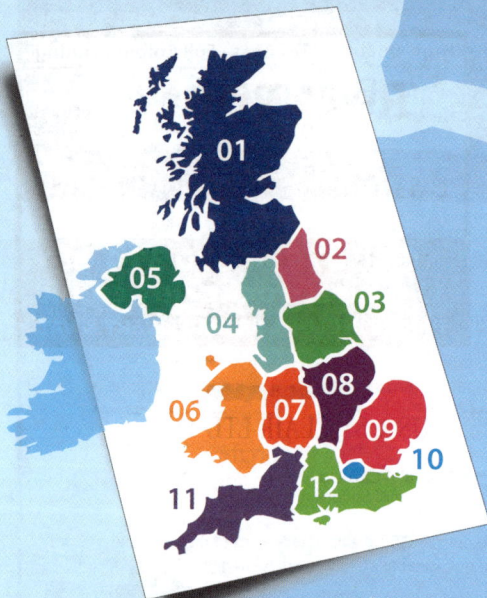

10

London City

Heathrow

The Business Supporting The Greater London Section for the 2012/13 Local Sourcing Directory is:

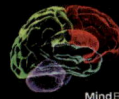

THE **GREEN** DIRECTORY

Accountancy

Stephen Rosser Chartered Accountants
43 Bridge Road , Grays
RM17 6BU **01375 396241**

Stewart & Partners
6 Regent Gate , Waltham Cross
EN8 7AF **08452 050011**

Accountants at Work

Garrett House , Brentford Middlesex , TW8 0QA 020 8568 5880

info@aaw.org.uk
www.accountantsatwork.co.uk

The Kingsmill Partnership
75 Park Lane , Croydon
CR9 1XS **02086 867942**

Aynesley Walters Cohen Ltd
16 South End , Croydon
CR0 1DN
02086 864488
graham.cohen@awcltd.co.uk
www.awcltd.co.uk

AN Perera & Co
173 Barnfield Avenue , Kingston upon Thames
KT2 5RQ **02089 745761**

Mat & Co Accountancy Services Ltd
264 High Street , Beckenham
BR3 1DZ **02086 583220**

E-Accountants Limited
36 Bardolph Road , Richmond
TW9 2LH **03303 004050**

Lieberman & Co
2L Cara House , 339 Seven Sisters Road
London , N15 6RD
020 8800 9296
mail@liebermanaccountants.co.uk
www.liebermanaccountants.co.uk

Accountancy

Garners
Bermuda House , Kingston upon Thames
Surrey , KT1 4EH
020 8943 2191
stephenf@garners.co.uk
www.garners.co.uk

Accreditation and Certification

H & K Safety Services Ltd
The Old Granary , Nr Ashford
TN26 6NU **01233 720113**

Acupuncture

West Dulwich Practice
Park Hall Road ,
London , SE21 8EH
0208 766 7324 or 07780821324
info@juliaquickacupuncture.com
www.juliaquickacupuncture.com

Advertising and Promotional Material

Creative Orchestra
206 Belgravia Workshops , London
N19 4NR **02072 722297**

Air Conditioning Systems

Mastercool (Southern) Limited
Systems House , Brentwood
CM13 3XL **01277 812615**

Taye Services Ltd
11 Parkhill Road , Chingford
E4 7ED **02089 250052**

A and A Cooling Ltd
143 Spencer Road , Isleworth
TW7 4BW **07920 055455**

ORAC, Oxford Refrigeration and Air Conditioning
79/81 Magdalen Road , Oxford
Oxfordshire , OX4 1RF
01865 424 424
sales@oracoxford.co.uk
oracoxford.co.uk

Trimair Ventilation
14 Seaforth Avenue , New Malden
KT3 6JP **02089 495410**

Air Conditioning Systems

BONAIR

SPECIALIST AIR CONDITIONING &
VENTILATION DESIGN CONTRACTORS

Bonair designs, builds, installs and maintains expertly
engineered, bespoke air conditioning systems for
commercial or industrial premises of any scale or complexity.

Tel: 0208 8785469
info@bonairltd.co.uk
www.bonairltd.co.uk
363A Upper Richmond Road, London, SW15 5QJ

Flair Development Ltd
71 Eversley Park Road, London
N21 1NT **07712 889943**

Air Source Heat Pumps

EDF Energy
40 Grosvenor Place, London
SW1X 7EN **08000 511905**

M V Construction and Renewables
37 Agnew Road, London
SE23 1DH **07931 332344**

Air Source Heat Pumps

Bonair Ltd
363A Upper Richmond Road, London
SW15 5QJ
0208 8785 469
info@bonairltd.co.uk
www.bonairltd.co.uk

**ORAC, Oxford Refrigeration and
Air Conditioning**
79/81 Magdalen Road, Oxford
Oxfordshire, OX4 1RF
01865 424 424
sales@oracoxford.co.uk
oracoxford.co.uk

Airport Transfers

Emerald Executive Cars
Harlow-Stansted
.............**01279 310562**

Park Lane
93 Bedford Lane, Feltham
TW14 9BU **02088 932222**

Page 393

Ambulance Services

LOCAL SECTION

THE GREEN DIRECTORY

eco airports

ECO FRIENDLY
AIRPORT TRANSFER

174 Brick Lane
Whitechapel
East London
E1 6RU
UK
ecominicabs@gmail.com

020 3597 0500
020 7247 7779

Airport Transfers

ECO Airports
174 Brick Lane , White Chapel
East London , E1 6RW
0203 597 0500
ecominicabs@gmail.com

(see full page advert for more information)

Havering Mini Cabs
222c South Street , Romford
RM11 2AD **01708 606060**

Ambulance Services

Aero Medical Ambulance Services
71 The Crescent , Abbotts Langley
Hertfordshire , WD5 0DR
07717478648
info@aeromedicalambulance.com
www.aeromedicalambulance.com
(see half page advert for more information)

Animal and Butchery Waste

Barwill and Co.
100 Thorney , Iver
Buckinghamshire , SL0 9AR
01895 440 630 or 07802 611741
barwill@btconnect.com

Architects

Ecovril Ltd
Fishing Cottage , Knebworth
Hertfordshire , SG3 6PY
07810 823918
ecovril@gmail.com
www.ecovril.com
(see full page advert for more information)

Parity Projects
Riverside Business Centre , London
SW18 4UQ **02088 746433**

Geddes Walker Architects
12 Denbigh Street , London
SW1V 2ER **07854 200114**

Architects

Blueprint.Vista
Architecture|Engineering|
Planning|Consultants|

Manpreet Matharoo

Tel: 07973 663 706
Web: www.blueprintvista.co.uk
Email: info@blueprintvista.co.uk

Assisting you with your architectural & building needs

S D Building Plans
5 Wilmington Avenue , Orpington
BR6 9BJ **01689 619068**

ARCH-Angels Architects Limited
128 Edward Street , Brighton
BN2 0JL **01273 267184**

Chestnut Planning
33 Trinity Church Road , Barnes
SW13 8ET **02082 558560**

Two Architectural
40 Copsfield Court , London
E18 2EF **07742 094002**

Prime Meridian
The Priory , Shepton Mallet
Somerset , BA4 5HS
01749 346699 or   0207 494 3522
dminns@prime-meridian.co.uk
www.prime-meridian.co.uk

Brunel Design Group
21-23 East Street , Fareham
PO16 0BZ **01329 238238**

Asbestos Handling and Removal

Asbestos Surveys & Advice
Cockenzie Business Centre , Cockenzie
EH32 0HL **01875 813999**

Abbey Asbestos Management Ltd
50 Penshurst House ,
NW5 3QH **02076 912099**

Asbestos Survey and Assesment

Asbestos Surveys & Advice
Cockenzie Business Centre , Cockenzie
EH32 0HL **01875 813999**

Page 396

ecovril

sustainable planning & design

Based in Hertfordshire, but with roots in Yorkshire and London, we deliver top quality planning and design service with a green heart.

Covering all the UK and on occasion abroad, we can take you through your project - From concept and design,through the planning system and on to project managent and completion if you wish, with the aim to provide the best outcome for you within your budget,

Our services include:
- **CAD design**
- **Green building design and specification**
- **Planning applications ingreenbelt, listed buildings, National Parks, Conservation areas, ANOB, etc.**
- **Off-grid planning and system design**
- **Materials specification**
- **interior design**
- **Structural detailing and specification**
- **Organisation of all specialist surveys**

Please see our website where you can view some of our current projects or call any time to have a chat about yours

www.ecovril.com

07966 138 474

THE GREEN DIRECTORY

Asbestos Survey and Assesment

Abbey Asbestos Management Ltd
50 Penshurst House ,
London , NW5 3QH
0207 6912 099 or   07941 000 711
team@abbeyasbestos.co.uk
www.abbeyasbestos.co.uk

Asbestos Training and Awareness

Asbestos Consulting & Training LLP
87A Castleton Road , Hope Valley
S33 6SB **07919 386738**

Audio Visual

NEC Display Solutions UK Ltd
1 Victoria Road , London
W3 6BL **02089 938111**

Rococo Systems & Design
26 Danbury Street , Islington
N1 8JU **02074 541234**

Biomass Energy and Biofuels

OHM Power Europe Ltd
Canada House , Harrow
HA4 9NA **08006 123260**

Stovesonline Ltd
Capton , Darmouth
TQ6 0JE **08452 265754**

Boilers and Water Heaters

S&L Plumbing, Heating & Building
2 Hazelbank Road , Catford
SE6 1TL **02086 984929**

Building and Construction

Professional Builders Ltd
57A Abbey Road ,
London , NW8 0AD
07545 469938
vinnykaka@gmail.com
www.professionalbuildersltd.com
(see full page advert for more information)

Building and Construction

Ecovril Ltd
Fishing Cottage , Old Knebworth
Hertfordshire , SG3 6PY
07966 138474 or   07810 823918
ecovril@gmail.com
www.ecovril.com

S&L Plumbing, Heating & Building
2 Hazelbank Road , Catford
SE6 1TL **02086 984929**

Avaneo Ltd
34 Downhills Way , Tottenham
London , N17 6BA
0800 0842588 or   07970 259 339
info@avaneo.co.uk
www.avaneo.co.uk

Burglar Alarms and Security Systems

Cryptex Security
Groupama House , Barnet
EN5 1NW **02084 499017**

Business Management Training

Premmit Associates
18A Norlands Square ,
London , W11 4PX
0207 2218176 or
reginald@premmit.com
www.premmit.com

Business Management, Coaching and Consultancy

Dave Sharman Associates
55 Mayhill Road , London
SE7 7JG **02083 052196**

Carpentry and Joinery

V O Kane Carpentry & Joinery
28 Warrender Road , London
N19 5EF **07803 173423**

Handmade Kitchen Co
18A Woodfield Terrace , Epping
CM16 6LL **01992 577998**

Catering Services & Design

Honey & Thyme

Ethically minded caterers, Specialising in Vegan and Vegetarian events. We use fair trade, Locally sourced ingredients, Organic when feasible.

You call, We cook. . . .Barbecues, Weddings, Family Parties and Corporate events.

Ethically minded caterers.....
Food adored from home and abroad.
www.skyecooks.co.uk
07939 592 724

CCTV and Surveillance

Cryptex Security
Groupama House , Barnet
EN5 1NW **02084 499017**

Chauffeur Services

Emerald Executive Cars
Harlow-Stansted
.............**01279 310562**

Cleaning and Hygiene Services

Ecotec Environmental Services Ltd
55 Cranworth Gardens ,
SW9 0NR **08006 226492**

Computer & IT Recycling

Techlogic UK Limited
450 Bath Road , Heathrow
UB7 0AE **08453 700028**

Computer Consultancy

Rephrase
298 Chartridge Lane , Chesham
HP5 2SQ **02033 974870**

Computer Maintenance

SOSPC and MAC
9 Chatsworth Gardens , London
W3 9LN **07756 496818**

Reflective IT.
55 Baker Street , London
W1U 8EW **02073 174535**

Morpheus Technologies Ltd
42 Handsworth Road , London
N17 6DE **07005 981244**

Computer Services

Route 22 Ltd
76 Campbell Road , Caterham
CR3 5JN **01883 370692**

Counselling , Advice and Psychotherapy

Mind & Behaviour Ltd
145-157 St John Street ,
London , EC1V 4PY
07717 478648
steven@mindbehaviour.com
www.mindbehaviour.com

Anne Fullam
Great Russell Street , London
WC1 3PP **02075 034586**

Angie Stevenson
Willow Walk , Farnborough
BR6 7AA **01689 824769**

Classic Counselling
88 Kingsway , Holborn
WC2B 6AA **02072 240299**

Marie Franks MSc MBACP (Accred)
Therapeutic Counsellor
Practice located within Swanley Osteopaths ,
BR8 8BQ **07984 896686**

Coupleworks
27 Monck Street , London
SW1 2AR **07884 064041**

Gary Holman Counselling
10 Roycroft Close , London
E18 1DZ **02085 057268**

A new, green, recurring revenue stream for your business

We help you temporarily reduce electricity consumed during times of peak demand by making minor adjustments to non-essential systems.

By reducing your consumption at peak times, you can help the UK avoid using expensive and polluting peaking power stations

National Grid pays you for this, as it is cheaper and produces less carbon than these peaking power plants

OFF

Cutting-edge energy intelligence

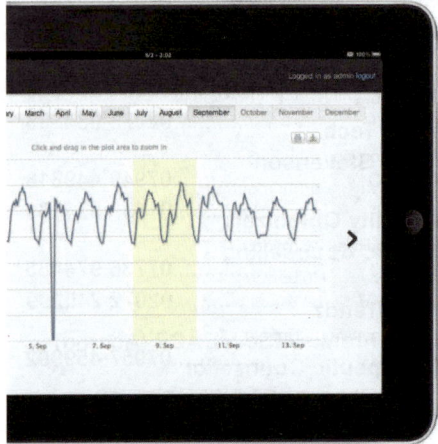

- A recurring annual revenue stream
- Your real time energy data with KiWi's online proprietary software
- Increased confidence in standby generation
- Contribution to a reduction in national carbon intensity
- All programme risks carried by KiWi Power
- **No cost to participate**

KiWiPOWER
demand management

www.kiwipowered.com
for more information

Counselling , Advice and Psychotherapy

Hilary Rock-Gormley
270 Lyham Road , London
SW2 5NP 07712 032814

Making the Difference Confidential Counselling Service
43A Pinner Hill Road , Pinner
HA5 3SD 07958 303487

Margaret Nightingale
20 Gavina Close , Morden
SM4 6AY 02086 870229

Courier Services

Anytime Removals and Couriers
Mortlake Road , Ilford
IG1 2SY 07940 445353

Bycaboy
Newland Court , London
EC1V 9NS 07809 767678

Fugal Express Couriers
4B Goldington Crescent , London
NW1 1UB 02073 871259

Demand Response (Electricity)

KiWi Power Ltd
45 Broadwick Street ,
London , W1F 9QW
0207 1831030   07584 132220
dtaylor@kiwipowered.com
www.kiwipowered.com
(see full page advert for more information)

Design 2 Print

The Marketing Practice
12 Kent House , Bexley
DA5 1LR 01322 310829

Digital and Electronic Branding

Miura
15c Micawber Street , London
N1 7TB 02075 667946

Display and Exhibition Boards

Aris Design & Management Ltd
270 London Road , London
SM6 7DJ 02088 352730

Document and Data Destruction

ShredSure Ltd
Union Yard , Erith
DA8 2AD 08000 743707

Double/Triple Glazing

Aspect Maintenance Ltd
Unit 4 Rufus Business Centre , Earlsfield
SW18 4RL 08432 163647

Drains, Drainage and Pipes

Aspect Maintenance Ltd
Unit 4 Rufus Business Centre , Earlsfield
SW18 4RL 08432 163647

Driving Schools

IAM. Drive and Survive.
IAM House , London
W4 5RG 08701 202910

E-commerce and Search Engine Optimisation (SEO)

Click Here Digital
6-8 Standard Place , Shoreditch
EC2 3BE 02071 832982

Z Designz
1 Campbell Court , Kingsbury
NW9 8AA 02083 57287

Tari Digital
25C Springfield Road , Harrow
HA1 1QF 02084 277599

Myrie Tech
Wallington
SM6 9JQ 07949 449818

Visibility Optimized
Mayfield Road , Croydon
CR7 6DJ 07736 974485

Web Trendz
14 Hadley Way , Enfield
N21 1AN 07957 459902

Datadial Ltd
8 Glenthorne Mews , London
N6 0LJ 02086 000500

Zine UK (Central London)
68 Lombard Street , London
EC3V 9LJ 07720 614049

THE GREEN DIRECTORY

THE GREEN DIRECTORY

E-commerce and Search Engine Optimisation (SEO)

Applied Inbound
15 Bindon Abbey , Bedford
MK41 0AZ 07760 757186

Eco Friendly Promotional Products

MJ Services
Building 329 , Shepperton
TW17 0QD 01932 593574

Ecology Surveys and Consultancy

Sussex Ecology
49-51 East Road ,
London , N1 6AH
07707 608 296
info@sussexecology.co.uk
www.sussexecology.co.uk

The Ecology Consultancy
6-8 Cole Street ,
London , SE1 4YH
020 7378 1914
enquiries@ecologyconsultancy.co.uk
www.ecologyconsultancy.co.uk

Darwin Ecology Ltd
8 Layton Lane , Shaftesbury
SP7 8EY 07748 843842

Make Natural Ltd (Ecological Services)
Research House , Middlesex
UB6 7AQ 07805 806616

Electrical and Electricians

Sensor Electrical Services
19 Sussex Road , Watford
WD24 5HL 07809 639424

Jack C Building Contractors
7 Lulworth Close , Harrow
HA2 9NR 07881 451715

Amsons Electrical Contractors Ltd
Unit 205 Fountayne Road , London
N15 4QL 07958 598331

IB Electrical (London) Ltd
22 South Court , Romford
RM1 1SY 02088 197553

Flair Development Ltd
71 Eversley Park Road , London
N21 1NT 07712 889943

Electrical and Electricians

Pawan Plumbing Ltd
24 Brook Road , Ilford
IG2 7EY 07961 106078

D Simmonds Electrical Services Ltd
39 Hevercrost , Eltham
SE9 3HA 08458 060668

Chesterton Electrical
8 Izane Road , Bexley Heath
DA6 8NX 02083 045706

EV Bullen & Son Ltd
Green Lane Business Park , London
SE9 3TL 02088 600030

ELECTROTEST
2A Eton Road , Orpington
BR6 9HE 02082 890000

Electrical Maintenance and Installation

Professional Builders Ltd
57A Abbey Road , London
NW8 0AD 07545 469938

Electronic Component Recycling

Exclusive Service Ltd
Unit 6 Crescent Court Business Centre , London
E16 4TG 02074 741990

Embroidery

Collisions Workwear
115 Hillingdon Hill , Uxbridge
UB10 0JQ 01895 272705

Alpha Embroidery Services Ltd
168 Railway Arches , London
E10 6JT 02085 392468

Clubrow Creations
24C Fairways Business Park ,
E10 7QB 02085 369130

Environmental Consultancy

Green Business Experts
69 Hungerdown , London
E4 6QJ 08442 720055

H & K Safety Services Ltd
The Old Granary , Nr Ashford
TN26 6NU 01233 720113

Environmental Consultancy

Isoquest
10 Fontmell Park , Ashford
TW15 2NW **01784 252275**

Exhibition Stands

Aris Design & Management Ltd
270 London Road , London
SM6 7DJ **02088 352730**

Fire and Smoke Detection

Ale Fire Systems Ltd
Unit 10 Wyndam Park , Midhurst
GU29 9RE **01730 815471**

Fire Risk Assessment and Training

**Firehouse Training and
Consultancy Ltd**
55 Waverley Avenue , London
TW2 6DQ **02033 764350**

Assured Safety & Health
109 Pegaxis House , Surbiton
KT6 4JX **02088 730976**

Chris Elliott Health & Safety
31 Coldershaw Road , London
W13 9EA **02087 283366**

Fire Safety Protection and Equipment

Multi-tech Fire & Security Ltd
Wyvern House , Great Bookham
KT23 3PD **01372 454221**

First Aid Training

Aero Medical Ambulance Service
71 The Crescent , Abbots Langley
WD5 0DR **07717 478648**

H & K Safety Services Ltd
The Old Granary , Nr Ashford
TN26 6NU **01233 720113**

Focus Training Anglia Ltd
Hockleys Business Centre , Clacton-On-Sea
CO15 4AE **01255 476589**

Flooring and Carpets

Floorsanding-Restoration Ltd
11 Loxton Road ,
London , SE23 2ET
020 8291 7305 or 07762 378 946
info@fsar.co.uk
www.floorsanding-restoration.co.uk

Food Hygiene

Chris Elliott Health & Safety
31 Coldershaw Road , London
W13 9EA **02087 283366**

Focus Training Anglia Ltd
Hockleys Business Centre , Clacton-On-Sea
CO15 4AE **01255 476589**

Gas and Central Heating (Domestic)

South London Heating Ltd
Mosslea Court , Penge
London , SE20 7AL
0208 778 1095 or 07880 527500
info@southlondonheating.co.uk
www.southlondonheating.co.uk
(see full page advert for more information)

S&L Plumbing, Heating & Building
2 Hazelbank Road , Catford
SE6 1TL **02086 984929**

Richland Management Ltd
8 Colton Road , Harrow
HA1 1SG **07888 727277**

Metro Maintenance Group
Stapleford ,
London , N17 6NA
07896 266058
info@metroheat.co.uk
www.metroheat.co.uk

Ramki Heating Ltd
237 Allenby Road , London
UB1 2HB **02088 134000**

C T Plumbing
38 Vereker Drive , Sunbury-On-Thames
TW16 6HF **01932 789117**

Waters Brothers Gas & Heating
Portsmouth Road , Esher
KT10 9PJ **07885 258384**

THE **GREEN** DIRECTORY

southlondon heating.co.uk

Delivering quality, reliable work in South London

We are Gas Safe registered and specialise in Energy Efficiency Heating installations with high efficiency condensing boilers,and on all relevant energy efficiency system set ups. We are experts in gas heating appliances.

South London Heating is an established company with over 20 years experience in the industry, catering to all domestic and business clients' central heating systems, gas services and plumbing requirements. We offer the highest quality workmanship and services for:

- Boiler installations
- Boiler replacements
- Boiler servicing & repairs
- Central heating installations
- Gas safety inspections
- Landlord safety certificates
- Power flushing

Contact : info@southlondonheating.co.uk
Tel : 0208 778 1095 - 07880 527 500

Gas and Central Heating (Domestic)

Gem Heating Services
44 Wrythe Lane , London
SM5 2RN **07837 189634**

Professional Builders Ltd
57A Abbey Road , London
NW8 0AD **07545 469938**

Ashville Inc Ltd
541A Kings Road , London
SW6 2EB **02077 360355**

Graphic Design

Mo Choy Design Ltd
40 Onslow Gardens , Wallington
SM6 9QN **02087 730024**

Rize Design
58 Lower Richmond Road , Wandsworth
SW15 1JT **07709 011535**

The Write Brothers
19 Dorset Drive , Edgware
HA8 7NT **02089 526544**

Moore-Wilson Ltd
19 Garrick Street , London
WC2E 9AX **02073 793300**

Glenn Hilling
44 Edenbridge Road , Enfield
EN1 2LW **02083 511672**

Mash Creative
186 Forest Road , Loughton
IG10 1EG **02032 555507**

Graphic Design

S2 Design and Advertising
4 Elm Park Road , London
SE25 6UA **02087 719108**

Osasp Graphic Design
Salcombe House , London
SE23 3YF **07507 373461**

Daniel Morgenstern
London
W1T 5ES **02073 886834**

Green Roofing

Folia (Europe) Ltd
Well End Road , Borehamwood
WD6 5NZ **02089 535827**

Optigreen Ltd
Unit 1F Ocean House, New Barnet
EN5 5FP **08455 650236**

Ground Source Heat Pumps

M V Construction and Renewables
37 Agnew Road , London
SE23 1DH **07931 332344**

ICAX Ltd
1 Berry Street , London
EC1M 5PS **02072 532240**

Head and Body Massage

Vaseem Gill MFHT
Leytonstone
E11 1LX **07956 365903**

Health and Safety

H & K Safety Services Ltd
The Old Granary , Nr Ashford
TN26 6NU **01233 720113**

Chris Elliott Health & Safety
31 Coldershaw Road , London
W13 9EA **02087 283366**

Assured Safety & Health
109 Pegaxis House , Surbiton
KT6 4JX **02088 730976**

Benchmark Site Solutions
8 Bowfell Drive , Basildon
SS16 6SB **01268 411983**

HSE Passport
Buckingham House , Aylsesbury
MP20 2LA **08450 557508**

Health and Safety

Essential Safety
119 White Horse Avenue , Halstead
CO9 1AP 07950 035651

ABC Health and Safety Ltd
1 Eythorne Court Barn , Dover
CT15 5AD 01304 206228

Grandis Consultants
67 Rowans , Welwyn Garden City
AL7 1NZ 07968 809127

Turner & Townsend
10 Bedford Street , Holborn & Strand
WC2E 9HE 02075 444000

Focus Training Anglia Ltd
Hockleys Business Centre , Clacton-On-Sea
CO15 4AE 01255 476589

Hosted Communications

InClouds Hosted Business Services
1st Canada Square , Canary Wharf
E14 5DY 08453 551200

Hypnotherapy

Change Made Easy
24 Red Down Road , Coulston
CR5 1AX 01737 550754

Nicola Dexter Stress Management Consultant & Hypnotherapist
24 Star Wharf , London
NW1 0QX 02073 830222

Insulation

Kingspan Tarec Industrial Insulation Ltd
Glossop Brook Road , Glossop
Derbyshire , SK13 8GP
0870 733 0021
info.uk@kingspantarec.co.uk
www.kingspantarec.com

Everything Energy
57 The Warren , London
KT4 7DH 02083 304711

Metropolitan Insulation
12 Cheshire Avenue , Lowstock Gralah
CW9 7UA 08000 284042

Lake & Pond Construction

Urban Oasis Landscapes
Allonby Drive , Harrow
HA4 7YU 01895 613757

Lamp Recycling

Recolight Limited
Suite 265 Purley Way , Croydon
CR0 0XZ 08456 017749

Landscape Design and Architecture

Urban Oasis Landscapes
Allonby Drive , Harrow
HA4 7YU 01895 613757

TENDERCARE NURSERIES
Southands Road , Uxbridge
UB9 4HD 01895 835544

Lawyers

Lawrence Graham LLP
4 More London Riverside ,
London , SE1 2AU
020 7759 6850 or 07725 279 524
david.ponsford@lg-legal.com
www.lg-legal.com

Low Energy Lightbulbs, Lighting and L.E.D.

Novel Energy Lighting
24 Kingston Road , London
Greater London , SW19 1JZ
0208-540-8287 or 07507-562-037
sales@novelenergylighting.com
www.novelenergylighting.com

Medical Checkups and Health Monitoring

Aero Medical Ambulance Service
71 The Crescent , Abbots Langley
WD5 0DR 07717 478648

Motivational and Life Coaching

Premmit Associates
18A Norlands Square , London
W11 4PX 02072 218176

GUS & ST CLAIR LTD
Painter & Decorator

Gus & St Clair Ltd
21 Silkmills Square
London
Greater London
E9 5NX
UK

Tel: 07773 932331

Motivational and Life Coaching

Trax to Work
London
N12 8QU 07958 029543

Networking and Cabling

InClouds Hosted Business Services
1st Canada Square , Canary Wharf
E14 5DY 08453 551200

Noise and Vibration Testing

Shaun Murkett
Acoustic Consultants Ltd
1 Clissold Road , Stoke Newington
N16 9EX 02079 237275

Office Cleaning and Cleaning Services

Office Revival Ltd
28 Kent House , Bexley
DA5 1LR 08081 203830

Exclusive Service Ltd
Unit 6 Cresent Court Business Centre , London
E16 4TG 02074 741990

Painting and Decorating

Aspect Maintenance Ltd
Unit 4 Rufus Business Centre , Earlsfield
SW18 4RL 08432 163647

Gus and St Clair Ltd
21 Silkmills Square ,
London , E9 5NX
07773932331
gusryan1@hotmail.co.uk

(see full page advert for more information)

Angels Decoration Ltd
28 Macdonald Road , London
N11 3JB 07588 226038

Paint The Town Green
70 Mysore Road ,
London , SW11 5SB
07956 834112 or 0207 228 4776
phil@paintthetowngreen.biz
www.paintthetowngreen.biz

Painting and Decorating

Michael Rose Painting Services
113 Constance Crescent , Bromley
BR2 7QG 07712 121359

Milena Ltd
11B Doyle Gardens , London
NW10 3DB 07900 996506

Prime Decorating
130 Chester Road , Watford
WD18 0RE 07903 579794

Payroll and Bookkeeping

Stephen Rosser Chartered Accountants
43 Bridge Road , Grays
RM17 6BU 01375 396241

NPS Services Ltd
17 High Street , London
E13 0AD 02085 035868

Accountants at Work
Garrett House , Brentford
TW8 0QA 02085 685880

Sara Graff & Co
28 Minchenden Crescent , London
N14 7EL 02088 826847

Shirley Grinter Ltd
51 Beaconsfield Road , London
SE9 4DS 02088 572376

Payroll People
37 Ellesmere Road , Chiswick
W4 3DU 02087 479575

HMA Ltd
Elmhurst , London
E18 2QH 02085 591989

1st Step Management Services Ltd
United House , Holloway
N7 9DP 08445 763808

Calculus Accounting Solutions Ltd
Upper Pelham , Chislehurst
BR7 5QE 0208 4673838

Verdi Bookkeeping Services Ltd
79 Maiden Lane , Camden
NW1 9YN 02074 824641

Page 411

THE GREEN DIRECTORY

Pest Control

Goodwin Pest Management
Hollywood House , Rochester
Kent , ME3 8AR
0800 634 2530
office@gpmpestcontrol.co.uk
www.gpmpest.com
(see full page advert for more information)

RPS Pest Control
E/7 Peak Hill , London
SE26 4LS 07824 341664

M C Pest Control
Bouverie Gardens , Croydon
CR8 4HL 07949 581949

Photography and Photographers

Jonathan Pollock Specialist Photography
Riverside Business Centre , London
SW18 ....02088 779493

Playground Design & Play Equipment

Urban Oasis Landscapes
Allonby Drive , Harrow
HA4 7YU 01895 613757

Plumbing Services

S&L Plumbing, Heating & Building
2 Hazelbank Road , Catford
SE6 1TL 02086 984929

Metro Maintenance Group
Stapleford , London
Greater London , N17 6NA
07896 266058
info@metroheat.co.uk
www.metromaintenancegroup.co.uk
(see full page advert for more information)

Portable Appliance and Fixed Wire Testing

Hometech Electrical Ltd
Gilberts Lodge , Epsom
KT17 1NK 01372 800026

Portable Appliance and Fixed Wire Testing

Cussens Electrical Services Limited
8 Marne Avenue , Welling
DA16 2EZ 02083 010751

JC Electrical UK Ltd
61 Sheldon Drive , Ruislip
HA 4 0UJ 02088 399561

PJC Maintenance Limited
7 North Orbital Road , Uxbridge
UB9 5EY 01895 835158

GSK Electrical Ltd
270 St Marys Lane , Upminster
RM14 3DD 08002 118548

1 Call Building Contractors Ltd
98B Berry Avenue , Watford
WD24 6RY 01923 354231

Jordan Testing Services
33 Bushbarns Chestnut ,
EN7 6EB 07903 560216

Sword Electrical Safety Ltd
49 Court Hill , South Croydon
CR2 9ND 02086 515231

Shannon Electrical Services
27 Milespit Hill , Barnet
NW7 2PJ 07966 313236

ELECTROTEST
2A Eton Road , Orpington
BR6 9HE 02082 890000

Printing, Design and Mailing Services

Captivat8 UK Ltd
Embassy House , Crowborough
East Sussex , TN6 2JL
01892 611500 or
simon@captiv8uk.co.uk
www.captiv8uk.co.uk
(see half page advert for more information)

Abbeyville Printing
1 Lansdowne Road , London
N170LL 02088 086789

Printing, Design and Mailing Services

Rockprint.co.uk
Kildare Road , Epsom Business Park
London , E16
07534 820314
info@rockprint.co.uk
www.rockprint.co.uk
(see full page advert for more information)

Kevin Williams
64 Crane Way , Twickenham
TW2 7NJ 07956 920270

Vertec Printing Services Ltd
1 Swan Road , Woolwich
SE18 5TT 02083 195200

Tangent Printers
52 London Road , Tooting
SW17 9HP 02086 489418

Rowcolour Limited
Unit 7 , Epsom
KT17 1JF 01372 745466

Printing, Design and Mailing Services

Print Express London
4 Sunnyside Terrace , London
NW9 5DL 02082 000600

Quddos Ltd
Manor Way Buisness Park , Swanscombe
Kent , DA10 0PP
01322 427277
sales@quddos.co.uk
www.quddos.co.uk

S.P. Litho Ltd
Thamesview Business Centre , Rainham
RM13 8BT 01708 529600

Promotional Items and Incentives

EMC Advertising Gifts
Derwent House , Whetstone
London , N20 0YY
0208 492 2200 or   0845 3451064
sales@emcadgifts.co.uk
www.emcadgifts.co.uk

Promotional Items and Incentives

Marketing Solutions
51 Castleton Road , Illford
IG3 9QW 02085 902703

Property Maintenance

ELECTROTEST
2A Eton Road , Orpington
BR6 9HE 02082 890000

Aspect Maintenance Ltd
Rufus Business Centre , Earlsfield
SW18 4RL 08432 163647

Drave Construction Limited
31 Albon House , Wandsworth
London , SW18 6AD
07957 703 264
draveconstructionltd@yahoo.co.uk

Publishing, Packaging and Corporate ID

Annex Design Limited
35 Hayes Hill Road , Bromley
BR2 7HH 02084 026793

Rain Water Harvesting

The Real Garden Company
83 Clarence Road , Horsham
RH13 5SL 07968 449329

Recycling

New Leaf Recycling Ltd
88 Bushey Road , London
SW20 0JH 02089 446866

Removal Services

Anytime Removals and Couriers
Mortlake Road , Ilford
IG1 2SY 07940 445353

Roofing Services

D & J Roofing
338 Lordship Lane ,
London , SE22 8LZ
020 8693 8822 or 07764 579 904
info@djroofing.co.uk
www.djroofing.co.uk

Roofing Services

Aspect Maintenance Ltd
Rufus Business Centre , Earlsfield
SW18 4RL 08432 163647

Safety Risk Assessment

Assured Safety & Health
109 Pegaxis House , Surbiton
KT6 4JX 02088 730976

Secretarial Service

BackUp Administration
Coulsdon , Surrey
.............07973 145443

Macsim Secretarial Services
46 Studios Road , Shepperton
TW17 0QW 01932 220199

Signs and Graphics

Aris Design & Management Ltd
270 London Road , London
SM6 7DJ 02088 352730

Advertising - Dawid Dubiel Sign Maker
84C Lee High Road , Lewisham
SE13 5PT 07977 015349

Ngwena
Unit 1 The Bronze Works , London
SE26 5AY 02086 596596

Signs 2 Print
Blythe Hill Lane , London
SE6 4UF 02083 140888

Signarama (Harrow)
227 Kenton Road , Harrow
HA3 0HD 02089 073864

Solar Panels and Photovoltaics

EDF Energy
40 Grosvenor Place , London
SW1X 7EN 08000 511905

M V Construction and Renewables
37 Agnew Road , London
SE23 1DH 07931 332344

I.C.IT Energy Solutions Ltd
North Greenwich Peninsula , London
SE10 0ER 02034 407012

Salisbury Electrical Engineers Ltd
23 Muswell Hill , London
N10 3PR 08006 335811

THE GREEN DIRECTORY

Solar Panels and Photovoltaics

Solar Mac 4
116 Humes Avenue , Hanwell
W7 2LP **07900 461334**

D & J Roofing
338 Lordship Lane ,
London , SE22 8LZ
020 8693 8822 or   07764 579 904
info@djroofing.co.uk
www.djroofing.co.uk

Pretty Green Energy Ltd
2 Scout Lane , London
SW4 0LA **08448 261333**

Solar Water Heating Systems

EDF Energy
40 Grosvenor Place , London
SW1X 7EN **08000 511905**

M V Construction and Renewables
37 Agnew Road , London
SE23 1DH **07931 332344**

Sports Grounds and Play Areas

Urban Oasis Landscapes
Allonby Drive , Harrow
HA4 7YU **01895 613757**

Stress Management

Change Made Easy
24 Red Down Road , Coulston
CR5 1AX **01737 550754**

Trax to Work
6 Woodside Grove , London
N12 8QU **07958 029543**

Taxi and Private Hire

Q Dell & LHR Express Cars Ltd
91 Station Road , West Drayton
Middlesex , UB7 7LT
01895 427621
julie@qdelllhr.co.uk
www.qdelllhr.co.uk
(see full page advert for more information)

Telecommunications

TSI Voice & Data
201 Lee Valley Technopark , London
N17 9LN **08707 373773**

InClouds Hosted Business Services
1st Canada Square , Canary Wharf
E14 5DY **08453 551200**

Accelerator Hosted IT Solutions Ltd
2nd Floor Marlborough House , Winchester
SO23 0HU **02079 933100**

Town Planning

ARCH-Angels Architects Limited
128 Edward Street , Brighton
BN2 0JL **01273 267184**

Tree Work and Surveys

Capital Trees Limited
33 Landsdowne Hill , London
SE27 0LP **07730 666396**

Red Squirrel Tree Surgery
97 Adelaide Grove , London
W12 0JX **02035 090108**

Website and Internet Services

1 Provide
59a Garston Cresent , Watford
WD25 0LD **07850 296476**

Your Online Setup
Suite 4 Galley House , Barnet
EN5 5YL **07970 524984**

ReedDesign
14 Shamrock Street , London
SW4 6HE **02077 388373**

Route 22 Ltd
76 Campbell Road , Caterham
CR3 5JN **01883 370692**

Peter Jones Internet Marketing Consultants
145-157 St John's Street , London
EC1V 4PW **07846 249538**

Designituk
56 Twining Avenue , Twickenham
TW2 5LP **03303 336186**

Bigfanta Ltd
Viglen House Business Centre , Wembley
HA0 1HD **02081 238206**

Page 417

Website and Internet Services

Web Temple Design Ltd
8-11 St John's Street , London
EC1M 4BF **02076 083003**

demoMedia Digital Ltd
8-11 St John's Lane , London
EC1M 4BF **02076 083000**

Bexley Web Services
The Old School House , Bexley Village
Kent , DA5 1LU
01322 529262
info@bexleywebservices.co.uk
www.bexleywebservices.co.uk

Window Cleaning

Office Revival Ltd
28 Kent House , Bexley
DA5 1LR **08081 203830**

Gaze-a-Glaze Ltd
Weatherbank House , London
SW6 3JD **02077 368030**

Big Green Book UK Ltd
Old Station Building
Oswald Road, Oswestry
Shropshire, SY11 1RE

Biggreenbook ©

Solutions to environmental problems exist, but where do you find them?

This is a question that occurred to ecologist, Stephen Lings in 2003, when he was looking to solve some problems for a local company.

So Steve started putting together a database of companies that can help solve all kinds of problems in our environment. Nine years on, that database has grown into one of the UK's largest business membership organisations.

Now when a company wants help to become sustainable they only have to look to one place www.biggreenbook.com.

But if you don't really know what to look for, then the unique **GET A QUOTE** feature of their website allows you to email an expert about your issues and get suitable suppliers contacting you.

It is an incredible free service, and is one that has helped companies, large and small, throughout the UK.

Over 45,000 organisations have used the Big Green Book website in the last year alone and with over 750,000 hits a month it is a highly visited site.

Big Green Book also runs a face-to-face clinic service, travelling around the country and visiting major trade shows and events. Directors from Big Green Book, supported by experts from within the membership, are on hand to answer question about business and the environment.

Currently Big Green Book is on a membership drive, with special deals for companies that sign up to promote their solutions to environmental and sustainability issues.

If you would like more information on how your company can join their team is very approachable and friendly. Just ask for Gary and you will see what we mean.

Page 419

With over 6,000 companies in 400 categories and sectors, the Big Green Book online directory is the place to start.

Call 01691 661 565
or email sales@biggreenbook.com
www.biggreenbook.com

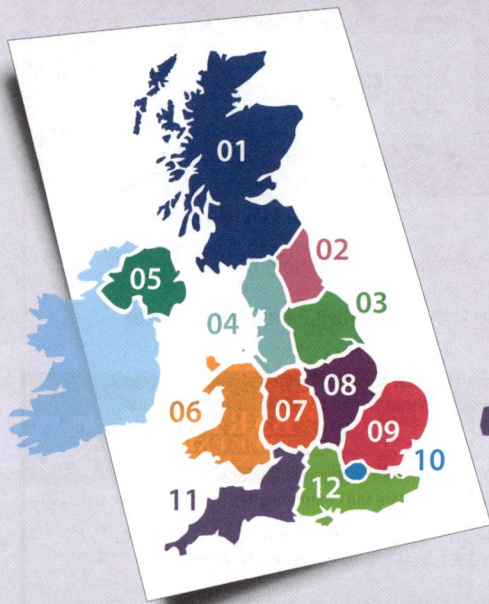

THE **GREEN** DIRECTORY

Accountancy

South Devon Accounting & Business Services Ltd
1.17 Torbay Innovation Centre , Torquay
Devon , TQ1 4BD
01803 321 284
david.vink@sdabs.co.uk
www.sdabs.co.uk

Peregrine Chartered Accountants
Old Bank , Bristol
BS39 7LE **01761 417414**

Lee Accounting
7 Templers Way , Newton Abbot
TQ12 3NX **01626 324994**

MG Associates
36 Victoria Road , Dartmouth
TQ6 9SB **01803 524960**

First Call Financials
Yate Campus , Yate
Gloucestershire , BS37 7PA
0333 577 9810
enquiries@firstcallfinancials.co.uk
www.firstcallfinancials.co.uk

Southwest Bookkeeping Services
14 St Fagen Court , Bristol
SN14 0SJ **01179 326147**

ADT Accountants and Taxation Advisors
24 Hayward Road , Bristol
BS16 4NY **01179 080523**

Munro Business Advisors
School House , Salisbury
SP5 2SU **07518 027031**

Peter Sanders
68 Hayle Terrace , Hayle
Cornwall , TR27 4BT
01736 755755
petersanders83@talktalk.net
www.charteredaccountants-cornwall.com

Best Accountancy Services
Bell Close , Plymouth
PL7 4PB **01752 338600**

Air Conditioning Energy Assessments

Dancold
24 Honiton Road , Exeter
EX1 3ED **01392 757499**

Air Conditioning Systems

Combined Property Solutions Ltd
13 Dyrham Close , Bristol
BS9 4TF **01179 096606**

Dancold
24 Honiton Road , Exeter
EX1 3ED **01392 757499**

Chilly Heat Ltd
Morelands Trading Estate , Gloucester
Gloucestershire , GL1 5RZ
0800 999 8881
info@chillyheat.co.uk
www.airconworld.co.uk
(see full page advert for more information)

ACAC (Bristol) Ltd
11- 12 Brighton Place , Bristol
BS15 1QY **01179 604122**

ACM Air Conditioning Ltd
6 Glenfeadon Terrace , Redruth
TR16 4JX **07816 832461**

Air Source Heat Pumps

Bellinus Ltd
Wolf Valley Business Park , Lifton
PL16 0JJ **01566 784181**

Exenergy Ltd
38 Rassau Industrial Estate , Wales
NP23 5SD **08005 26107**

Airport Transfers

ASAP Getuthere
31 Brimley Vale , Newton Abbot
TQ13 9DA **01626 833912**

Airline Taxis
The Courtyard , Yeovil
TA16 5NH **01935 414444**

Alternative and Renewable Energy

1 World Solar Ltd
35 Cobourg Road ,
Bristol , BS6 5EE
0117 941 1663 or   07971 102 750
info@1worldsolar.co.uk
www.1worldsolar.co.uk

T H White - Energy
Williams Road , Devizes
SN10 3EW **01380 723040**

Wessex Ecoheat Ltd
Old Rope Walks , Bridport
DT6 3BE **01308 485396**

Anaerobic Digestion and Biogas

Methanogen UK Ltd
127 Rampart Road , Salisbury
SP1 1JA **07753 571371**

Architects

D and J May Architectural Services
Deer Park , Barnstaple
EX31 4JS **01271 850488**

**Chedburn Dudley Building
Conservation & Design**
Limpley Mill , Bath
BA2 7FJ **01225 859999**

Easton Bevins
436-440 Gloucester Road , Bristol
BS7 8TX **01179 427876**

Robert Rowett Architectural Services
2B Old Amenity Buildings , Lostwithiel
PL22 0HG **01208 873323**

Edward Davies Studios Ltd
21 Tyndalls Park Road , Bristol
BS8 1PQ **07714 719718**

Archara
Liberation Station, St Helier
JE2 3AS **01534 719700**

Architects

Geoff Sellick
ARCHITECTURAL & INTERIOR DESIGN

30 years experience in top quality residential
architectural and interior design. Personable,
approachable and professional service

*Offices in Dartmouth, Ashburton and Wiveliscombe
covering Devon & Somerset*

www.geoffsellick.com   geoffsellick@me.com
01803 834990   07855 371911

**Singleton Design Architectural
Services**
32 Castle Street , Tisbury
SP3 6SN **01747 870767**

Malcolm Ness Ltd
Crossways Church Road , Spaxton
Somerset , TA5 1BZ
01278 671302 or   07795 254999
malcolmnessarchitect@gmail.com
www.malcolmnessarchitect.co.uk
(see full page advert for more information)

CB Design
18 Reynell Avenue , Newton Abbot
TQ12 4HE **01626 212148**

John Hardy Chartered Surveyor
Kings Weston House , Bristol
Avon , BS11 0UR
0800 810 1040
john@kingswestonhouse.co.uk

(see full page advert for more information)

Asbestos Handling and Removal

Maylarch Recycling Ltd
Andoversford Industrial Estate , Cheltenham
GL54 4LB **01242 821450**

**Westcountry Environmental
Services Ltd**
Kingsmill Road , Saltash
PL12 6LD **01752 651053**

Page 425

South West

LOCAL SECTION

THE GREEN DIRECTORY

Asbestos Survey and Assesment

Westcountry Environmental Services Ltd
Kingsmill Road , Saltash
PL12 6LD 01752 651053

Asbestos Consultancy Salisbury Ltd
Rushdene , Salisbury
SP5 3BD 01722 710604

Asbestos Training and Awareness

Encompassed Ltd
Meldrum Lodge , Bristol
BS40 5JH 01934 853803

Independent Asbestos Training Providers
PO BOX 870 , Taunton
TA1 9GX 08002 118498

Biomass Energy and Biofuels

Stovesonline Ltd
Capton , Darmouth
TQ6 0JE 08452 265754

Wessex Ecoheat Ltd
Old Rope Walks , Bridport
DT6 3BE 01308 485396

Building and Construction

Marmot Associates LLP
Higher Tor Farm , Newton Abbot
TQ13 7PD 01364 631566

Architectural Concepts
2 Tredanek Close , Bodmin
PL31 2PJ 01208 76214

Mitchell Architects Ltd
5 Church Street , Plymouth
PL3 4DT 01752 606007

Heads Apart Property Maintenance & Repair
Henleaze House ,
Bristol , BS9 4PN
0117 9898208 or 07811149095
info@heads-apart.co.uk
www.heads-apart.co.uk

Building and Construction

Argyll Design Partnership
Hillside House , Keynsham
Bristol , BS31 2DR
0117 986 8634
paulcampbell@argylldesign.co.uk
www.argylldesign.co.uk

Lionel Gregory Limited
The Fulcrum Business Park , Poole
BH12 4NU 01202 723157

David G Emery RIBA
Willows , Bristol
BS20 7RW 01275 849628

Building Envelope Evolution
Lakside House , Chippenham
SN14 8HF 01179 373937

Cleaning and Hygiene Services

G.A Helliar & Son Ltd
7 Lufton Heights , Yeovil
BA22 8 UY 01935 477747

Avalon Cleaning
87 Bere Lane , Glastonbury
BA6 8BE 08000 807872

Crown Clean Services
7A Resugga Green Lane , St Austell
PL26 8YR 01726 852217

Cleaning Products

Solution Cornwall Ltd
Cardrew Industrial Estate , Redruth
TR15 1SS 01209 204343

Compost

Eco Sustainable Solutions Ltd
Chapel Lane , Christchurch
BH23 6BG 01202 593601

Computer Maintenance

Yeovil Computers
..............07901 978198

Bridgeman Technologies
EX36 3DR 01172 305670

JMV Solutions Ltd
1 Ben Lears Acre , Liverton
TQ12 6GF 01626 821160

Computer Maintenance

Compu-Tech
11 Balmoral Crescent , Okehampton
EX20 1GN 01837 659714

Computer Services

Impact IT Solutions (UK) Ltd
Londonderry Farm Workshop , Bristol
BS30 6EL 01173 700801

MCC Systems
Longrock Industrial Estate , Penzance
TR20 8NX 01736 362730

Mousewise
Uphill Road North , Weston -Super-Mare
BS23 4ND 01934 643962

Absolutely PC Limited
The Grove Industrial Estate , Bristol
BS34 5BB 08450 745689

D and L IT Recycling Ltd
Quinceborough Farm , Bude
Cornwall , EX23 0NA
01288 361 154 or
admin@dlit.co.uk
www.dlit.co.uk

Computer Software

SwiftTec
68 Andrew Allan Road , Wellington
TA21 9DY 01823 478226

Counselling , Advice and Psychotherapy

Christopher Pollock Counselling
47 Claredon Avenue , Trowbridge
BA14 7BW 01225 808755

**Integrative Therapies
(Raymond Mansfield)**
Rose Cottage , Stock-Sub-Hamdon
TA14 6PS 01935 824595

Ear_4_You
3 Broomfield Hall , Bridgewater
TA5 2DZ 01278 671679

Esther Smith
8 Rosemount Lane , Bath
BA2 4NE 01225 319122

Counselling , Advice and Psychotherapy

**Fast Pace Consultancy
(Dr Penny Rawson)**
55 Cleeve Park , Minehead
BA23 6JF 08450 213278

Counselling Between Ourselves
Rowden Farm , Newton Abbot
TQ13 7TX 01364 621249

Tina Welch
47 Bowel Street , Honiton
EX14 1LZ 07811 110293

Gemma Mason
Gemstone consultancy , Trowbridge
BA14 7SJ 07974 134265

Joanne Lindsay Counselling
14 Lyngford Road , Taunton
TA2 7EQ 01823 259881

Lodestar Coaching Ltd
122 Westbury Leigh , Westbury
BA13 3SH 01373 301215

Courier Services

ILS Distribution Ltd
Unit 9 Kingsford Business Park , Cullompton
EX15 2AU 08002 118187

Design 2 Print

Print 2 Media Ltd
Unit 11a Miller Business Park , Liskeard
PL14 4DA 08455 390172

Document and Data Destruction

Elm Tree Recycling
4 Blackhorse Lane , Bristol
BS16 6TD 01179 407597

Data Shredding Services
38 Pound Lane , Steyning
BN44 3JD 01903 814949

Drains, Drainage and Pipes

Carnon Valley Transport
Carnon Valley , Truro
TR3 6LG 01872 862139

Driving Schools

Philip Chappell Driving Tuition
Cullompton
EX15 2ES 07731 147836

Ecology Surveys and Consultancy

Habitat Aid Ltd
Hookgate Cottage , South Brewham
BA10 0LQ 01749 812355

Darwin Ecology Ltd
8 Layton Lane , Shaftesbury
SP7 8EY 07748 843842

Cornwall Environmental Consultants Ltd
Five Acres , Truro
TR4 9DJ 01872 245510

Abbas Ecology
Brooklands Farm , Dorchester
Dorset , DT2 7AA
07500 781973
info@dorsetecology.co.uk
www.dorsetecology.com

Acorn Ecology Ltd
The Granary , Clyst St Mary
Exeter , EX5 1DJ
01392 366512
info@acornecology.co.uk
www.acornecology.co.uk

Tree Research Ltd
Hetherley Cottage , Cold Ashton
Wiltshire , SN14 8JU
07979 770 907 or 01225 891 614
charlie@treeresearch.co.uk
www.treeresearch.co.uk

Encompass Ecology Ltd
Bow Hill , Exeter
EX4 1LQ 01392 424231

Electrical and Electricians

Jose & Blackler Ltd
Threemilestone Industrial Estate , Truro
TR4 9LD 01872 222565

DM Hawkins Electrical
31 Berkeley Close , Bristol
BS16 6UL 01179 109383

Electrical and Electricians

Sabre Electrical Solutions
126 North Road , Bath
BA2 5DL 07733 227666

Neutral Ground Electrics
3 Hoxton Road , Torquay
TQ1 1JG 07748 631633

Air Conditioning & Electrical Services Ltd
26 Merrymeet , Exeter
EX4 2JP 01392 811733

Mainstones
Unit 4 Station Road , Bruton
BA10 0EH 01749 812316

J Webb Electrical Services
Bramble Cottage , Ilminster
TN19 0JD 01460 57000

G R S Electrical Services Ltd
62 Salisbury Road , Bristol
BS16 5RP 01179 149887

CRS Electrical
Unit D3 Avondale Works , Bristol
BS15 1PA 01179 352994

Keith Lewis Electrical Services
3 Pembroke Street , Swindon
SN1 3LY 07886 366490

Electrical Maintenance and Installation

A and L Electrical Ltd
18 Sutherland Place , Bristol
Avon , BS8 2TZ
0117 973 3284
adam@aandlelectrical.co.uk
www. aandlelectrical.co.uk

MBE Solutions
7 Saddleback Close , Calne
SN11 8HW 07590 277786

Muzzell Lighting
11 Hooe Hill , Plymouth
PL9 9QG 01752 491489

D T Electricals
11A Rowley Road , Torquay
TQ1 4PX 07846 113471

Pro-Safe Electrix
53 Pendarves Street , Camborne
TR14 8NP 07817 766996

LOCAL SECTION South West
THE GREEN DIRECTORY

Electrical Maintenance and Installation

Connectrix Electrical South West
Hydeaway , Taunton
TA2 8BX **07989 771092**

S J F Electrical
22 Meddon Street , Bideford
EX39 2EF **01237 470554**

NAC Electrical Services
12 Emleigh Road , Bristol
BS16 9ET **01179 059960**

Soundfit
The Shaftsbury Centre , Swindon
SN2 2AZ **07810 203764**

A-Z Electrics
11 Middlemill Lane , Exeter
EX15 1JP **07951 210310**

Electronic Component Recycling

D and L IT Recycling Ltd
Quinceborough Farm , Bude
EX23 0NA **01288 361154**

Embroidery

Badge Design Embroidery
Crofts End Industrial Estate
Bristol , BS5 7UW
01179 525856
grev@badge-design.co.uk
www.badge-design.co.uk

Ravenspring Ltd
Ford Road , Totnes
TQ9 5LQ **01803 867092**

Sew Good
Glenhurst , Weston Super Mare
BS23 2UR **01934 632283**

Phoenix Promotions Ltd
1 Woodridge Close , Hayle
TR27 6DQ **01736 850634**

Special Tees
Unit 1 The Market House , St Austell
PL25 5QB **01726 70767**

Unicorn Embroidery Design
4 Fourwinds , Devizes
SN10 4PJ **01380 816427**

Go-Logo
Stagg House , Inchbrook
GL5 5EZ **01453 833823**

Employment Law

Steren Limited
35 Treeve Cane , Hayle
TR27 5DQ **01736 759140**

Energy Assessors & Consultants

Dorset Surveyors Ltd
26 Wallace Road , Poole
BH18 8NG **08458 721335**

Energy Performance Certificates

Dorset Surveyors Ltd
26 Wallace Road , Poole
BH18 8NG **08458 721335**

Energy Performance Services
11 Village Farm Close , Bude
EX23 0HN **01288 361821**

Caroline de Mancha Stevens
The Granary , Ilminster
Somerset , TA19 0HT
01460 52309 or 07812 893529
caroline@fortnum.eclipse.co.uk

Keith Marjason
Marbear , Crediton
EX17 6BE **07970 791838**

South Wilts Home Inspections
Swan Cottage , Warminster
BA12 0SP **01985 850180**

Eagle i Services
13 Park Road , Bristol
BS16 5LB **07846 684559**

Energy Saving Heating

NRG 8 Ltd
Peartree Business Centre , Ferndown
BH21 7PT **08448 009938**

Environmental Consultancy

Buckland Energy Projects Ltd
Albany House , Salisbury
SP1 2PH **07855 947998**

Acorn Environmental Health and Safety Ltd
BSS House , Swindon
SN2 2PJ **03334 560999**

Exhibition Stands

ECO Display Systems Ltd
Little Common Farm , Trowbridge
BA14 0TX 01225 777619

External Wall Insulation

C R Building & Plastering
62 Agnes Close , Bude
EX23 8SB 01840 230988

Fair Trade Products

The Friendly Trading Company
Whiteways Cottage , Wootton Bassett
Wiltshire , SN4 7RX
01793 407 040
friendlytrading@msn.com
www.friendlytrading.co.uk

Fair Trade Wholesale

The Friendly Trading Company
Whiteways Cottage , Wootton Bassett
SN4 7RX 01793 407040

Financial Services

Steren Limited
35 Treeve Cane , Hayle
TR27 5DQ 01736 759140

Fire and Smoke Detection

Bristol Fire
Covert End , Bristol
BS37 4PR 01454 315779

Fire Risk Assessment and Training

Safety and Fire Consultancy
97 Chatsworth Road , Swindon
SN25 4UJ 01793 728681

KBM Fire Safety Services
17 Queens Crescent , Bodmin
PL31 1QP 01208 73001

Fire Marque
34 Paxmans Road , Westbury
BA13 4HS 01373 820592

Safe Track Associates Ltd
Unit 12 Greenway Business Centre , Bristol
BS10 5PY 01179 083860

Fire Risk Assessment and Training

Bristol Fire
Covert End , Bristol
BS37 4PR 01454 315779

West Country Health & Safety Services Ltd
Cove Lodge , Torpoint
PL11 2PQ 01752 657313

Fire Safety Protection and Equipment

Green Light Safety Consultancy Ltd
Suite 2 Poseidon House , Plymouth
Devon , PL4 0SN
01752 604713
enquiries@greenlightsc.co.uk
www.greenlightsc.co.uk

Bristol Fire
Covert End , Bristol
BS37 4PR 01454 315779

First Aid Training

West Country Health & Safety Services Ltd
Cove Lodge , Torpoint
PL11 2PQ 01752 657313

Flashings for Solar Systems

Deks Distribution UK
West End Trading Estate , Bristol
BS48 4DJ 01275 858866

Fleet Driver Training

UK Global Road Safety Ltd
Waterwells Drive , Gloucester
GL2 2AT 08449 106255

Flooring and Carpets

Empire Flooring (South West) Ltd
Unit 6 Hope Yard, Newquay
Cornwall , TR7 1NN
01637 852455
info@empireflooringltd.com
www.empireflooringltd.com

THE **GREEN** DIRECTORY

corporate identity
branding
brochures
internal literature
catalogues
direct mail
websites
new media
exhibitions
advertising
point-of-sale

For over 20 years Herrstein Design have been providing clients with clear, practical design ideas right across the marketing mix; from corporate identity to sales literature to website design. We believe in the strength of a well designed corporate identity. Our skills have helped our clients gain a key competitive edge by presenting strong brand values to their customers. The examples shown are an overview of how we have helped clients with design to create consistent and compelling visual communications.

herrstein design

est. 1991

If you would like to discuss how successful design can help your next project, please contact us:

tel: 01225 446891

e info@herrstein.com   w www.herrstein.com

Food Waste Processing

Eco Sustainable Solutions Ltd
Chapel Lane , Christchurch
BH23 6BG **01202 593601**

Fuel Saving Products

PALE Fuel Systems Ltd
West Point Business Park , Chippenham
SN14 6RB **08451 162828**

Gas and Central Heating (Domestic)

DME
5 Meadlands , Bath
BA2 9AJ **01225 873947**

Geothermal Energy

Mimer Energy Ltd
Falmouth Business Park , Falmouth
TR11 4SZ **02081 441662**

Graphic Design

Herrstein Design
24 Gay Street , Bath
Somerset , BA1 2PD
01225 446891
info@herrstein.com
www. info@herrstein.com

(see full page advert for more information)

Stuart Lansdowne
Malago Cottage , Falmouth
TR11 5QN **01326 340197**

Ammonite Design Associates
The Old Piggery , Beaminster
DT8 3NS **01308 862112**

Bean-Creative.co.uk
North Street Workshops , Stoke-sub-Hamdon
TA14 6QR **01935 822902**

Peter Skeet Design and Print
The Studio , Tiverton
EX16 5HW **01884 257222**

Q-Ball Media
Minera Way , Newton Abbott
TQ12 4PY **01626 332552**

Identities of Distinction
The Granary , Exeter
EX5 1DJ **01392 833003**

Graphic Design

Mindvision Media Limited
Malmesbury Business Park , Malmesbury
SN16 9JU **01666 826226**

Colin Harrison Design Limited
19 Bader Park , Melksham
SN12 6UF **08450 943558**

Revival Design Consultants
28 Fore Street , lostwithiel
PL22 0BL **01208 873944**

Green Roofing

Sedum Green Roof
Heseltine Carp Ltd , East Knoyle
SP3 6EY **01747 830176**

Ground Source Heat Pumps

Kensa Engineering Ltd
Mount Wellington Mine , Truro
TR4 8RJ **08456 804328**

Nu-Heat UK Ltd
Heathpark House , Honiton
Devon , EX14 1SD
01404 549 770 or 0800 731 1976
info@nu-heat.co.uk
www.nu-heat.co.uk

Health and Safety

Safety and Fire Consultancy
97 Chatsworth Road , Swindon
SN25 4UJ **01793 728681**

Acorn Environmental Health and Safety Ltd
BSS House , Swindon
SN2 2PJ **03334 560999**

SCT Solutions
Wixford Business Park , Bidford on Avon
B50 4JS **01789 774715**

First Aid Medical Services
80-88 Eyre Lane , Sheffield
S1 4RB **07729 010034**

Safe Track Associates Ltd
Unit 12 Greenway Business Centre , Bristol
Avon , BS10 5PY
0117 908 3860 or 07977 562376
neil@safetrackassociates.co.uk
www.safetrackassociates.com

THE GREEN DIRECTORY

Health and Safety

West Country Health & Safety Services Ltd
Cove Lodge , Torpoint
PL11 2PQ **01752 657313**

Green Light Safety Consultancy Ltd
Suite 2 Poseidon House, Plymouth
PL4 0SN **01752 604713**

InterFace
Oakley , Barnstaple
EX31 4JG **07712 587238**

Management & Safety Training Ltd
6 Briar Mead , Yatton
BS49 4RE **01934 865144**

CWE Training Ltd Asbestos
Lintham House , Bristol
BS15 9GB **08458 387107**

Health and Social Care

West Country Health & Safety Services Ltd
Cove Lodge , Torpoint
PL11 2PQ **01752 657313**

Hotels,Guest Houses and Hospitality

The George Inn
Main Street , Black Awton
Devon , TQ9 7EG
01803 712 342
ruth@blackawton.eclipse.co.uk
www.blackawton.com

Hypnotherapy

Lodestar Coaching Ltd
122 Westbury Leigh , Westbury
BA13 3SH **01373 301215**

Illustration, Art and Design

Artwork by Pennyr
55 Cleeve Park , Minehead
BA23 6JF **08450 213278**

Insulation

Exenergy Ltd
38 Rassau Industrial Estate , Wales
NP23 5SD **08005 26107**

Insulation

Therm-Eco EWI Ltd
39 Marsh Green Road , Exeter
EX2 8PN **01392 424898**

Energywise (Bristol) Limited
Unit 34 Bonville Business Centre , Bristol
BS4 5QR **01179 716662**

WS Insulations Ltd
Unit 5 Mendip View Business Park , Hewish
BS24 6RX **08447 360103**

Diamond Bead Ltd
Unit 1 Granary Court , Cullompton
EX15 1BS **01884 820683**

Insurance

Coversure Insurance Services Bude
12 Burn View , Bude
Cornwall , EX23 8BZ
0800 3081012
bude@coversure.co.uk
www.coversure.co.uk/branch/bude

Landscape Design and Architecture

Cornwall Environmental Consultants Ltd
Five Acres , Truro
TR4 9DJ **01872 245510**

Landscaping and Ground Maintenance

S L P Vegetation Solutions
235 Greggs Wood Road , Tunbridge Wells
TN2 3HS **07540 552501**

Living Walls

MMA Architectural Systems Ltd
Broadway House , Midsomer Norton
BA3 4BH **08451 300135**

Low Energy Lightbulbs, Lighting and L.E.D.

Kudos Business Technologies Limited
Units 3 & 5 The Old Saw Mill , Bristol
BS40 6PE **01761 463181**

Motivational and Life Coaching

Lodestar Coaching Ltd
122 Westbury Leigh , Westbury
BA13 3SH 01373 301215

Nestboxes

Habitat Aid Ltd
Hookgate Cottage , South Brewham
BA10 0LQ 01749 812355

Networking and Cabling

Talkwire Ltd
Kingsbury Square , Melksham
SN12 6HL 01225 899861

Cable Network & Accessories Ltd
CE Building , Westbury
BA13 4JR 01373 858200

Noise and Vibration Testing

Robin Mackenzie Partnership Ltd
42 Collington Road , Edinburgh
EH10 5BT 01315 573327

Office And Retail Furniture

Bristol OFFICE PRODUCTS
Woodview House , Bristol
BS9 2HX 01179 685016

Office Cleaning and Cleaning Services

Home Sweep Home
2 Cleeve House Cottages , Melksham
SN12 6PG 01380 828653

Office Stationery

Bristol OFFICE PRODUCTS
Woodview House , Bristol
BS9 2HX 01179 685016

GreenBuying.co.uk
Festival House , Cheltenham
GL50 3SH 08452 178995

Office Supplies

Accord Office Supplies
Unit 22 Bridge Mead , Swindon
SN5 7TL 08451 308800

Office/Shop Fitters

A and L Electrical Ltd
18 Sutherland Place , Bristol
BS8 2TZ 01179 733284

Focus Interiors Ltd
Wellsway Works , Bath
BA3 3RZ 01761 420055

Painting and Decorating

Wayne Skinner
19 Burford Avenue , Swindon
SN3 1BU 07535 092399

Joe Wiseman Decorators
2 Stringfellow Close , Chard
Somerset , TA20 1EY
07737 578568
joewiseman@live.co.uk

J. Connerty Painting and Property Maintenance
15 Lysley Close , Chippenham
SN15 3UJ 07720 320927

Tony Layard
27 Downside Close , Warminster
BA12 6AS 07941 759297

Paul Jenkins
Treholden Poughill , Bude
EX23 9EQ 07967 131985

Chris Jones & Son Contract Decorators
136 Westpark , Wadebridge
PL27 6AS 01208 815798

Swindon Decorators
79 Kingshill Road , Swindon
Wiltshire , SN1 4LH
01793 420259 or 07067 030469
danielj.rowe@virgin.net
www.swindondecorators.co.uk

Jaqui's Handy Woman Service
6 Brismar Walk , Plymouth
PL6 5SQ 01752 429528

Nigel Toy & Son
4 Brook Place , Penryn
TR10 8LJ 01326 375121

Duet Decorators
109 Moorland , Weston Super Mare
BS23 4 HU 01934 641171

THE GREEN DIRECTORY

Partitioning Services

Credo Carpentry Solutions Ltd
Meadow View Cottage , Newquay
TR8 4AW **07800 963702**

Payroll and Bookkeeping

**South Devon Accounting &
Business Services Ltd**
Lymington Road , Torquay
TQ1 4BD **01803 321284**
Peregrine Chartered Accountants
Old Bank , Bristol
BS39 7LE **01761 417414**

SinglePoint BookKeeping Services
6 Jolliffe Avenue , Poole
BH15 2HF **01202 649997**

Chevalier Services Ltd
4 Honeysuckle Close , Calne
SN11 9US **07753 632483**

Accounts On Us
67 Beech Avenue , Swindon
SN2 1JZ **01793 511169**

Southwest Bookkeeping Services
14 St Fagen Court , Bristol
Avon , SN14 0SJ
0117932 6147 or 07761 699146
info@southwestbookkeeping.co.uk
www.southwestbookkeeping.co.uk

Business Control
Red Lion Yard , Bath
BA2 2PP **01225 840538**

The Brand Partnership
16 Maylings Farm Road , FAREHAM
Hampshire , PO16 7QU
01329 232892 or 01329 440007
enquiries@thebrandpartnership.co.uk
www.thebrandpartnership.co.uk

Walbrook Bureau Services Ltd
34 High Street , Bristol
BS9 3DZ **01179 419000**

FF Services
The Old Manse , Tisbury
SP3 6LG **01747 870791**

Pest Control

Falcon Pest Control
19 Beaufort Road , Bristol
BS16 6UQ **01179 041756**

Pest Control

Baroque (SW) Ltd
Orchard Cottage , Plymouth
PL9 0DY **01752 862908**

Camelot Pest Control
Higher Church Farm , Somerton
TA11 6BU **01458 851607**

South Devon Environmental Services(South Devon Pest Control)
61 Seymour Drive , Dartmouth
Devon , TQ6 9GE
07593 333625
sdeservices1011@hotmail.com

(see full page advert for more information)

M.A.D Totally Green Pest Control
Launceston
Cornwall
01566 782472 or 07521 649122
searle328@btinternet.com
www.madtotallygreenpestcontrol.co.uk

Kapow Pest Control
Overhill , Frome
BA11 3QZ **01373 813721**

A 2 Z Pest Control
Christow Road , Axebridge
BS26 2XP **01934 822210**

Abee Pest Control
Fielding Bristol Road , Chippenham
SN14 6NA **01249 653797**

Sentinel Pest Control
Queensgate House , Exeter
EX4 3SR **08009 997898**

LOCAL SECTION **South West**

Page 437

THE **GREEN** DIRECTORY

THE **GREEN** DIRECTORY

Photography and Photographers

Monkey Puzzle Repro Art
Mount Pleasant Eco Park , Porthtowan
TR4 8HL 01209 890333

Portable Appliance and Fixed Wire Testing

West Kernow Electrical Installations
8 Furry Way , Helston
TR13 8SN 01326 722757

Baker Electrical
73 Severn Drive , Taunton
TA1 2PW 01823 336286

Midas Electronics Ltd
4 Northwick Road ,
Bristol , BS35 4HF
01454 632 967 or 07762 323 367
chrisgray@midaselectronics.co.uk
www.midaselectronics.co.uk

S Chapman Electrical Contractors
86 St Andrews Road , Exmouth
EX8 1AS 01395 260585

Posters

Zig Design
Belle Vue , Holsworthy
EX22 6EF 01409 253799

Pre Design Advice

Steve Eastland Design Limited
Hope House , Kerswell
EX15 2EL 01884 266437

Printing, Design and Mailing Services

Emtone Print Ltd
Locksbrook Road Trading Estate , Bath
BA1 3DZ 01225 330894

Westprint
Clystcourt , Exeter
EX5 1SA 01395 233442

Nick Walker Printing Ltd
The Old Workhouse , Kingsbridge
TQ7 1EQ 01548 852812

Printing.com Plymouth
Unit 2 Discovery Wharf , Plymouth
PL4 0AU 01752 255100

Printing, Design and Mailing Services

C and S Print Services
Becks Business Park, Weston Super Mare
BS23 3TJ 01934 622240

Quay Media Solutions Ltd
35 Kestrel Court , Portishead
BS20 7AN 01275 390550

Salisbury Printing
71A Greencroft Street , Salisbury
Wiltshire , SP1 1JF
01722 413330
info@salisburyprinting.co.uk
www.salisburyprinting.co.uk

Jack Harris Design & Print
2 Biddiblack Way , Bideford
EX39 4AY 08455 198502

Mail Boxes Etc
3 Edgar Buildings , Bath
BA1 2FJ 01225 483777

Monkey Puzzle Repro Art
Mount Pleasant Eco Park , Porthtowan
Cornwall , TR4 8HL
01209 890 333
info@monkeypuzzleart.co.uk
www.monkeypuzzleart.co.uk

Profit and Loss Management

Steren Limited
35 Treeve Cane , Hayle
TR27 5DQ 01736 759140

Property Maintenance

Neils Property Maintenance Ltd
44 Welsford Avenue , Wells
BA5 2HX 07734 282958

Markley Contracting Ltd
18 Witham Way , Swindon
SN2 7NN 01793 680587

Recycled and Refilled Printer Cartridges

Cartridge World (Street)
The Bayliss Centre , Street
BA16 0EX 01458 841260

Recycling

Childrens Scrapstore
Scrapstore House , Bristol
BS2 9LB 01179 143005

Europlastix Ltd
Ashleigh House , Bridgwater
TA6 7QL 01278 423544

Maylarch Recycling Ltd
Andoversford Industrial Estate , Cheltenham
GL54 4LB 01242 821450

Elm Tree Recycling
4 Blackhorse Lane , Bristol
Avon , BS16 6TD
01179 407597
elmtreerecycling@aol.com
www.elmtreerecycling.com

JB Confidential
Station House , Kings Wympton
EX37 9EU 08451 364904

**Cornwall Cullet Ltd
(General Recycling)**
The Glass Works , Redruth
TR16 5HY 01209 719800

Roofing Services

BCB Roofing Ltd
Hillside Farm , Chippenham
SN15 5EB 01666 510977

Safety Risk Assessment

Synapse Safety Ltd
4 Ploughman Way , Plymouth
PL8 2JE 01752 880781

Safe Track Associates Ltd
Unit 12 Greenway Business Centre , Bristol
BS10 5PY 01179 083860

Saw Milling and Timber Supplies

Duchy Timber Limited
Downend , Loswithiel
Cornwall , PL22 0RB
01208 872338 or   01404 815878
sales@duchytimber.co.uk
www.duchytimber.co.uk

Screen and T Shirt Printing

21st Century Screen Printers
Units 4-5b Coventry Farm Estate , Torquay
TQ2 7HX 01803 875088

Print 'n' Stitch
Unit 2 The Yarn Barn , Paignton
Devon , TQ3 2TP
01803 666010
sales@printnstitch.co.uk
www.printnstitch.co.uk

Secretarial Service

HW Secretarial Services
138 Chiphouse Road , Bristol
BS15 4TZ 01179 871152

Steren Limited
35 Treeve Cane , Hayle
TR27 5DQ 01736 759140

Precis
Unit 1 Brookside Court , Bodmin
PL30 4LN 01208 850729

Out of Hours Typing Ltd
21 Champford Lane , Wellington
TA21 8BH 01823 662814

**Hunt's Word Processing &
General Admin**
84 Widgery Road , Exeter
EX4 8AX 01392 251940

Septic Tanks

Signs and Graphics

Bradley Signs
The Maisonette , Paignton
TQ3 1NT 01803 529603

THE GREEN DIRECTORY

Signs and Graphics

Sign & Design
Western Farm , Bridgwater
TA7 9BG **01458 210623**

Frenzy Designs
Timsbury Workshop Estate , Bath
Avon , BA2 0HQ
01761 470639 or 07836371566
val@frenzydesigns.fsnet.co.uk
www.frenzydesigns.co.uk

Lime Design
Maida Vale Business Centre, Cheltenham
GL53 7ER **01242 232599**

Perranporth Signs and Graphics - Cornwall
The Industrial Estate Station Road , Perranporth
TR6 0LH **01872 572282**

Skips and Skip Hire

Allmead Waste Management
Broadmead Lane Ind Est , Bristol
Avon , BS31 1ST
0117 9059874
hazel.shaw@allmead.co.uk
www.allmead.co.uk

Bu-Mar Skip Hire
Vale Mill , Redruth
TR16 4HG **01209 219810**

Solar Energy

My Power UK
Gamma Three , Cheltenham
GL54 5EB **08002 949246**

All Powered Up Ltd
Lower Whiddon , Beaworthy
Devon , EX21 5AX
01409 221769
nick@allpoweredup.co.uk

(see full page advert for more information)

Paul O'Brien Solar Installations
Unit 6 Brookgate , Bristol
BS3 2UN **01179 533234**

Deks Distribution UK
West End Trading Estate , Bristol
BS48 4DJ **01275 858866**

Solar Energy

Greenshop Solar Ltd
Cheltenham Road , Stroud
Gloucestershire , GL6 7BX
01452 772030
enquiries@greenshopsolar.co.uk
www.greenshopsolar.co.uk

JHS Solar Solutions
Cherwell Business Village , Banbury
OX16 2SP **08453 024779**

Solar Panels and Photovoltaics

Enlighten Systems Ltd
2 Mill Road , Exeter
EX2 6LX **01392 254435**

My Power UK
Gamma Three , Cheltenham
Gloucestshire , GL54 5EB
0800 294 9246 or 07793 579047
benharrison@mypoweruk.com
www.mypoweruk.com

Bellinus Ltd
Wolf Valley Business Park , Lifton
PL16 0JJ **01566 784181**

Deks Distribution UK
West End Trading Estate , Bristol
BS48 4DJ **01275 858866**

Greenstart Solar Solutions
Unit B Allerton Road , Bridgewater
Somerset , TA6 4PN
07973 406795
bob.greenstart-energy@uwclub.net

(see full page advert for more information)

AAECO Ltd
37 Chamberlain Street , Wells
BA5 2PQ **07775 803032**

Gendex Ltd
Unit 1 Holden Road , Poole
BH16 6LT **01202 625588**

NRG 8 Ltd
Peartree Business Centre , Ferndown
BH21 7PT **08448 009938**

Mainstones
Unit 4 Station Road , Bruton
BA10 0EH **01749 812316**

Looking for renewable energy?

GreenStart

Thermodynamics

Hot water in the sun, rain, snow and even overnight. Works 24 Hrs a day, 365 days a year

Solar PV

Produce your own electricity and earn at least 8% on your investment

Heat Pumps

Free energy form the Ground and air to heat your home, Up to 70% savings on oil & LPG Gas bills

Biomass Boilers

Wood-fuelled heating systems, also called biomass systems, burn wood pellets, chips or logs to provide central heating & hot water.

Remember the sun will never send you an energy bill

We work with Private and Commercial Clients

MCS

REA✓

Tel: **01278 427879** | Fax: **01278 433004**
E-mail: **gres-ltd@uwclub.net**
www.greenstartenergy.co.uk

Solar Panels and Photovoltaics

Woofenden Construction Limited
Glimsters Farm , Collumpton
EX15 2AD **01844 266055**

Solar Water Heating Systems

Miller & Symons
2 Luxton Road , Newton Abbott
TQ12 6YQ **07871 063055**

Paul O'Brien Solar Installations
Unit 6 Brookgate , Bristol
BS3 2UN **01179 533234**

Bellinus Ltd
Wolf Valley Business Park , Lifton
PL16 0JJ **01566 784181**

Deks Distribution UK
West End Trading Estate , Bristol
BS48 4DJ **01275 858866**

NRG 8 Ltd
Peartree Business Centre , Ferndown
BH21 7PT **08448 009938**

HotSpot Solar
4 Alkerton Grange Cottages , Eastington
GL10 3AF **01453 826200**

Exenergy Ltd
38 Rassau Industrial Estate , Wales
NP23 5SD **08005 26107**

Greenshop Solar Ltd
Cheltenham Road , Stroud
GL6 7BX **01452 772030**

Wessex Ecoheat Ltd
Old Rope Walks , Bridport
DT6 3BE **01308 485396**

Stress Management

**Integrative Therapies
(Raymond Mansfield)**
Rose Cottage , Stock-Sub-Hamdon
TA14 6PS **01935 824595**

Surveyors

PWH Associates (Barnstaple) Ltd
16 Castle Park Road , Barnstaple
EX32 8PA **01271 326335**

Marmot Associates LLP
Higher Tor Farm , Newton Abbot
TQ13 7PD **01364 631566**

Suspended Ceilings - Installation and Manufacture

Credo Carpentry Solutions Ltd
Meadow View Cottage , Newquay
TR8 4AW **07800 963702**

Sustainable Building Services and Supplies

Woofenden Construction Limited
Glimsters Farm , Collumpton
EX15 2AD **01844 266055**

Building Envelope Evolution
Lakside House , Chippenham
SN14 8HF **01179 373937**

Tax Advice and Taxation

Steren Limited
35 Treeve Cane , Hayle
TR27 5DQ **01736 759140**

Taxi and Private Hire

Travel Guardians
3 Martins Close , Wells
BA5 2CS **07811 409725**

A J Cars
5 Knightlands Lane , Langport
TA10 9HR **07770 978326**

Airline Taxis
The Courtyard , Yeovil
TA16 5NH **01935 414444**

Page 444

Stress Management

JOYCE HOWITT

MBACP *(Accred)*, UKRCP Registered Independent Counsellor/Psychotherapist.

- **Dip Clinical and Pastoral Counselling**
- **Advanced Cert in Counselling**
- **Dip Creative CBT; Cert Supervision**

- **Confidential, Non Judgmental, Caring Counselling Service**

I am based in Plympton, Plymouth but also see clients in and near Totnes. I also offer Telephone Counselling for those who live in other areas. I can offer both short and long term therapy

My counselling approach is integrative which means that I draw on the theoretical counselling approach which is the most appropriate for your needs.

Our initial session (*an hour*) costs £15, and gives you the opportunity to outline the areas of concern, and to decide whether you wish to make further appointments.

Subsequent sessions cost £25. Concessions may be available. Areas of Speciality; Abuse, Anger Management; Anxiety & Depression; Bereavement & Loss; Childhood Related Issues; Relationships; Low Self Confidence; Low Self Esteem; Stress Management; Termination, Abortion, Miscarriage; Work Related Issues

I am also a qualified, experienced Supervisor of Counsellors including those in training.

Telephone: 01752 642 441 Mobile: 07596 008840
Email: joyce.howitt@mail.com
www.counsellinginplymouth.co.uk

THE GREEN DIRECTORY

Taxi and Private Hire

A P Taxi Co.
2 Sparrow Road , Totnes
TQ9 5PR 01803 840404

Capital City Taxis
3/4 Isambard Parade , Exeter
EX4 4BX 01392 433433

Torbay Cab Co. Ltd
Peaceful Cottage , Torquay
TQ2 5EX 01803 292292

The Green Taxi Company
1 Meadow Drive , Sidmouth
EX10 0DN 01395 568111

Telecommunications

JJ Services
6 Aller Park Road , Newton Abbot
TQ12 4NG 01626 365540

Talkwire Ltd
Kingsbury Square , Melksham
SN12 6HL 01225 899861

Derek Wood Associates Ltd
68 Riverside Way , Bristol
BS15 3TF 01179 612938

Indigo Telecom Group
Castlegate Business Park , Caldicot
NP26 5AA 01291 435500

Faces UK Ltd T/A Beta Telecoms
16 Bulwark Avenue , Chepstow
NP16 5QG 01291 620189

Telecom Services
Gillingham
SP8 ....01747 822324

Telephone Answering & Virtual Office Services

Red Virtual Office Ltd
1 Barton Court , Highworth
Wiltshire , SN6 7AG
01793 862000 or 07974 649363
denis@redvirtualoffice.biz
www.redvirtualoffice.biz

Timber Frame Buildings

Building Envelope Evolution
Lakside House , Chippenham
3N14 8HF 01179 373937

Timber Frame Buildings

Milner Associates
129 Cumberland Road , Bristol
Avon , BS1 6UY
0117 945 3260 or 07801 340 231
martin@milnerassociates.co.uk
www.milnerassociates.co.uk

Merlin Timber Frame Ltd
The Coach House , North Curry
TA3 6JZ 01823 490700

English Oak Buildings Ltd
Bassett Farm , Bath
BA2 7BJ 01225 789978

Town Planning

Architectural Concepts
2 Tredanek Close , Bodmin
PL31 2PJ 01208 76214

Jon Hughes Architectural Services
Well Park Barn , Wadebridge
PL27 7JA 01208 814250

EJFP Planning
49 Bannawell Street , Tavistock
PL19 0DP 01822 851010

Training and Apprenticeships

JTL
Stafford House , Orpington
BR6 0JS 08000 852308

Tree Work and Surveys

Green Planet Tree Services
23 Chestnut Walk , Bristol
BS13 7RJ 07974 771409

Chestnut Trees
22 Powderham Road , Exeter
EX2 9BS 01392 424288

Greenhills Tree Services
43 Milton Crescent , Tavistock
PL19 9AL 01822 616792

Wood-Land South West Ltd
Quatock Lodge , Bridgwater
TA5 1HD 07980 664126

Wessex Tree Consultancy
Ayford Land , Marshfield
SN14 8AB 01258 91730

Tree Work and Surveys

Smart Trees
5 Preddy's Lane , Bristol
BS5 8TD 01173 224031

Heartwood Tree Care
108 Kilmersdon Road , Radstock
Somerset , BA5 3QR
07810 371593
heartwoodtreecare@hotmail.com

Adrian Feeney Tree Surgery
28 Brooklyn Road , Bath
BA1 6TE 01225 460492

Jeremy Hawkins Tree Surgeon
19 Rogers Meadows , Marlborough
SN8 1OZ 07980 536156

Tree Research Ltd
Hetherley Cottage , Cold Ashton
Wiltshire , SN14 8JU
07979 770 907 or 01225 891 614
charlie@treeresearch.co.uk
www.treeresearch.co.uk

Trees, Plants & Seeds

Habitat Aid Ltd
Hookgate Cottage , South Brewham
BA10 0LQ 01749 812355

Underfloor Heating

NRG 8 Ltd
Peartree Business Centre , Ferndown
BH21 7PT 08448 009938

Waste Management and Disposal

Maylarch Recycling Ltd
Andoversford Industrial Estate , Cheltenham
GL54 4LB 01242 821450

Website and Internet Services

SOKP Media
116 Commercial Road , Swindon
SN1 5BD 01793 292171

Flair Web Design
25 Oak Road , Fordingbridge
SP6 3BL 01425 650294

Website and Internet Services

Zig Design
Tony Hart , Holsworthy
EX22 6EF 01409 253799

Clubnet Search Marketing
Tamar Science Park , Plymouth
PL6 8BX 08452 996005

Dino Digital Ltd
45 Friezewood Road , Bristol
BS3 2AD 07866 929640

Quality Website Design
Netton House , Plymouth
PL8 1HV 08450 941632

Carn Gerrish Creative
16 Bristol Vale , Bristol
BS3 5RJ 01179 666448

Sandbox Media Ltd
The Tobacco Factory , Bristol
Avon , BS3 1TF
0117 966 7115
andy@sandboxmedia.co.uk

(see full page advert for more information)

Distinctive UK
43 Bridge Street , Taunton
TA1 1TP 01823 321860

Ojo Solutions Ltd
39a Lyncombe Hill , Bath
BA2 4PQ 08004 681550

Wind Energy

InterFace
Oakley , Barnstaple
Devon , EX31 4JG
07712 587238
ma@interfacewsm.com

Window Film

Tinting Express
New Estate House , Barnstaple
EX31 3AL 01271 322857

THE GREEN DIRECTORY

South West

LOCAL SECTION

Page 448

THE GREEN DIRECTORY

Flexible Web Solutions

- Domain Services
- Managed Hosting
- Virtual Servers
- Backup Solutions
- Support Packages

Scan the QR code or visit:
hostingdept.co.uk/big-green-book
for details on **special offers**

www.**hostingdept**.co.uk

GREENER TIMES
>SUSTAINABLE SOLUTIONS MAGAZINE

*Old Station Building
Oswald Road, Oswestry
Shropshire, SY11 1RE*

SUBSCRIBE TO THE UK'S BEST GREEN BUSINESS, LIFESTYLE AND SUSTAINABILITY MAGAZINE

If you enjoy reading the Greener Times magazine, why not take advantage of our special subscription rates and save yourself some money?   Each issue of Greener Times is enjoyable, informative reading that will also make you think!

As well as articles on environmental issues that can affect you at home as well as at work; there are interviews with celebrities like Gareth Southgate and successful businesses such as Stagecoach, quizzes that the whole family can get involved with and current affairs relating to local communities and businesses, all with an environmental and sustainable theme i.e. The Green Deal, The Renewable Heat Incentive (RHI) etc.

There is also a 'Whats On?' list of forthcoming shows and events that we will be attending where you can come along and meet us in person.

It costs just **£4.20 + P&P** Or if you want to save some money you can subscribe for a year for just **£42 + P&P** *(payable by monthly or annual direct debit)* Instruction to Greener Times Publishing Ltd

Page 449

DON'T MISS AN ISSUE, SUBSCRIBE TODAY!

£42 + P&P

01691 661 565
info@greener-times.co.uk
www.greener-times.co.uk

THE GREEN DIRECTORY

01
02
03
04
05
06
07
08
09
10
11
12

12

Canterbury

Brighton

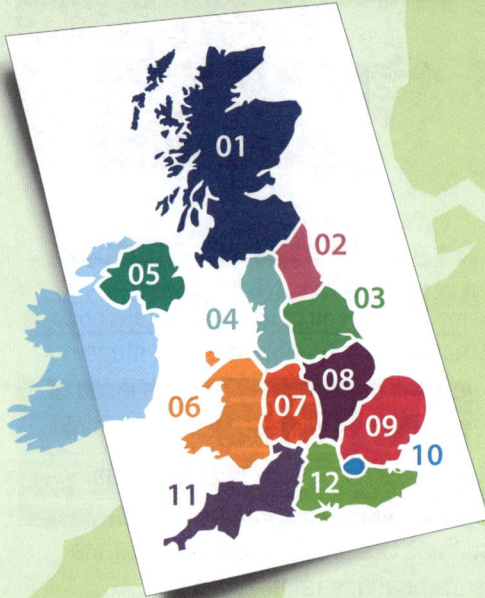

The Business Supporting The South East of England Section for the 2012/13 Local Sourcing Directory is:

THE GREEN DIRECTORY

THE GREEN DIRECTORY

Accountancy

Wellington Coaching
PO Box 3425 , Wokingham
RG41 2ZY **08707 664982**

Accountancy People
Wentworth , Freshwater
PO40 9QS **01983 718455**

Windsor Head Accountants & Business Advisors
14 Buttermere Drive , Basingstoke
RG22 5LD **01256 331801**

Smith & Williamson
No. 1 Bishops Wharf , Guildford
Surrey , GU1 4RA
01483 407100
janice.clay@smith.williamson.co.uk
www.smith.williamson.co.uk/guildford

Vale And West
Victoria House , Reading
RG1 1TG **01189 573238**

Wood & Associates LLP. Chartered Certified Accountants.
Spectrum House , Hove
BN3 5AA **01273 724537**

Knight and Company
11 Castle Hill , Maidenhead
SL6 4AA **01628 631056**

JT-Accounting
Caversham
Berkshire , RG4 6LA
07768 726226 or 0118 946 3831
juliette@jt-accounting.co.uk
www.jt-accounting.co.uk

Peter Auguste & Co.
1 Dukes Passage , Brighton & Hove
BN1 1BS **01273 727376**

Kinrade & Co.
14 Kingsgate Close , Maidstone
ME16 0JT **01622 686283**

Accreditation and Certification

H & K Safety Services Ltd
The Old Granary , Nr Ashford
TN26 6NU **01233 720113**

Administration and Payroll Software

Cashflow Manager (UK) Ltd
Suite 10 Courtyard Offices , Witham
CM8 3GA **08451 300611**

Advertising and Promotional Material

Promotional Sourcing International Ltd
Glade House , Mortimer Common
RG7 2JX **01189 333331**

Route Marketing Limited
Sandwich Industrial Estate , Sandwich
CT13 9LY **01227 722722**

Air Conditioning Energy Assessments

ECO Climate Control Ltd
20 Little Oxley , West Malling
ME19 5QU **01732 321633**

Air Conditioning Systems

EAC Services
Home Farm , Hurtmore
GU8 6AD **01483 812240**

ORAC, Oxford Refrigeration and Air Conditioning
79/81 Magdalen Road , Oxford
Oxfordshire , OX4 1RF
01865 424 424
sales@oracoxford.co.uk
oracoxford.co.uk

Right Climate Air Conditioning Ltd
Unit Y Canna Enterprise , Aldershot
GU12 5QF **08005 677800**

Total Contracting Services
John Wilson Business Park , Whitstable
CT5 3QY **01227 277719**

Tamco Ltd
70 Churchill Square , West Malling
ME19 4YU **01732 897969**

D.W Smith Services Ltd

Specialists in the design and installation of air-conditioning ventilation and air source heat pumps

We specialise in the design and installation of air-conditioning, ventilation and heating systems at highly competitive rates.

Commercial EPCs

We are also commercial energy assessors and can carry out Energy Performance Certificates (EPC's) on all types of commercial premises.

We offer a nationwide service and can provide solutions for any type of building project. We have over 18 years experience within the industry, and as such have the expertise to offer the perfect response to any enquiry.

Installations

Wall Mounted - This unit is often used in small offices, domestic applications or server rooms. It is the cheapest type of air-conditioner and is the quickest to install. The unit normally hangs on the wall about 100mm below ceiling level and blows hot or cold air from the bottom louvre.

Floor mounted - This unit is used when there is no ceiling or wall space. It can sit directly on the floor or be turned through 90 degrees to hang from the ceiling. It is slightly more expensive than a wall unit. Air is blown through the top grille.

Cassette - This is the most commonly used type of air-conditioner, mainly in large offices or shops. It is fitted in the false ceiling with only the white fascia grille visible. Air is distributed in four directions from the louvres, hence giving a better air distribution throughout the room. This unit is more expensive than a floor or wall unit.

Ducted - This unit normally sits above the false ceiling and has the advantage of being able to serve more than one room, via ductwork and ceiling grilles. It is the most expensive individual unit but saves costs for multiple rooms.

We are approved installers of

DAIKIN   MITSUBISHI ELECTRIC   HITACHI Inspire the Next   TOSHIBA

www.dwsmithservices.co.uk

| Tel: 0845 643 4652 | Fax: 0845 643 4652 |
| Mobile: 07711 859 421 | Email: dws49@hotmail.com |

Page 453

Air Conditioning Systems

D.W Smith Services Ltd
12 Vectis Road , New Milton
Hampshire , BH25 7OF
0845 643 4652
dws49@hotmail.com
www.dwsmithservices.co.uk
(see full page advert for more information)

Air Temperatures Controlled Ltd

Santon , Newbury
Berkshire , RG14 7EP
01635 550806
07917 148002
info@atc-limited.co.uk
www.atc-limited.co.uk

Just Cold Services Ltd
117 Old Farleigh , South Croydon
CR2 8QD **08442 492929**

Heating & Cooling Solutions Ltd
Appledown Barn , Southampton
SO32 2AE **01489 860667**

SJM Air Conditioning Ltd
Felcourt Road , Felcourt
RH19 2LP **0800 9557333**

MBS Environmental Services Ltd
146 Rock Avenue , Gillingham
ME7 5PR **07969 217896**

Air Source Heat Pumps

BritishEco Ltd
Unit 1A Oaklands Business Centre , Wokingham
RG41 2FD **08452 570041**

Go Eco Consultancy Co Ltd
University of Southampton , Southampton
SO16 7NP **08456 026461**

Ice Energy
Oakfields Industrial Estate , Eynsham
Oxfordshire , OX29 4TH
01865 882202
pwatson@iceenergy.co.uk
www.iceenergy.co.uk

Air Source Heat Pumps

ORAC, Oxford Refrigeration and Air Conditioning
79/81 Magdalen Road , Oxford
Oxfordshire , OX4 1RF
01865 424 424
sales@oracoxford.co.uk
oracoxford.co.uk

D.W. Smith Services Ltd
12 Vectis Road , New Milton
BH25 7OF **07711 859421**

Heating & Cooling Solutions Ltd
Appledown Barn , Southampton
Hampshire , SO32 2AE
01489 860667 or 07831 210611
info@heating-cooling.co.uk
www.heating-cooling.co.uk

Heat Pump Installations Ltd
Manor Way Industrial Estate , Woking
GU22 9JX **01483 750447**

Airport Transfers

The Executive Car Company
62 Kemp Lock Crescent , Brighton
BN41 2AD **01273 410752**

Emerald Executive Cars
Harlow-Stansted
.............**01279 310562**

Alternative and Complimentary Therapies

Shila Jassal
58 Bryant Road , Rochester
ME2 3ES **01634 718664**

Alternative and Renewable Energy

NRG Renewables
The Oast , Chart Sutton
ME17 3SA **01622 609070**

Catchin Rays Ltd
59 Guildford Road , Aldershot
GU12 6BQ **08000 88066**

Architects

Quadria Ltd
38 Stafford Road , Wallington
SM6 9AA **02086 471915**

Architects

Easton Bevins
436-440 Gloucester Road , Bristol
BS7 8TX **01179 427876**

Ace Designs Ltd
143 Station Road , Liss
GU33 7AJ **01730 894988**

M2 Architecture
4 Queensgate , Fareham
PO16 0NW **01329 288911**

Cadsquare Limited
Great Bramshot Barns , Fleet
GU51 2SF **01252 786580**

South Coast Architectural Technology Ltd
4th Floor Melbury House , Bournemouth
BH8 8ES **01202 421190**

Telion Architectural Design LLP
Telion House , Woking
GU21 8UH **01483 488230**

Studio Heathfield Limited
Parallel House , Guildford
GU1 2AB **01483 230760**

Wildcry Technical Services
1 Bealing Close , Southampton
SO16 3AW **07879 641047**

Roger Wilkinson Architectural & Building Services
Bailie Gate Industrial Estate , Wimborne
BH21 4DB **01258 857350**

Asbestos Handling and Removal

Maylarch Recycling Ltd
Andoversford Industrial Estate , Cheltenham
GL54 4LB **01242 821450**

Ductclean (UK) Ltd
Cambridge Cottages , High Cross
Hertfordshire , SG11 1BB
0870 112 9196
info@ductclean.co.uk
www.ductclean.co.uk

Asbestos Survey and Assesment

Hastings Environmental Services
2 Windmill Drive , Brighton
BN1 5HG **01273 262388**

Asbestos Survey and Assesment

AV Asbestos Limited
Manor Lees House , Reading
RG5 3DA **08458 332660**

Alpha Surveys Ltd
Wychwood , Bodiam
TN32 5UW **01580 860301**

Asbestos Training and Awareness

Pelham Safety Services Ltd
14 Pelham Terrace , Gravesend
DA11 0JJ **01474 537496**

Ductclean (UK) Ltd
The Yard ,
Hertfordshire , SG11 1BB
0870 112 9196
info@ductclean.co.uk
www.ductclean.co.uk

Audio Visual

Catchin Rays Ltd
59 Guildford Road , Aldershot
GU12 6BQ **08000 88066**

Badges, Emblems, Medals and Awards

Promotional Sourcing International Ltd
Glade House , Mortimer Common
RG7 2JX **01189 333331**

Biomass Energy and Biofuels

BritishEco Ltd
Unit 1A Oaklands Business Centre , Wokingham
RG41 2FD **08452 570041**

Stovesonline Ltd
Capton , Darmouth
TQ6 0JE **08452 265754**

Boilers and Water Heaters

Alpha Heating Innovation
Nepicar House , Wrotham Heath
TN15 7RS **08448 718760**

Heat-Tec 2000 Ltd
57 Corkscrew Hill , West Wickham
BR4 9BA **07802 976778**

Building and Construction

Upfold Construction
Station Approach , Godalming
GU8 5TB 01483 600335

M Wilson Builders
20 Willow Road , Redhill
RH1 6LW 01737 221574

calfordseaden LLP
St Johns House , Orpington
BR6 0JX 01689 888222

Lionel Gregory Limited
The Fulcrum Business Park , Poole
BH12 4NU 01202 723157

Kent Turf Care
2 Sedley Close , Aylesford
ME20 7JG 01622 213012

F.J. Malcolm Mair
5 Cottage Hill , Crowborough, East Sussex
TN6 3JL 01892 852976

Burglar Alarms and Security Systems

Pro-Tech Security Systems
16 Pevensey Road , Eastbourne
BN21 3HP 01323 419496

Business Management, Coaching and Consultancy

Riverside Practice
45 Cayfield Road , Gillingham (Medway)
ME7 2QY 01634 855807

Wellington Coaching
PO Box 3425 , Wokingham
RG41 2ZY 08707 664982

IMAGO Transformational Change Ltd
148 Binfield Road , Bracknell
RG42 2AY 07789 176796

Carpentry and Joinery

Handmade Kitchen Co
18A Woodfield Terrace , Epping
CM16 6LL 01992 577998

McKays Carpentry & General Builders
19 St Nicholas Close , Canterbury
CT2 0WT 01227 711942

Westgate Joinery
Sycamore House , Ringmer
BN8 5SY 01273 814555

Carpet and Floor Care

Natural Carpet Care
18 Willingdon Road , Upperton
BN21 1TH 01273 634177

Catering Services & Design

NileRose Catering
12 Broadmark Avenue , Rustington
BN16 2HQ 01903 850525

CCTV and Surveillance

Pro-Tech Security Systems
16 Pevensey Road , Eastbourne
BN21 3HP 01323 419496

CD and DVD Duplication

The Duplication Service
3B Sturdee Place , Hastings
TN34 3AJ 01424 863981

Promotional Sourcing International Ltd
Glade House , Mortimer Common
RG7 2JX 01189 333331

Chauffeur Services

Emerald Executive Cars
Harlow-Stansted
.............01279 310562

Your Executive Car Ltd
Farnborough
GU14 8ER 08006 123414

Cleaning and Hygiene Services

Rainbow Domestic Services Ltd
38 Foredown Drive , Portslade
BN21 2BB 01273 417988

Top Mops (Contract Cleaning) Ltd
Unit B6 Spithead Business Centre , Sandown
PO36 9PHH 01983 400202

Clothing for Schools

School Uniform Direct
22A Howard Business Park , Waltham Abbey
EN9 1XE 01992 763679

T G R Workwear Ltd
Sanderson Centre , Gosport
PO12 3UL 02392 528066

Company Networking

Forever Living Products
Salisbury
SP4 6BH 07740 911401

Compost

KPS Composting Services Ltd
KPS House , Scanyes Hill
RH17 7PR 01444 831010

Computer & IT Recycling

Techlogic UK Limited
450 Bath Road , Heathrow
UB7 0AE 08453 700028

Computer Consultancy

Fahrenheit Consultancy Services Ltd
49 Jubilee Road , Wimbourne
BH21 3NH 01202 901741

HACCS T/A Netplay
School Lane , Gillingham
SP8 4QW 01747 228287

Computer Consultancy

Punchedcard Ltd
Moor Park Farm , Liss
GU33 7BX 05602 559319

Technologies & Solutions Ltd
Olivier House , Steyning
BN44 3RE 01903 814188

Entrust IT Ltd
Unit 1, The Doughty Building , Ringwood
BH24 1NZ 08703 830045

Computer Maintenance

keepITsimple Consultancy Ltd
9 Burnside Crescent , Lancing Sompting
BN15 9TN 01903 868122

ITSA (UK) Ltd
57 Allenby Road , Maidenhead
SL6 5BG 08452 300710

GTI Computers
219 Victory House , Portsmouth
PO1 1PJ 08455 438077

NAH Computer Services
65 Rugby Road , Worthing
BN11 5NB 07932 704546

Entrust IT Ltd
Unit 1, The Doughty Building , Ringwood
BH24 1NZ 08703 830045

Alton IT Support Ltd
The Alton Business Centre , Alton, Hampshire
GU34 2PP 01420 559800

DRT Technologies
4a Priory Street , Dover
CT17 9AA 01304 202622

Computer Services

Warren IT Services Ltd
Unit 12, The Glenmore Centre , Folkestone
CT19 4RJ 01303 770216

PC Pal
1 Marlpit Cottages , Wadhurst
TN5 6UW 01892 640999

ITSA (UK) Ltd
57 Allenby Road , Maidenhead
SL6 5BG 08452 300710

Alpha IT
400 Thames Valley Park Drive , Reading
RG6 1PT 01189 664588

Computer Services

Nova IT Solutions Ltd
New Bond House , London
W15 1DX 08000 194525

Vermillion Technology Ltd
6 Vulcan Way , Sandhurst
GU47 9DB 01252 873142

DSNetworx Ltd
68 North Acre , Andover
SP11 6QD 01264 724897

Vecta Computer Services
11 Spanners Close , Chale Green
PO38 2HY 01983 551319

PC Computer Services
16 South Avenue , Bognor Regis
PO21 3QS 01243 820840

iRepair Systems Ltd
9 Hassock Wood Business Centre , Basingstoke
RG24 8UQ 01256 468264

Counselling , Advice and Psychotherapy

Sonia Willmot Counselling and Business/ Life Coaching
Woodbine Cottage , Newbury
RG20 8QG 01488 638774

Kunu Gordon Counselling and Therapy
Guildford Natural Health Centre , Guildford
GI1 3UQ 01483 300400

Sue Pallenberg Psycotherapy Counselling Practice
6 Burydale Lane , St Albans
AL2 2PJ 01727 875212

Erika's Counselling
31 Priory Road , Southampton
SO17 2HT 02380 559183

Sonia Mackenzie Counselling
24 Gordon Road , Folkestone
CT20 3LD 01303 489652

Jacqueline Anderiesz-Tyrrell & Inspire
Inspire , Portsmouth
PO4 9JB 02392 297582

Jean Carrington
19 Glenrose Avenue , Bedford
MK44 2SB 01234 306784

Penny Carter
67-69, The Centre for Counselling , Bromley
BR1 3AA 07880 735868

Counselling , Advice and Psychotherapy

Louise Martin
30 Tamworth , Bracknell
RG12 0TU 07966 578453

Trubshaw Counselling
21 Elm Road , Winchester
SO22 5AG 07736 509794

Lodestar Coaching Ltd
122 Westbury Leigh , Westbury
BA13 3SH 01373 301215

Currency Exchange

Excel Currencies Ltd
20 Copperfields Centre , Dartford
DA1 2DE 01322 221121

Design 2 Print

Print on Anything UK Ltd
143 Wigmore Road , Gillingham
ME8 0TH 01634 260700

RP Printers
The Warehouse , Bournemouth
BH1 3SH 01202 557917

Palm Tree Design & Print Ltd
Palm Tree House , Southampton
SO19 8PP 02380 442686

Display and Exhibition Boards

Cerberex
Little Dale Workshops , Cranbrook
TN17 2LS 01580 212939

Document and Data Destruction

PHS Datashred
Unit J Acorn Industrial Park , Crayford
DA1 4FL 08003 764422

ShredSure Ltd
Union Yard , Erith
DA8 2AD 08000 743707

Data Shredding Services
38 Pound Lane , Steyning
BN44 3JD 01903 814949

Drains, Drainage and Pipes

Robert Clark Associates Ltd
Willow Cottage , Rustlington
BN16 3EE 01903 778945

—

Drilling, Boring and Site Investigations

W T Specialist Contracts Ltd
Bird-In Eye Yard , Uckfield
TN22 5HA **01825 768111**

Driver, CPC, Periodic Training

WRRS Solutions
Greenacres , Reading
RG7 1QX **01189 888426**

E-commerce and Search Engine Optimisation (SEO)

SDX Digital Solutions
6 Chetwode Way , Poole
BH17 7JF **07779 679081**

Caroline Gowans
6a London Road , Petersfield
GU31 4BD **01730 268414**

Radweb
12 Acorn Business Centre , Portsmouth
PO6 3TH **03333 444505**

Pegu Design
Flackley Ash Farm Cottage , Rye
TN31 6TB **01797 230962**

Chrave Technology Ltd
6A Brokes Road , Reigate
RH2 9LP **07816 966169**

WSI Internet Solutions Ltd
Talbot Oaks Technical Centre , Upper Basildon
RG8 8NJ **01491 830134**

RedGreenBlue Web Design & Marketing
15 Holmes Road , Reading
RG6 7BH **01189 267182**

Direct Design Studio
Two Furlongs , Esher
KT10 9AA **01372 466666**

The Web Maverick
1 Houston Road , Surbiton
KT6 5RL **02087 866903**

RYH Web Design
Rochester
ME2 4QJ **07837 722832**

Ecology Surveys and Consultancy

Azure Ecology
518A Sheppards Lodge , Petworth
GU28 9NE **07761 154345**

Darwin Ecology Ltd
8 Layton Lane , Shaftesbury
SP7 8EY **07748 843842**

Abbas Ecology
Brooklands Farm , Dorchester
Dorset , DT2 7AA
07500 781973
info@dorsetecology.co.uk
www.dorsetecology.com

Sussex Ecology
49-51 East Road ,
London , N1 6AH
07707 608 296
info@sussexecology.co.uk
www.sussexecology.co.uk

Oak Bay Ecology
16 Waters Edge Fold , Manchester
OL1 4QJ **07775 186757**

Electric Cars

Evergreen Consulting
Brighton Hill , Basingstoke
RG22 4LM **07711 252974**

Electrical and Electricians

Andrews Electrical Services
Unit 16 Aztec Centre , Poole
BH17 0RT **01202 675525**

JF Electrical & Testing Solutions Limited
4 Highwood Close , Yateley
GU46 6DG **01252 890245**

Acer Projects (S.E.) Ltd T/A Acer Electrical
The Wattles , Whitstable
CT5 3JX **01227 793793**

One Electrical Safety Services
268 Southampton Road , Portsmouth
PO6 4QD **07722 091409**

She's Electric, He's Not
1 Cambridge Place , Brighton
BN2 0HB **07590 724935**

Electrical and Electricians

T&J Bateman Ltd
10 Harwood Close , Southampton
SO40 3FT   ....

Thomas Frederick Electrical Ltd
21 Mountfield Close , Meopham
DA13 0UJ **01732 823557**

Electrical Building Systems
The Clock Tower , Weybridge
KT15 3NZ **01932 350681**

Knightfall Electrical Ltd
Blue Coates Yard , Maidstone
ME15 6LD **07769 157598**

RJS Electrical (UK) Ltd
35 Fairborne Way , Guildford
GU2 9GB **07793 586776**

Electrical Maintenance and Installation

Elec-Trick
19 Station Road , Christchurch
BH23 1QY **07830 410649**

Mark Black Electrical Contractors Ltd
1 Trinity Road , Ventnor
PO38 1NL **01983 857129**

Embroidery

T G R Workwear Ltd
Sanderson Centre, Gosport
PO12 3UL **02392 528066**

Oak Apple Embroidery
Oak Apple House , Sherbourne
DT9 5EW **01963 251645**

Alison Wynne Embroidery
21 Ruskin Way , Wokingham
RG41 3BP **01183 262532**

Aries Embroidery Ltd
Fareham Enterprise Centre , Fareham
PO14 1TH **01329 314766**

KTEES Clothing Ltd
Units 15-16 Northern Galleries , Fareham
PO14 1AH **01329 822583**

Energy Assessors & Consultants

Dorset Surveyors Ltd
26 Wallace Road , Poole
BH18 8NG **08458 721335**

Total Environmental Management
4 Lakeside Business Park , Sandhurst
GU47 9DN **01252 878722**

Altechnica
85 Waterside , Milton Keynes
MK6 3DE **01908 668797**

Energy Performance Certificates

Dorset Surveyors Ltd
26 Wallace Road , Poole
BH18 8NG **08458 721335**

H I Southern
P.O. Box 128 , Brighton
BN51 9BU **01273 302304**

D & S Energy
10 Little Walton , Sandwich
CT13 0DW **01304 620674**

D.W. Smith Services Ltd
12 Vectis Road , New Milton
BH25 7OF **07711 859421**

Environmental Consultancy

Total Environmental Management
4 Lakeside Business Park , Sandhurst
GU47 9DN **01252 878722**

QSUK Ltd
Venture House , Bracknell
RG12 1WA **08004 589421**

Eagle Eye Environmental Solutions
The Old Dairy , Ventnor
PO38 3EN **01983 840778**

H & K Safety Services Ltd
The Old Granary , Nr Ashford
TN26 6NU **01233 720113**

Ecosys
23 Baden Road , Brighton
BN2 4DP **01273 245587**

Environmental Consultancy

HSE Advisor Ltd
28 Castle Street , Dover
CT16 1PN **01304 600999**

PMB Management Ltd
83 Stoneham Close , Reading
RG3 4HD **01189 431463**

Event Organisers

The Northern Home Show
Carnah Events Ltd , Tadworth
KT20 7HZ **08445 611230**

Exhibition Display Banners

Cerberex
Unit 5B Little Dale Workshops , Cranbrook
TN17 2LS **01580 212939**

Exhibition Stands

442 Graphics Ltd
Rushton Farm House , Wokingham
RG40 5RE **01189 795442**

Cerberex
Unit 5B Little Dale Workshops , Cranbrook
TN17 2LS **01580 212939**

Vivid Pixel
Mereworth Business Centre, Wateringbury
ME18 5LW **01622 814066**

Fences, Fencing & Decking

ABA Solutions
20 Buccaneer Close , Reading
RG5 4XP **01189 699830**

Chase Fencing Supplies
Station Hill , Tonbridge
TN11 8JD **01892 870882**

County Landscaping
Horton Depot , Slough
SL3 9PE **07710 441442**

Financial Auditing

Peter Auguste & Co.
1 Dukes Passage , Brighton & Hove
BN1 1BS **01273 727376**

Financial Services

Smith & Williamson
No. 1 Bishops Wharf , Guildford
Surrey , GU1 4RA
01483 407100
janice.clay@smith.williamson.co.uk
www.smith.williamson.co.uk/guildford

Adlam Accountancy Services
22 Grange Road , Ramsgate
CT11 9LR **01843 851319**

Fire and Smoke Detection

Ale Fire Systems Ltd
Wyndham Park , Midhurst
GU29 9RE **01730 815471**

Multifire Maintenance Services Limited
Suite 2B Beta House , Rochester
ME2 4HU **01634 735465**

Fire Risk Assessment and Training

QSUK Ltd
Venture House , Bracknell
RG12 1WA **08004 589421**

Bravanark Ltd
The Lodge , Reading
RG2 7PP **01189 541700**

IC Safety Consultancy Ltd
68 Winchester Street , Basingstoke
RG25 3HY **01256 771878**

Firehouse Training and Consultancy Ltd
55 Waverley Avenue , London
TW2 6DQ **02033 764350**

Fire Safety Protection and Equipment

Fire Safety Protection and Equipment

FireCare Solutions
Aden House , Eastleigh
SO53 2EN **02380 269833**

Flash Point Fire Protection
111 Testwood Lane , Southampton
SO40 3QR **07917 060076**

Fireguard Services (N.M) Ltd
Unit 1 Milton Business Centre , New Milton
BH25 6RH **01425 616139**

First Aid Supplies

Train2Protect(T2P) International Ltd
7 Dickens Road , Rochester
ME1 2JR **08000 438827**

First Aid Training

Train2Protect(T2P) International Ltd
7 Dickens Road , Rochester
ME1 2JR **08000 438827**

H & K Safety Services Ltd
The Old Granary , Nr Ashford
TN26 6NU **01233 720113**

First Response Learning Limited
21 Bramber Road , Seaford
BN25 1AG **08009 990100**

Train Aid Ltd
Northside Coach House , Reigate
RH2 9DZ **01737 211228**

Food and Drink

Greenfields Hog Roast Ltd
Sunnycliff , Andover
SP11 7LU **01264 359422**

Food Hygiene

QSUK Ltd
Venture House , Bracknell
RG12 1WA **08004 589421**

Train Aid Ltd
Northside Coach House , Reigate
RH2 9DZ **01737 211228**

Gas and Central Heating (Domestic)

Martin Environmental Services Ltd
Unit 1 Forward Way , Rochester
ME1 3QX **01634 668397**

Plumb-Seal Heating
7 Athelstan Road , Hastings
TN35 5JB **01424 422745**

James Whitear Plumbing & Heating
132 Milward Road , Hastings
TN34 3RT **01424 427702**

Geothermal Energy

Nicholls Boreholes.co.uk
Brownings Barn , Kirdford
RH14 0LW **01403 820750**

Graphic Design

TL&L Design Ltd
Avondale House , Woking
GU21 8UA **01483 747911**

Bravanark
HEALTH AND SAFETY
TRAINING AND SUPPORT
*Let your safety be our business
with a sensible approach*

Health and Safety Training - A Legal Requirement or Just Nice To Have

The training of staff is critical to the ongoing health and safety performance of the business. Staff at all levels need to understand how to carry out their tasks safely and to be aware of the health effects they are likely to be at risk to, should they not observe their instructions, supervision and training.

Safety training has clear benefits:

- Less time investigating accident.
- Better productivity.
- Fewer replacement staff costs.
- Less sickness absence.
- Less equipment / machinery damage.
- Lower insurance premiums
- Improved bottom line.
- Less down time

IOSH accredited Training courses we provide:
Managing Safely and Working Safely.

General Health and Safety training in:
Manual Handling – Risk assessments – Office Safety – Warehouse Safety –
General Workplace Safety – Employee induction – Accident Investigation
We offer either in-house or as open courses for all industries

Welcome to Bravanark Ltd.
Based in Reading, our aim is to ensure that our clients can demonstrate robust health and safety compliance through the provision of tailored, professional health and safety compliance services.

Our consultants are experienced Safety Practitioners who will work with you to achieve your health and safety goals.

Visit our website for further details or Contact us to on 01189541700

Graphic Design

10% Discount
Just quote BGB2012

SWATT
design ltd

Affordable Graphic Design

Professional Service

Specialists in Design for Print

ADVERTISING   BRANDING   BROCHURES
CATALOGUES   PACKAGING   POINT OF SALE
PROMOTION   VEHICLE LIVERY

www.swatt-design.co.uk

Vivid Pixel
Unit 1E , Wateringbury
ME18 5LW 01622 814066

Graphic Force Ltd
39 Narromine Drive , Reading
RG31 7ZL 01183 750705

White Cat Design Ltd
Leamington Court , Basingstoke
RG23 7HE 01256 892952

Marsh Graphic Design
The Studio , Scaynes Hill
RH17 7NG 01444 831314

Munkee Bum
39 Narromine Drive , Reading
RG31 7ZL 01183 750705

Route Marketing Limited
The Centre , Sandwich
CT13 9LY 01227 722722

Paw Design Solutions
158 Marrowbrook Lane , Farnborough
GU14 0AD 01252 521609

Green Roofing

Sussex Green Roofs
Brighton
BN1 9GG 07834 488632

Ground Source Heat Pumps

BritishEco Ltd
Unit 1A Oaklands Business Centre , Wokingham
RG41 2FD 08452 570041

Go Eco Consultancy Co Ltd
University of Southampton , Southampton
SO16 7NP 08456 026461

Ice Energy
Unit 2 Oakfield House , Eynsham
Oxfordshire , OX29 4TH
01865 882202
pwatson@iceenergy.co.uk
www.iceenergy.co.uk

Habitat Management.

JDB Contractors & Son Ltd
Timbermill Yard , Eversley
RG27 0PY 01189 733943

Head and Body Massage

Gentle Touch Therapies
Crookhorn
PO7 8AQ 07876 550047

Health and Beauty Products

Heidi Organic
61 Playstool Road , Sittingbourne
ME9 7NL 07592 599411

Health and Safety

Bravanark Ltd
The Lodge , Reading
Berkshire , RG2 7PP
0118 954 1700
enquiry@bravanark.co.uk
www.bravanark.co.uk
(see full page advert for more information)

Shea Occupational Health Ltd
8 Homewood , Slough
SL3 6AU 07872 590245

Page 465

THE GREEN DIRECTORY

THE GREEN DIRECTORY

Health and Safety

HSE Advisor Ltd
28 Castle Street , Dover
CT16 1PN 01304 600999

AMW Health & Safety Ltd
75 Inhurst Avenue , Waterlooville
PO7 7QT 02392 233322

MJZ Health & Safety Management
9 Prince Andrew Road , Maidenhead
SL6 8QQ 07957 888750

PMB Management Ltd
83 Stoneham Close , Reading
RG3 4HD 01189 431463

Active Safety Associates
39 Tindale Close , South Croydon
CR2 0RT 02086 516601

de Silva Safety Services
23 Helmsdale , Bracknell
Berkshire , RG12 0TA
01344 441494 or 07813 542756
info@desilvasafetyservices.co.uk
www.desilvasafetyservices.co.uk

IC Safety Consultancy Ltd
68 Winchester Street , Basingstoke
RG25 3HY 01256 771878

Cunningham Consulting
1 Edwards College , South Cerney
GL7 5TR 01285 862831

Hypnotherapy

Lodestar Coaching Ltd
122 Westbury Leigh , Westbury
BA13 3SH 01373 301215

The Clinical Hypnosis Institute
26 Ewell Avenue , West Malling
ME19 6NN 01732 846374

Hancocks Hypnotherapy
Southampton
SO17 1RT 02380 582245

Insulation

Marmox UK Ltd
101-103 Caxton House , Chatham
ME5 7NP 01634 835290

Insulation Shop
49 Gladstone Road , Portslade
BN41 1LJ 08455 441077

Insurance

Oakland Insurance Services
25 Lintot Square , Horsham
RH13 9LA 01403 888193

Cassey Miller James Ltd
1A Waltham Court , Reading
RG10 9AA 01189 406175

**P & A Taximeters /
Motor Trade Insurance**
6 Foundation Unit , Guildford
GU1 1SF 01483 535353

**Coversure Insurance Service
Portsmouth**
4 Westbrook Centre , Portsmouth
PO7 8SF 08003 081104

Investment

Top Marks Partnership
42 Gloucester Road , Bewbury
Berkshire , RG14 5JR
07768 400866
adrian@topmarkspartnership.co.uk
www.topmarkspartnership.co.uk

Land Reclamation, Site Clearance and Groundworks

JDB Contractors & Son Ltd
Timbermill Yard , Eversley
RG27 0PY 01189 733943

Landscape Design and Architecture

Openview Landscape Design Ltd
The Studio , Tenterden
Kent , TN30 7AU
0800 0778633
enquiries@openviewlandscapes.co.uk
www.openviewlandscapes.co.uk
(see full page advert for more information)

Adam S Bailey Garden Design
3 Riverside, Eynsford
DA4 0AE 07912 647012

THE GREEN DIRECTORY

Landscaping and Ground Maintenance

Thompson Estate Maintenance
Classic House , Alfold
GU6 8HP **08445 610578**

S L P Vegetation Solutions
235 Greggs Wood Road , Tunbridge Wells
TN2 3HS **07540 552501**

Openview Landscape Design Ltd
Homewood Road , Tenterden
Kent , TN30 7AU
0800 0778633
enquiries@openviewlandscapes.co.uk
www.openviewlandscapes.co.uk

Andrews Landscaping
8A Upper Edgeborough Road , Guildford
GU1 2BG **01483 546228**

Andrew Montgomerie Landscape Contractors
Dairy House , Sevenoaks
TN14 7UD **01959 524375**

County Landscaping
Horton Depot , Slough
SL3 9PE **07710 441442**

Brymarts Ltd
16 Thorold Close , South Croydon
CR2 8SA **02086 514157**

Kent Turf Care
2 Sedley Close , Aylesford
ME20 7JG **01622 213012**

Rymer Landscaping Ltd
18 Hangleton Lane , Brighton
BN41 2FQ **01273 416660**

Dan Storey Landscape
75 Victoria Park Road , Bournemouth
BH9 2RD **01202 522779**

Legionella

Clearwater Safety Solutions Ltd
1 Queens Mount , Mayfield
TN20 6LH **01825 710002**

Mobile Phones

Green Mobile Ltd
Broadham House , Hindhead
GU26 6PT **08452 333333**

Mobility and Living Aids

Nordic Care Services Limited
307-309 Lombard House , Canterbury
CT1 2NF **01227 479293**

Motivational and Life Coaching

Lodestar Coaching Ltd
122 Westbury Leigh , Westbury
BA13 3SH **01373 301215**

Sue Millett
66 Drum Mead , Petersfield
GU32 3AQ **08454 563892**

Music, Theatre and Entertainment

Lost Vegas
40 Nutley , Bracknell
RG12 7HE **01344 752050**

Networking and Cabling

Hayes Communication Services
Studio 8 , Hastings
TN38 0BJ **08454 742937**

Blade Direct
74a Upton Road , Slough
SL1 2AW **01753 673717**

Systems Cabling Ltd
64 Upper Mulgrave Road , Cheam
SM2 7AJ **02083 951390**

Noise and Vibration Testing

Acoustic Associates Sussex Ltd
8 Highdown House , Shoreham-by-Sea
BN43 5PB **01273 455074**

Office And Retail Furniture

Mount Industries
Barton Park Ind Est , Eastleigh
SO50 6RR **02380 612841**

Office Stationery

Office Hut
Noble House , Gerrards Cross
SL9 8SU **08453 104497**

Office Supplies

Accord Office Supplies
Unit 22 Bridge Mead , Swindon
SN5 7TL **08451 308800**

THE GREEN DIRECTORY

Office Supplies

Siam Ltd
Eastlands Court , Basingstoke
RG24 8FA **08456 838414**

Osteopathy

Amblecote Osteopathy and Aromatherapy Total Health
4 Chapel Hill , Reading
Berkshire , RG31 5DG
0118 841 1212
email@amblecote-osteopathy.co.uk
www. amblecote-osteopathy.co.uk
(see full page advert for more information)

Packaging

Promotional Sourcing International Ltd
Glade House , Mortimer Common
RG7 2JX **01189 333331**

Painting and Decorating

Premier Decorating Services
19 B Bourne Court , Brighton
BN1 8QQ **07930 851655**

Palmers Decorating
62 Baring Road , Hensbury Head
BH6 4DT **07748 640269**

Rowe and Martin, Decoration and Restoration
1 Church Square , Broadstairs
Kent , CT10 1HB
01483 224016
simon.martin@rowemartin.co.uk
www.rowemartin.co.uk
(see full page advert for more information)

P. Godman
No 1 Bourne Road , Bromley
BR2 9PB **02084 605181**

Darren Roberts Painter & Decorator
11 Ashlodge Close , Guildford
GU12 6JU **07889 436186**

High Maintenance Decorators
1 Stuart House , Bracknell
RG42 1UA **07980 399034**

Partitioning Services

AC Interior Projects Ltd
53 William Street, Herne Bay
CT6 5NR **03333 210986**

South East Partitioning Ltd
Sunnybank House , Crowborough
TN6 1XG **01892 667348**

Castle Interiors
17 The Castle , Horsham
RH1 5PX **01403 218422**

EG Silverthorn and Sons Ltd
20 Metuchen Way , Southampton
SO30 0JZ **02380 658813**

Paving and Driveways

County Landscaping
Horton Depot , Slough
SL3 9PE **07710 441442**

Payroll and Bookkeeping

Sabre Business Systems Limited
16 Ruscombe Gardens , Slough
SL3 9BG **01753 540809**

AFH Payroll Solutions Ltd
Unit B3 Brownings Farm , Uckfield
TN22 5HG **01825 891049**

Matthews Hanton Limited
93 Aldwick Road , Bognor Regis
PO21 2NW **01243 861521**

Adlam Accountancy Services
22 Grange Road , Ramsgate
CT11 9LR **01843 851319**

Munro Business Advisors
School House , Salisbury
SP5 2SU **07518 027031**

RFL Bookkeeping Services
Riverview Padmore House , East Cowes
PO32 6LP **01983 209915**

Kinrade & Co.
14 Kingsgate Close , Maidstone
ME16 0JT **01622 686283**

The Brand Partnership
16 Maylings Farm Road , Fareham
PO16 7QU **01329 232892**

Peter Auguste & Co.
1 Dukes Passage , Brighton & Hove
BN1 1BS **01273 727376**

ROWE & MARTIN
DECORATION & RESTORATION

Rowe and Martin Design Decoration and Restoration Ltd are committed to the use of natural, eco paints and wood finishes. Uncompromising in our environmental standards, our specialist team can advise you on the best product for you and the environment.

We aim to ensure that materials used contain natural raw components from environmentally managed sources, produced using a sustainable ecological cycle. We also have an unparalleled track record in design restoration and decoration of many landmark buildings, galleries and monuments using artisan techniques.

If you require a single room repainted or a complete property makeover we can easily adjust to your unique specification.

For a commitment free quote please
Contact 01843 260473 or 07973 238126
or email: enquiries@rowemartin.co.uk

Page 472

THE GREEN DIRECTORY

Payroll and Bookkeeping

C.M.S. Bookkeeping Services
20 Wellington Cottages , Cranbrook
TN18 5EL 01580 754511

Pest Control

All Brook Pest Control
54 Allbrook Knoll , Eastleigh
SO50 4RY 07712 896212

Pestatak Ltd
Peanhill Park , Whitstable
CT5 3BJ 01227 768189

Force 10 Pest Control
1 St Martins Road , Eastbourne
BN22 0LG 07540 625737

Guest and Sons Ltd
Cherry Trees , Cranbrook
TN18 4XB 01580 753357

Advanced Pest Control
28 Lower Cippenham Lane , Slough
SL1 5DF 07825 647266

M B Pest Services
7 Primrose Road , Andover
SP11 9TJ 07584 201121

Clear Round Pest Service
76 Parsonage Estate , Petersfield
GU31 5HL 01730 821500

No More Pests
1 Hazlewood Close , Ashford
TN27 8NY 07931 505224

Goodwin Pest Management
Hollywood House , Rochester
ME3 8AR 08006 342530

Pest Force (Dorset)
7 Lufton Heights , Yeovil
BA22 8UY 01202 366741

Photography and Photographers

Robert Hughes Photography & Design
51 Reeves Way , Wokingham
RG41 2PS 01189 787615

Clive Woodley Photography
Old London House , Knockholt
TN14 7JE 01959 532613

Plastering and Tiling

P. Godman
No 1 Bourne Road , Bromley
BR2 9PB 02084 605181

Plumbing Services

NRG Plumbing
The Oast , Chart Sutton
ME17 3SA 01622 609070

Thatcham & Newbury Maintenance Services
34 Green Lane , Thatcham
RG19 3RG 01635 826770

Portable Appliance and Fixed Wire Testing

BES Electrical
14 Trinity Road , Weymouth
DT4 8TJ 07776 026182

PTP Testing
114 Albert Street , Slough
SL1 2AY 07818 227365

PATTCO Ltd
43 Southampton Road , Ringwood
BH24 1HE 08000 850482

Hannington-Gilbert & Co Ltd
24 North Ridge Park , Hastings
TN35 4PP 01424 428696

MJG P.A.T Services
17 Holmwood Court , Hassocks
BN6 8AS 01273 844761

Kent PAT Testing
9 Taylor Road , Snodland
ME6 5HH 07792 566125

Advanced PAT Testing
105 Fleet Road , Dartford
DA2 6JF 01322 270006

Emerald Electrical Services (SE) Ltd
352 Cheriton Road , Folkestone
CT19 4DS 01303 248163

ELECTROTEST
2A Eton Road , Orpington
BR6 9HE 02082 890000

Pothole and Road Repairs

Andrew Montgomerie Landscape Contractors
Dairy House , Sevenoaks
TN14 7UD 01959 524375

Pressurisation Systems & Vacuum Degassing

Reflex UK
Stablegate , Waterlooville
PO8 8TS **02392 240816**

Print Management

Foundry Press
Foundry Lane , Horsham
RH13 5PX **01403 216120**

Printed School Bags, P.E. Bags and Rucksacks

Promotional Sourcing International Ltd
Glade House , Mortimer Common
RG7 2JX **01189 333331**

Printing, Design and Mailing Services

Captiv8 UK Ltd
Embassy House , Crowborough
East Sussex , TN6 2JL
01892 611 500
enquiries@captiv8uk.co.uk
www.captiv8uk.co.uk

Print on Anything UK Ltd
143 Wigmore Road , Gillingham
ME8 0TH **01634 260700**

Foundry Press
Foundry Lane , Horsham
West Sussex , RH13 5PX
01403 216120 or 07788 724411
brucephillips@foundry-press.co.uk
www.foundry-press.co.uk
(see full page advert for more information)

Wimborne Print Centre
16 East Street , Wimborne
BM21 1DT **01202 885881**

Colour Inc.
Basingstoke Business Park, Basingstoke
RG22 4AU **01256 843151**

PEP The Printers
127 Tarring Road , Worthing
BN11 4HE ....**01903 535353.**

Rowcolour Limited
Epsom Business Park , Epsom
KT17 1JF **01372 745466**

Printing, Design and Mailing Services

Ashford Print
102 Ellingham Industrial Centre , Ashford
TN23 6LZ **01233 630110**

Copy That Printing
25 Spur Road , Portsmouth
PO6 3DY **02392 375737**

Oyster Press
110 John Wilson Business Park , Whitstable
CT5 3QY **01227 772605**

Profit and Loss Management

JTA Business Services
Winnersh , Wokingham
RG41 5XP **07860 513181**

Promotional Items and Incentives

New Media Branding
New Media House , Sevenoaks
Kent , TN13 1YH
0845 520 0660 or 01732 45 00 66
sales@newmediabranding.com
www.newmediabranding.com

Trophies & Gifts
16 Whatmer Close , Sturry
CT2 0JJ **01227 710638**

Thames & Solent Publicity Ltd
Campbell Court , Bramley
RG26 5EG **01256 882912**

Promotional Sourcing International Ltd
Glade House , Mortimer Common
RG7 2JX **01189 333331**

Pumps and Pumping Equipment

Active Pump Services Ltd
Rudford Industrial Estate , Arundel
West Sussex , BN18 0BD
01903 734030
nigel@activepumpservices.co.uk
www.activepumpservices.co.uk

Recycled and Refilled Printer Cartridges

Impact Inkjet & Toner Recycler
19 Trubridge Road , Rochester
ME3 9EN **01634 255400**

THE **GREEN** DIRECTORY

Looking for a green printing company?

Foundry Press are a high quality, full-service green printers for all your litho and digital printing.

foundrypress

Enabling you to communicate your messages through print

Unit A, Foundry Lane
Horsham RH13 5PX
01403 216120
info@foundry-press.co.uk
www.foundry-press.co.uk

Recycled and Refilled Printer Cartridges

BJW Computers
PO Box 557 , Maidstone
ME14 4LY 01634 684333

Cartridge World Reading
225 Caversham Road , Reading
RG1 8BB 01189 599000

The Print Store
96 High Street , Newport
PO30 1BQ 01983 532891

Recycling

Maylarch Recycling Ltd
Andoversford Industrial Estate , Cheltenham
GL54 4LB 01242 821450

GHS Recycling Ltd
32 Ackworth Road , Portsmouth
PO3 5JP 02392 670399

Steve Butler Cable Recycling
22 Haviland Road , Wimborne
BH21 7RG 01202 896058

Kingsnorth Waste Management
17 Kingsnorth Industrial Estate , Rochester
ME3 9ND 01634 253557

Hazchem Waste Disposal
Lasham Depot , Alton
GU34 5SQ 01256 385910

Refrigeration

New World Solar Solutions Ltd T/A Sunstruck Energy
Unit 7 Skein Enterprise Park , Wrotham
Kent , TH15 7LB
01732 822414 or 07972 249652
matthew@sunstruckenergy.co.uk
www.sunstruckenergy.co.uk

Total Contracting Services
John Wilson Business Park , Whitstable
CT5 3QY 01227 277719

Robins Refrigeration Ltd
Units 18 A-B Chapman Way , Tunbridge Wells
TN2 3EF 01892 537291

Renewable Energy Training.

Wagner Solar UK Ltd
Unit 2 Keynor Farm , Chichester
PO20 7NQ 01243 649035

Roofing Services

Richard Soan Roofing Services
Davey's Lane , Lewes
East Sussex , BN7 2BQ
01273 486110
enquiries@richardsoan.co.uk
www.richardsoan.co.uk
(see full page advert for more information)

John Nicholson Ltd
1B Vittlefields , Newport
PO30 5QL 01983 524222

BJN Roofing (Contractors) Ltd
Gladstone House , Horsham
RH12 2NN 01403 255155

Safety Risk Assessment

R S Safety Management Ltd
2 Southcote Drive , Camberley
GU15 1JL 01276 24690

WRRS Solutions
Greenacres , Reading
RG7 1QX 01189 888426

Sheq On Line Ltd
Connaught Road , Woking
GU24 0EU 08454 657475

Screen and T Shirt Printing

New Media Branding
New Media House , Sevenoaks
TN13 1YH 08455 200660

Cavaliers Custom T-Shirts + Embroidery
Reading Small Business Centre , Reading
RG1 7BX 01189 574885

KTEES Clothing Ltd
Units 15-16 Northern Galleries , Fareham
PO14 1AH 01329 822583

Screen Machine
68A Station Road , Winstable
CT5 1LF 01227 272288

Secretarial Service

Flying Finger
47 Greenways , High Cliffe
BH23 5BB 01425 270252

Sewage and Effluent Products and Services

Bio-Bubble Technologies Ltd
Unit L, Fishers Grove , Portsmouth
Hampshire , PO6 1RN
02392 200 669
sales@bio-bubble.com
www.bio-bubble.com

Signs and Graphics

Eberhardt Signs Quality Sign Solutions
2 Prospect Road , Portsmouth
PO1 4QY 02392 824624

Signarama (Heathrow, West London)
530 London Road , Ashford
TW15 3AE 01784 257043

Signarama (Reading)
89-91 Basingstoke Road , Reading
RG2 0HA 01189 311388

Chilli Graphics
Dairy Farm House , Lewes
BN8 6NB 01273 858763

Phil Croxford Signs and Graphics
Follygate , Chichester
PO20 8JT 01243 673993

Solar Energy

Silverstream Solar Limited
181 Silverdale Drive , Waterlooville
PO7 6DX 08007 101170

Stonegrove Limited
Boyd Industrial Estate , Rochester
ME2 4DZ 01634 291151

Windscout Ltd
Lyde Arundel , Hereford
HR4 7SN 01172 302789

Ardenham Energy Ltd
Cane End Lane , Aylesbury
HP22 5BH 08003 698980

Supreme Solar Systems Ltd
AllensYard, Aldingbourne
PO20 3UA 01243 544548

Sungod Solar Limited
24 Nelson Villas , Westgate-on-Sea
CT8 8BN 08002 889027

Solar Energy

Sunny Future Solar
Belle Vue Enterprise Centre , Aldershot
GU12 4QW 01252 343609

Solar Synthesis Limited
88 Meads Street , Eastbourne
BN20 7RS 01323 886980

Solex UK
225 Seafield Road , Bournemouth
BH6 5LL 03309 992324

Solar Panels and Photovoltaics

BritishEco Ltd
Unit 1A Oaklands Business Centre , Wokingham
RG41 2FD 08452 570041

IBC SOLAR UK LTD
4300 Nash Court , Oxford
OX4 2RT 01865 337230

Ice Energy
Unit 2 Oakfield House , Eynsham
OX29 4TH 01865 882202

New World Solar Solutions Ltd T/A Sunstruck Energy
Skein Enterprise Park , Wrotham
Kent , TH15 7LB
01732 822414 or 07972 249652
matthew@sunstruckenergy.co.uk
www.sunstruckenergy.co.uk

Wildwood Renewable Energy Systems Ltd
The Croft , Billericay
CM12 9SN 01277 656750

Emerald Electrical Services (SE) Ltd
352 Cheriton Road , Folkestone
CT19 4DS 01303 248163

Eco Warriors Solar
Limners Lease , Compton
GU3 1DJ 01483 811663

LC Energy Solutions Ltd
352 Havant Road , Portsmouth
PO6 1NE 02392 367057

Sphere Energy Solutions Ltd
36b London Road , Bagshot
GU19 5HN 08005 677629

Solar Panels and Photovoltaics

GHE Solar
Stags Grange Farm , Newbury
Berkshire , RG14 2TF
01635 200142
linda@ghesolar.co.uk
www.ghesolar.co.uk
(see full page advert for more information)

Solar Water Heating Systems

BritishEco Ltd
Unit 1A Oaklands Business Centre , Wokingham
RG41 2FD **08452 570041**

Wildwood Renewable Energy Systems Ltd
The Croft , Billericay
CM12 9SN **01277 656750**

Staff and Work Wear

New Media Branding
New Media House , Sevenoaks
TN13 1YH **08455 200660**

T G R Workwear Ltd
Sanderson Centre , Gosport
PO12 3UL **02392 528066**

Suspended Ceilings - Installation and Manufacture

AC Interior Projects Ltd
53 William Street , Herne Bay
CT6 5NR **03333 210986**

South East Partitioning Ltd
Sunnybank House , Crowborough
TN6 1XG **01892 667348**

Specialized Interiors Ltd
11 Hilliat Fields , Abingdon
OX14 4JE **01235 525526**

Castle Interiors
17 The Castle , Horsham
RH1 5PX **01403 218422**

EG Silverthorn and Sons Ltd
20 Metuchen Way , Southampton
SO30 0JZ **02380 658813**

Sustainable Water Supplies

Water Matters (EU) Ltd
4 St Johns Court , Keynsham
BS31 2AX **01189 401233**

Telecommunications

Swan Telecom
47 Canterbury Road , Worthing
BN13 1AN **01903 264500**

ECL Telecom
47 Prideaux Road , Eastbourne
BN21 2NB **08702 421718**

Accelerator Hosted IT Solutions Ltd
2nd Floor Marlborough House , Winchester
SO23 0HU **02079 933100**

X Kommunications Ltd
268 Bath Road , Slough
SL1 4DX **08454 58810**

Avocet Telecom Ltd
Suite 3 Pine Court, Bournemouth
BH1 3DH **01202 789977**

Telemarketing

Route Marketing Limited
Sandwich Industrial Estate , Sandwich
CT13 9LY **01227 722722**

Timber Frame Buildings

Rookery Barns Ltd
Hartley Wood Farm , Oakhanger
GU35 9JW **01420 488870**

Town Planning

Cadsquare Limited
Great Bramshot Barns , Fleet
GU51 2SF **01252 786580**

Red House Design
Rose Cottage , West Stourmouth
CT3 1HS **01227 721779**

F.J. Malcolm Mair
5 Cottage Hill , Crowborough, East Sussex
TN6 3JL **01892 852976**

ARCH-Angels Architects Limited
128 Edward Street , Brighton
Sussex , BN2 0JL
01273 267184 or
info@aaarchitects.co.uk
www.aaarchitects.co.uk

White & Sons
39-41 Station Road East , Oxted
RH8 0BD **01883 723680**

Page 480

Town Planning

Griffin Lascelles Associates
54 Cranmoore Road , Mytchett
GU16 6EW **01252 516414**

Tree Work and Surveys

Eagle Trees
Creative Media Centre , Hastings
TN34 1HL **07903 663751**

Brighton Tree Specialists
16 Chapel Mews , Hove
BN3 1AR **01273 719522**

Bartlett Consulting
Shenley Lodge Farm , Radlett
WD7 9BG **01707 649018**

Landmark Tree Surgery
Boveney Court Farm , Windsor
SL4 6QG **01628 630071**

Bartlett Tree Experts (Guildford)
New Pond Road , Guildford
GU3 1JR **01483 546582**

JDB Contractors & Son Ltd
Timbermill Yard , Eversley
RG27 0PY **01189 733943**

Fellam Tree Services
15 Morelands Court , Waterlooville
Hampshire , PO7 5PP
02392 640737
fellamtrees@yahoo.co.uk
www.fellamtreeservices.co.uk
(see full page advert for more information)

Island Wide Tree Work & Grounds Maintenance Ltd
1 Lee Brickyard Cottage , Yarmouth
PO41 0XN **01983 761766**

The Tree Wise Men
17 Alexandra Road , Addlestone
KT15 2PQ **01932 851856**

Tree Care Consultancy
61 Allnora Avenue , Worthing
BN12 4LR **07969 104421**

Trophies and Engraving

Promotional Sourcing International Ltd
Glade House , Mortimer Common
RG7 2JX **01189 333331**

Underfloor Heating

Underfloor Heating Systems Ltd
68 Castleham Road , St Leonards-on-Sea
East Sussex , TN38 9NU
01424 851111 or 07811 931224
rob.stabbins@underfloorheating.co.uk
www.underfloorheating.co.uk

PRM Solutions Ltd
98 Hurst Road , Horsham
RH12 2DT **01403 265503**

Green Heat
Valley View Business Park , Andover
SP11 6LU **01264 350481**

Ice Energy
Unit 2 Oakfield House , Eynsham
OX29 4TH **01865 882202**

Thermotec
10 Menzies Road , Hastings
TN38 9BB **01424 205544**

Vehicle Cleaning and Car Washes

Onedrywash (SJK Products Ltd)
James Place , Crawley
RH10 6GA **01293 533064**

Vehicle Leasing and Rentals

Green Motion Luton
London Luton Airport , Luton
LU2 9PE **01582 246750**

Video and Filming

The Internet Video Company
IVC Studios , Winchester
SO21 1BQ **01962 779020**

Cracking Media
713 Wimborne Road , Bournemouth
BH9 2AU **01202 532522**

Waste Management and Disposal

Maylarch Recycling Ltd
Andoversford Industrial Estate , Cheltenham
GL54 4LB **01242 821450**

All Waste Matters
Joseph Wilson Industrial Estate , Whitstable
CT5 3PS **01227 280777**

THE GREEN DIRECTORY

12

LOCAL SECTION **South East**

Page 482

THE **GREEN** DIRECTORY

Waste Management and Disposal

A1 Group Wokingham
Silver Birches , Wokingham
RG41 4SP **01189 894652**

Water Coolers

Wingham Well Spring
Watercress Lane , Kent
CT3 1NS **08009 553398**

Water Wells & Bore Holes

Nicholls Boreholes.co.uk
Brownings Barn , Kirdford
RH14 0LW **01403 820750**

Website and Internet Services

Mustard Design Ltd
Coles Yard Barn , Clanfield
PO8 0RN **02392 596450**

Target Ink Ltd
The Warehouse , Tunbridge Wells
TN4 0PG **01892 544549**

SLP IT Ltd
181 Saunders Lane , Woking
GU22 0NT **07786 266725**

Volia Creations Ltd
Station Mill , Winchester
SO24 9JQ **01962 732158**

Wildeyebrow Design
20 Mercury Close , Southampton
SO16 8BH **07980 803570**

Peak Web Design
58 Brook Street West , Reading
RG1 6BB **07918 172128**

Sky Blue Pink Web Design Ltd
Rocklands Place , Nr Hertmonceux
BN27 1RS **01323 831673**

A1 IT Web Design
68 Albion Road , Canterbury
CT10 2UR **01843 604664**

Web of Knowledge Ltd
Unit 4 Mays Yard, Waterlooville
PO8 0YP **02392 593487**

Independent Design Ltd
The Design & Image Studio , Arundel
BN18 0AG **01903 610078**

Wildlife Protection and Conservation

JDB Contractors & Son Ltd
Timbermill Yard , Eversley
RG27 0PY **01189 733943**

Wind Energy

Marine Electronic Installations Ltd
15 The Slipway , Portsmouth
PO6 4TR **02392 326366**

BritishEco Ltd
Unit 1A Oaklands Business Centre , Wokingham
RG41 2FD **08452 570041**

Consuta Training Ltd
Culver Cottage , Newport
Isle of Wight , PO30 2NJ
0330 660 0262
info@consuta.com
www.consuta.com

Renewable Advice Ltd
Unit 1 Moorside Business Park , Winchester
SO23 7RX **07884 181204**

Window Film

GP Window Films
Worthing House , Basingstoke
RG23 8PX **08450 037260**

Pabrofilm
Cruise Terminal 1 , Dover
CT17 9TF **01304 204950**

Southgate Solar Controls
9 St Johns Road , Southampton
SO30 4AF **01489 788443**

Solar Shield Ltd
Unit 10 Swan Business Park , Dartford
DA1 5ED **08451 306232**

*Big Green Book UK Ltd
Old Station Building
Oswald Road, Oswestry
Shropshire, SY11 1RE*

Biggreenbook ®

Solutions to environmental problems exist, but where do you find them?

This is a question that occurred to ecologist, Stephen Lings in 2003, when he was looking to solve some problems for a local company.

So Steve started putting together a database of companies that can help solve all kinds of problems in our environment. Nine years on, that database has grown into one of the UK's largest business membership organisations.

Now when a company wants help to become sustainable they only have to look to one place www.biggreenbook.com.

But if you don't really know what to look for, then the unique **GET A QUOTE** feature of their website allows you to email an expert about your issues and get suitable suppliers contacting you.

It is an incredible free service, and is one that has helped companies, large and small, throughout the UK.

Over 45,000 organisations have used the Big Green Book website in the last year alone and with over 750,000 hits a month it is a highly visited site.

Big Green Book also runs a face-to-face clinic service, travelling around the country and visiting major trade shows and events. Directors from Big Green Book, supported by experts from within the membership, are on hand to answer question about business and the environment.

Currently Big Green Book is on a membership drive, with special deals for companies that sign up to promote their solutions to environmental and sustainability issues.

If you would like more information on how your company can join their team is very approachable and friendly. Just ask for Gary and you will see what we mean.

With over 6,000 companies in 400 categories and sectors, the Big Green Book online directory is the place to start.

Page 483

Call 01691 661 565
or email sales@biggreenbook.com
www.biggreenbook.com

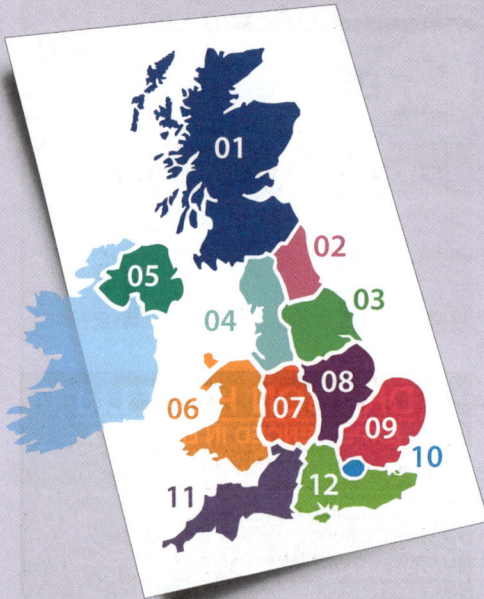

01
02
03
04
05
06
07
08
09
10
11
12

13
Edinburgh
Belfast
Cardiff
London

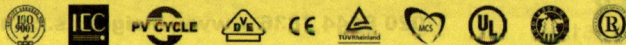

LOCAL SECTION National

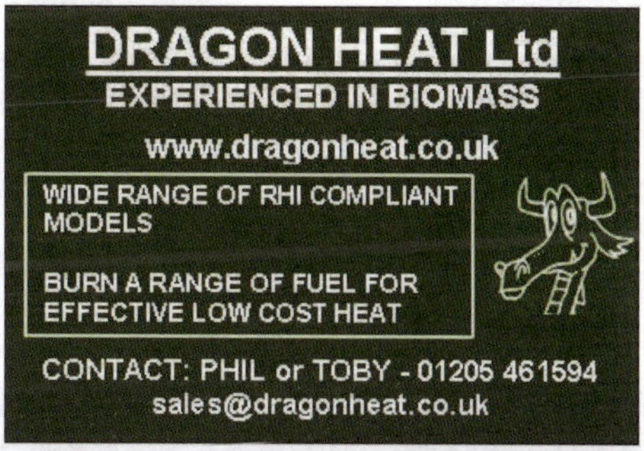

Page 485

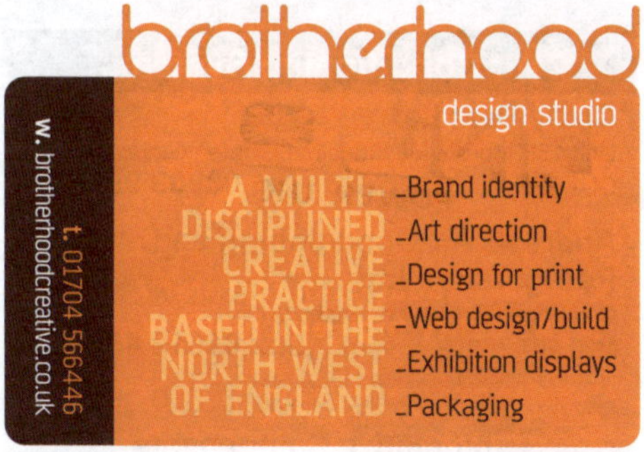

THE GREEN DIRECTORY

Access Control and Entry Systems

Atmos Heating Systems
TBS Depot , Daventry
NN11 4ES **01327 871990**

Accountancy

Precis
Unit 1 BrooksideCourt , Bodmin
PL30 4LN **01208 850729**

Accreditation and Certification

ISO Assured Ltd
69-73 Crossgate , Cupar
KY15 5AS **08456 190860**

Acoustic Products

Hush (UK) Limited
44 Canal Street , South Sefton
L20 8QU **01519 332026**

Silvaperl
Albion Works , Gainsborough
DN21 2QB **01427 675094**

Acoustic Wall Panels And Tiles

Green Footprint Solutions
14 Inham Fields Close , Gunthorpe
NG14 7FH **01159 665546**

Air Conditioning Systems

Chilly Heat Ltd
Unit 15B Morelands Industrial Estate , Gloucester
GL1 5RZ **08009 998881**

Andrews Air Conditioning and Refrigeration Ltd
Claverton Road , Wythenshaw
M23 9FT **01619 458599**

Interactive Components
2A Patrick way , Aylesbury
Buckinghamshire , HP21 9XH
01296 425656 or 07836 694643
interactive@bucksnet.co.uk

(see full page advert for more information)

M K Air Conditioning Services Ltd
The Arches , Stoke on Trent
ST4 2RP **01782 551000**

Air Source Heat Pumps

BritishEco Ltd
Unit 1A Oaklands Business Centre , Wokingham
RG41 2FD **08452 570041**

EDF Energy
40 Grosvenor Place , London
SW1X 7EN **08000 511905**

Atmos Heating Systems
TBS Depot , Daventry
NN11 4ES **01327 871990**

**Kingspan Environmental
(was Kingspan Renewables)**
Tadman Street , Wakefield
WF1 5QU **01924 376026**

Viessmann Limited
Hortonwood 30 , Telford
Shropshire , TF1 7YP
01952 675000
info-uk@viessmann.com
www.viessmann.co.uk

Husky Heat Pumps
Unit 17 Dalweb Trading Estate , Southport
Merseyside , PR9 8DF
01704 509596
sales@huskyheatpumps.co.uk
www.huskyheatpumps.co.uk
(see full page advert for more information)

Ice Energy
Unit 2 Oakfields Industrial Estate , Eynsham
OX29 4TH **01865 882202**

Radiant Heating Solutions Ltd
Hougham , Grantham
NG32 2HZ **01400 250572**

Solartech Ltd
Unit 2 Sterling Business Park , Buckingham
Buckinghamshire , MK18 1TH
0845 838 2477
info@solartech.org.uk
www.solartech.org.uk
(see half page advert for more information)

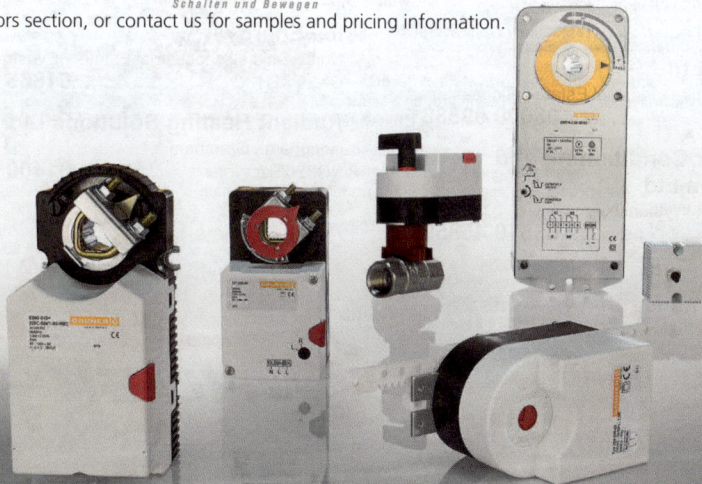

Air Source Heat Pumps

Underfloor Warehouse Ltd
Unit V2 Winchester Avenue , Blaby
Leicestershire , LE8 4GZ
0116 258 1410
enquiries@ufw.co.uk
www.ufw.co.uk

Airport Transfers

Benchmark Cars
52 Church Street , Leeds
LS23 6DN 07774 608860

Alternative and Renewable Energy

Bidwells
Bidwell House , Cambridge
CB2 9LD 01223 559406

Dulas Ltd
Unit 1 Dyfi Eco Park , Machynlleth
SY20 8AX 01654 705000

Alternative and Renewable Energy

Natural Sparx
313-333 Rainham Road , Dagenham
Essex , RM10 8SX
0845 218 6938
marketing@naturalsparx.co.uk
www.naturalsparx.co.uk
(see half page advert for more information)

Matrix Energy Systems
23 Lathkill Close , Sheffield
S13 8DI 07931 801904

Linuo Power UK
Rotterdam House , Newcastle-upon-Tyne
NE1 3DY 01912 064144

Oak Apple Renewable Energy Ltd
Oak Apple Road , Leeds
LS12 6QA 01132 708052

T H White - Energy
Williams Road , Devizes
SN10 3EW 01380 723040

Page 489

LOCAL SECTION National

THE GREEN DIRECTORY

THE GREEN DIRECTORY

Alternative and Renewable Energy

Travis Perkins Plc
Lodge Way House , Northampton
Northamptonshire , NN5 7UG
01604 752 424
marketing@travisperkins.co.uk
www.travisperkins.co.uk

Solartech Ltd
Unit 2 Sterling Business Park , Buckingham
Buckinghamshire , MK18 1TH
0845 838 2477
info@solartech.org.uk
www.solartech.org.uk
(see half page advert for more information)

Ecoliving Ltd
60 High Craighall Road , Glasgow
G4 9UD **08453 013121**

Worcester Bosch Group
Cotswold Way , Wardon
WR4 9SN **08448 929900**

Anaerobic Digestion and Biogas

Methanogen UK Ltd
127 Rampart Road , Salisbury
Wiltshire , SP1 1JA
07753 571371
info@methanogen.co.uk
www.methanogen.co.uk

Architects

Building Design Chartered Architects
3 Connaught Road , Eastbourne
East Sussex , BN21 4PY
01323 410095 or 01323 417234
info@building-design.co.uk
www.buildingdesignsussex.com
(see full page advert for more information)

Parity Projects
Unit 230/231 Riverside Business Centre , London
SW18 4UQ **02088 746433**

Cadsquare Limited
Unit 7 & 8 Great Bramshot Barns , Fleet
GU51 2SF **01252 786580**

Architects

Prime Meridian
The Priory , Shepton Mallet
Somerset , BA4 5HS
01749 346699 or 0207 494 3522
dminns@prime-meridian.co.uk
www.prime-meridian.co.uk

Synergy Architects Ltd
8 Euston Place , Leamington Spa
CV32 4LN **01926 450391**

Asbestos Handling and Removal

Asbestos Surveys & Advice
Suite 5a Cockenzie Business Centre , Cockenzie
EH32 0HL **01875 813999**

D J Cleaning Ltd
43 White Gap Road , Cottingham
HU20 3XF **01430 827491**

Asbestos Survey and Assesment

Asbestos Surveys & Advice
Suite 5a Cockenzie Business Centre , Cockenzie
EH32 0HL **01875 813999**

Asbestos Training and Awareness

Asbestos Consulting & Training LLP
87A Castleton Road , Hope Valley
S33 6SB **07919 386738**

ActOn Group
Miskin Manor Estate , Pontyclun
CF72 8ND **08456 436201**

XL HAZMAT LTD
16 Rosemary Drive , Derby
DE24 0TA **01158 882797**

cnm training solutions ltd
14 Trent Place , Darlington
DL1 5TA **01325 353151**

Encompassed Ltd
Meldrum Lodge , Bristol
BS40 5JH **01934 853803**

Independent Asbestos Training Providers
PO BOX 870 , Taunton
TA1 9GX **08002 118498**

BUILDING DESIGN
CHARTERED ARCHITECTS

Building Design: Chartered Architects Practice

Building Design is one of the leading architects practices for the Sussex area. We work for both commercial & residential customers on projects located across the UK to deliver innovative, practical, sustainable and economic design solutions.

The success of our practice, lies in our specialist eco knowledge, application of latest innovations in construction and attention to client requirements.

As a registered Green Architects practice we have a special focus in promoting sustainable design that delivers a better living environment, energy efficiency and cost benefits. Please call us on 01323 410095 and let us work with you on your next new build project, property conversion or refurbishment.

www.buildingdesignsussex.com
Telephone: 01323 410095 **Email:** info@building-design.co.uk
Address: 3 Connaught Road, Eastbourne, East Sussex BN21 4PY

Page 494

THE GREEN DIRECTORY

Audio Visual

Hyde AV
17 Puckleside , Basildon
SS16 5XD 07540 615125

Backing Gates

Fabdec Limited
Grange Road , Ellesmere
SY12 9DG 01691 627210

Biomass Energy and Biofuels

BritishEco Ltd
Unit 1A Oaklands Business Centre , Wokingham
RG41 2FD 08452 570041

NNFCC
Biocentre , York
YO10 5DG 01904 435182

Dulas Ltd
Unit 1 Dyfi Eco Park , Machynlleth
SY20 8AX 01654 705000

Biomass Energy and Biofuels

Dragon Heat Ltd
Loves Lane , Boston
Lincolnshire , PE20 2EU
01205 461594   or   07811147803
sales@dragonheat.co.uk
www.dragonheat.co.uk
(see full page advert for more information)

Viessmann Limited
Hortonwood 30 , Telford
Shropshire , TF1 7YP
01952 675000
info-uk@viessmann.com
www.viessmann.co.uk
(see half page advert for more information)

Ecovision Systems Ltd
Barley Court , Tetbury
GL8 8TQ 01666 501580

OHM Power Europe Ltd
Canada House , Harrow
HA4 9NA 08006 123260

Biomass Energy and Biofuels

Advanced wood heating systems from Viessmann

- Manual and automated wood boilers for commercial and domestic use
- Vitoligno 300-P pellet boiler. Output from 4 to 48 kW
- Pyromat wood boiler for logs, waste wood, woodchips and pellets. Output from 35 to 170 kW
- Pyrot rotating combustion boiler for pellets, woodchips and shavings. Output from 100 to 540 kW
- Pyrotec fully automated wood boiler with grate combustion. Output from 390 to 1250 kW

Available now, for more information please see our website or email us at, info-uk@viessmann.com
www.viessmann.co.uk

Viessmann Limited • Telford • Telephone 01952 675000

Efficiency Plus

VIESSMANN
climate of innovation

LOCAL SECTION National

THE **GREEN** DIRECTORY

Biomass Energy and Biofuels

Lauderdale Renewables Ltd
The Old Post Office , Earlston
Berwickshire , TD4 6BS
01896 849 829 or 07808 689 668
info@lauderdalerenewables.com
www.lauderdalerenewables.com

Matrix Energy Systems
23 Lathkill Close , Sheffield
S13 8DI 07931 801904

Worcester Bosch Group
Cotswold Way , Wardon
WR4 9SN 08448 929900

Boilers and Water Heaters

Atmos Heating Systems
TBS Depot , Daventry
NN11 4ES 01327 871990

Fabdec Limited
Grange Road , Ellesmere
SY12 9DG 01691 627210

Alpha Heating Innovation
Nepicar House , Wrotham Heath
TN15 7RS 08448 718760

Heatwell
Edward House , Hucknall
NG15 7JD 01159 681273

Radiant Heating Solutions Ltd
Hougham , Grantham
NG32 2HZ 01400 250572

Builders Merchants

Travis Perkins Plc
Lodge Way House , Northampton
Northamptonshire , NN5 7UG
01604 752 424
marketing@travisperkins.co.uk
www.travisperkins.co.uk
(see half page advert for more information)

Buildbase
Gemini One , Cowley
Oxford , OX4 2LL
01865 871700 or 07788 717884
gogreen@buildbase.co.uk
www.gogreenatbuildbase.co.uk
(see full page advert for more information)

Builders Merchants

E H Smith
Westhaven House , Solihull
West Midlands , B90 4NH
0121 713 7100
mark.mallinder@ehsmith.co.uk
www.sustainablebuildingmaterials.co.uk
(see full page advert for more information)

Jewson Ltd
Merchant House , Coventry
Warwickshire , CV3 2TT
0800 539 766 or 07525 672771
steven.a.smith@jewson.co.uk
www.jewson.co.uk
(see half page advert for more information)

Building & Roofing Products

Gradena Ltd
Beevor Street , Barnsley
South Yorkshire , S71 1HN
07799 635283
info@gradsol.com
www.gradsol.com
(see full page advert for more information)

Building and Construction

Green Footprint Solutions
14 Inham Fields Close , Gunthorpe
NG14 7FH 01159 665546

Building Conservation and Preservation

Elden Minns & Co Ltd
453 Glossop Road , Sheffield
S10 2PT 01142 662458

Building Integrated Photovoltaics(BIPV)

Radiant Heating Solutions Ltd
Hougham , Grantham
NG32 2HZ 01400 250572

Worcester Bosch Group
Cotswold Way , Wardon
WR4 9SN 08448 929900

Page 497

THE **GREEN** DIRECTORY

Builders Merchants

GO GREEN AT BUILDBASE

Buildbase offer the Total Solution for choice, expertise and innovation from suppliers to installers and end users.

- **Renewable Energies**
- **Water Management & Recycling**
- **Air Management**
- **Environmental Heating Products**
- **Sustainable and Recycled Building Products**

BUILDBASE THE TOTAL SOLUTION

For you local branch visit:

www.gogreenatbuildbase.co.uk

Business Management, Coaching and Consultancy

Positive Management Services
17 Whitbourne Hall , Worcester
WR6 5SE **01886 822222**

Canals and Waterways

The Planning Company
51 Battenhall Rise , Worcester
WR5 2DE **01905 360277**

Canopies, Carports & Covered Walkways

GRP Canopies plc
Edgcott House , Aylesbury
Buckinghamshire , HP18 0QW
0800 783 3835 or 07878 846697
jd@123v.com
www.123v.com

Catering Equipment and Supplies

Environmental Products & Services Ltd
5 Shepherd's Drive , Newry
BT35 6JQ **02830 833081**

Catering Services & Design

Restaurant Design Associates Limited
5 Apollo Court , Hebburn
NE31 2ES **07872 831131**

Chauffeur Services

Benchmark Cars
52 Church Street , Leeds
LS23 6DN **07774 608860**

Cleaning Products

GreenBuying.co.uk
Festival House , Cheltenham
GL50 3SH **08452 178995**

Solution Cornwall Ltd
Unit 10D Cardrew Industrial Estate , Redruth
Cornwall , TR15 1SS
01209 204343
nick@solution-uk.com
www.worldofclean.co.uk
(see full page advert for more information)

Cleaning Products

Eco EZEE
West Hill Manor Barn , Welford
NN6 6HF **01858 575454**

Computer & IT Recycling

Computer Recycling Technologies Ltd.
11A Trident Industrial Estate , Warrington
WA3 6AX **01925 813030**

Computer Services

Softcraft Computer Services Ltd
Norwich House , Norwich
NR28 9AL **01692 535355**

Computer Software

SwiftTec
68 Andrew Allan Road , Wellington
TA21 9DY **01823 478226**

Cooling Products

Fabdec Limited
Grange Road , Ellesmere
SY12 9DG **01691 627210**

Currency Exchange

Excel Currencies Ltd
20 Copperfields Centre , Dartford
DA1 2DE **01322 221121**

Demand Response (Electricity)

KiWi Power Ltd
45 Broadwick Street
London , W1F 9QW
0207 1831030 or 07584 132220
dtaylor@kiwipowered.com
www.kiwipowered.com
(see full page advert for more information)

Design 2 Print

Eight Days A Week Print Solutions
3 Church View , Sandiacre
NG10 5EA **01159 399797**

THE **GREEN** DIRECTORY

A new, green, recurring revenue stream for your business

We help you temporarily reduce electricity consumed during times of peak demand by making minor adjustments to non-essential systems.

By reducing your consumption at peak times, you can help the UK avoid using expensive and polluting peaking power stations

National Grid pays you for this, as it is cheaper and produces less carbon than these peaking power plants

OFF

Cutting-edge energy intelligence

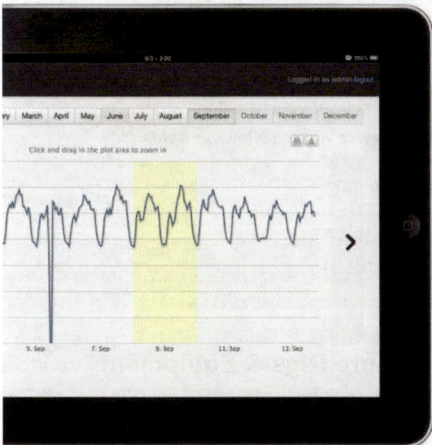

- A recurring annual revenue stream
- Your real time energy data with KiWi's online proprietary software
- Increased confidence in standby generation
- Contribution to a reduction in national carbon intensity
- All programme risks carried by KiWi Power
- **No cost to participate**

KiWiPOWER
demand management

www.kiwipowered.com
for more information

THE GREEN DIRECTORY

Development

Jumpstart (Scotland) Ltd
6 Atholl Crescent , Edinburgh
EH3 8HA **01312 402900**

Display and Exhibition Boards

Aris Design & Management Ltd
270 London Road , London
SM6 7DJ **02088 352730**

Cerberex
Unit 5B Little Dale Workshops , Cranbrook
TN17 2LS **01580 212939**

Exantia Display Systems
9 Muirhead Quay , Barking
IG11 7BW **02085 071612**

Document and Data Destruction

PHS Datashred
Unit J Acorn Industrial Park, Crayford
DA1 4FL **08003 764422**

Drilling, Boring and Site Investigations

Hughes Geothermal Ltd
Leebotwood , Church Stretton
Shropshire , SY6 6LU
01694 751251
office@hughesdrilling.co.uk
www.hughesdrilling.co.uk
(see half page advert for more information)

E-commerce and Search Engine Optimisation (SEO)

NSM Web Design Ltd
8 Consett Innovation Centre , Consett
DH8 5XP 08456 432667

Eco Friendly Promotional Products

MJ Services
Building 329 , Shepperton
TW17 0QD 01932 593574

Ecology Surveys and Consultancy

WWT Consulting
Wildfowl & Wetlands Trust , Slimbridge
GL2 7BT 01453 891222

Naturally Wild Consultants Limited
Office 8 Evans Business Centre, Middlesbrough
Cleveland , TS6 6UT
0845 260 1107 or   07817 634 504
graeme.skinner@naturallywild.co.uk
www.naturallywild.co.uk

Herpetosure
Piper Hole Farm , Melton Mowbray
LE14 4SS 01664 444660

Habitat Aid Ltd
Hookgate Cottage , South Brewham
BA10 0LQ 01749 812355

Access Ecology Ltd
Unit R1b Sheaf Bank Business Park , Sheffield
S2 3EN 01142 587819

Encompass Ecology Ltd
Bow Hill , Exeter
EX4 1LQ 01392 424231

Oak Bay Ecology
16 Waters Edge Fold , Manchester
OL1 4QJ 07775 186757

Ecology Surveys and Consultancy

The Ecology Consultancy
6-8 Cole Street , London
Greater London , SE1 4YH
020 7378 1914
enquiries@ecologyconsultancy.co.uk
www.ecologyconsultancy.co.uk

Ecotoxicology

NCIMB Limited
Ferguson Building , Bucksburn
Aberdeen , AB21 9YA
01224 711 100
enquiries@ncimb.com
www.ncimb.com

Electric & Plug In Vehicle Charging Systems

Charging Solutions Ltd
Border Chase , Nr Alberbury
SY5 9AN 08432 890125

Electric Cycles

Pedego Europe
Walnut Tree House , Stonehouse
GL10 3PW 02032 394722

Electrical and Electricians

JP Electric Services Ltd
30 Pope Garden , Stafford
ST17 9LS 01785 603279

Interactive Components
2A Patrick Way , Aylesbury
HP21 9XH 01296 425656

Corts Electrical Limited
27 Durkar Rise , Wakefield
WF4 3QB 07939 252611

Embroidery

Jaslyn Embroidery & Print Ltd
Unit D2 Innsworth Technology Park , Gloucester
GL3 1DL 01452 731336

KTEES Clothing Ltd
Units 15-16 Northern Galleries , Fareham
PO14 1AH 01329 822583

Carlisle Embroidery Ltd
8b Port Road Business Park , Carlisle
CA2 7AF 01228 597649

DAVID CRADDOCK
Consultancy Services

MOTIVATIONAL AND LIFE COACHING

David Craddock Consultancy Services
10 Smokies Way
Biddulph
Staffordshire
ST8 6TZ

Tel: 01782 519925

Employee Share Schemes

David Craddock Consultancy Services
10 Smokies Way , Biddulph
Staffordshire , ST8 6TZ
01782 519925
d.craddock@virgin.net
www.davidcraddock.com
(see full page advert for more information)

Energy Assessors & Consultants

Total Environmental Management
4 Lakeside Business Park , Sandhurst
GU47 9DN 01252 878722

Energy Saving Heating

Ecopod Heating Systems Limited + Belfry Group Limited
Unit 12 Cameron Court , Warrington
WA2 8RE 01925 633311

Worcester Bosch Group
Cotswold Way , Wardon
WR4 9SN 08448 929900

Energy Saving Products and Services

Schneider Electrics Ltd
Stafford Park 5 , Telford
TF3 3BL 08706 088608

Energenie
Unit 5 Harolds Close , Harlow
CM19 5TH 01279 422022

MS Electronics
Unit 5 Harvey Close , Basildon
SS13 1EY 03336 661176

Ecopod Heating Systems Limited + Belfry Group Limited
Unit 12 Cameron Court , Warrington
WA2 8RE 01925 633311

Big Green Smile Ltd
First Floor , Amersham
Buckinghamshire , HP6 5BX
01494 727 575
nbuhler@biggreensmile.com
www.biggreensmile.com

Radiant Heating Solutions Ltd
Hougham , Grantham
NG32 2HZ 01400 250572

Energy Saving Products and Services

Worcester Bosch Group
Cotswold Way , Wardon
WR4 9SN 08448 929900

Environmental Consultancy

D J Cleaning Ltd
43 White Gap Road , Cottingham
HU20 3XF 01430 827491

Buckland Energy Projects Ltd
Albany House , Salisbury
SP1 2PH 07855 947998

Environmental Strategies Limited
81 Harland Way , Hull
HU16 5P 01482 841164

Green Business Experts
69 Hungerdown , London
E4 6QJ 08442 720055

Total Environmental Management
4 Lakeside Business Park , Sandhurst
GU47 9DN 01252 878722

Naturally Wild Consultants Limited
Office 8 Evans Business Centre, Middlesbrough
Cleveland , TS6 6UT
0845 260 1107 or 07817 634 504
graeme.skinner@naturallywild.co.uk
www.naturallywild.co.uk

GeoCon Site Investigations Ltd
15 Belmont Drive , Stockport
SK8 5EA 08445 043901

The Planning Company
51 Battenhall Rise , Worcester
WR5 2DE 01905 360277

Environmental Training and Awareness

Liverpool Environmental Training
41-51 Greenland Street , Liverpool
L1 0BS 01517 083563

Environmental Water Treatment

IWTM
86 Maldon Road , Chelmsford
CM2 7DS 01245 471875

Event Organisers

The Northern Home Show
Carnah Events Ltd , Tadworth
KT20 7HZ **08445 611230**

Exhibition Display Banners

Cerberex
Unit 5B Little Dale Workshops , Cranbrook
TN17 2LS **01580 212939**

Exantia Display Systems
9 Muirhead Quay , Barking
IG11 7BW **02085 071612**

Exhibition Stands

The Exhibition Hub.Com
42 High Street , Tilbrook
Cambridgeshire , PE28 0JP
01480 861777 or 07809 451073
info@theexhibitionhub.com
www.theexhibitionhub.com

Aris Design & Management Ltd
270 London Road , London
SM6 7DJ **02088 352730**

Unique Exhibitions Limited
Whitebirk Industrial Estate , Blackburn
BB1 5UA **08450 704456**

Cerberex
Unit 5B Little Dale Workshops , Cranbrook
TN17 2LS **01580 212939**

Smart XS Limited
35 Chesterton Close , Redditch
B97 7CG **01527 457784**

Exantia Display Systems
9 Muirhead Quay , Barking
IG11 7BW **02085 071612**

External Wall Insulation

C R Building & Plastering
62 Agnes Close , Bude
EX23 8SB **01840 230988**

Fire Risk Assessment and Training

Fire Risk Management Solutions Ltd
27-29 Wellhouse Road , Barnoldswick
BB18 6DB **01282 876336**

Springboard Safety Services
18 Turnberry Avenue , Wrexham
LL13 9GG **07805 112019**

Fire Risk Assessment and Training

Miles Safety Ltd
502 Fullwood Road , Sheffield
S10 3 QD **01142 302200**

Fire Safety Protection and Equipment

Silvaperl
Albion Works , Gainsborough
DN21 2QB **01427 675094**

Springboard Safety Services
18 Turnberry Avenue , Wrexham
LL13 9GG **07805 112019**

Fireplaces & Woodstoves

Fireplace Products
Lower Barn Farm , Rayleigh
Essex , SS6 9ET
01268 200139
sales@fireplaceproducts.co.uk
www.fireplaceproducts.co.uk
(see full page advert for more information)

First Aid Supplies

Train2Protect(T2P) International Ltd
7 Dickens Road , Rochester
ME1 2JR **08000 438827**

First Aid Training

Medrock Training Ltd
2 Carr Gate , Billinghay
LN4 4HD **08000 433822**

Train2Protect(T2P) International Ltd
7 Dickens Road , Rochester
ME1 2JR **08000 438827**

First Response Learning Limited
21 Bramber Road , Seaford
BN25 1AG **08009 990100**

B & D M Johnson
7 Riverdown , March
PE15 8RA **07980 884218**

First Aid Academy
2 Railway Road, Urmston
M41 0XL **08443 571426**

Springboard Safety Services
18 Turnberry Avenue , Wrexham
LL13 9GG **07805 112019**

Flashings for Solar Systems

Deks Distribution UK
West End Trading Estate , Bristol
BS48 4DJ 01275 858866

Radiant Heating Solutions Ltd
Hougham , Grantham
NG32 2HZ 01400 250572

Fleet Driver Training

UK Global Road Safety Ltd
Kestrel Court , Gloucester
GL2 2AT 08449 106255

Food Hygiene

Key Consultancy Services Ltd
15 Bulwer Road , Leicester
LE2 3BW 07849 414285

Fuel Saving Products

Motrak Fleet Monitoring
Minton Hollins Building , Stoke On Trent
ST4 7RY 01782 221100

Clean Drive Systems uk Ltd
98 Uplands , Leicester
LE2 4ND 07812 743232

Greenfoot Global
117 Greenwood , Preston
PR5 8JY 07595 643797

Funding

Jumpstart (Scotland) Ltd
6 Atholl Crescent , Edinburgh
EH3 8HA 01312 402900

Garden Sculptures

Sculptures by Karen Williams
15 East Street , Nottingham
NG10 2DH 01158 492977

Geothermal Energy

Hughes Geothermal Ltd
Leebotwood , Church Stretton
SY6 6LU 01694 751251

Earthtest Energy
Bridge Mills , Holmfirth
HD9 3TW 01484 681314

Geothermal Energy

Mimer Energy Ltd
Unit 1 Falmouth Business Park , Falmouth
TR11 4SZ 02081 441662

Worcester Bosch Group
Cotswold Way , Wardon
WR4 9SN 08448 929900

Graphic Design

Sugar Salt Media
17 Gwynt Mews , Cardiff
CF11 9LZ 07972 610393

K I Designs Ltd
44 Hall Farm Drive , Twickenham
London , TW2 7PQ
07971 543764
info@kidesigns.co.uk
www.kidesigns.co.uk

BigStuff Media
Dunston Hole Farm , Chesterfield
S41 9RL 01246 261617

SWATT Design Ltd.
23 Hadleigh Gardens , Eastleigh
SO50 4NP 07789 076364

Green Roofing

Green Footprint Solutions
14 Inham Fields Close , Gunthorpe
NG14 7FH 01159 665546

Silvaperl
Albion Works , Gainsborough
DN21 2QB 01427 675094

Nimrod Environmental Ltd
14 Haigh Lane , Barnsley
South Yorkshire , S75 4BZ
01924 830961 or 07843 680483
enquiries@nimrodenvironmental.co.uk
www.nimrodenvironmental.co.uk

The Better Roofing Company
35 Coverdale Road , Lancaster
LA1 5PY 07972 815797

Optigreen Ltd
Unit 1F Bentley Way, New Barnet
EN5 5FP 08455 650236

Green Roof Systems
Unit 5 Churchfield Court , Nottingham
NG5 9JL 07702 882234

Green Roofing

Greenroofs are part of our sustainable future.

The leading independent UK supplier of green roofs have the expertise to provide environmental solutions within the urban landscape.

01242 620905
www.sky-garden.co.uk
enquiries@sky-garden.co.uk

Ground Source Heat Pumps

BritishEco Ltd
Unit 1A Oaklands Business Centre , Wokingham
RG41 2FD **08452 570041**

ICAX Ltd
1 Berry Street , London
EC1M 5PS **02072 532240**

Kensa Engineering Ltd
Mount Wellington Mine , Truro
TR4 8RJ **08456 804328**

REHAU Ltd
Hill Court , Ross-on-Wye
HR9 5QN **01989 762600**

Viessmann Limited
Hortonwood 30 , Telford
Shropshire , TF1 7YP
01952 675000
info-uk@viessmann.com
www.viessmann.co.uk
(see full page advert for more information)

Ground Source Heat Pumps

Nu-Heat UK Ltd
Heathpark House , Honiton
EX14 1SD **01404 549770**

Ecoliving Ltd
60 High Craighall Road , Glasgow
G4 9UD **08453 013121**

Radiant Heating Solutions Ltd
Hougham , Grantham
NG32 2HZ **01400 250572**

Fusion G Source Ltd
Smeckley Wood Close , Chesterfield
S41 9PZ **01246 262721**

Go Geothermal Ltd
Unit 3 Ridgeway , Newton Aycliffe
DL5 6SP **01388 720228**

Earthtest Energy
Bridge Mills , Holmfirth
HD9 3TW **01484 681314**

Health and Beauty Products

Forever Young Yorkshire. Group
Moore Farm , York
YO60 7QZ **01904 468088**

Health and Safety

WRRS Solutions
Greenacres , Reading
Berkshire , RG7 1QX
0118 988 8426
edward@wrrsconsultancy.co.uk
www.wrrsconsultancy.co.uk

Page 511

Key Consultancy Services Ltd
15 Bulwer Road , Leicester
LE2 3BW **07849 414285**

TL Safety Ltd
4 Wenlock Close , Bolton
BL6 7PE **07749 838367**

D G B Health & Safety Solutions
PO Box 122 , Bingley
BD16 9BF **07900 431649**

Bravanark Ltd
The Lodge , Reading
RG2 7PP **01189 541700**

Securing A Family Environment (S.A.F.E.) Limited
399-401 High Street , London
E15 4QZ **07557 432582**

The ground source heat pump range from Viessmann

Using energy from the earth our ground source heat pump range features outputs from 5.8 - 58.9 kW

Vitocal 200-G
- Output from 5.8 to 9.7 kW
- High COP value from 4.3 to 4.4
- 60°C flow temperature
- Vitotronic 200 controller

Vitocal 300-G
- Output from 5.9 to 58.9 kW
- Available as brine/water or water/water
- High COP value from 4.6 to 6.3
- Can be cascaded

Vitocal 222-G and 242-G
- Compact brine/water models
- Output from 5.9 to 10 kW
- Very quiet sound power level of 43 dB
- High COP value up to 4.3

Available now, for more information please see our website or email us at, info-uk@viessmann.com
www.viessmann.co.uk

Viessmann Limited • Telford • Telephone 01952 675000

VIESSMANN
climate of innovation

Health and Safety

Paramount Health and Safety Ltd
39 Mayflower Close , Basingstoke
RG24 8XS 01256 334419

Positive Management Services
17 Whitbourne Hall , Worcester
WR6 5SE 01886 822222

S.I.S (GB) Ltd
Hanover House , Liverpool
L1 3DZ 01512 853884

Heat Detection

Fabdec Limited
Grange Road , Ellesmere
SY12 9DG 01691 627210

Heat Recovery and Ventilation Systems

Fabdec Limited
Grange Road , Ellesmere
SY12 9DG 01691 627210

Heat Transfer Fluids

Kilfrost
32 Gallowgate , Newcastle upon Tyne
NE1 4SN 01434 323184

Hosted Communications

InClouds Hosted Business Services
1st Canada Square , Canary Wharf
E14 5DY 08453 551200

Housing Adaptions

Jordan Shaw
Alloa Business Centre , Alloa
FK10 3SA 08450 550323

Insulation

THE **GREEN** DIRECTORY

Insulation

Green Footprint Solutions is committed to the supply of Insulation and Construction materials that have the least impact on the environment

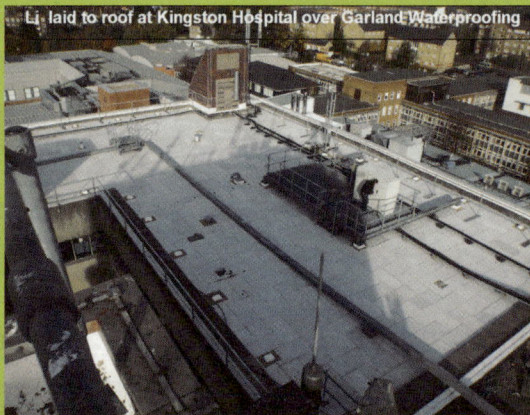

Li- laid to roof at Kingston Hospital over Garland Waterproofing

Projects Completed using Extruded Polystyrene Insulation and GFS Li Board

We promote and advise on the specification of thermal Insulation products, in new and refurbished buildings to Construction (Private & Public) , Anaerobic digestion, Agriculture and Horticulture industries

Tel: 0115 966 5546 Web: www.greenfs.co.uk
Email: info@greenfs.co.uk

Insulation

Green Footprint Solutions
14 Inham Fields Close , Nottingham
Nottinghamshire , NG14 7FH
0115 966 5546
info@greenfs.co.uk
www.greenfs.co.uk
(see full page advert for more information)

Insulation Shop
49 Gladstone Road , Portslade
East Sussex , BN41 1LJ
0845 544 1077
insulationshop@gmail.com
www.insulationshop.co

Silvaperl
Albion Works , Gainsborough
Lincolnshire , DN21 2QB
01427 675094
catherine.white@william-sinclair.co.uk
www.william-sinclair.co.uk
(see half page advert for more information)

Kingspan Tarec
Industrial Insulation Ltd
Glossop Brook Road , Glossop
Derbyshire , SK13 8GP
0870 733 0021
info.uk@kingspantarec.co.uk
www.kingspantarec.com

Sprayseal Contracts Ltd
Bollin House , Mobberley
WA16 7LX 01565 872303

Devana Insulation Ltd
34 Mill Road , Cambridge
CB24 5PY 01954 201834

Marmox UK Ltd
101-103 Caxton House , Chatham
ME5 7NP 01634 835290

UK Solar Energy Group Ltd
Belfry House , Hertford
SG14 1BP 02080 902390

Excel Industries Ltd
Maerdy Industrial Estate , Rhymney
NP22 5PY 01685 845200

AOK Insulation Ltd
36 Grainger Road Industrial Estate , Southend
SS2 5DD 08458 381508

Insurance

M G P Group
99 Seymour Road, Manchester
M16 0ND 07747 621055

Jelf Group
Chequers Close , Malvern
WR14 1BF 01684 571835

Independent Warranty
20 Billing Road , Northampton
NN1 5AW 01604 604511

Investment

Jumpstart (Scotland) Ltd
6 Atholl Crescent , Edinburgh
EH3 8HA 01312 402900

Japanese Knotweed

Herpetosure
Piper Hole Farm , Melton Mowbray
LE14 4SS 01664 444660

Nimrod Environmental Ltd
14 Haigh Lane , Barnsley
South Yorkshire , S75 4BZ
01924 830961 or 07843 680483
enquiries@nimrodenvironmental.co.uk
www.nimrodenvironmental.co.uk

Key and Asset Management Systems

Keytracker Limited
Keyper House , Rowley Regis
B65 0JY 01215 599000

Lamp Recycling

Recolight Limited
Suite 265 Purley Way , Croydon
CR0 0XZ 08456 017749

Landscaping and Ground Maintenance

CR Swift Landscaping Ltd
8 Over Road , Longstanton
Cambridgeshire , CB24 3GP
01954 288870 or 07889 110415
steve@swiftlandscaping.co.uk
www.swiftlandscaping.co.uk
(see full page advert for more information)

THE **GREEN** DIRECTORY

Lawyers

Lawrence Graham LLP
4 More London Riverside
London , SE1 2AU
020 7759 6850 or 07725 279 524
david.ponsford@lg-legal.com
www.lg-legal.com

Living Walls

MMA Architectural Systems Ltd
Broadway House , Midsomer Norton
BA3 4BH **08451 300135**

Low Energy Lightbulbs, Lighting and L.E.D.

Kudos Business Technologies
The Old Saw Mill , Ubley
BS40 6PE **01761 463181**

Ledi Solutions Limited
Kingsway Industrial Estate , Luton
Bedfordshire , LU1 1LP
01582 488800 or 07540 872545
paul@ledisolutions.co.uk
www.ledisolutions.co.uk

LED Switchover Ltd
Unit D3C Edgefold Industrial Estate,
Bolton , BL4 0JW
0161 850 0906 or 0207 798 1606
lynda.thorpe@britektechnologies.co.uk
www.ledswitchover.co.uk
(see full page advert for more information)

Novel Energy Lighting
24 Kingston Road , London
Greater London , SW19 1JZ
0208-540-8287 or 07507-562-037
sales@novelenergylighting.com
www.novelenergylighting.com

OCIP Energy Ltd
Montpellier House , Cheltenham
GL50 1TY **01242 250633**

Magazine Publishers

Energy Now
County House , Worcester
WR1 1HB **01905 616665**

Milking Equipment

Fabdec Limited
Grange Road , Ellesmere
SY12 9DG **01691 627210**

Mobility and Living Aids

Nordic Care Services Limited
307-309 Lombard House , Canterbury
CT1 2NF **01227 479293**

Motivational and Life Coaching

David Craddock Consultancy Services
10 Smokies Way , Biddulph
ST8 6TZ **01782 519925**

Nestboxes

Habitat Aid Ltd
Hookgate Cottage , South Brewham
BA10 0LQ **01749 812355**

Networking and Cabling

Talkwire Ltd
Kingsbury Square , Melksham
SN12 6HL **01225 899861**

InClouds Hosted Business Services
29th Floor 1st Canada Square , Canary Wharf
E14 5DY **08453 551200**

Softcraft Computer Services Ltd
Norwich House , Norwich
NR28 9AL **01692 535355**

Noise and Vibration Testing

Red Acoustics Ltd
Suite 3 Cottam Lane Business Centre , Preston
PR2 1JR **01772 722182**

Page 517

LOCAL SECTION National

THE GREEN DIRECTORY

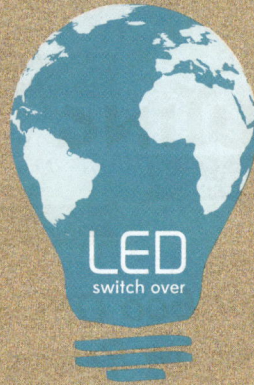

Off Grid Power

Office And Retail Furniture

Mount Industries
Barton Park Ind Est , Eastleigh
SO50 6RR 02380 612841

Diamond Office Furniture Limited
No 4 East Wing , Harlow
CM19 5TJ 01279 406756

Office Stationery

GreenBuying.co.uk
Festival House , Cheltenham
Gloucestershire , GL50 3SH
0845 217 8995
mroper@greenbuying.co.uk
www.greenbuying.co.uk
(see full page advert for more information)

Office Hut
Noble House , Gerrards Cross
SL9 8SU 08453 104497

Office Supplies

Accord Office Supplies
Unit 22 Westmead Industrial Estate, Swindon
Wiltshire , SN5 7TL
01793 553921
kchild@accordoffice.co.uk
www.accordoffice.co.uk
(see full page advert for more information)

Outdoor/Street Furniture

Sustainable Options
Unit 11 Riverside Place , Leeds
LS9 0RQ 01132 492222

Painting and Decorating

Solver Painters
39 Edinburgh Place , Cheltenham
GL51 7RH 07561 520255

Painting and Decorating Supplies

Eco EZEE
West Hill Manor Barn , Welford
NN6 6HF 01858 575454

International Paint - Akzonobel
Stoneygate Lane , Gateshead
Tyne & Wear , NE10 0JY
0191 469 611
proactivecoatings@akzonobel.com
www.international-pc.com
(see full page advert for more information)

Payroll and Bookkeeping

Unicorn Bookkeeping Service
2 Normont Gardens , Newcastle upon Tyne
NE4 8AP 01912 731593

The Three Little W s Limited
17 Sidney Street , Blyth
NE24 2RD 01670 362316

1st Step Management Services Ltd
United House North Road , Holloway
N7 9DP 08445 763808

Peter's Bookkeeping Services
Dean and Chapter Industrial Estate, Ferry Hill
DL17 8LN 01740 664730

Payserve Limited
9 Arran Close , Sleaford
NG34 8FY 01529 417129

Payroll and Bookkeeping

Numiracle Ltd
28 Friars Wharf , Gateshead
NE10 0QX **01914 479094**

Adkins & Morris (Rugby) Ltd
23a High Street , Welford
NN6 6HT **01858 571197**

Whitesides Payroll Solutions
6-7 Feast Field , Leeds
LS18 4TJ **01132 582437**

Calculus Accounting Solutions Ltd
Upper Pelham , Chislehurst
BR7 5QE **02084 673838**

Payroll People
37 Ellesmere Road , Chiswick
W4 3DU **02087 479575**

Plumbers Merchants

Travis Perkins Plc
Lodge Way House , Northampton
Northamptonshire , NN5 7UG
01604 752 424
marketing@travisperkins.co.uk
www.travisperkins.co.uk

Buildbase
Gemini One , Cowley
OX4 2LL **01865 871700**

Plumbing Services

Environmental Products & Services Ltd
5 Shepherd's Drive , Newry
BT35 6JQ **02830 833081**

Pollution & Fire Water Containment Equipment

Environmental Innovations Ltd
The Innovation Farm , Nr Bishop Stortford
CM22 7QU **01279 600440**

Plumbers Merchants

Posters

Zig Design
Bell Vue , Holsworthy
EX22 6EF 01409 253799

PR and Media Management

Gravitas Public Relations
7 Lansdown Place , Cheltenham
GL50 2HU 01242 211000

Pre Design Advice

Steve Eastland Design Limited
Hope House , Kerswell
EX15 2EL 01884 266437

Pressurisation Systems & Vacuum Degassing

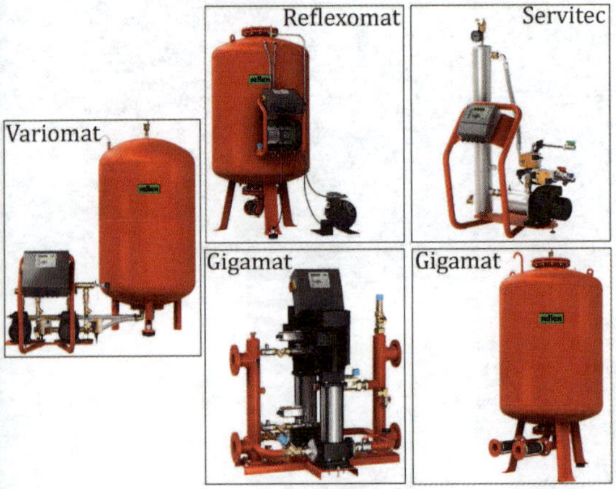

Reflex UK
Stablegate , Waterlooville
Hampshire , PO8 8TS
0239 224 0816 or
dan.testar@reflex.co.uk
www.reflex.de
(see half page advert for more information)

Print Management

Foundry Press
Unit A Foundry Lane, Horsham
RH13 5PX 01403 216120

Trade Search UK Ltd
Unit 16 Globe Industrial Estate , Grays
RM17 6ST 01375 768515

Printing, Design and Mailing Services

Ruddocks
56 Great Northern Terrace , Lincoln
LN5 8HL 01522 529591

Loyalty Matters Ltd (printing.com)
104 Station Parade , Harrogate
HG1 1HQ 01423 857900

Pace Print
19 South Clerk Street , Edinburgh
EH8 9JD 01316 670737

Easy Green Print.com
Pony Road , Oxford
OX4 2SE 01865 395252

Pressurisation Systems & Vacuum Degassing

AT GMP WE LIKE TO KEEP THINGS SIMPLE.

WE HAVE 2 PASSIONS:

1: To provide our clients with the **BEST QUALITY** design & print at affordable prices. Quality is a necessity not a luxury in today's marketplace.

2: To offer this service in such a way that it has the **LEAST DETRIMENTAL IMPACT ON OUR ENVIRONMENT.**

HOW DO WE ACHIEVE THIS?

We carbon balance all our print projects by planting broadleaf trees in local community woodlands, enhancing the communities and their environs.

Contact **Roger Parry,** a 2009 Scottish Sustainable Development Forum Green List Champion:

07841 429 775

e: roger.parry@gmpprint.co.uk
www.gmpprint.co.uk
office: 0131 629 0071

OUR PRODUCT EXPERTISE INCLUDES INDOOR & OUTDOOR SIGNAGE LARGE & SMALL FORMAT POINT OF SALE POSTERS BANNERS FLYERS BROCHURES EXHIBITION STANDS

LOCAL SECTION National

Page 525

THE GREEN DIRECTORY

THE GREEN DIRECTORY

Printing, Design and Mailing Services

GMP Print Solutions
Unit 17 , Loanhead
Midlothian , EH20 9LZ
0131 629 0071
roger.parry@gmpprint.co.uk
www.gmpprint.co.uk
(see full page advert for more information)

Creative Images
Brackig , Bridgend
CF31 2JF **01656 645110**

Stephens & George Print Group
Goat Mill Road , Merthyr Tydfill
CF48 3TD **01685 388888**

Print 2 Media Ltd
Unit 11a Miller Business Park , Liskeard
PL14 4DA **08455 390172**

BPM-UK (Print Bromsgrove)
26 Stratford Road , Bromsgrove
B60 1AP **01527 872436**

Print Express London
4 Sunnyside Terrace , Edgeware Road
NW9 5DL **02082 000600**

Promotional Items and Incentives

New Media Branding
New Media House , Sevenoaks
TN13 1YH **08455 200660**

MR Products
94a Greenfield Business Centre , Holywell
CH8 7GR **01352 717917**

Perfect Promotional Products Limited
36 Coniston Close , Rushden
NN10 8NL **01933 420624**

Trophies & Gifts
16 Whatmer Close , Sturry
CT2 0JJ **01227 710638**

EMC Advertising Gifts
Derwent House , Whetstone
London , N20 0YY
0208 492 2200   or   0845 3451064
sales@emcadgifts.co.uk
www.emcadgifts.co.uk
(see full page advert for more information)

Quality Management (ISO Accreditation)

Des Bennett Consultants Ltd
66a The Wroe , Peterborough
PE14 8AN **01945 587205**

Rain Water Harvesting

Nu-Heat UK Ltd
Heathpark House , Honiton
EX14 1SD **01404 549770**

GRP Canopies plc
Edgcott House , Aylesbury
Buckinghamshire , HP18 0QW
0800 783 3835 or 07878 846697
jd@123v.com
www.123v.com

Recruitment and Employment Services

Positive Management Services
17 Whitbourne Hall , Worcester
WR6 5SE **01886 822222**

Recycling

Amaryllis
Amaryllis House , Chelmsford
CM2 6TE **08448 006326**

Europlastix Ltd
Ashleigh House , Bridgwater
TA6 7QL **01278 423544**

Dyfed Recycling Services
Dafen Industrial Estate , Llanelli
SA149RQ **01554 772478**

Renewable Energy Training.

Wagner Solar UK Ltd
Unit 2 Keynor Farm , Chichester
PO20 7NQ **01243 649035**

Easy MCS Ltd
Viscount House , Chester
CH4 8RH **08444 146041**

Research

Jumpstart (Scotland) Ltd
6 Atholl Crescent , Edinburgh
EH3 8HA **01312 402900**

Recycled, Recyclable, Alternative Energy Organic & Biodegradable Products

We will find the perfect product for your Green promotions

5oz Cotton Shopping Bags

HARPER FENTON
Art materials

Natural and black, red, yellow, pink or navy cotton shopping bags all at 5oz weight with long handles.

Bio S! Ballpen

Remade from 80% compostable material in a choice of 9 frosty colours all with white frosty barrel.

Corn Calculator

Pocket calculator made from corn starch and powered by solar energy.

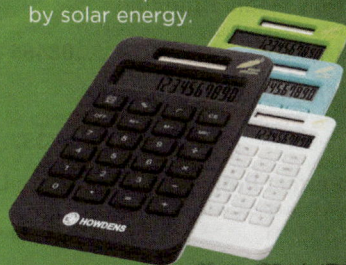

ECO OPTION

A5 Notebook & Pen

A5 size notebook with 80 sheets of lined paper includes a matching coloured ballpoint.

Call: 020 8492 2200
0845 345 1064
Email: sales@emcadgifts.co.uk
Web: www.emcadgifts.co.uk

emc
advertising gifts

Page 527

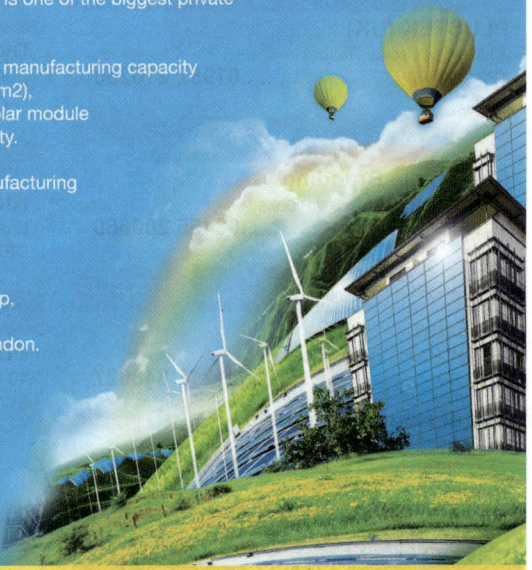
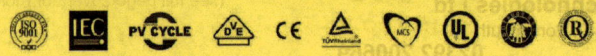
LOCAL SECTION National

THE GREEN DIRECTORY

Reuse and Reduction

GreenBuying.co.uk
Festival House , Cheltenham
GL50 3SH 08452 178995

Roofing Services

Green Roof Systems
Unit 5 Churchfield Court , Nottingham
NG5 9JL 07702 882234

Safety and Convenience Products

Heatshot Limited
Unit 1 Sovereign Business Park , Leeds
LS10 1AW 07814 503566

Kaizen Distribution Services Ltd
98 Uplands Road , Leicester
LE2 4NQ 07812 743232

Safety Risk Assessment

Hodgins Smith Consulting
151 West George Street , Glasgow
G2 2JJ 01292 678484

Scanners

PLUSTEK (UK)
33 Mayfair Grove , Telford
TF2 9GJ 01952 210280

Screen and T Shirt Printing

New Media Branding
New Media House , Sevenoaks
TN13 1YH 08455 200660

Secretarial Service

VA Extra
11 Croft Road , Birmingham
B26 1SG 01217 848627

Out of Hours Typing Ltd
21 Champford Lane , Wellington
TA21 8BH 01823 662814

Sewage and Effluent Products and Services

Bio-Bubble Technologies Ltd
Unit L, Fishers Grove , Portsmouth
PO6 1RN 02392 200669

Signs and Graphics

Direct Signs (UK) Ltd
Venture Court , Hinckley
LE10 3BT 01455 230122

Aris Design & Management Ltd
270 London Road , London
SM6 7DJ 02088 352730

Ngwena
Unit 1 The Bronze Works , London
SE26 5AY 02086 596596

SK Signs & Labels
Temple Farm Industrial Estate , Southend On Sea
SS2 5RR 01702 462401

Blizzard Graphics
Unit 6b Runway Farm , Kenilworth
CV8 1NQ 01676 533000

Mark Latchford Screen and Digital Print Ltd
Unit 10E Alstone Trading Estate, Cheltenham
GL51 8HF 01242 584588

Exantia Display Systems
9 Muirhead Quay , Barking
IG11 7BW 02085 071612

Skips and Skip Hire

Dyfed Recycling Services
Dafen Industrial Estate , Llanelli
SA14 9RQ 01554 772478

Solar Accessories

Klober Limited
East Midlands Distribution Centre, Castle Donnington
DE74 2HA 08007 833216

Solar Energy

EDF Energy
40 Grosvenor Place , London
SW1X 7EN 08000 511905

Linuo Power UK
Rotterdam House , Newcastle-upon-Tyne
Tyne & Wear , NE1 3DY
0191 206 4144
info@linuouk.com
www.linuouk.com
(see full page advert for more information)

My Power UK
Gamma Three , Cheltenham
GL54 5EB 08002 949246

Page 529

Solar Energy

Nu-Heat UK Ltd
Heathpark House , Honiton
EX14 1SD 01404 549770

Deks Distribution UK
West End Trading Estate , Bristol
BS48 4DJ 01275 858866

Uniq Renewable Energy Solutions Ltd
The Barn , Gringley-On-The-Hill
S. Yorkshire , DN10 4RA
01777 816379 or 07713 575249
ures@live.co.uk
www.ures.co.uk

T J Warr Electrical
34 Marlborough Road , Manchester
M41 5GQ 07793 046262

Trust Renewable
Bradley Mill , Halifax
HX4 8BH 01422 382822

Radiant Heating Solutions Ltd
Hougham , Grantham
NG32 2HZ 01400 250572

Worcester Bosch Group
Cotswold Way , Wardon
WR4 9SN 08448 929900

IGREEN Energy
Sarn Farm , Oswestry
SY10 7AU 01691 662279

Solar Panels and Photovoltaics

BritishEco Ltd
Unit 1A Oaklands Business Centre , Wokingham
RG41 2FD 08452 570041

Linuo Power UK
Rotterdam House , Newcastle-upon-Tyne
Tyne & Wear , NE1 3DY
0191 206 4144
info@linuouk.com
www.linuouk.com
(see full page advert for more information)

The Better Roofing Company
35 Coverdale road , Lancaster
LA1 5PY 07972 815797

GreenTech
Unit F3 Holly Farm Business Park, Kenilworth
CV8 1NP 08455 194277

Solar Panels and Photovoltaics

Deks Distribution UK
West End Trading Estate , Bristol
BS48 4DJ 01275 858866

Viessmann Limited
Hortonwood 30 , Telford
Shropshire , TF1 7YP
01952 675000
info-uk@viessmann.com
www.viessmann.co.uk

EOS Energy
Senator House , Southam
CV47 0NA 08456 080680

Affordable Renewables
Chamberlayne Road, Bury St. Edmunds
Suffolk , IP32 7EY
08000 320944
richard@affordablerenewables.org.uk
www.affordablerenewables.org.uk
(see half page advert for more information)

IBC SOLAR UK LTD
4300 Nash Court , Oxford
OX4 2RT 01865 337230

Underfloor Warehouse Ltd
Unit V2 Winchester Avenue , Blaby
Leicestershire , LE8 4GZ
0116 258 1410
enquiries@ufw.co.uk
www.ufw.co.uk

Solar Water Heating Systems

BritishEco Ltd
Unit 1A Oaklands Business Centre , Wokingham
RG41 2FD 08452 570041

Atmos Heating Systems
TBS Depot , Daventry
NN11 4ES 01327 871990

**Kingspan Environmental
(was Kingspan Renewables)**
Tadman Street , Wakefield
W.Yorkshire , WF1 5QU
01924 376026
richard.andrews@kingspan-renewables.com
www.kingspansolar.com

Solar Water Heating Systems

Deks Distribution UK
West End Trading Estate , Bristol
BS48 4DJ 01275 858866

Viessmann Limited
Hortonwood 30 , Telford
Shropshire , TF1 7YP
01952 675000
info-uk@viessmann.com
www.viessmann.co.uk

Affordable Renewables
Chamberlayne Road , Bury St. Edmunds
IP32 7EY 08000 320944

NSA Solar Thermal Ltd
Unit 3 Coal Cart Road , Leicester
LE4 3BY 01162 675835

The Better Roofing Company
35 Coverdale Road , Lancaster
LA1 5PY 07972 815797

EZ Solar
Ditton Mill House , Cleobury Mortimer
DY14 0DH 01299 270011

Solar Water Heating Systems

Underfloor Warehouse Ltd
Unit V2 Winchester Avenue , Blaby
Leicestershire , LE8 4GZ
0116 258 1410
enquiries@ufw.co.uk
www.ufw.co.uk

Radiant Heating Solutions Ltd
Hougham , Grantham
NG32 2HZ 01400 250572

Spray Foam Insulation.

BASF Polyurethenes UK Ltd
Wimsey Way , Alfreton
Derbyshire , DE55 4NL
07557 012683
bilal.mohyuddin@basf.co.uk
www.walltite.basf.co.uk
(see full page advert for more information)

Staff and Work Wear

New Media Branding
New Media House , Sevenoaks
TN13 1YH 08455 200660

Surveyors

John Hardy Chartered Surveyor
Kings Weston House , Bristol
Nationwide , BS11 0UR
0800 810 1040
john@kingswestonhouse.co.uk
www.john-hardy.co.uk
(see full page advert for more information)

Bradley-Mason LLP
Evans Business Centre , Harrogate
HG3 2XA 01423 534604

Sustainable Bathroom Equipment.

Ecotoilets
The Canal Shop , Rugby
Warwickshire , CV21 4PW
01327 844442
richard@ecotoilet.org.uk
www.ecotoilet.org.uk
(see full page advert for more information)

Sustainable Materials

The Bongtree
Unit W8 , Hartlepool
Cleveland , TS25 5TG
07958491876   or   07917460330
info@thebongtree.co.uk
http://www.thebongtree.co.uk/
(see full page advert for more information)

Sustainable Water Supplies

Water Matters (EU) Ltd
4 St Johns Court , Keynsham
BS31 2AX 01189 401233

Tanks and Cylinders

Fabdec Limited
Grange Road , Ellesmere
SY12 9DG 01691 627210

Taxi and Private Hire

Telecommunications

Talkwire Ltd
Kingsbury Square , Melksham
SN12 6HL 01225 899861

TSI Voice & Data
201 Lee Valley Technopark , London
N17 9LN 08707 373773

InClouds Hosted Business Services
29th Floor 1st Canada Square, Canary Wharf
E14 5DY 08453 551200

BlueBox Communications Ltd
Network House , Bolton
BL1 6AH 01204 494950

The Complete Solutions Group Ltd
Moss Road , Manchester
M32 0AZ 08443 443443

Complete ICT
Twyford House , Stoke on Trent
ST5 9QH 01782 200030

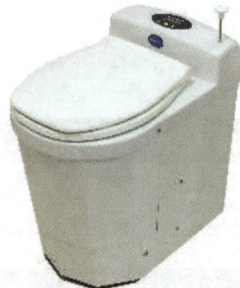

Page 538

THE **GREEN** DIRECTORY

RED

**Telephone Answering and Personal Assistant Service
Day to day business support without the cost of
hiring staff!**

Want to create more time?
Managing your business effectively means being able to delegate
tasks to others.
The RED Virtual PAs can take care of all those tedious or time-consuming
parts of running a business that you hate!

Want to create a great first impression?
We all appreciate how much first impressions count.
Our RED PAs help busy people like you every day!
We make your callers feel welcome by taking the time to listen to their
enquiry, giving you the time to work ON your business instead of IN it!

Want to help the environment?
Hiring a Virtual Assistant over an employee reduces travel time and
therefore reduces your carbon footprint!
You will be able to run your business from a smaller space.
Less space to light, less space to heat and less space to fill with machines.
By the very nature of what we do, we have embraced digital technology
and while we're not yet 100% paperless, we certainly use less than most
traditional offices.

Go **GREEN,** use **RED**

📞 **01793 862000
0800 458 3367**

✉ pateam@redvirtualoffice.biz

🐦 @REDvirtualPAs

🌐 redvirtualoffice.biz

RED Virtual Office Services
All the benefits of having Staff - without the headaches

Telephone Answering & Virtual Office Services

Red Virtual Office Ltd
1 Barton Court , Highworth
Wiltshire , SN6 7AG
01793 862000 or 07974 649363
denis@redvirtualoffice.biz
www.redvirtualoffice.biz
(see full page advert for more information)

Thermal Insulation

Knauf Insulation Ltd
PO Box 10 , St Helens
WA10 3NS **08700 668660**

Total Homefix Solutions
Unit 15 Ollerton Business Park , Childs Ercall
TF9 2DB **08006 121170**

Timber Frame Buildings

MBC Timber Frame Ltd
Cahir Business Park , Cahir
.............**07909 667241**

Building Envelope Evolution
Lakside House , Chippenham
SN14 8HF **01179 373937**

Benfield Advanced Timber Frame Technology
1 Symondscliffe Way ,
Caldicot , NP26 5PW
01291 437050
info@benfieldattgroup.co.uk
www.benfieldattgroup.co.uk
(see full page advert for more information)

Town Planning

The Planning Company
51 Battenhall Rise , Worcester
WR5 2DE **01905 360277**

Tracking Systems

Motrak Fleet Monitoring
Minton Hollins Building , Stoke On Trent
ST4 7RY **01782 221100**

Complete ICT
Twyford House , Stoke on Trent
ST5 9QH **01782 200030**

Training and Apprenticeships

JTL
Stafford House , Orpington
BR6 0JS **08000 852308**

Tree Work and Surveys

RGS Tree Services. Arboricultural Consultants
52 Millway , Northampton
Northamptonshire , NN5 6ES
01604 581044
robert.rgs@virgin.net
www.rgs-treeservices.co.uk
(see half page advert for more information)

Trees, Plants & Seeds

Q Lawns
Corkway Drove , Thetford
IP26 4JR **01842 880010**

Habitat Aid Ltd
Hookgate Cottage , South Brewham
BA10 0LQ **01749 812355**

Turf and Top Soil.

Q Lawns
Corkway Drove , Thetford
Norfolk , IP26 4JR
01842 880010 or 01842 828266
sales@qlawns.co.uk
www.enviromat.co.uk

Underfloor Heating

Atmos Heating Systems
TBS Depot , Daventry
NN11 4ES **01327 871990**

Green Heat
Valley View Business Park , Andover
SP11 6LU **01264 350481**

Ice Energy
Unit 2 Oakfields Industrial Estate , Eynsham
OX29 4TH **01865 882202**

GES Underfloor Heating Systems Ltd
Pentre Meurig Road , Carmarthen
SA33 6AA **01267 237920**

Ecovision Systems Ltd
Barley Court , Tetbury
GL8 8TQ **01666 501580**

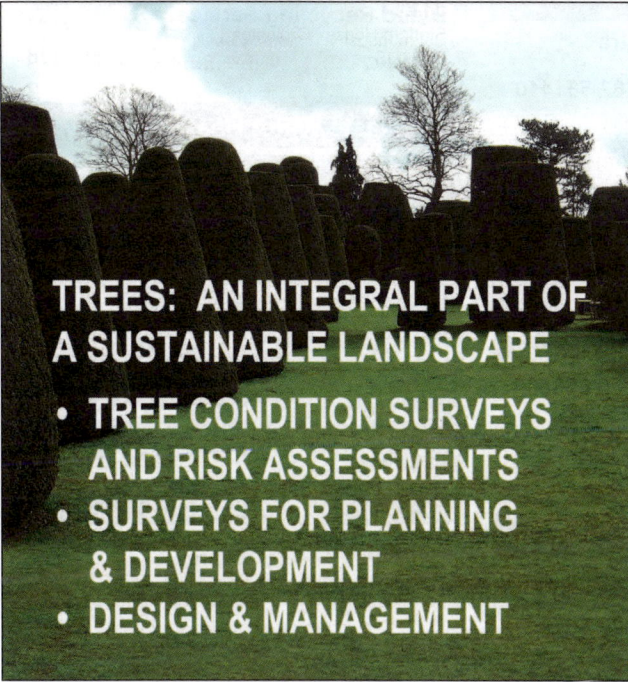

THE GREEN DIRECTORY

Underfloor Heating

**UFW Limited -
The Renewable Energy Centre**
Unit V2 Winchester Avenue , Blaby
LE8 4GZ **01162 581410**

Underfloor Heating Systems Ltd
68 Castleham Road , St Leonards-on-Sea
East Sussex , TN38 9NU
01424 851111 or 07811 931224
rob.stabbins@underfloorheating.co.uk
www.underfloorheating.co.uk

Universal Construction Products

Dragonboard
Grosvenor House , Mold
CH7 1EJ **01352 700088**

Vehicle Accident Management and Recovery

FARG - Green
PCLE House , Swinton
M27 9HF **07825 506250**

Vehicle Cleaning and Car Washes

Tammer UK Ltd
34 Greenhey Place , Skelmersdale
WN8 9SA **01695 727994**

Vehicle Cleaning Equipment

Tammer UK Ltd
34 Greenhey Place , Skelmersdale
Lancashire , WN8 9SA
01695 727994
sales@tammer.co.uk
www.tammeruk.co.uk
(see half page advert for more information)

Vehicle Leasing and Rentals

Go Green Car and Van Rental
10-30 Nantwich Road , Crewe
CW2 6AD **08002 987957**

Waste Machinery

Orwak Environmental Services
Unit 6 Alpha industrial Park , Smethwick
B66 1BZ **01215 657436**

Waste Management and Disposal

Dyfed Recycling Services
Dafen Industrial Estate , Llanelli
SA149RQ **01554 772478**

Waste Water Heat Recovery

Water Coolers

Evapure
Unit 4 KG Business Centre , Northampton
Northamptonshire , NN3 8DF
08000 935237 or 07976 243298
leo@eva-pure.co.uk
www.eva-pure.co.uk

Water Saving Products and Services

Ecotoilets
The Canal Shop , Rugby
CV21 4PW **01327 844442**

Tammer UK Ltd
34 Greenhey Place , Skelmersdale
Lancashire , WN8 9SA
01695 728191
sales@tammer.co.uk
www.tammeruk.co.uk
(see full page advert for more information)

Water Treatment and Purification Systems

B & V Water Treatment
Hartlands Business Park , Daventry
NN11 8YH **08443 727344**

LOCAL SECTION National

Page 543

THE **GREEN** DIRECTORY

Website and Internet Services

Venti Venti Media Ltd
7-9 Rosebery Parade , Ewell
KT17 2EJ **02034 411688**

Primo Website Design
Manchester (Central) , Manchester
M13 9AB **01612 744513**

Clubnet Search Marketing
Tamar Science Park , Plymouth
PL6 8BX **08452 996005**

Designed By Dave
35 Fernhill Lane , Harlow
CM18 7JL **01992 350600**

NSM Web Design Ltd
8 Consett Innovation Centre , Consett
DH8 5XP **08456 432667**

demoMedia Digital Ltd
8-11 St John's Lane , London
EC1M 4BF **02076 083000**

Jellis Design
225 Ravenhead Road , St. Helens
WA10 3LR **01744 21246**

Wind Energy

Ecotricity Group Ltd
Unicorn House , Stroud
Gloucestershire , GL5 3AX
0845 230 6102
mark.neveu@ecotricity.co.uk
www.ecotricity.co.uk
(see full page advert for more information)

BritishEco Ltd
Unit 1A Oaklands Business Centre , Wokingham
RG41 2FD **08452 570041**

GreenTech
Unit F3 Holly Farm Business Park , Kenilworth
CV8 1NP **08455 194277**

Drakes Renewables
118 Lower Luton Road , Harpenden
AL5 5AN **07866 494952**

Dulas Ltd
Unit 1 Dyfi Eco Park, Machynlleth
SY20 8AX **01654 705000**

Evance Wind Turbines Ltd
Unit 6 Weldon Road, Loughborough
LE11 5RN **01509 215669**

FuturEnergy Limited
Ettington Park Biz Centre , Stratford Upon Avon
CV37 8BT **01789 450280**

Wind Energy

Consuta Training Ltd
Culver Cottage , Newport
PO30 2NJ **03306 600262**

Renewable Advice Ltd
Unit 1 Mooreside Business Park, Winchester
SO23 7RX **07884 181204**

Worcester Bosch Group
Cotswold Way , Wardon
WR4 9SN **08448 929900**

Window Film

Solar Control Films Ltd
Unit 18 The Weavers, Newark
NG24 4RY **01636 613222**

GP Window Films
Worthing House , Basingstoke
RG23 8PX **08450 037260**

Solar Shield Ltd
Unit 10 Swan Business Park, Dartford
DA1 5ED **08451 306232**

Wood Recycling and Waste

Jericho Wood Recycling
Unit 8 Metro Triangle , Birmingham
B7 5QT **01213 285082**

Q Lawns
Corkway Drove , Thetford
IP26 4JR **01842 880010**

Sandersons Eco Fuel
Unit 2 , Four Crosses
SY22 6ST **01691 830075**

Wood Stoves & Eco Fuels

Sandersons Eco Fuel
Unit 2 , Four Crosses
SY22 6ST **01691 830075**

LOCAL SECTION National

THE GREEN DIRECTORY

notes

notes. | D D | M M | YYYY

notes

DD | MM | YYYY   notes.

notes

notes.   D D | M M | YYYY

notes

DD | MM | YYYY

notes.

notes

notes.

D D | M M | YYYY

notes

notes.   D D | M M | YYYY

DD | MM | YYYY

GREENER TIMES

> SUSTAINABLE SOLUTIONS MAGAZINE

Old Station Building
Oswald Road, Oswestry
Shropshire, SY11 1RE

SUBSCRIBE TO THE UK'S BEST GREEN BUSINESS, LIFESTYLE AND SUSTAINABILITY MAGAZINE

If you enjoy reading the Greener Times magazine, why not take advantage of our special subscription rates and save yourself some money?   Each issue of Greener Times is enjoyable, informative reading that will also make you think!

As well as articles on environmental issues that can affect you at home as well as at work; there are interviews with celebrities like Gareth Southgate and successful businesses such as Stagecoach, quizzes that the whole family can get involved with and current affairs relating to local communities and businesses, all with an environmental and sustainable theme i.e. The Green Deal, The Renewable Heat Incentive (RHI) etc.

There is also a 'Whats On?' list of forthcoming shows and events that we will be attending where you can come along and meet us in person.

It costs just **£4.20 + P&P** Or if you want to save some money you can subscribe for a year for just **£42 + P&P** (payable by monthly or annual direct debit) Instruction to Greener Times Publishing Ltd

DON'T MISS AN ISSUE, SUBSCRIBE TODAY!

£42 + P&P

01691 661 565
info@greener-times.co.uk
www.greener-times.co.uk